BAHADUR SHAH ZAFAR
AND
THE WAR OF 1857 IN DEHLI

BAHADUR SHAH ZAFAR
AND
THE WAR OF 1857 IN DEHLI

SYED MAHDI HUSAIN

AAKAR

BAHADUR SHAH JAFAR
Syed Mahdi Husain

First Published, 1958
Reprinted with a new Preface by Mushirul Hasan, 2006

ISBN 81-87879-91-2

Published by
AAKAR BOOKS
28 E Pocket IV, Mayur Vihar Phase I, Delhi-110 091
Phone : 011-2279 5505 Telefax : 011-2279 5641
aakarbooks@bol.net.in; www.aakarbooks.com

Printed at
Mudrak, 30 A, Patparganj, Delhi-110 091

CONTENTS

Illustrations and Maps

PREFACE

Dr. Syed Mahdi Husain was a distinguished historian of medieval India. He wrote a number of important books, specially on the Tughlaq period. His biography of Muhammad bin Tughlaq, in particular, is a reference book that sets at rest many of the speculative theories about that ruler. Likewise, his editing of Ibn Battuta's *Rehla* and Isami's *Futuhu's Salatin* bear testimony to his scholarship.

Dr. Mahdi Husain's profound scholarship is reflected in yet another major scholarly enterprise, *Bahadur Shah Zafar and the War of 1857 in Dehli*. Published in 1958, this authoritative book was reviewed extensively in scholarly journals.

Even though much literature on Bahadur Shah Zafar and the 1857 revolt exists, Mahdi Husain's book continues to be of considerable relevance to the historians of Modern India. It is rich in details, and offers a dispassionate interpretation of the 1857 revolt. The book brings alive, to the present-day reader, the trauma of living in 1857, a trauma that people like Syed Ahmad Khan and the poet Mirza Ghalib experienced.

In 2007, we shall recall the heroism of the freedom-fighters and invoke their memories. On that occasion, we would do well to remember that it was Bahadur Shah Zafar who was the rallying point for those who revolted against the British rulers. It is also worth remembering that he was a visible symbol of composite culture – the hallmark of Delhi's life – and of Hindu Muslim unity.

The timely reprint of this book will, I hope, generate more research on Delhi's social and cultural life and place in perspective the changes ushered in by British rule and the responses they triggered in north India.

For me, the publication of this book brings back happy memories.

Mahdi Husain Sahib was a close friend of my father, Professor Mohibbul Hasan. As a child, I remember his visits to our house – 'Prince Mansion' in Calcutta. He would invariably come to us with Professor A.B.M. Habibullah, a foremost historian of medieval India. In Aligarh, too, Mahdi Husain Sahib used to stay with us in Haider Villa. I remember his exhortations to me on Islam. He did not want me to 'deviate' like my father had done. I also remember his attachment to my mother, who took care of his needs.

Mushirul Hasan

ABBREVIATIONS

A.G.H.G.	...	*Afsana-i Gham Aur Hangama-i Ghadr*
A.S.I.R.	...	*Archæological Survey of India Reports*
D.G.	...	*Dastan-i Ghadr*
D.N.	...	*Delhi News*
F.D.	...	*Foreign Department*
G.D.A.	...	*Ghadr-i Dehli Ke Afsane*
H.I.M.	...	*History of Indian Mutiny*
I.H.R.C.	...	*Indian Historical Records Commission*
I.M.	...	*Indian Mutiny*
J.P.H.S.	...	*Journal of Pakistan Historical Society*
L.Q.E.J.	...	*Lal Qile Ki Aik Jhalak*
M.P.	...	*Mutiny Paper*
N.L.	...	*Naziriya Library*
N.S.D.	...	*Narrative of the Siege of Delhi*
P.D.	...	*Punjab and Delhi in 1857*
P.L.	...	*Press-List*
Pr.Tr.B.S.	...	*Proceedings of the Trial of Bahadur Shah*
R.I.D.	...	*Records of the Intelligence Department*
R.F.	...	*The Rise and Fall of Muhammad bin Tughluq*
S.B.	...	*Safinatu'l Bihar*
S.L.D.S.P.	...	*Selections from the Letters, Despatches and other State Papers in the Military Department of the Government of India*
T.B.	...	*Tarikh-i Baghawat-i Hind*
S.M.R.	...	*Sepoy Mutiny and the Revolt of 1857*
Tel.	...	*Telegram*
T.H.	...	*Tarikh-i Hindustan*
T.M.	...	*Twilight of the Mughuls*
T.N.N.	...	*Two Native Narratives of the Mutiny in India*
T.U.A.S.I.	...	*Tarikh-i 'Uruj-i 'Ahd-i Saltanat-i Inglishiya*

PREFACE

In my childhood I used to hear stories about the Mutiny (*Ghadr*[1]) of 1857 from my revered father who had witnessed it as a boy of 13, then living with his parents in Dehli. One day, while narrating the story he said feelingly, 'We were compelled to leave Dehli our paternal home and all our belongings, afraid of the plundering raids of the Telingas and fled to Alwar where we found shelter and we did not return until many years after the fall of Dehli and restoration of peace'. In this manner was awakened in me some curiosity about the so-called *Ghadr* but I had no time to think seriously of it until the 18th of November 1956 when I wrote an article on 'Emperor Bahadur Shah II and his role in the War of 1857' for the *Amrita Bazar Patrika.* It is reproduced below together with its criticism which appeared subsequently in the same paper.

Emperor Bahadur Shah II: His Role in the War in 1857.

The last Mughul Emperor of *Dehli* (this spelling is strictly according to the chronicles and is in fact truly Indian. *Delhi* is the English spelling) commonly known as Bahadur Shah Zafar was the second son of Akbar Shah and his Rajput wife Lal Bai. He was a great scholar of Persian, a marvellous calligrapher and a gifted poet of Urdu with Zafar as his pen-name. He composed many ghazals in Urdu as well as diwans some of which are available in printed form: He also wrote a çommentary on Shaikh Sa'di's *Gulistan.*

He ascended the throne in 1837 when he was 62 years old. Since his accession he remained for the most part in Dehli Fort as a pensioner of the East India Company and

[1] *Ghadr*—a Hindustani equivalent for the Mutiny, meaning perfidy, treachery and base ingratitude—became after the fall of Dehli a popular expression to denounce the Rising of 1857.

had nothing to do with the administration of the city and country which remained entirely in British hands. He was a very quiet man of sufi disposition. His activities were confined to writing books, holding discourses in poetry and visiting the shrine of sufi saints like the dargah of Hazrat Nizamu'ddin Auliya and that of Shaikh Qutbu'ddin Bakhtiyar Kaki where he had built a palace called Zafar Mahal. From this Zafar Mahal he used to watch the annual Hindu-Muslim fair or picnic called *Phul Walon Ke Sair* which he had inaugurated. This national fair continued to be held in the precincts of the Qutb shrine even after Bahadur Shah regularly every year until the year of communal fury, *i.e.* 1947. It was restored through the efforts and sacrifice of Mahatma Gandhi.

He joins the Rebels.

When on 10th May 1857 the Indian contingents commonly known as Telinga—perhaps because their officers came from the Telingana territory—rose in a body against the British at Mirath and secured arms and booty by reckless killing and loot, Bahadur Shah II of Dehli knew nothing about the matter. In the morning of 11th May they arrived in Dehli and the revolt spread to all classes of people in the city. In the morning of 12th May the Telingas called on the aged and infirm Emperor Bahadur Shah in the Fort. They implored him to accept their services in the cause of Mughul rule which they said they were anxious to restore. In spite of his old age Bahadur Shah accepted their request. Along with his sons Zaheeru'ddin Mirza Mughul and Mirza Jawan Bakht and other able-bodied members of the royal family he went in cavalcade from the Fort up to Chandni Chowk. There he stopped near the gate of what was then known as Begum Ka Bagh and addressed the Telinga army saying, 'I am with you wholeheartedly. But I possess neither a treasure nor an army. If I get back my dominion I shall bestow gifts on you in right royal manner'. They replied, '*Huzur*! we require neither wealth nor army. We only want this much—and this is our earnest desire—that *Huzur* may kindly give us the support of your name. We shall lay down our lives at your feet. We want to see you recover your Indian dominion and we should thereby earn a good name for ever.' The Emperor said in reply, 'Whatever I possess is at your disposal. Eat and drink out of my provision. And with a bold heart turn these adversaries (the English) out of India and make my coin current.' Immediately a gold coin was struck with the following verse engraved on it:

Bazar zad sikka nusrat tarazi
Siraju'ddin Bahadur Shah Ghazi

(Siraju'ddin Bahadur Shah Ghazi
struck gold coin as a sign of victory)

Emperor's Patriotism

In the morning of 13th May the Emperor held a durbar in the Diwan-i Khass of the Dehli Fort. The durbar was attended by all the officers of the Telinga army. But in the course of the arrangements they made there for the capture of the city, for the conveyance of ammunition and other details they dictated their own terms which the Emperor accepted and he assured them of his espousing their cause which was the cause of India's liberation provided they proved obedient to his orders, behaved properly and observed discipline. Presumably the Emperor had strong misgivings about the Telingas and feared that they would misbehave and would ultimately make his position worse. That in spite of his misgivings he did not disappoint the Telingas and accepted their request speaks volumes for Bahadur Shah's patriotism and his desire for the liberation of India. He had no personal ambition left for he was now extremely old and had been used to living the life of a dervish.

In the afternoon of the same day the Telingas brought 60 Englishmen, ladies and children as prisoners before the Emperor and wanted his permission to kill them. The Emperor dissuaded them from killing innocent people. And he ordered those ladies and children to be taken to the Fort and looked after.

New Government Set Up

On 14th May, the English having evacuated the city of Dehli, a kind of national government was set up there.

All Hindu and Muslim officers, Raos and Rajas were called to attend the Court. The Emperor desired co-operation from all and sent circular letters to the jagirdars and amirs requesting them to come over. But there was little response; and amirs like Aminu'ddin Ahmad Khan and Ziyau'ddin Ahmad Khan of Loharu attended the court but made lame excuses and went away. Most of the remaining amirs and jagirdars who had been approached sent in messages alleging their inability to leave their estates in the midst of turmoil.

On 15th May another durbar was held and new officers of the Indian Army of Liberation were appointed. The supreme command of this army was given to Zaheeru'ddin Mirza Mughul and a subordinate command was taken by the queen Zinat Mahal Begum. Mirza Jawan Bakh, a son of the Emperor and the queen, was made wazir. Two Hindu officers stand out prominent in the list. One was the Rao Sahib of Pargana Dadri and another was a chieftain named Sai Mall. The Rao Sahib was awarded a royal robe and put in charge of the commissariat and transport while Sai Mall was appointed commander of a battalion and charged to seize the British provisions. When shortly after Sai Mall was killed, his maternal grandson Puran Mall succeeded him in the office.

Rebel Army's Excesses

But in spite of the Indian Army of Liberation thus formed, the Indians were not united. Some of them carried tales to the British who had established their camp on the Ridge, now known as Fatehgarh or Jitgarh. Among such tale carriers is found the name of a Muslim, *viz.* Agha Jan and of a Hindu called Mohan Lall. They are said to have opened secret correspondence with the British.

For the next four months Bahadur Shah held the trembling throne of Dehli while he himself was trembling under the weight of years and for fear of the disobedient and irresponsible army who had already proved wayward and were committing blunders every day.

On 16th May they requested the Emperor to make over the aforesaid English prisoners to them and they wanted to kill them all. The Emperor ordered the army not to do

took the prisoners out of the jail and making them stand before the Naqqarkhana killed them all with swords. This was not all. The Telingas began to lay hands even on their own countrymen. They attacked Munshi Mohan Lall and plundered the house of Munshi Gobind Dass whom they suspected of being pro-British.

At this stage rumours were set afloat— and no wonder were engineered by certain schemers—that the queen Zinat Mahal Begum and a leading Amir Hakim Ahsanullah Khan had on their own account opened secret correspondence with the British. But this is mere hearsay. The truth of the matter is that the queen Zinat Mahal Begum continued true to the cause her royal husband had espoused.

Meanwhile the war between the British on the Ridge and the Indians and their Emperor in the city of Dehli was in progress. Skirmishes and fighting continued until the 14th September on which fateful day the British succeeded in storming Dehli. On hearing of this, Bahadur Shah burst into tears and said, 'I had foretold this calamity. At long last these ungrateful men have ruined me in my old age. However today I shall go personally to the battlefield to fight.' Saying this the 84-year-old Emperor buckled his armour and rode out of the Fort. But the British guns were booming and bullets were ceaselessly falling all around. Some of the men of the now broken Army of Liberation persuaded the aged Emperor to go back into the Fort. He retired. The war was over; and in the course of the next four days the rump of the Indian army melted away.

LAST OF THE TIMURS

On 19th September Emperor Bahadur Shah found himself alone. And fearing a bitter fate awaiting him he sent out the queen and other ladies and some princes in the darkness of the night from the Fort to some unknown place. Alone he remained dismayed in the Fort for the rest of the night. On the morrow he left it quietly and went straight to the shrine of Hazrat Nizamu'ddin Auliya. He sat down by the side of the sacred tomb and burst into tears. After a short time he looked to the custodian of the shrine and said, 'I had told you this much before. These luckless rebel soldiers are wayward. They have no stamina, no discipline and no powers of endurance. I had apprehensions from the beginning; now they have come true. These soldiers have fled before the English. Brother! although I am a retired fakir yet in my veins runs that great blood which would keep me fighting if I took to it, to the last drop of it in my body. My forefathers have seen worse days than these and they never lost heart. But I have read the writing on the wall. I see with my own eyes the fast approaching tragic end of our glory. Now there is not a shadow of doubt left that of the great house of Timur I am the last mark and trail seated on the throne of India. The lamp of Mughul dominion is fast extinguishing; it would remain but a few hours more. Since I know this definitely why should I cause more bloodshed unnecessarily? Hence I left the Fort. The country belongs to God; He may give it to whomsoever He likes.' Saying this he delivered into the custody of the shrine a box which alone he had carried with himself on leaving the Fort. This box contained three hairs from the sacred beard of Prophet Muhammad—a holy relic which had passed on as sacred from father to son in the house of Timur since the 14th century A.D. (8th century Hijra). Then the Emperor felt relieved and said, 'It is more than a day that I took my last meal. Give me something to eat.'

BANISHED TO RANGOON

Some coarse food was readily presented and he took some hasty morsels and then left for the mausoleum of Humayun which stood a few furlongs from there. He took shelter near his ancestor's tomb. But he was pursued immediately by the British troops and arrested by Hodson who captured also two of the sons of the Emperor and one grandson. They surrendered to him but in spite of their surrender they were shot dead by Hodson. Bahadur Shah was taken into the Fort and tried. After a long trial the judges decided that Bahadur Shah was guilty of abetting murder. As a result he was deposed and banished to Rangoon in December 1858 where he lived and died as a dervish (1862).

HERO AND MARTYR

It follows from the above that Bahadur Shah was not only a great patriot and hero but a martyr in the cause of India's liberation. He combined in his person qualities of fakir and king and did no harm to anyone. He might have succeeded in expelling the Englishmen had there been union among the Indians. It was his misfortune that he was born in a disunited India and the closing years when life had gone out of the Mughul rule. But he had a genuine love for India and plunged himself into a whirlpool of disasters for the sake of his countrymen. He was a symbol and standard-bearer of Hindu-Muslim unity. And it is a fact that during the short period of his nominal and ineffective rule the Musalmans had abandoned cow-slaughter.

Amrita Bazar Patrika, Nov. 28, 1956

Letter to the Editor

Martyr or Traitor

Sir,—Prof. Mahdi Husain, M.A., Ph.D. (London) D. Lit. (Paris) wrote an article on the above subject in the Sunday 'Amrita Bazar Patrika' of November 18, last. The account we are told is based on contemporary Persian sources. But as he has not said anything to indicate the nature of these sources it is not possible to discuss in detail the facts stated by him or the views and sentiments based thereon.

There is however one passage which cannot go unchallenged, particularly as the real facts are contrary to what he has said and demolish the whole structure he has sought to construct. The passage runs as follows: 'Rumours were set afloat and no wonder were engineered by schemers —that the queen Zinat Mahal Begum and a leading amir Hakim Ahsanullah Khan had on their own account opened secret correspondence with the British. But this is a mere hearsay. The truth of the matter is that the queen Zinat Mahal Begum continued true to the cause her royal husband had espoused'. Fortunately for history, but unfortunately for the two illustrious persons involved we have positive evidence to prove that these rumours were only too true. A book published in 1858 contains a number of letters written during the siege of Delhi by H. H. Greathed Commissioner of Mirat who was appointed by the Lieutenant-Governor of North-West Province as his Political Agent at Delhi attached to the Field-Force. In a letter dated Camp Delhi August 23, 1857 he writes, 'An emissary came out from Zeenut Mahal the favourite wife of the king, a great political personage offering to exercise her influence with the King to bring out some arrangement'. In another letter dated August 19, 1857 Greathed says, 'I am beginning to get letters from the princes declaring they have been all along fondly attached to us and they want to know what they can do for us'.

Prof. Mahdi Husain is quite right when he says that Zinat Mahal continued true to the cause her royal husband had espoused for Bahadur Shah himself led the way to such treacherous intrigues with the English. Immediately after the Mutineers from Mirat arrived at Delhi and Bahadur Shah accepted their leadership he sent post-haste a secret message to the British Lieutenant-Governor at Agra informing him of the situation. This fact is mentioned by Jiwan Lall Munshi who was at Delhi at the time in his Persian narrative which has been translated by Metcalfe. Hakim Ahsanullah admits in his evidence at the trial of Bahadur Shah that he sent the message on behalf of the King asking for the help of British troops to put down the sepoys. According to the written statement of Chunni Lal published in the proceedings of the trial of Bahadur Shah the sepoys intercepted a letter written by Ahsanullah Khan and bearing his own seal in which he offered to the British to make over all the soldiery now in Delhi. Ahsanullah when confronted with the letter said it was a forgery.

During my recent visit to London I came across a letter from the British Commander of the forces besieging Delhi dated 4th July 1857 in which he refers to a proposal made by Ahsanullah on behalf of Bahadur Shah that if the British guaranteed his pension he would secretly admit the British troops inside the Fort of Delhi through Jer-darojah, a private entrance, into the palace. So the sepoys were quite right in suspecting the loyalty of Ahsanullah and Bahadur Shah, and we can well understand why they threatened to take away Zinat Mahal Begum and keep her as a hostage for the loyalty of Bahadur Shah.

According to Prof. Mahdi Husain 'Bahadur Shah was not only a great patriot and hero but a martyr in the cause of India's liberation'. If we understand the meaning of English words, Bahadur Shah has not the least claim to be called a hero, a patriot or a martyr. The only epithet applicable to Bahadur Shah is traitor. The queen Zinat Mahal, the princes and Ahsanullah who all—to use Prof. Husain's words—'continued true to the cause espoused by Bahadur Shah', also deserve to share the epithet equally with him.

Sd. Dr. R. C. Majumdar,
Professor of Ancient Indian History and Culture,
Nagpur University, Nagpur

On reading the above letter I wrote a commentary of my article; and after sending the same for publication to the *Amrita Bazar Patrika* I pursued further studies and researches. After several months of ceaseless work at different places—Calcutta, Patna, Rampur and Dehli—I wrote this book entitled *BAHADUR SHAH II AND THE WAR OF 1857 IN DEHLI WITH ITS UNFORGETTABLE SCENES.* Seven of its never-to-be-forgotten scenes which, if reiterated, will enable the student to acquire proper understanding and insight (জ্ঞান ভুজ্ঞান) are reproduced below.

First scene.—From 14th to 26th May while news poured in at the Royal Palace of the march of British troops from Mirath, Emperor Bahadur Shah continued to advise his Army to make an attack on Mirath and expel the English completely from that city and its environments. But his advice went unheeded and the English exploited the situation; they concentrated troops at Baghpat, thus threatening to attack Dehli. In the course of the next four days (27th to 30th May) they fortified their position, and Wilson marched with his divisions from Mirath in the direction of Dehli reaching Ghaziu'ddin Nagar near the Hindan at daybreak on 30th May. There they encountered some opposition from the Badshahi Army (*Sipah-i*

Shahi) who made an attack according to plan but were repulsed; another attack made on 31st May proved equally ineffective. The victorious British troops advanced to Alipur where they fortified themselves as well as at Baghpat (4th June).

Second scene.—On 8th June took place the battle of Badli-ki-Serai which was again a victory for the British resulting in the British occupation of Hindu Rao's house and the Flagstaff. Now they began to look confidently forward to conquering Dehli, and 7,000 British and allied soldiers held themselves ready to fall from the heights of the Ridge upon the city below at any suitable moment. But on 9th June the Badshahi Army made a grand attack on the Ridge; and fighting continued the whole day, the shells from the Badshahi artillery falling on the Ridge ceaselessly till 11th June.

Third scene.—On 12th and 13th, and again on the 17th and 23rd June, the Badshahi Army made fresh attacks, heedless of the loss of lives and property inflicted by the British who had meanwhile burnt a Royal battery as well as the village of Kishangarh. Believing that 23rd June—the centenary of Plassey—was the last day of the British Raj in India the Badshahi Army rushed fiercely that day on the British Camp and severe fighting ensued at the Sabzi Mandi, but they were not favoured by luck and the Sabzi Mandi area fell to the British. Still the Badshahi Army pulled themselves together and advanced to make a fresh attack on the British Camp (30th June); and they became distinctly hopeful and courageous after the arrival of General Bakht Khan on 2nd July.

Fourth scene.—On 3rd July General Bakht

Khan fell on the British at Alipur and he did so again on the 4th. From 5th to 8th July no attack could be made because the British troops had destroyed the Najafgarh canal bridge and the rains had set in, but a fresh attack was made on the 9th when over 200 British soldiers were killed. In the course of this attack, it is said, the Badshahi Army made a vain appeal in the name of India to the Indian gunners in the British artillery and urged them to come over to their side.

Fifth scene.—From 10th to 13th July while there was no fighting, huge ammunition and stores convoys from the Indian Princes reached the British Camp and 300 Sikh artillerymen also arrived to reinforce them. But the Badshahi Army were not dismayed. On 14th July they fell on the enemy's camp at the Sabzi Mandi but were driven back. Four days later they made another attack at the same Mandi though fresh reinforcements of Sikh cavalry and large convoys of ammunition and stores had reached the British Camp the same day. Fighting was held up for the next four days (July 19-22) on account of the incessant rains. The Badshahi Army made a sally on 23rd July and occupied Ludlow Castle. But a rift having occurred in their ranks quarrels broke out. For this reason there was no fighting till the 2nd of August when the Emperor raised their drooping spirits and inspired them with new zeal. As a result they made a severe attack on the enemy but there was no appreciable success. Fighting ceased for the next two days (4th and 5th August) only to be resumed on the 6th; and after 11 days' continuous action it ceased again for three days (19th to 21st August), the arrival of fresh reinforcements for the British from the Punjab having changed the programme. Under the leadership of Nicholson the British now held out a new threat of a sweep on Dehli. But the Badshahi Army who had been preparing for a fresh grapple were surprised and defeated by Nicholson on the 26th. This was followed by a cessation of fighting for the next ten days during which period there came for the British another instalment of reinforcements and ammunitions from Mirath and Firozpur, and some troops also came from Jind.

Sixth scene.—On 8th September the Qudsia Bagh and Ludlow Castle were seized by the British; and an attempt made by the Badshahi Army to recover these places proved abortive. Then the British fortified the Ludlow Castle and constructed a battery in front of it; they also began to make serious preparations for the grand assault which had long been in the offing. On 11th and 12th September they bombarded and destroyed the Kashmiri Gate Bastion and their shells began to fall into the city. On the 13th all the British batteries began simultaneously to fire on the city and the strength of the Badshahi Army fell from 60,000 to less than 10,000 while that of the British rose from the pre-Badli figure of 1,700 to 8,000.

Seventh scene.—On 14th September began the planned assault. The British assailants seized the Kashmiri, Kabuli and Mori Gates and destroyed the Water Bastion. At the same time they bombarded the Royal Palace and Salimgarh. The assault continued on the 15th and 16th; the bombardment of the Royal Palace and Salimgarh also continued, and the street fighting which now began continued through the 17th, 18th and 19th. On that fateful day General Bakht Khan broke his camp outside the Lahori Gate and went away. On 20th September the Emperor was captured at Humayun's tomb; he was betrayed into British hands by his elderly kinsman, Mirza Ilahi Bakhsh.

In all the above scenes Bahadur Shah's is the most important figure[1], the cynosure of all eyes, of friends as well as of foes, of the army and the inhabitants of Dehli as also of the British officers and their allies.[2] All the time Bahadur Shah was assailed by formidable difficulties, the most telling of all being an empty treasury. Since May 1857 the British Government had stopped payments of all kinds to him. He was unable to pay his own servants and to provide for his large family. One day, it is reported, his daughter Nawab Khatun Zamani Begum was compelled to ask Banarsi Lal, the Royal treasurer, for a loan of Rs. 15. Such was the financial strain but Bahadur Shah held his head high and lowered not the cause for which he had accepted the leadership of the sepoys. He did not sell that cause at any price and resisted all kinds of baits and fears. Great were the temptations that dallied before him; greater still were the threats that were held out to him through repeated warnings; and sure was the destruction of himself and his household that threatened him in adhering to the Fort and fighting the English amidst the greatest financial strains and all kinds of drains on his resources. One day, it is said, he found one of the chieftains intriguing with the British. Thereupon he expressed his disapproval and said angrily, 'Until the English at Nynee Pul are not

[1], [2] *Cf.* p. 427 *infra.*

killed, I shall consider you their friend and that you are in treacherous communication with them. It is a great pity that for a few hours' security in the world you barter your eternal welfare; go off to Nynee Pul; complete your work there and return'.[1] There was sincerity even in his rebuke and his expressions impressed the friend and foe alike. A British spy warned the British on the eve of their grand assault of Dehli against their laying severe hands on the Royal house after the fall of the city;[2] such was the popularity which Bahadur Shah enjoyed. Greathed too was impressed. While speculating on 17th-18th September that the Palace is being defended by the King's own troops he said, 'But our shells must be knocking them about most unpleasantly and there will soon be a hole in the wall. If the King wishes to have the lives of his family and his own spared, he had better surrender the Palace and I should be glad to save that slaughter[3]. Bahadur Shah did not surrender the Palace and fighting continued through the following day. Then in utter helplessness he left the Fort and fled in the direction of Humayun's tomb, not in the direction of the Qutb which he might have preferred in ordinary circumstances. Humayun's tomb lay in the neighbourhood of the shrine (*dargah*) of Nizamu'ddin Auliya where he wanted to stop in order to deposit the Box containing the Sacred Hairs of Prophet Muhammad. Making enquiries on the spot I came to know that Bahadur Shah's arrival with the said Box was strongly believed in the Dargah circles; and I was told that the Box was still preserved in the store room (*toshakhana*)

---

[1] *Delhi News,* File 135; dated 4th-7th September 1857.

[2] *Delhi News,* File 141; 11th September 1857.

[3] Greathed—*Letters written during the seige of Delhi,* pp. 284-285.

of the Dargah and that it was exhibited to the public every year on 11th Rabiu'l Awwal, one day before the Prophet's birthday after the *Asr* prayer. That holy day happened to fall during my stay in the city on Sunday, 6th October 1957. I took my camera, and just at the moment the believers were exhibiting the Sacred Box I snapped it. It is also believed in the Dargah circles that Bahadur Shah was anxious to avoid public notice of his visit to the shrine with the object of saving it from desecration and pillage at the hands of the unscrupulous British soldiers. Accordingly he manoeuvred his flight from the Fort in such a manner that the performance has remained a mystery ever since, the details being not disclosed even to men like Hakim Ahsanullah Khan and Maulvi Fazl Haq. As a result speculation arose and some preposterous reports sprang.[1]

Zakaullah who always disparaged[2] Bahadur Shah has incidentally remarked that while the British were a solid mass like a wall of steel, the Indians were hopelessly divided. While one party was fighting nominally under the leadership of Bahadur Shah another party was with the British. And this party which was a hundred times stronger—for they included the Indian Princes—and more useful, for they comprised (i) the menials without whose essential services the British could not stand in the battlefield even for a day, and (ii) the spies who were sending all kinds of news about the weaknesses of the King and his army daily and hourly from the city of Dehli to the British Camp. These spies went about in disguise in the Royal Camp, in the city and the Palace and suggested to the British

---

[1] *Vide* (i) J.P.H.S., January 1958, pp. 12 ff.
(ii) P. 374 *infra*, footnote 2.

[2] *Vide* p. 307 *infra*.

when and at which part of the city, they should make the final assault.[1]

Regarding Bahadur Shah some reports capable of prejudicing certain minds also proceeded from some anti-Bengali sources. General Bakht Khan with whom Bahadur Shah had identified himself and to whom he confided all kinds of powers is reported to have imprisoned 50 Bengalis, accusing them of maintaining correspondence with the British.[2] Further the report says that Bakht Khan imprisoned every Baboo who could read and write English.[3] According to another news 'some Bengalis who had been suspected were taken prisoner in Dehli and General Bakht Khan undertook to report about their conduct to the Commander-in-chief[4]'. Further it is reported that the Kotwal of Dehli wrote to Mirza Mughul the commander-in-chief 'to remove the 12 Bengalis under arrest to the Fort, there being no accommodation in the Kotwali[5]'. These alleged anti-Bengali moves may have affected in some parts of this country the attitude against Bahadur Shah even after a hundred years. When in 1957 every detail of the story was examined and the incident of 11th May, for instance, was telescoped, it was inferred that 'Bahadur Shah had not the courage to confront an unruly crowd and he sent Captain Douglas instead[6]'. But it is a fact that subsequently he confronted the unruly crowds more than once. On 7th August 1857

---

[1] (i) Zakaullah—T.U.A.S.I., pp. 616, 699.
(ii) M.P. Box 15, No. 6, August 16, 17, 20, 1857; No. 104, August 21, 1857; No. 12, August 26, 1857; No. 14, August 28, 1857; No. 17, September 13, 1857; Box 16, No. 18, September 4, 1857; No. 23, September 8, 1857.

[2], [3] *Delhi News*—July 25, 1857.

[4] M.P. Box 57, Aug. 30-31, 1857; Nos. 381-383.

[5] *Idem,* Box 103, July 21, 1857; No. 175.

[6] Sen, S. N.—*Eighteen Fifty-Seven,* p. 70.

when much larger crowds of the sepoys attacked Hakim Ahsanullah Khan and wanted to kill him he pulled the latter safely out of the jaws of death[1]. Again on 2nd September 1857 he confronted them when there was a great tumult in the Palace about the distribution of pay. Two companies actually surrounded the Royal apartments. Bahadur Shah rushed into the crowds who were clamouring for pay, and said courageously, 'I never called you together, nor do I want you, nor have I any money to pay you.'[2] If he did not go out in the morning of May the 11th to confront the unruly crowd in question, the reason was that he did not then want to compromise his position by starting a massacre of Englishmen indiscriminately while the character of the rising was yet dubious and ominous. In fact he then found himself in a dilemma. He knew that success in the career on which the sepoys had embarked without making preparations was impossible. He also knew that he was surrounded on all sides by the British officers and spies. Says Cave-Browne the British chaplain attending the troops at Dehli, 'The King had at first been taken by surprise; the spirit of insurrection which he had evoked had broken out before the preconcerted time. The thought of the strong European garrison at Mirath and of the dire retribution which might come from that quarter made him cautious. He hesitated before compromising himself. Messengers were despatched on camels along the Mirath road to give immediate intimation of the advance of any European force. About the middle of the day (11th May) they returned to the Palace and reported

[1] (i) Zakaullah—T.U.A.S.I., p. 664.
(ii) *Delhi News,* August 7, 1857.
(iii) Metcalfe—T.N.N., pp. 186-187.

[2] *Delhi News,* September 5, 1857.

that not a soldier was within 20 miles. The old king now took courage. Mr. Rotton in his *Siege of Delhi* (p. 20) also mentions this circumstance. Another and a stronger guard was sent down under a son and a grandson of the King to demand the immediate surrender of the Magazine in the King's name. On this being refused scaling ladders were sent out from the Palace and planted against the walls along the main road[1]'.

This was a correct reading of the Royal mind made by Cave-Browne. Similarly he made another reading when he reported about Bahadur Shah's letter addressed to the Maharaja of Patiala[2]; and this letter which was betrayed by the Maharaja is also attested by two telegrams[3]. Then Greathed testifies to the Emperor's endeavours to secure general support for the war. 'The King of Delhi', says he, 'has written to the mutineers at Lucknow to come here and assist in taking the batteries[4]'. According to Hakim Ahsanullah

"[1]Cave-Browne—P.D., Vol. I., pp. 362-363.

[2] Says Cave-Brown, 'The Maharaja of Patiala . . . . no sooner received this letter from the Lion's Mouth at his palace gate than he at once with unhesitating loyalty forwarded it to Mr. Barnes for transmission to the Commissioner.'

Cave-Browne—P.D., I, pp 224-225.

[3] Tel. No. 8 of 27th May 1857 from the Secretary to the Chief Commissioner, Punjab, Rawalpindi, to the Government of India, Foreign Department, gives the translation of this letter and says that the Maharaja of Patiala delivered the original to the Commissioner, Cis-Sutlej States. *Vide P. L. of Mutiny Papers of 1857-1858 in Punjab Secretariat*, p. 39. Another telegram No. 139 of 23rd May 1857 tends to elucidate the contents saying, 'The letter from the King of Delhi to the Maharaja of Patiala invited the Maharaja to rise'. *Idem*, p. 30.

[4] Greathed—*Letters written during the seige of Delhi*, p. 134.

Khan the Emperor 'addressed letters to the troops at Nimuch and Firozpur and received petitions from the regiments at Jhansi, Dinapur, Allahabad, Aligarh, Muthra, Bulandshahr, Roorki, Farrukhabad, Hansi, Sirsa, Karnal, Nasirabad, Saugor, Jubbulpur, Ambala, Phillaur, Jallandar, Sealkote, Jhelum, Rawalpindee, Loodhiana, Gurgaon, Rewari, Badshahpur, Rohtak, Hissar, Bijnor, Bareilly and Mainpuri. All these regiments were invited to proceed to Dehli at once[1]; and circular letters to this effect were despatched to Rao Bhara the ruler of Kutch Bhoj, to Ranjit Singh, Chief of Jaisalmir and to Raja Gulab Singh of Jammu'[2].

Then it is contended that Bahadur Shah lacked military knowledge and personal bravery[3]. But the incident from which, on the authority of Muinu'ddin Hasan the above inference has been drawn was related differently by Mukand Lal, the Emperor's private secretary, before the Military Tribunal. Muinu'ddin Hasan, indeed, had said, 'The mutineers represented to the King that the sepoys were reluctant to attack the English and demanded his presence in the field. This he promised to give. A large force was ordered to assemble in the evening. The King headed the force and passed by the Dehli Gate and showed himself to the assembled troops. Passing by the Lal Diggi Tank he went towards the Lahore Gate. One of the Palace dependents was substituted for the King who secretly retired to the city by a back way. This show of force ended in nothing. The troops gradually moved back to their own quarters and the threatened attack ended in smoke'[4]. To

---

[1] *Pr. Tr. B.S.*—pp. 168-175.

[2] *Op. Cit.*, pp. 151-152.

[3] S.M.R., pp. 119-120.

[4] Metcalfe.—T.N.N., p. 68.

Mukand Lal the Judge advocate put the following question: 'Did the Prisoner on any occasion go out of the Palace for the purpose of encouraging the troops to fight against the English?' 'Yes' replied Mukand Lal, 'two days after the assault, *viz.*, on the 16th September he went in an open litter in the direction of the Magazine at the head of the army; but had scarcely proceeded 200 yards beyond the Palace when he halted for an hour and then returned, the army in the meantime dispersing.' 'Do you know', said the Judge Advocate, 'what induced the Prisoner to halt after proceeding so short a distance and to what was it generally attributed?' 'He', replied Mukand Lal, 'had gone out with the army in order to dislodge the British from the city; when the troops became engaged, he stayed to encourage them[1]'.

There is some lacuna in both of these narratives; both are incomplete and each tends to stress a feature. Mukand Lal says: 'The King had gone out with the army in order to dislodge the British from the city: when the troops became engaged, he stayed one hour[2] to encourage them'. Muinu'ddin Hasan says that the King went towards the Lahore Gate and then he secretly retired by a back way. From the information given by Hakim Ahsanullah Khan who was present on that occasion it appears that on his arrival in the battlefield

[1] *Pr. T. B. S.*—p. 104.

[2] If he stayed in the battlefield one hour he could not have remained there with his lips sealed. He was in the habit of speaking to the sepoys. He always made some remarks addressing the batterymen whenever he visited Salimgarh. *Vide* Metcalfe—T.N.N., pp. 145, 154, 159, 163, 169, 181, 198, 203, 204, 206.

the Emperor noticed signs of insincerity among the sepoys; so he returned to the Palace. The story runs as follows:

'Next day Maulvi Sarfaraz Ali and Maulvi Abdul Ghafur and many Maulvis from outside came to the King after 12 o'clock and importuned him to ride forth and take his troops with him otherwise the sepoys would make a disturbance asking, 'Why does not the King send out his servants to attack the Ridge (*Pahari*) if he is in truth the enemy of the English? Although the order has been given (to attack the *pahari*) yet the King's servants never advance beyond the Lahori Gate. True some boys went out one day with the sepoys and their officer was wounded and died. The Kamona (?) youth, *i.e.* Sirdar went out daily to the attack. He too, 4 days ago, was severely wounded. In short they continued to talk thus until the King, unable to help himself, set out.

'At this moment some officers of the army came up. Having gone out of the Fort by the Dehli Gate they stopped at the Ellenborough Tank (Lal Diggi)'. 'As soon as I heard the news', continues Hakim Ahsanullah Khan, 'I went too. At that time people about the King said, 'Advance and place the guns on the further side of the magazine. The cavalcade was about to move on when I remonstrated and said, "Pray don't advance but return to the Fort for balls are flying about here even."

'After much discussion about the time of afternoon prayers the cavalcade returned to the Fort. I said, 'These people bring disgrace on Your Majesty for nothing. You never ought to have ridden forth! God forbid that the sepoys should take Your Majesty out to the front of the battle, and then run off and you be taken prisoner. Never. You had better mused over what they say'.[1]

It is commonly believed that Hakim Ahsanullah Khan had ingratiated himself with the British[2]. But there is no documentary evidence available to convict him; rather there are some records which testify to the honest performance of duties on his part. His letters—written during the war to Lala Debi Prasad directing the latter to arrange for the supply of food to the cavalry and infantry of the Badshahi Army proceeding to give battle to the English[3]—are a case in point. His own memoirs do not go beyond showing that suspicions were cast on him of sending news to the British; but he successfully removed the suspicions from the minds of his accusers by swearing on the Quran and saying, 'I will never write anything[4]'. Nor had he a hand in the explosion of the Magazine at Churiwalan on 7th August 1857. Says Jiwan Lal, 'A great number of officers, assembled in the court, said, 'We are satisfied that the Hakim had nothing to do with the explosion of gunpowder[5]'. Nor had he written the seditious letter which the sepoys once attributed to him[6]. Says Chunni Lal, 'Ahsanullah Khan declared it was a forgery got up by some persons and impressions on it were from counterfeit seals of gypsum; and they (Ahsanullah Khan and Mahbub Ali Khan) took off their signets and threw before the soldiers. They further swore by the Quran that the seals on the paper were not theirs and that the document was a forgery[7]'.

---

[1] J.P.H.S., January 1958, pp. 30-31.

[2] *Vide* p. 422 *infra.*

[3] M.P., Box 151, Nos. 9-11-15

[4] J.P.H.S., January 1958, pp. 5, 7.

[5] Metcalfe—T.N.N., p. 191.

[6] *Pr. Tr. B. S.*, p. 111.

[7] *Ibid.*

Subsequently when the Emperor went to inspect the Salimgarh fortifications he assured the soldiers that he was associated with them in a common cause and desired them to place every confidence in the Hakim. He told them that he would slay with his own hands any European they might seize and bring to him. On hearing this the troops were convinced and Hakim Ahsanullah was fully exculpated[1]. Bahadur Shah held the British spies responsible for endeavouring to bring the Hakim into bad odour. On another occasion he challenged the Hakim's accusers to bring forth a single objectionable letter with a genuine seal of the latter and he promised to change his opinion about him and punish him with his own hands. That differences of some kind did exist between the Hakim and his benevolent Royal master has been shown elsewhere[2]. Here it may be recalled that when on the occasion of Bakar-'id the Emperor banned cow-slaughter and ordered that 'if any Musalman should do so he would be blown away from a gun and whoever on the part of a Musalman helped to kill a cow would also be killed[3].' Hakim Ahsanullah Khan demurred to such an order and said he would consult the Maulvis. On hearing this the Emperor became very angry, closed the audience and retired to the private apartments[4]'. Hakim Ahsanullah Khan had also clashed with his Royal master in respect of the conferment of military commands and khilats on the Princes and strongly opposed him in the matter of

---

[1] *Ibid.*

[2] *Vide* p. 53 *infra.* It should be noted that Hakim Ahsanullah Khan who had no knowledge of the cold war that his Royal master had been waging with the East India Company since 1837 never rose to the height of Bahadur Shah's political intelligence.

[3], [4] Metcalfe—T.N.N., p. 170.

awarding Royal consent to the murder of the English prisoners, so persistently demanded by the sepoys[1]. That in spite of all this the Emperor did not like to give up the Hakim is a question which calls for an answer. In my opinion the answer lies in the character of Bahadur Shah which has been discussed in this book[2] and also in the fact that Hakim Ahsanullah Khan was the scion of a sufi family and was himself a man of sufi persuasion. He had enjoyed an unsullied reputation for many years in the Dehli territory and had been appointed court physician by Akbar Shah who extolled him and reposed great confidence in him[3]. Bahadur Shah did the same. He liked Hakim Ahsanullah Khan not only for his professional skill but also for his scholarship and literary pursuits. He considered him indispensable not only as physician but also as editor of his manuscripts and the supervisor of the Royal press and publications. The *Precis of Palace Intelligence* says:

> 'In the evening (Tuesday, 7th January 1851) Hakim Ahsanullah Khan presented the works of His Majesty printed in several volumes for inspection. His Majesty directed that the Princes and others should be informed that they could purchase any of the works at 5 rupees per volume'[4].

Cognizance must also be taken of the details available about the character of the sepoys, their unbalanced judgment and habitual suspicions. They suspected everyone of being in league with the English. Begin-

---

[1] J.P.H.S., January 1958 p. 6 ff.

[2] Chapter I.

[3] Syed Ahmad—*Tazkira-i Ahl-i Dehli,* pp. 46-47.

[4] MS. Miscellaneous, N. A.

ning with Mahbub Ali Khan[1] and Hakim Ahsanullah Khan[2] they charged everyone in the Royal court and Family—Nawab Hamid Ali Khan[3], Maulvi Sadru'ddin[4], the Princes[5] who were their commanders of their own choice and Queen Zinat Mahal Begum[6]. In the last instance General Bakht Khan[7] and even the Emperor were drawn in the whirlpool[8]; none was spared and all were suspects in their eyes. This was a case of over suspicion which only betrays a diseased mind and a guilty conscience, the more so because they did not know their own duties and were incapable of distinguishing a friend from a foe. While they strongly suspected their best friends and would have them killed,—they were, and remained uniformly, blind to the army of mischievous British spies that wrought havoc in their midst.

Regarding Zinat Mahal Begum, on whom fell the brunt of the sepoys' suspicions, the treatment that the British Authorities extended to her after the fall of Dehli is highly suggestive. In their eyes she was as much a convict as Bahadur Shah himself. They treated her equally cruelly and plundered her house, seized her personal hoardings as well as the security paper which Hodson had given her. Such was her fate at the hands of the British because she had been kind to their enemies—the sepoys. She had arranged of her own accord for the supply of food to the sepoys in the battlefield and had shown her readiness more than once to pay the Royal servants and the Army out of her private purse. Saiyed Jameelu'ddin, editor of the *Sadiqul Akhbar,* admired her for her spirit of self-

---

[1], [2] Metcalfe—T.N.N., p. 59.

[3], [4] (i) *Pr. Tr. B. S.,* p. 109.

(ii) Metcalfe—T.N.N., p. 191.

[5], [6], [7], [8] *Op. cit.*

sacrifice saying: 'The queen is prepared to pay the sepoys' pay out of her private purse[1]'. If she had expressed a desire for a peaceful settlement with the British, it was at bottom the same as Bahadur Shah's to help the 'mutineers' by interceding for them with the British authorities. With the same object she subsequently proposed a settlement through Mirza Ilahi Bakhsh[2].

It should also be noted that at the time of the uprising in Dehli she gave evidence of her humanity by endeavouring to protect a helpless European girl who had sought shelter with her. To this effect she made a statement before Captain Davies in the Rangoon prison[3]. She claimed for herself the credit of writing a letter to the Governor of the North-West Provinces. This tends to explain the charge brought against her of 'opening secret correspondence with the British[4]'. But she failed to impress Captain Davies who continued to treat her as a convict.

Among the new sources of information which have been drawn upon in this book and could not find a place in the Chapter on Sources[5], the following deserve particular notice here:

(i) *Zafar-uz Zafar or Fath Nama-i Angrezi*[6].
(ii) *Khiyban-i Tasawwuf*[7].
(iii) *List of Documents drawn up at the National Archives of India in connection with the centenary celebrations on 21st August, 1957*.

[1] M.P.—Box 4-6, Vol. 4; also see p. 305 *infra*.
[2] *Vide* p. 100 *infra*.
[3] *Vide* p. 421 *infra*.
[4] *Cf*. p. xix *supra*.
[5] *Vide* p. 282 *infra*.
[6] MS. 129, Oriental Library, Bankipur.
[7] Raza Library, Rampur.

(iv) *Azamgarh Proclamation.*

(v) *Letter of an English Officer written after the fall of Dehli.*

(i) *Zafar-uz Zafar* (literally victory over Bahadur Shah Zafar) is a manuscript No. 129 of the Bankipur Library giving in Persian verse the story of the War of 1857 in Dehli by Francis Godlieu Quins or Franz Gottieb Kuen[1] (1777-1861)—a Persian-Urdu poet of German race commonly known as Frasoo which was his pen-name. Describing him as a good poet of Urdu, the author of the *European Shuara-i Urdu* says that Frasoo's father named Augustan was employed under Begum Samru[2]. The manuscript written clearly in Persian *nast'aliq* script comprises 2,380 verses[3] which the poet composed in the course of one year (May 1857-May 1858[4]). He says that immediately on their arrival from Mirath Bahadur Shah called the mutineers to a personal interview, and speaking his mind to them made them swear to fight the English[5]. Then Frasoo describes the distress of the Europeans (white people) and his own misfortunes at the hands of the black (*siyahan*[6]). For having given shelter in his native village of Harcharanpur to some Englishmen—namely Hewett, Forrest, Gramhir, Batson, Carteret, Gough and Thomas—he was seized by the sepoys headed by Shah Mall[7], Nirpat Singh and Laj Ram Jat. They bound

---

[1] *Vide* (i) I.H.R.C. (1942), xix.

(ii) *Bengal, Past and Present,* 1955, July-December, pp. 89-91.

[2] Sardar Ali—*European Shuara-i Urdu,* p. 22.

[3] These verses in the MS. 129, Bankipur Library have been numbered by me for the first time.

[4] Frasoo—*Fath Nama,* F. 98 b.

[5] *Vide* p. 103 *infra.*

[6], [7] *Fath Nama,* F. 85b. Verses 2014-2026 ff.

him hand and foot and beat him severely and plundered his house[1]. He was ransomed by a *mahajan* of Banali village[2] and was finally saved by Dunlop, William and Trumble—the British officers who setting out from Mirath for Dehli happened to arrive in time in the vicinity of Harcharanpur[3]. It was the personal notes, news-letters and despatches of the said British refugees and rescuers, besides his own bitter experiences that formed the chief sources of Frasoo's book[4]. To these may be added the stories that were related to Frasoo by the inhabitants of Sonhara village under the leadership of Ismail, Ram Bhai and Jasudi, the confirmed rebels who had roused many villages against the British and had worked in unison with the Jats and Musalman inhabitants of Harcharanpur, Nanwa, Kazim, Nanuhan, Sarkhlan, Bajrol, Johri, Bajwarah, Pothi, Dhanaura, Bodhera, Pois, Gorana, Naglagulab, Baroli Bali, Banali Baghon, Santokhpur, Halvari, Barauth, Osaikh, Nadir, Aslat and Aslat Kharmast[5]. In the end Frasoo says,

دریں ملک بیگانه و دشمن اند
ایں هند و مسلماں هر یک تن اند
طرفدار هند و مسلماں شود
یکے طرف دیگر دگر آں شود

The English are (considered as) strangers and

[1] *Op. cit.*

[2] *Cf.* Telegram of 21st July 1857 which says, 'Shah Mall Jat has been attacked and killed with 6,000 followers by the Mirath Force. (*Press-List of Mutiny Papers of 1857-1858* in *the Punjab Secretariat,* p. 166.)

[3] *Fath Nama;* verses 2154-2250

[4] *Idem,* F. 75b.

[5] *Idem,* F. 85b.

enemies in this country. The Hindus and Musalmans, though apparently two communities, really form one nation, one siding with the other[1].

(ii) *Khiyaban-i Tasawwuf* (a venue of sufism) is the title of Bahadur Shah's masterpiece on Shaikh S'adi's *Gulistan*. It is a voluminous work of 759 pages of large size printed in 1259 Hijra[2], *i.e.* 6th year of Bahadur Shah's reign under the supervision of Hakim Ahsanullah Khan. I have seen and used a copy of it at the Raza Library, Rampur.

The *Khiyaban-i Tasawwuf* opens with a sermon in Arabic after which the Royal author says, 'I was yet the Heir-Apparent during the reign of my illustrious father Akbar Shah when I wrote several books including notably the *Lughat-o Istilah-i Dakhani* also called *Talifat-i Abu Zafari* in 3 volumes published in 1226 Hijra[3]. I had compiled it after a close study of many reliable works. . . . . Many commentaries on Shaikh S'adi's works have been written but his true meaning, mission and message as a sufi of the Suharwardi order have not been brought out at all'. In other words the *Khiyaban-i Tasawwuf* is the first research work in this line. In it every saying of Shaikh S'adi's has been carefully examined and explained, and a suitable commentary is given with many quotations from the Holy Quran, Hadis and the maxims of Hazrat Ali as well as from the history of Islam and Islamic world. In the end the author gives a chronogram, saying:

بنوشت ولیعہد شہ اکبر ثانی
چوں شرح گلستاں پئے تبیاں تصوف

[1] *Idem*, verses 2226-2227.

[2] 1843 A.D.

[3] 1811 A.D.

چوں کرد قلم لفظ بخرد در بر آمد
تاریخ مع نام خیابان تصوف

(When the Heir-Apparent of Emperor Akbar II had written the commentary of the *Gulistan* containing a profound study of sufism, his pen scribbled the word *'bakhirad'* which together with the name *Khiyaban-i Tasawwuf* turned out a chronogram).

(iii) Out of the 40 documents which the given List of Documents contains the 7th, 11th, 12th, 16th, 17th, 18th B, 19th, 20th, 31st A, 32nd, and 34th bring into relief some of the points which have been discussed in this book.

The 7th is a call to jihad made by Maulvi Liyaqat Ali of Allahabad. 'A weaver by birth and schoolmaster by profession, Liyaqat Ali assumed leadership of the inhabitants of Allahabad and strove to establish the new order of which Emperor Bahadur Shah was the champion'.

(Foreign, 31st December, 1858, No. 1752)

The 11th is a proclamation from the Peshwa's archives issued by the Maratha Brahmins, calling on all the Brahmins of the Deccan between the age of 16 and 32 as well as all those who could use the sword to serve as soldiers in the Peshwa's army.

(Foreign Supplement, 30th December 1859, No. 651)

The 12th is an 'inflammatory Persian placard posted on a mosque at Hyderabad, calling on the government and people of Hyderabad to declare war on the English.'

(Secret, December 18, 1857, No. 252-53)

The 16th reproduces an order issued by Mirza Mughul, the commander-in-chief, to all the officers enjoining that whoever took anything from any citizen without payment was liable to capital punishment.

(Mutiny Papers, 50-309, July 13, 1857)

The 17th gives one instance out of many showing that cow-slaughter was completely prohibited on the occasion of Bakar'id (2nd August 1857). The proclamation to this effect issued by Mirza Mughul the commander-in-chief was confirmed by Emperor Bahadur Shah. The Emperor's autograph in ink is clearly visible.

(Mutiny Papers, 50-309, July 13, 1857)

The 18th reproduces the Royal order sent to the commander-in-chief asking him to arrest all those who plundered Dehli.

(Mutiny Papers, 43, 24. June 27, 1857)

The 18th B gives one out of the many instances of the steps taken by Emperor Bahadur Shah to maintain order and to suppress law-breaking. In this case Mirza Mughul the commander-in-chief is particularly ordered to warn the people of Dehli against counterfeiting coins.

(Mutiny Papers, 57. No. 542)

The 19th and 20th are a confirmation of the role that the Dehli Newspapers of 1857 played in making the War popular. The reader will find occasional references to this effect in the course of this book.

(Mutiny Papers, Collection No. 2 and Box No. 1)

The 31st A announces the decision of the inhabitants of the historic Doaba, particularly the tract between Etawa and Fatehpur, to fight the English.

(Pol. December 30, 1859. Suppt. 626)

The 32nd is a double document illustrating Rani Lakshmi Bai's protests against the annexation of Jhansi. It also gives her letter to Dalhousie dated December 21, 1854 and her memorial to the Court of Directors, saying that her people did not want a change of rulers.

(Foreign, March 2, 1855. No. 75 KWA)

The last document No. 34 reproduces the Rani's letter in Marathi addressed to the Peshwa dated 14th February 1858 soliciting the Peshwa's help against the English.

(Foreign, December 30, 1858. Supplement Nos. 617-54, K.W.A.)

(iv) AZAMGARH PROCLAMATION[1]

It being clear as the noonday sun that Hindoos and Masulmans have been ruined by the faithless Infidels, it becomes necessary for every ambitious and aspiring man and for those devoted to this cause (especially for Kings and Chiefs who have been created by God expressly for the purpose of taking care of the people and of their rights) to sacrifice their lives and fortunes for improving the condition of the people. Several of the Princes of Dehli have with this view,

---

[1] The heading under which this Proclamation appears in the Records is this: *Translation of a Proclamation issued by the Rebels.* Political Consultations, 8th October, 1858,

Azamgarh is a town near the Gogra with Ballia to the east, Jaunpur and Ghazipur to the south, and Faizabad and Gorakhpur in the north.

travelled for the last several years in all quarters of Hindoostan, Persia and Afghanistan and one of them has succeeded in bringing the Persian and Afghanistan forces to this quarter of the globe.

It must be known that I, Aboo Moozuffer Sirajooddeen Buhadoor Shah Ghazee, Emperor of Hindoostan have determined to kill and extirpate the Christians[1] and to preserve and protect the public and after travelling a good deal have arrived here and planted the standard of Mahomed, for rallying around it not only Musulmans but Hindoos who, from the time of my forefathers were faithful and obedient subjects and who have joined me in killing the Christians[1] and to raise alike their standard of Muhabeer[2]. I am glad to proclaim that several Mohomedans and Hindoos have since joined us and assisted in exterminating the Christians, and that a force from the west[3] is very shortly expected to join and reinforce our cause. I therefore publish the following articles for general information and guidance and make known that any one who has not the means of defraying the expenses, may receive succour from the Imperial Treasury on making his wants known.

It should be further remembered that the books of Hindoo and Mahomedan Religion prophesy that after this year the British reign will end in Hindoostan and in several other places; every man should therefore remove from his mind the fear of its continuance, and

---

[1] The term 'Christian' in the given translation is wrong and seriously misleading. It has been shown above (pp. 58-103) that Emperor Bahadur Shah II was no bigot and did not dislike the Christians. The term Christian should be replaced by 'British'.

[2] *I.e.* Mahavira.

[3] *I.e.*, Arabia and Iran.

should join our cause thus obtaining some benefit to himself, otherwise he will repent, and that in a short time. (*Couplet*: Do not waste time when you can make your fortune by immediately joining us, for the time is precious and once lost can never be restored).

Keep in mind that the outrages committed by our force are inseparable from Civil Warfare, and be assured that they will not continue long, though the well-wishers of the British may speak to the contrary about the continuance of such outrages for ever. Every man should present himself to us and state his grievances when immediate redress will be given and all his losses made good from the Imperial Treasury after the establishment of our reign.

1st. *Zamindars*! It is very well known that the British assess lands very highly and this has been the cause of your ruin. Besides, when sued by a mean labourer or a male or female servant, you are summoned without investigation to attend to their court and are thus dishonured and degraded, and when you have to prosecute a case in their court you are put to the expense of doing so on stamp paper and have to pay court fees which are ruinous. Besides this you have to pay a percentage for roads and schools—all these grievances will be removed in our reign and the powers of all Zamindars thereby increased, and their complaints decided agreeably to the Shari'a and Shastra. It is therefore incumbent on you to make common cause with us; and those of you who will supply men and money to help us to kill these Christians and to meet the expenses of our Troops, will receive a perpetual remission of half the revenue of their Ilaqas, and those who supply only men or money will receive a remission of one quarter of the revenue for good· such as have, during the British rule lost their lands and will now join in this common cause will be replaced in possession of their lands and remission of a quarter of the Revenue will also be granted.

2nd. *Merchants*! You are also well aware that the faithless British have appropriated to themselves the monopoly of all lucrative trade such as indigo, opium, cloth . . and left the less remunerative merchandise to you, and when you have to resort to their courts you have to pay large sums for stamp papers and court fees; moreover they realize money from the public in the shape of postage and school funds and you, like the Zamindars, are degraded by being summoned to their courts and imprisoned or fined on the assertion of men and low people. But during the King's Reign all these inconveniences will be put a stop to, and every description of trade, whether by sea or land, left to native merchants (Hindoos and Musalmans) and men will be posted at each stage on the road for your protection at the King's expense. Besides every assistance shall be given to the poorer members of your class. It is therefore necessary for you to assist us with men and money.

3rd. *Men of Service*! You likewise well know that in the Civil and Military Department, all the less lucrative and dignified situations are given to natives and the well paid and honourable ones to Europeans, for instance in the Military Line the highest post that a native attains is that of a Subadar on a salary of 60 or 70 Rupees a month and in Civil that of a Sadr Ameen on a salary of 500 Rupees—and jageers, rewards, maafees etc. are not known to be in existence while during our reign, the offices of Colonels, Generals, etc. which are now given to the Europeans only, and the ranks of Pansadee, Shash Huzaree, Punj Hazaree, Haft Hazaree, Sepah Salar in the military and those of Collector, Magistrate, Judge, Sadr Dewanee, Secretary, Governor-General, etc. in the Civil Departments and the situations of Wizarat, Qazi, Sifarat, Sooba, Nizamat Dewanee and yielding lacs of rupees will be granted to the natives of this country. Besides Jageers rewards 'maafees, etc. will be bestowed on them; moreover it should be well understood that by remaining with the Christians you will be called Infidels in this world, and will forfeit your prospects in the next, and if any of you die while fighting against the British, you will gain a name in this world and obtain endless happiness in the next, therefore every one now in the service of the Firangees should leave them and join us and their salaries will at present be doubled or tripled and they will hereafter be promoted to higher grades. If any one cannot openly leave British employ they should secretly assist us as much as lies in their power. If any Telingas or Sawars, who have killed Christians and gone to their homes will come and join us, they will be paid, sepoys at 3 as. a day and Sowars at 8 and 12 as. besides the double *batha* and the monthly pay given by the Firangees. If any others will accept employment under us, they will get for the present as follows:—

Matchlockmen	2 as. a day
Each man with sword and shield ...	1½ as. a day
Sowar with a full size horse ...	8 as. a day
Sowar with poney	6 as. a day

But after the settlement of our rule they will get as follows:—

Each Sepoy ...	8 and 10 Rs. per month
Each Sowar ...	25 and 30 Rs. per month

4th. *Artizans*! You are also well aware that the Europeans import every sort of article from Europe leaving but a small trade in your hands, while in our reign every article will be manufactured by you which will tend to your benefit and profit. Besides the Emperor and his Chiefs will require precious articles which you will supply and which will greatly enhance your profits. You should therefore leave the British and join us and secure the good will of both God and man.

5th. *Scholars of both creeds of Hindoos and Musalmans*! (*Maulvies and Pundits*!) You are aware that the British are opposed to your religion and as the present is a Religious War you should join us and gain the good will of your Creator, otherwise you will be considered 'Sinners'. If you will join us you will receive maafees and lands from the Emperor.

It should be borne in mind that if any one of the above-mentioned classes of the people, after reading or hearing this Proclamation still adhere to the British, his property etc. will be confiscated and he and his family put to the sword.

Dated Uurutha (*sic*) Ilaqa Azamgarh (*Azimgurah*), the 16th Muharram[1] 1275, corresponding with 3rd Bhadoon 1265 Fuslee.

True Translation.
Sd. J. D. Forsythe,
Secretary to the Chief Comm. Oude.

The legend of Bahadur Shah

The above proclamation proves that the legend of Emperor Bahadur Shah II lived after his exit. Much before August 1858/Muharram 1275—the date

[1] 25th August, 1858 A.D.

of the Proclamation—he had been tried and found guilty by the British. While they were making plans to exile him from India, an attempt was made by Prince Firoz Shah—a direct descendant of Bahadur Shah I—who was still at war with the British to rally the Indians in the name of the Emperor. Therefore he issued the so-called Azamarh Proclamation which was in fact a replica of Emperor Bahadur Shah II's Proclamation of 25th August 1857, already described in this book. To this effect I have invited the reader's attention in footnote 3(ii) on page 103 *infra*.

The story of Prince Firoz Shah lies outside the scope of this book. But he had an ideology similar to that of Bahadur Shah II. Both were intensely anti-British and endeavoured to enlist the support of the foreign princes in their war against the East India Company. By his trip to the Middle East on the eve of the outbreak of 1857 and afterwards on being defeated by the British on Indian soil by his retiring to Mecca where he died (1877/1294), Prince Firoz Shah proved that the War of 1857 in Dehli amounted to an armed Revolution and that it was not a mere local revolt of a few discontented sepoys in British employ.

(v) *Letter*[1] *of an English Officer written after the fall of Dehli*

'Upon examining the apartments occupied by the King and his chief officers in the Palace many

[1] Charles Ball—H.I.M., Vol. I, p. 524.

papers were found that threw a liight upon the intended proceedings of the rebel monarch; and from them it appeared that the kind of government to be permanently established for the city and immediately surrounding country was more of the nature of a military than of a Mohammedan government. It seems to have been a sort of constitutional monarchical milocracy. The King was king and honoured as such like a constitutional monarch; but instead of a parliament, he had a a council of soldiers in whom power rested and of whom he was in no degree a military commander. No Arabic or Persian names, forms or terms appear to have been introduced; but on the centrary the English terms and modes of business were generally adopted. All petitions seem to have been presented to the King; but the great authority to which almost all of them on all matters both civil and military were referred (by order endorsed on petition) was the Court—a body composed of a number of colonels, a brigade-major and a *seketur* (secretary) which latter functionary seems to have been the most important personage in Dehli. All the colonels etc. were sepoys who made their mark or at best signed in rough Hindoo characters. Very regular muster-rolls of regiments were kept up and authenticated in due form by the colonel adjutant and quartermaster. From these documents it also appears that they went so far into detail as to fill up the places of the European sergeant majors and quartermaster sergeants.

'One sepoy colonel had presented to the King a kind of memorandum on the best mode of administering the country after getting rid of the Firangees. First and foremost he advises His Majesty to collect as much money as he can from any quarter by any means whatever, as a capital to start upon. Second he proposes that the future administration should be based on British model; and then in many headings he goes into details evincing considerable thought and shrewdness. There was also among the papers a very long and enthusiastic account of the destruction of the European garrison of Fatehgarh. A petition was found from a man who sought to be appointed collector of the district in the rear of our army on a solemn pledge that he would collect the revenue and stop the supplies of the Europeans or if not, would submit to be blown from a gun; but the prudent order is to be considered when the hill (British position) is taken! There were also many communications from native Princes who either promised or temporised much'.

Before closing this preface I solemnly declare that in writing this book I have been moved by no passion other than a burning desire to ascertain the truth. I have conducted the researches embodied in this book in the light of the following verse of the *Rajtarangini*:

হলায়ঃ সঃএব গুণবান্ রাগদ্বেষ বহিষ্কৃতঃ
ভূতার্থ কথনে যস্য স্থেয়স্যেব সরস্বতী

(A writer of real parts is he whose narration of past events is free from anger and malice, and is firm like the word of the supreme arbiter—Saraswati.)

Now I let this unpretentious work of mine prepared under the most difficult circumstances swim or sink on its own merits. The reader is requested to note that the references to the Boxes in the footnotes of this book pertain to the actual contents of the Bastas. I have checked the alleged number of papers in many of the

Bastas at the National Archives and have found that the alleged number does not always tally with the actual number of papers in a given Basta.

I have disapproved of the wrong spellings of proper names and have preferred Kanpur to Cawnpore, Lakhnao to Lucknow, Mirath to Meerut and Dehli to Delhi, editing the texts accordingly wherever possible. In connection with 'Dehli' and 'Delhi' the reader's attention is particularly invited to an appendix on the subject in the *Rehla of Ibn Battuta*[1]. There it has been shown that the correct Indian spelling is Dehli. With the establishment of the East India Company's rule, Delhi—the result of a corrupt spelling[2]—came to be regarded as the official spelling and crept into the postal guides by the middle of the 19th century. Hunter noticed this in 1869. In 1871 he prepared a scheme for 'a revised orthography of the Indian towns and villages' wherein he suggested *'Dehli'* as the correct spelling[3] to be adopted by the British Government. But his suggestion was not accepted, and 'Delhi' was notified as the authorized spelling.

I thank all those who have helped me in the course of my labours, particularly the top-ranking officers of the National Archives of India and of the Raza Library, Rampur. I also thank Shri V. S. Puri, Keeper of Records, Punjab Government, who enabled me to use the Scripts of the *Delhi News* (May—September 1857) and the photographic copies of *Atkinson's Prints of the War of 1857 in India*. I am grateful to Shri C. L. Sharma Tuleki, who kindly built into regular maps my

---

[1] *The Rehla of Ibn Battuta*, G.O.S., pp. 287-289.

[2] Cunningham—A.S.I.R., I, p. 161.

[3] Hunter, W.W.—*Guide to the Orthography of Indian Proper Names with a list showing the true spelling of Post Towns and Villages in India*, (Calcutta, 1871, p. 32.)

sketches of the War in Dehli. In one of these I have used the term 'National trenches' in order to express adequately the thought of Emperor Bahadur Shah II on the subject[1]. I am convinced that he considered the War of 1857 in Dehli as the national war, looking upon both the communities—Hindus and Musalmans—as forming one nation[2].

I am also grateful to Father Courtois of St. Xavier's College, Calcutta who very kindly corrected the proofs. Lastly I thank Professor M. M. Namazie of Calcutta University who read through the Arabic parts of this book.

National Archives of India, Mahdi Husain
Delhi, December 1957

P.S.—(i) In the *Bengal, Past and Present* (Jubilee Number 1957) I have read two articles—'A new account of the siege of Delhi,' and 'Some unpublished documents regarding the Mutiny of 1857.' But Syed Mubarak Shah's narrative which is the theme of the first article falls in line with Jiwan Lal's and Mu'inu'ddin Hasan's diaries for it was also prepared to please the British masters. In the second article there is nothing new as far as Bahadur Shah II is concerned. Already those 'unpublished documents' have been discussed in this book. Regarding the Rani of Jhansi the given documents tend to show that she too was shocked at seeing the blunder and misbehaviour on the part of the sepoys and consequently faced like Bahadur Shah himself a critical situation. She acquitted herself as best she could, but she was never unpatriotic.

(ii) The photo referred to in the footnotes of pages 280 and 281 of this book has not been included.

Calcutta University M.H.
November 1958

---

[1] *Vide* p. 34, footnote 2, *supra*.

[2] *Cf.* p. xxviii, *supra*.

When the book was completed and already in the press I lighted upon some old publications in Bengali containing contemporary or quasi-contemporary and modern Bengali thought on the subject matter of this work. Different kinds of evidence also came into my hands. I decided to incorporate all this under six headings at the end of the Preface.

I Bengali Thought as Expounded In

(i) Durga Das Bandopadhyaya's *Vidrohe Bangali* (বিদ্রোহে বাঙ্গালী)[1]

(ii) Rajani Kanta Gupta's *History of the Sepoy War* (সিপাহী যুদ্ধের ইতিহাস)[2]

(iii) Panch Kori Bandopadhyaya's *History of the Sepoy War* (সিপাহী যুদ্ধের ইতিহাস)[3]

(iv) Nagendra Nath Basu's *Encyclopaedia* (বিশ্বকোষ)[4]

(v) Ram Pran Gupta's *Mughul Dynasty* (মোগল বংশ)[5]

(vi) Ananda Bazar Patrika's *India's First War of Independence* (ভারতের প্রথম স্বাধীনতা সংগ্রাম)[6]

---

1 Calcutta, 1924 A.D./1331 B.S.
2 ,, 1897 A.D.
3 ,, 1909 A.D.
4 ,, 1904 A.D
5 ,, Ditto.
6 ,, May 10th, 1949 A.D.

(vii) Parichaya's *Bengali Folklore of 1857* (১৮৫৭র লোকগীতি)[1].

(i) Born in 1835 A.D. at Karnal in an orthodox Brahman family of West Bengal Durga Das inherited from his father Shiva Chandra—a cavalryman in the British army—his fervent devotion to the English. In 1851 when Shiva Chandra died Durga Das was employed in the British military service at Sultanpur. In 1856 he was posted at Bareilly where on the outbreak of the Mutiny (31st May 1857) his house was plundered by the sepoys who knew him as a friend of the English. He fled for his life seeking shelter in a local temple. Meanwhile a 'national' government[2] was formed with Bahadur Shah as Emperor, Khan Bahadur Khan as Nawab Nazim, Shobha Ram—a

---

[1] পরিচয় August 1957.

Some of these works, which are out of print or rare, were secured for me by Maulvi Mu'inu'ddin Husayn. I thank him for his kindness.

[2] This government must be called 'national' considering among other facts the following letter, dated 17th March 1858 of Saunders, the Commissioner, Dehli, to the Secretary to the Commissioner, Punjab, saying: 'I have the honour to forward a copy of the vernacular Proclamation issued by Khan Bahadur Khan, Nawab of Bareilly calling upon the Hindus to unite and make a common cause with the Musalmans against the British' (*Freedom Struggle in Uttar Pradesh,* I, p. 441). It should also be noted that Disraeli in the British Parliament had depicted the Rising of 1857 in India as a national revolt'. (*Idem,* p 486). And according to an eyewitness 'Bahadur Shah was acclaimed Emperor by not less than 10,000 people of Bareilly' (বিদ্রোহে বাঙ্গালী p. 143).

staunch Hindu—as Diwan and Bakht Khan as commander-in-chief, and Durga Das was invited to join it. He was offered the post of Chief Accountant in the commissariat with a salary of Rs. 1000 per mensem[1]. But he was planning secretly to flee from Bareilly and join the British at Naini Tal[2]. He declined to accept the post and fled. In spite of his planned flight he was arrested on the way and his life was endangered more than once. He was, however, saved on all occasions by his Muslim friends—namely Muhammad Safi, a Sepoy officer, Hafiz Ni'mat Khan, a cousin of Khan Bahadur Khan, and Chhunney Miyan, son of Hafiz Ni'mat Khan and son-in-law of Khan Bahadur Khan. Chhunney Miyan also saved the life of Kashi Prasad, younger brother of Durga Das, besides six other Bengalis[3], all of whom were to be killed under the orders of Khan Bahadur Khan. Then Chhunney Miyan enabled Durga Das to resume his journey to Naini Tal which he reached towards the close of 1857 with a treasure of Rs. 25,000—a present[4] for the British entrusted by Shiv Raj

---

[1] Durga Das—বিদ্রোহে বাঙ্গাল p. 117.

[2] Durga Das justified his attitude of firm loyalty to the English, saying, 'I have eaten the salt of the English' (*Idem*, p. 148). Similar was the case with Munshi Jiwan Lal. *Vide* p. 316 *infra*.

[3] *Idem*, pp. 340, 361.

[4] *Idem*, pp. 372, 375, 378.

Singh, the Raja of Kumaon. From the British camp he marched at the head of a squadron organized by himself to fight the sepoys. He killed many of them and seized Haldwani[1] as well as Kaladhungi[2] (February 1858)[3].

Durga Das considered the British rule in India as 'Ram Raj[4]' and looked upon the Rising of 1857 as an attempt on the part of the degenerate Musalmans to destroy Hindu society[5]. He disliked Khan Bahadur Khan for his anti-Bengali measures[6] and the following order of his: 'Whosoever in Bareilly knows English must be arrested.[7] He also disliked Bakht

---

[1] *I.e.*, a place roughly 3 miles west of the Gola river in Naini Tal district.

[2] Kaladhungi stands about 12 miles north-west of Haldwani.

[3] This was the final acquisition of Haldwani and Kaladhungi for the British who appear to have occupied Haldwani in part in October 1857. Afterwards sporadic fighting continued until the given date. (*Idem*, p. 502; *cf. District Gazetteer of Naini Tal,* p. 230).

[4] Durga Das—বিদ্রোহে বাঙ্গালী, p. 217.

[5] *Idem, cf.* pp. 215-216.

[6] Khan Bahadur Khan is reported to have said, 'The Bengalis are the gurus of the English and should not be trusted (*Idem,* p. 224). Fearing lest the Bengalis of Bareilly should go over to Naini Tal to join the British he prevented them from leaving the city unless they wanted to take their families to Bengal. (*Ibid*).

[7] This order applied to all, *i.e.,* to the Hindus as well as to the Musalmans and was not intended for the Bengalis only. But Durga Das's statement before Bakht Khan that he could maintain the accounts in English only for he knew no language other than English (p. 117)—although he knew five languages, *i.e.* Bengali, English, Persian, Urdu, and Hindi —made Bakht Khan as well as Khan Bahadur Khan suspicious.

Khan who had issued a similar order at Dehli. 'Bakht Khan', he remarked, 'is a rustic, highly conceited and extremely selfish. In my opinion he is not a good man. To meet his own needs he would flatter one enormously, otherwise his heart is as hard as stone'[1]. And Maulvi Fazl Haq[2] was equally disliked since the latter had ordered Durga Das, who was arrested in the course of his flight to Naini Tal and suspected as an agent of the British, 'to be blown up at the mouth of a gun'[3]. But Durga Das doted on the British spies who brought him news pleasing to his heart. Says he:

> 'At the time of war spy service is highly essential and indispensable; it serves as a great divine weapon. I am of opinion that without spies the British could not stand in any war even for a day, particularly so in the Sepoy War. In this war the spies were the entire life; they were the essence of life; they constituted the thread of life. To a talented spy greater respect was shown than even to a worshipful deity, not only respect but also immeasurable love and equally immeasurable devotion, indulgence, affection and motherly care. At the sight of a spy (my) heart was filled with joy. I longed to take him into my arms and bestow on

---

[1] *Idem*, pp. 91, 92, 114.

[2] After the fall of Dehli, Maulvi Fazl Haq had escaped to Lakhnao whence he appears to have proceeded to Naini Tal district. According to the information given by Durga Das, Maulvi Fazl Haq was the commander-in-chief of the Sepoy Army at Haldwani and was a very important officer (বিদ্রোহে বাঙ্গালী —, pp. 261, 264, 270, 272, 277, 278, 455).

[3] *Idem*, p. 272.

him my warm embraces. And I used to drink in his nectar-like words coming out of his moon-like bright mouth to my heart's content'[1].

The reader may well speculate what kind of news was so highly welcome to Durga Das! From the interest that according to his own account the British officers at Naini Tal evinced in the nature of Hindu-Muslim relations it would appear that the news really sought for in the British camp was about the 'expected or planned' outbreak of communal riots in the Badshahi army. And enquiries to that effect were made in the presence of Durga Das. We are told that a certain spy gave in reply a glowing account of the fight and bloodshed between the Hindus and Musalmans of Bareilly[2].

It would not be out of place if reference were here made to the letters issued by the British officers during the war of 1857 in order to inflame communal feelings among the Hindus and Musalmans. According to one such letter they authorized 'the sum of Rs. 50,000 to be expended in an attempt to raise the Hindu population of Bareilly against the Musalman rebels'[3].

(ii) Basing his account on those British writers who took the spies' reports verbatim, Rajanikanta Gupta says:

> 'Impatient through fear and desperation he (Bahadur Shah) used sometimes in his durbar and in the presence of nobles to uproot his white beard and moustache. Then pulling off

---

[1] Translated by the writer from the বিদ্রোহে বাঙ্গালী p. 448.
[2] *Idem*, pp. 459-460.
[3] *Freedom Struggle in Uttar Pradesh*, I, p. 472.

his turban from his head he used to tear it into pieces . . . A prince named Mirza Mughul having supported the English cause was compelled to appear before the Sepoys' court'.[1]

Finally as a necessary link in the supposed chain of the pro-British intrigues of Bahadur Shah the author reproduces the well-known but mischievous story that 'the aged king offered to admit the British troops into the Fort through a secret gate'[2].

At the end of his book the author reproduces two addresses that the rajas and zamindars of Bengal presented to Lord Canning after the war of 1857, saying:

'My Lord—we, the undersigned Rajas, Zamindars, Talookdars, Merchants and other Natives of Bengal, take the earliest opportunity, on the retaking of Delhi, to offer your Lordship in Council our warmest congratulations on the signal success which has attended the British arms, under circumstances unparalleled in the annals of British India......

'Happily remote from the scene of the outrages which have darkened the aspect of the land ...we have derived sincere consolation from the reflection that in Bengal proper there has been no disturbance, not even a symptom of disaffection; but that on the contrary the people have

---

[1] Translated by the writer from Rajanikanta Gupta's সিপাহী যুদ্ধের ইতিহাস, p. 110.

[2] Such is the essence of the 'unpublished documents' given in the *Bengal Past and Present* of 1957. And the above quotation shows that the contents of these unpublished documents had permeated Bengal before 1897, *vide* p. lvi *supra*.

maintained that loyalty and devotion to the British Government which led their ancestors to hail, and as far as they could, to facilitate, the rising ascendancy of that power......

' . . . . So entirely have they identified their interests with those of their Rulers, that the natives of Bengal, men, women and children, have in every part of the scene of the mutinies, been exposed to the same rancour, and treated with the same cruelty, which the mutineers and their misguided countrymen have displayed towards the British within their reach . . . .'[1]

(iii) Panch Kori Bandopadhyaya says :

'The Hindu-Muslim culture, which at the advent of the British had disappeared never to come back, still had left a hope of its recovery; and in the hope to recover it and restore that well-organized society in its proper place was made the beginning of the Sepoy War.

'To liberate themselves and the country from the high-handedness and insults of Lord Dalhousie's the sepoys throughout India recklessly and without thinking of the consequences jumped into the ocean of war . . .

'When the sepoys resolved to uproot the British power they lost much of their time in determining who would rule the empire and finally settled that the old feeble Bahadur Shah be again their ruler. This was settled among the Hindus and Musalmans since Bahadur Shah had been well-known and profoundly familiar to them for a long time. To save themselves and the country

---

[1] Translated by the writer from Rajanikanta Gupta's সিপাহী যুদ্ধের ইতিহাস. pp. 303-304.

from the government of the British strangers, such a determination was made; and having been once made nobody receded . . .

'Bahadur Shah was a man of patience, endurance and peace . . . He was bold like his father and did not like to lower himself and damage his pride and self-respect by accepting the condition demanded by Auckland in the way of increasing the Royal allowance'[1].

(iv) Nagendra Nath Basu says :

'Many still hold that he (Bahadur Shah) was the organizer of the Sepoy revolt of 1857.'[2]

(v) Ram Pran Gupta says :

'In 1857 while Bahadur Shah, grandson of Shah Alam, was living in Dehli enjoying the allowance given by the British the sepoys armed themselves to fight the British. Bahadur Shah joined the sepoys. For this crime of his the British, after extinguishing the sepoy revolt, banished him to Rangoon. There he remained in exile until a few years ago death came to his rescue and he left this world to enjoy everlasting peace. . . In this manner disappeared from India the name of Timur's dynasty.

ক্ব গতাঃ ধরণীপালাঃ স্বসৈন্যবলবাহনাঃ
বিয়োগ সাক্ষিণী যেষাং ভূমিরদ্যাপি তিষ্ঠতি

O rulers of the world (India) ! Where have you gone, you who possessed armies with might and main? India is missing you with a

[1] Translated by the writer from Panch Kori Bandopadhyaya's সিপাহী যুদ্ধের ইতিহাস, pp. 112-115.

[2] Translated from বিশ্বকোষ (Fifteenth Part), p. 447

heavy heart till today and the whole world stands as a witness to the loss that she has suffered'[1].

(vi) Ananda Bazar Patrika says :

'Having depicted India's First War of Independence as 'Sepoy Mutiny' the British rulers and historians have made a futile effort at undermining its historical importance and making light of it . . . While in England the Industrial Revolution was in progress the British brought in the machinery and mill devils; and in order to satisfy the overwhelming appetite of these devils, necessity arose to steal from India her economic prosperity. They began to destroy the cottage industry of India and turned her into a supplier of raw material. And the goods manufactured in the British factories were dumped in the Indian markets . . .

'Further, as a result of the British colonial policy and commercial exploitation the Indian masses were ruined . . . Even at this stage the British ambition did not stop. In the attempt to convert all the Indians into Christianity they undertook as a sacred duty to secure paradise for the peoples of India, rich with their mighty traditions of history. In the daily life of the Indians the English oppression began to tell . . . Not content with extracting money directly or indirectly from the people the British began to punish them with or without cause even to the extent of torturing them to death; and this became a regular practice. As a reaction from this political, economic and social revolution, the Indian mind in the

---

[1] Translated by the writer from Ram Pran Gupta's মোগল বংশ, p. 361.

preliminary stage was embittered against British rule. The sepoys only added fuel to the fire of the century-old malice and rage of the people.

'On account of the oppression exercised on the Mughul Emperor Bahadur Shah, the Musalmans of Dehli became ready to raise the standard of rebellion. The leaders of the War of Indian Independence selected Bahadur Shah as their commander who made an appeal to the Indians—Hindus and Musalmans—to cut off the chain of slavery through their combined efforts, sacrifice and bloodshed. Through a proclamation he promised to remove the grievances of the people by making a sacrifice of self. The people in a majority responded to his call. He gave further evidence of his patriotism to the Hindus by writing personal letters[1] to the rajas of Jodhpur, Bikaner, Alwar and others, as shown below:

> 'To drive away the Firangis from India by any means and at any cost is my only desire. I want to see the whole of India free and independent. Certainly it is not my desire to rule the country for myself by driving away the enemy. If you, rajas, draw your swords to drive away the enemy and then form a confederacy and government I would gladly entrust the sovereignty to you and will thus be freed from responsibility'[2].

---

[1], [2] For confirmation of these letters, see pp. 181, 182 footnotes, *infra*.

(Translated by the writer from ভারতের প্রথম স্বাধীনতা সংগ্রাম —Ananda Bazar Patrika).

(vii) Under the heading of 'Bengali Folklore of 1857' a scholar[1] in the *Parichaya* says :

রেঙ্গুনে নির্বাসিত জীবন কাটাবার সময় ইংরাজ অফিসার তাঁকে ব্যঙ্গ করে বলেছিলেন ঃ

দমদমে মেঁ দম নেহি হ্যয়ে খয়ের মাঙ্গো জান কী
বাস জফর বাড়চল চুকি অর তৈর হিন্দুস্থান কী

বাহাদুর শাহ প্রত্যুত্তরে বলেছিলেন ঃ

গাজিয়োঁ মেঁ জব তলক বাকি হ্যয় লৌ ইমান কী
তখতে লণ্ডন তক চলেগী তরবারী হিন্দুস্থান কী,[2]

Translation of the above by the writer

'While he was pining as an exile in Rangoon the British officers mocked at Bahadur Shah, saying :

'The batteries have no strength left, O Zafar ! the firing of Indian guns as also the plying of India's sword is over. Now you should make entreaties for your life's safety.'[3]

To this mockery Bahadur Shah replied saying :

'As long as there remains even a spark of Faith in the valiant soldiers, so long they will continue to fight and the sword of India will ply until they seize the throne of London.[4]'

The fact that the contents of the above-mentioned Urdu verses formed part of the Bengali folklore is a

---

[1] মহাশ্বেতা ভট্টাচার্য

[2] পরিচয় —A Bengali journal—(August 1957), p. 72.

[3], [4] *Cf.* pp. 45-46, *infra*.

pointer to the kind of feeling and belief then current in certain parts of Bengal.

II A Verse of Bahadur Shah Zafar

عالم صورت میں تو میں صورت آدم میں ہوں
عالم معنی میں لیکن اور ہی عالم میں ہوں[1]

'In the world of forms I am in human form.
But in the world of spirits I am in a different state.'

This verse of Bahadur Shah Zafar's was exploited after the fall of Dehli. It supplied the necessary material for the grotesque figure depicted in the *Asbab-i Ghadr*.[2]

[1] Bahadur Shah Zafar—*Diwan-i Awwal.*

[2] *Vide,* p. 49 *infra.*

III Prince Firoz Shah—a true warrior in the cause of India's liberation—speaks :

> '. . . . and I who am the grandson of Abu Zafar Siraju'ddin Bahadur Shah Ghazi, Emperor of India, having in the course of tour come here to extirpate the infidels residing in the eastern part of the country and to liberate and protect the poor helpless people now groaning under iron rule, have by the aid of the *mujahideen* erected the standard of Muhammad and persuaded the orthodox Hindus who had been subject to my ancestors and have been and are still accessories in the destruction of the English, to raise the standard of Mahavir . . . . '

The above proclamation of Prince Firoz Shah which is the famous Azamgarh proclamation has now been published under the heading of 'Proclamation of Bahadur Shah[1]. It shows that Prince Firoz Shah was neither a nephew[2] nor a son[3] of Bahadur Shah II; he was his grandson.

---

[1] *Freedom Struggle in Uttar Pradesh*, I, pp. 453-458.

[2] It has been contended that Prince Firoz Shah—son of Nizam Bakht, a direct descendant of Bahadur Shah I—was a nephew of Bahadur Shah II (*Freedom Struggle in Uttar Pradesh*, II, Editor's Appendix, p. 655.)

[3] It has also been contended, that Prince Firoz Shah was a son of Bahadur Shah II's. He was 'one of the chief rebels in the outbreak of 1857 and the British Government offered a reward of 10,000 rupees for his apprehension. It was reported that he made his appearance in the Serony jungles. Some Arabs who have recently arrived at Haiderabad, state that he is now (1866) in Arabia and supports himself by begging among the rich merchants'. (Beale, T. W.—*Oriental Biographical Dictionary* (1881), p. 83.)

The following is another proclamation of Prince Firoz Shah which throws light on his role in the War even after the exit of his royal grandfather, Bahadur Shah II . . . . It also shows that he was waging the war of India's liberation and independence. He speaks :

> 'O Hindoostanee Brethren ! . . . . Before the commencement of these calamities of the English I went on a pilgrimage to Mecca; on my return when I arrived at . . . and saw the condition of the English, I thanked God. As I am by nature a seeker after religious excellence, just and equitable and the obstructor of tyranny, therefore enticing the people to rebellion as I came along I travelled from Bombay to Gwalior, intending first to arrange and consolidate affairs and then to fight . . . . . 130,000 men, old and new soldiers, have been induced to swear to join me and I will soon, collecting all these, purify the land from all Nazarenes[1] . . . .
>
> 'The reason of the delay there has been in burying the English is that the commands of God have been disregarded inasmuch as the soldiers have wickedly put women and children to death, and have without the orders of their leaders, given themselves to loot in such a way that they generally convert victory into defeat and the common people have been much oppressed. When you have rectified these faults, you will succeed as I have promised you. . . . . .

[1] *I.e.* the English.

'. . . Therefore again I urge you and urge you one and all to join me, prompted only by the desire of doing God's work.

'. . . On the day and date I will march from the city, let all who wish, come then.

'. . . My advice is this : abandon every other work; give your life to your beloved or death will take it. Decide which of these alternatives is preferable'.[1]

IV More Contemporary Evidence

(i) His Majesty watched lion and elephants' and hounds' fight and rewarded handsomely Mir Fath Ali Khan who showed great bravery in killing the lion. His Majesty granted him the title of Nasru'ddaula Saiyed Fath Ali Hoshiyar Khan Bahadur Ghazanfar Jang.

(*M.P.* Vol. 12, No. 18).

(ii) His Majesty[2] insisted on Europeans taking off their shoes when they entered his presence.

(*Freedom Struggle in Uttar Pradesh,* p. 61).

(iii) His Majesty[3] granted the title of Dilawaru'l Mulk Raja Gulab Singh Bahadur Fath Jang to Gulab Singh, ruler of Jammu and Kashmir.

(*Idem.,* pp. 87-88).

(iv) *Sepoys addressing Bahadur Shah on their arrival from Mirath*:

'You are the king of both the worlds—terrestrial and spiritual . . . The English have been ruling on your behalf . . . A dispute

---

[1] (i) *Abstract N.W.P. Narrative Foreign,* 1858.
(ii) *Freedom Struggle in Uttar Pradesh,* I, pp. 462-463.

[2], [3] The text has 'King of Delhi'.

> between the Government and the Indian soldiers ensued . . . This dispute now has been continuing for the last four months . . . . We have circulated letters in our regiments of the Infantry and Cavalry to the effect that the entire army should totally refuse to honour the order and leave service, and in case any stringent measures are taken a *revolt should break out on one and the same date all over India*'

(*Freedom Struggle in Uttar Pradesh,* I, p. 405).

(v) ' . . . a document has been discovered at Dehli containing the names of all those to whom the King of Dehli has for many years past been in the habit of making presents of money. It is affirmed that the document contains the names of men in almost every regiment throughout the late Bengal Army and of many native functionaries in high civil employ.'

(*Freedom Struggle in Uttar Pradesh,* I, pp. 400-1 and *Friend of India,* January 7, 1857, p. 8).

(vi) *Proclamation of Nana Sahib*[1].

'Tyranny, wickedness and injustice having been practised by the Kafir (*Kaffur*) English on the faithful and sin-fearing, I have been commissioned by God to punish the Kafirs by annihilating them to re-establish the Hindu and Musalman kingdoms as formerly and to protect our country. . . .

---

[1] *A History of the Freedom Movement in India,* Bombay Vol. I, (1957), p. 254.

'. . . This proclamation is published by order of Ullee Shan[1] Bundeegan[2] Ulee Hoozoor[3], the Emperor of Dehli'[4].

V Rabindra Nath Tagore's Thought

(in original Bengali)

'সেদিন বিদ্রোহের ঝটিকার মধ্যে দেখিয়াছি. কত বীরপুরুষ উৎসাহে প্রজ্জ্বলিত হইয়া স্বকার্য সাধনের জন্য সেই গোলমালের মধ্যে ভারতবর্ষের প্রদেশের মধ্যে যুঝা-যুঝি করিয়া বেড়াইয়াছেন। সিপাহী যুদ্ধের সময়ে অনেক বীর তাঁহাদের বীর্য অযথা পথে নিয়োজিত করিয়াছিলেন একথা স্বীকার করিলেও মানিতে হইবে যে তাঁহারা যথার্থ বীর ছিলেন। পৃথিবীর মহা মহা বীরের নামের পার্শ্বে তাঁহাদের নাম লিখা উচিত। কিন্তু ভারতবর্ষের কি দুর্ভাগ্য, এমন বীরেরও জীবনী বিদেশীয়দের পক্ষপাতী ইতিহাসের পৃষ্ঠা হইতে সংগ্রহ করিতে হয়। আমরা সিপাহী-যুদ্ধ সময়ের অনেক বীরের নামোল্লেখ করিতে পারি, যাঁহারা ইউরোপে জন্মগ্রহণ করিলে ইতিহাসের পৃষ্ঠায়, কবির সঙ্গীতে, প্রস্তরের প্রতিমূর্ত্তিতে, অভ্রভেদী স্মরণস্তম্ভে অমর হইয়া থাকিতেন'[5]

রবীন্দ্রনাথ

Translation of the above by the writer

'The other day I looked through the stormy scenes of the Rebellion (of 1857) and visualized many a brave man, roused to action through zeal, marching about

---

[1], [2], [3] *I.e.*, عالی شان بدگان عالی حضور (His Majesty).

[4] Panta Pradhan Peshwa, according to Dr. P. M. Joshi. (*Idem*, p. 253.)

[5] Taken from Mani Bagchi's *History of the Sepoy War* –সিপাহী যুদ্ধের ইতিহাস), **Calcutta, 1957.**

and struggling amidst the chaos that reigned from province to province of India.

'It has been contended that during the Sepoy War many stalwarts spent their energies to the point of bravery improperly. Even if this contention were accepted, this much must be conceded that those sepoys were really brave. Their names deserve to be recorded by the side of the bravest and greatest heroes of the world.

'How unfortunate is this country that the life story of such heroes has to be collected from the pages of the biassed history written by the foreigners. Of the Sepoy war period we can specify the names of many brave warriors, who if they had been born in Europe, would have been immortalised in the pages of history, in the lyric verses of the poets and on marble statues and lofty monuments'.

Rabindra Nath

INTRODUCTION

In their work *L'Insurrection de l'Inde* Fonvielle and Legault explain the nature and objective of the War of 1857 saying, 'Is it necessary to reproduce exactly the allegations of the British press and to assert that the revolution which has broken out in India is without cause? Is it correct to say that the Indians are not interested in this and the revolt of the sepoys is only a military mutiny without an echo from the people of India? Is it correct to say that this revolution could not have been foreseen, and that there were no forebodings of it and that England—just, beneficent and paternal—was relying on the goodness of her administration but she only met with ungratefulness? No; all this is a fallacy and must be given up; let no one be deceived by this empty phraseology. The hour of Indian vespers is soon going to strike. Discontent has invaded all classes of the Indian population; they are going to make common cause with the sepoys. And while deploring the barbarities and atrocities of the awakening of the people of India, sworn to this great cause, it must be admitted that there exist in their favour numerous and considerably extenuating circumstances.'[1]

The above is one out of the numerous quotations given in a contemporary French work[2] which makes it clear that the outbreak of 1857 had been foreseen in

---

[1], [2] Fonvielle et Legault—*L'Insurrection de l'Inde,* Paris (1858).

Des Sentiments de Justice et d' Humanite de l' Angleterre dans la Question Indienne (Paris, 1857), p. 115.

England as well as in France where it was believed that it would be not only a military mutiny but also a rebellion of the Indian people against a century-old British maladministration[1] and tyranny, flagrant instances of which had been seen by Sir Charles Napier, conqueror of Sind, and are reproduced in French. His letter dated 30th May, 1850, addressed to a higher officer of the Company says:

'No, no, I'll not concede to you that we are strong, just or punctilious (strictly following the rules) or that we take from the people only that which law empowers us to take or that we pay them (their dues) all the months. We do not pay ourselves, nor do we pay others. Here is a fact: the coolies who were called to carry the baggages of the governor setting out on a journey are forcibly made to come over from long distances and meet at Simla. They are each paid two annas per day and are treated with great cruelty. But I understand that by the negligence of the officers and perhaps also through defalcation, 8,000 to 10,000 of these coolies who had been employed for carrying and transporting the luggage of a certain Englishman going out of India have not obtained even those miserable wages of theirs for three years. In Calcutta you live

---

[1] In their account of the causes of the Indian Mutiny (1857) the French compilers of *Des Sentiments de Justice et d'Humanite de l' Angleterre dans la Question Indienne* (p. 83) say, 'According to the narrative of the unlucky English passengers who arrived from India by the *Colombo* the causes of the rebellion lay in the long series of violences and frauds which had been committed by the officers of the East India Company on the Indians. Such was the belief of the Indians. They also believed that the officers of the East India Company had exceeded all bounds in their attempt to satisfy their unbridled ambition and their thirst for gold and power.'

in an enchanted circle. You know the Indian government only in theory, just as if you were the governor-general. The atrocities which are committed here baffle description. You cannot know that much from your book-shelves of Calcutta but I, who have travelled over all parts of the country sometimes on foot and sometimes on horseback, have been seeing the condition of the Indians for years.

'I placed Sind under good authority but when I left the country the government of Bombay introduced in it all kinds of iniquities and wrongs in spite of the good-natured Mr. Pringle who succeeded me as commissioner . . . I had left Sind contented but now it has been made unhappy and discontented. To remove the political disaffection that has set in, the Government has employed military force. Therefore I do not associate myself with the praises that you bestow on the Indian government; my opinion is just the reverse . . . .

'We force the Indian to work at the plough and we force him to walk thousands of miles carrying the luggage of the English soldiery. The Indian peasant loses his harvest, his land remains uncultivated and his family perishes; his oxen, overworked by the soldiers, fall on the way and he does not receive a farthing as compensation for this. His broken plough is left on the way and he is dragged to shoulder another plough whose master has fled away in desperateness. And after six or eight months the peasant is sent back ruined to his house where he used formerly to live happily and peacefully before our arrival there. There he may find his wife and children alive; but if the wife is beautiful, he will (have the misfortune to) hear that the European magistrate has taken her for himself.

'I am told that these magistrates have no scruples about taking the Indian women. The only thing one might say in their favour is that they do not openly practise severity and violence *vis- à-vis* the women as the Indians do'.[1]

Sir Thomas Munro held similar opinion about British administration in 1822; and having also studied the psychology of the Indian people and army he made a prediction about the war of 1857, 35 years before the actual outbreak. He said:

> 'The army will not wait for the long process of the spread of education and the growth of freedom. It will hurry to do things which it will consider practical for subverting the government and recovering its national independence, the achievement of which the press will teach them before long to consider their duty. They will experience great difficulty in finding leaders . . . A military revolt which will come about through some temporary or partial causes can be suppressed but a movement which arises from a change in the character of troops and from systematic opposition becomes irresistible. We shall never be able to recover our present ascendancy; all confidence in the Indians will be destroyed. After one series of civil and sanguinary wars, rather amidst mutinies and massacres coming off alternatively we would be compelled to leave the country . . . In this struggle we will have no support from the people. The traders and shopkeepers whose interests we have promoted may

[1] *Des Sentiments* pp. 67-70. Mangin, A—*La Revolte au Bengale en* 1857 *et* 1858 pp. 110-112.

desire our success; they cannot help doing otherwise. It will be only to deceive ourselves if we believe that gratefulness to, and love for, our government will raise a considerable number of Indians to rally to our side, should a war break out with the army'.[1]

Now, among the numerous factors and circumstances that eventually led to the outbreak of this war must also be noted the prevalent Indian belief that the Company's life had terminated and that a changeover had been decreed by Providence. The *Bengal Hurkaru and India Gazette* reports that the sepoys of the Bengal army 'take much unnecessary pains to procure the services of foretellers or soothsayers . . . The principal question asked of them by these misguided men (Hindus as well as Mahomedans) refers to the duration of British rule over this country, whether it has not come to its end . . . . The professors of the mysterious art . . . state gravely thus. The Joteesh Shastras limit the prevalence of the Christian (*melacho*) power over this country to one hundred years . . Those one hundred years are over.'[2] And the *Bombay Times* reports[3], "To-day is the centenary of the battle of Plassey; and according to a prevalent belief the last of our rule. To-day is positively the last day appointed for a rising of the Musalman population for the recovery of the empire." On hearing of these predictions the Hindus exclaimed, "On the departure of the English from this land, we will offer one hundred lac of beasts for being sacrificed at the shrine of the mighty Kalee." Such is the conduct of the Hindus,

---

[1] *Op. cit.* pp. 91-94.

[2] *Bengal Hurkaru and India Gazette,* June 1, 23, 1857.

[3] *Op. cit.* June 23, 1857.

while among the Musalmans there are few who wish prosperity to the British Government. The greater portion of them are actually dancing with joy at the probable prospect of its destruction'[1]. Then comparing the mutinies of 1857 with the Vellore mutiny of 1806 the *Bengal Hurkaru* correspondent said:[2]

> 'The Vellore mutiny was an explosion originating in very similar persuasions. On that occasion a new head-dress had been introduced which offended the sepoys, partly by its resemblance to the European hat and partly from the belief that hog's skin was employed in the manufacture of the cockade. Political disaffection too had its share in the revolt; and just as intrigues of the king of Oude are spoken of . . . at the present time, the machinations of Tipu's family . . . . were referred to 50 years ago . . . . Now in the mutinies of 1857 the old fable has been revived and circulated; and it is extensively believed that the sepoys and the people are to be coerced into a profession of Christianity and that the use of the unctuous cartridges is but the first part of the organized system for the accomplishment of this dreaded end . . . . In 1806 partly through the action of hired emissaries who assumed the varied guise of wandering devotees and partly by clandestine correspondence conveyed through special messengers, an insurrectionary spirit under the pretext of violent interference with their religion was simultaneously fomented at far distant places —Palamcottah, Bangalore, Nandydroog, Bellary,

---

[1], [2] *Bengal Hurkaru,* June 1, 3, 23. 1857.

Cf Mangin, A—*La Revolte au Bengale en 1857 et 1858* p. 128

Wallajabad and Hyderabad. Something identical with this has been discovered in the widespread ramifications of the recent mutinous spirit extending over 1600 miles from Calcutta to Peshawar and leavening more or less with treasonable poison every intervening station. Now, during months past, have not Mahomedan and Brahmanical strangers—men of suspicious port and mien—been noticed prowling about the cantonment bazars and entering the sepoy lines at Barrackpore and all the principal stations? Again has not correspondence of a treasonable kind been actually intercepted? Revolt against the Firangi was preached in 1806 as well as in 1857 by men under the guise of saints and fakirs. As in 1806, so in 1857 the British Government counted on the good results of *divide et impera* policy which had been introduced in the army . . . . . Our position in India has been very largely strengthened since those times. The cavalry at Murshidabad could have been confidently relied upon, if necessary, to act against their brethren of the line—a circumstance in some degree explained by the preponderance of Musalmans in one of these arms and Hindus in the other'.

But the Indian sepoys had now become alive to the situation. They realized that they had been divided and weakened and shabbily treated, and scantily paid although they had been fighting the Englishman's battles over a century and securing him victories. They knew how little reliance could be placed on British promises. The British government had given them a pledge not to send them out to oversea expeditions but several Indian regiments had been compelled to go across the sea to Burma; to crown all they were even bulleted ruthlessly by British officers. In these circumstances the sepoys, conscious of their overwhelming numbers and strength and believing that the Firangis wanted to destroy their caste and religion, determined to kill the foreigners or to expel them. In its issue of 24th June 1857 the *Bengal Hurkaru* reproduces the unforgettable reply that the sepoys gave on hearing of the Company's assurances to remove their grievances. 'WE WILL NOT ALLOW THE COMPANY TO REIGN OVER US', said they in one voice. And in order to enlist the support of their compatriots, the civil population, they issued and circulated a proclamation which ran as follows:

> 'Be it known to all the Hindoos and Mahomedans, the subjects and servants on the part of the officers of the English forces stationed at Dehli and Mirath that all the Europeans are united in this point, first to deprive the army of their religion and then by the force of strong measures to christianise all the subjects. In fact it is the absolute order of the Governor-General to serve out cartridges made up with swine and beef fat; if there be ten thousand who resist this, to blow them up; if fifty thousand, to disband them.
>
> 'For this reason we have merely for the sake of the faith concerted with all the subjects and have not left one infidel of this place alive and have constituted the Emperor of Dehli upon this engagement that whichever of the troops will slaughter all their European officers and people, and pledge allegiance to him, shall always receive double salary. Hundreds of cannon and immense treasure have come to hand; it is therefore requi-

site that all subjects will unite cordially with the army, take courage and not leave the seed of these devils in any place.

'All the expenditure that may be incurred by the subjects in furnishing supplies to the army, they will take receipts for the same from the officers of the army and retain them by themselves; they will receive double price from the Emperor. Whoever will at this time give way to pusillanimity and allow himself to be overreached by these deceivers and depend upon their word, will experience the fruits of their submission like the inhabitants of Lakhnao. It is necessary that all Hindus and Mahomedans should be of one mind in this struggle and make arrangements for their preservation with the advice of some creditable persons. Wherever the arrangements shall be good and with whomsoever the subjects shall be pleased those individuals shall be placed in high offices in those places.

'And to circulate copies of this proclamation in every place as far as it may be possible, let it not be understood to be less than a stroke of the sword that this proclamation be stuck up at a conspicuous place in order that all Hindus and Mahomedans may become appeased and be prepared. If the infidels now become mild it is merely an expedient to save their lives. Whoever will be deluded by these frauds, he will repent. Our reign continues. Thirty rupees to a mounted and ten rupees to a foot soldier will be the salary of the new servants of Dehli.'[1]

---

[1] *Bengal Hurkaru,* June 13, 1857.—This proclamation was first published in an Urdu paper *Doorbin* (June 8, and

This proclamation should be read together with the following proclamation of Bahadur Shah II:

'Let it be known to all the rajas and chiefs of India: Whereas you are noted for your all-round goodness, virtues and liberality and whereas the different creeds of India are sponsored by your good sense and right approach, you are hereby reminded that God has created you to maintain through your efforts His different religions. It is incumbent on you to know well, and adhere to, the tenets and teachings of your respective religions. It is by destroying the enemies who have tampered with your religion that you can be true to God and justify in His eyes the high positions He has given to you all. . . . . It is written in your sacred books that death is better than apostasy; and such is verily the ordainment of God—a truth which everybody, high and low, clearly knows.

'Now these Englishmen want to destroy all the religions; and in order to tamper with India's different creeds they have had books written, published and distributed by means of the clergymen who go about preaching their own tenets. It is worth your while to notice what different tricks the English have been playing in order to destroy our religions: first they have ordered that when a man dies his widow can re-marry; secondly the ancient practice of performing *sati* the Englishmen have abolished; thirdly they have openly declared and brought home to the people that they would be recipients of Government honours and

---

then in another Urdu paper *Sultanul Akhbar* (June 10, 1857). Subsequently it was communicated under the heading of 'A Seditious Proclamation' to the editor of the *Bengal Hurkaru*.

distinctions if they join their fold and embrace their religion. They have also advised the people to attend the churches and listen to the sermons. Over and above all this they ordered that only the true heirs of their body would be entitled to succeed to the rajas' *gaddi* and that no recognition would be accorded to the children of adoption although the Shastras permit ten different kinds of heirs. By this means the British Government aim at seizing your States and jagirs just as they have seized Lakhnao and Nagpur. Besides this, they have issued compulsory orders that prisoners in jail should eat the chapatis; many of the prisoners did not agree to eat the chapatis and have died of starvation, but many have been compelled to eat those chapatis whereby they have lost their caste. And when this trick of the English did not answer they got the powdered bones mixed in sugar so that the unsuspecting people, on eating the same, lose their caste and faith. Further the British Government arranged the sale of a mixture of small pieces of bone and meat in open market. In short, they have adopted and tried every means to impair our religions. Some Bengalis decided to watch and follow the lead of the army and to embrace the religion of the English should the army do so. Thereupon the English ordered the Brahmans and top-ranking men of society to cut the cartridges prepared out of the animal fat. On receiving this order the Musalman sepoys thinking that by so doing their Hindu colleagues would lose caste sympathised with them and refused to cut the cartridges. The Englishmen shot them down as well as all those who had similarly refused to cut the cartridges. Seeing this great tyranny the sepoys started killing Englishmen and they killed the Firangis wherever found. By the grace of God and divine aid the sepoys are still busy in the pursuit of similar plans so that a few Englishmen who might have still lingered in odd places may also be destroyed. It is our firm belief that, should Englishmen still remain in India and survive this killing, then surely they would in return kill all the inhabitants of this country and annihilate our religions. As for those of our fellow-countrymen—and they are not many—who are still supporting the English and are fighting their battle it can be easily said that there is no hope for their redemption; the English will surely destroy their faith and religion,

'In these circumstances we ask you what measures have you adopted to protect your faith and lives. If you and we unite in holding one and the same opinion, we can verily destroy these Englishmen, and thereby we can save our country and faith since all of you desire the common weal of Hindus and Musalmans. Verily the English are the enemies of both. Therefore in the hope of supporting the cause of your religion and in order to repulse the common enemy it is hereby announced by means of this Printed Firman that the Hindus and Musalmans must unite AND JOIN HANDS—the Hindus solemnizing this union by taking an oath of the sacred Ganges, Tulsi and Salgram and the Musalmans by swearing on the Quran—to save their own lives and religions, considering it their duty to kill the English.

'Inasmuch as the slaughter of cows is a curse and insult according to the Hindu religion, the leading Musalmans have decided and resolved that, should the Hindus zealously join hands with the Musalmans in killing the Englishmen, they would immediately and from that very day abandon the slaughter of cows and oxen. Afterwards, if a Musalman were found acting contrary to the said decision and resolve (that is indulging in cow-slaughter), he would be considered an outlaw beyond the pale of the Quran; eating of beef on the part of such a Musalman would be tantamount to eating pork. As for the Hindus failing to make up their minds to kill the English their sin in the eyes of God would be as grave as cow-slaughter and beef-eating.

'In order to grind their own axe the Englishmen also would make an equally solemn pledge and promise to abstain from tampering with the Hindu religion, but no wise man can now be duped by them. Englishmen are noted for their false promises, craftiness and cunning. The moment their object is achieved they cast their promises and pledges to the winds.

'Therefore, never rely on the word of Englishmen. And rest assured that never again will you be able to avail yourselves, of such an opportunity which has now presented itself'.[1]

The above proclamations give a true picture of the substantive Hindu-Muslim unity which in my opinion is the most important of all the numerous scenes of the drama of the mutinies

[1] In the *Mahariba-i Azeem* (p. 385) of Pandit Kanhiya Lal as well as in the *Tarikh-i Baghawat-i Hind* (p. 102) published in 1859 at Agra by Dr. Mukand Lal, this proclamation appears under the title of 'Firman of the Emperor of Dehli'. It also appears in part under the heading of *Dharam Ki Fath Ka Khat* (Letter announcing victory of Dharma) in some Mutiny Papers (Box 194, No. 30). Some points from it are also noticeable in a letter written jointly by the Hindus and Musalmans and published by Maulvi Qutb Shah at Bareilly (*Ibid*). And it has much in common with the proclamation issued subsequently by a Mughul Prince of Dehli the so-called Azamgarh Proclamation (N. A., F. D., Pol. Cons., No. 196, October 8, 1858).

and War of 1857. Without it there would have been neither a mutiny nor a war. And it was this phenomenon of Hindu-Muslim unity which the British Government from the beginning considered a potential danger and had been endeavouring since 1821 to obviate. In 1821 a British officer[1] wrote in the Asiatic Journal, '*Divide et impera* should be the motto of our Indian administration, whether political, civil or military[2].' Accordingly the British Government 'favoured the Hindus sometimes, then it favoured the Musalmans, again the Hindus and so on as occasion required.' In 1843 Lord Ellenborough openly adopted the policy of favouring the Hindus saying, 'I cannot close my eyes to the belief that this race (Musalman) is fundamentally hostile to us and therefore our true policy is to conciliate the Hindus'.[3] To execute this policy he brought from Kabul the spurious gates of the temple of Somnath, supposed to have been taken away by Mahmud of Ghazni. In token of his special kindness to the Hindus Ellenborough then announced that the gates of the Somnath temple would be restored. 'The progress of the gates' procession from Firozpur to Somnath, he wrote, 'would be one great national triumph; and their restoration to India would endear the Government to the whole people. . . I would make the most of the recovery of the gates of the temple, treating it ostensibly as a great military triumph but knowing very well that the Hindus would value it as the guarantee of the future security of themselves and their religion against the Musalmans'. According to the eye-witness accounts the procession created a great stir in the country and excited Hindu-Muslim feeling in spite of the fact that the whole

---

[1], [2], [3] Caveeshar, S.S.—*India's Fight for Freedom*, p. 427.

thing was a farce, no gates having been actually taken away from the Somnath temple by Mahmud.[1] Elated by their success and hopeful of thus keeping alive the sense of bitterness and conflict between the Hindus and Musalmans, the British Government persisted in the pursuit of their policy. And a little before the outbreak of the Mutiny of 1857, John Coke, commandant at Moradabad, observed, 'Our endeavours should be to uphold in full force the (for us fortunate) separation which exists between the different religions and races, not to endeavour to amalgamate them. *'Divide et impera'* should be the principle of Indian Government'.[2] So confident had the British now become that they considered the phenomenon of Hindu-Muslim unity chimerical. Holloway who participated in the War of 1857 observed, 'The British never conceived that the Hindus and Musalmans could unite over any question. . . It was deemed quite as an impossible occurrence for the 'Hindus and Musalmans to agree upon a question of public interest as it was for fire and water to agree when brought into contact with each other. This assumption has proved a fallacy. For both these representatives of the religious bodies perfectly agreed whilst prosecuting the scheme for overthrowing our dominion in the East'.[3]

From the disasters of the War of 1857 the British were quick to learn a great lesson. They orientated their old policy of divide and rule with the object of making the attainment of Hindu-Muslim unity really

[1] *Op. cit.* Also see Nazim, M—*The Life and Times of Sultan Mahmud of Ghazna* pp. 16, 124 n. For the Arabic inscriptions on these gates see J.B.A.S., xii, Pt. I, 1843 p. 76-77.

[2] Caveeshar, S.S.——*India's Fight for Freedom* p. 427.

[3] Holloway—*Essays on Indian Mutiny* pp. 18-19.

impossible for all times. In the words of Pandit Nehru,[1] 'it was from 1857 onwards that the British rulers consolidated their empire in India by following a deliberate policy of dividing the people on the basis of religion, thus striking at the very root of the conception of nationhood'.[2] The British scholars made choice extracts from the numerous Persian manuscripts of Muslim period of Indian history and translated the same literally into English without adequate commentaries. These translations were not only inexact but also seriously misleading for the texts were almost incomplete. And the manuscripts from which the extracts were made were also inexact, blurred and unscientific for they had been written for the most part by the Turks who had

---

[1] *Statesman*—May 11, 1957.

[2] In essence religion and nationhood are not incompatibles.; and religion in Medieval India was never the cause of discord among the people. On the contrary religion then proved indispensable in the building of communal harmony as is proved by the progress of the Bhakti movement and the words and deeds of the many Sufi saints and Indian apostles from Ramanuja to Guru Nanak. The same was true of the Mughul period down to Bahadur Shah II.

In the post-Mutiny period, however, the British changed or 'communalised' the Indian outlook towards religion to such an extent that racial hatred sprang, and discord between the two communities became the order of the day. The *Statesman* of May 1942 tells us, . . . 'Communal riots have frequently broken out at Dacca, Ahmadabad, Bombay and Cawnpore and in the Punjab. Even private quarrels, say with a tongawala or with a boy thief as was recently the case at Dehra-Dun and Delhi respectively, develop into communal riots. At Bhiwani in the Punjab trouble originated in a communal ill-feeling in a school where students made demonstrations on communal lines against masters belonging to different communities. There was a general outbreak of violence, and 8 people were killed and 43 injured'.

accepted Islam mainly with the object of satisfying their ambition for worldly power and for the sake of enjoying the facilities which Islam was supposed to afford of indulgence in war and plunder. They considered their military campaigns in this country as sacred Islamic injunctions, and delighted to brandish a militant Islam not only in their trade as swordsmen but also in the domain of historiography. Their numerous chronicles reflected the destructive ideology of those ulama whom a 14th-century emperor,[1] condemned as 'godless and greedy'. In these chronicles almost all the kings of medieval India—warrior or no warrior—have been portrayed as *mujahideen* (jihad makers), ever ready to wage war with the Hindus and extirpate idolatry by demolishing idol-houses. Out of such chronicles extracts were made according to their own policy, choice and interest by the British scholars, headed by Sir Henry Elliot of mid-19th century. He undertook to prove that the age which followed the Hindu period of Indian history was one of unmitigated oppression and bigotry from which the Hindus were rescued by the benign intervention of the British.[2] And according to the famous saying—*har 'aib kih sultan bepasandad hunar ast*—books to that effect were also written, *e.g.* the *Muntakhabatu-t Tawarikh* in which the author Munshi Sada Sukh Dehlawi highly praised the British rule and condemned the Musalmans.[3] And the legacy of Sir Henry Elliot has continued till to-day; as a result two

[1] Muhammad bin Tughluq—*Memoirs,* R.F., p. 173.

[2] (i) Elliot—*History of India as told by its own historians,* Vol. I, pp. xii—xiii.

(ii) *Idem,* Vol. II, Reprinted at Aligarh. Supplement by Khaliq Nizami.

[3] *Op. cit.,* Vol. viii, p. 405.

features stand out clearly in post-British historiography. The first is the tendency to praise unduly the British rule including Dalhousie's annexationist policy.[1] The second important feature is the implicit reliance, placed while conducting researches in Indian history, on English translations of Persian, Arabic and Urdu texts. Mention might here be made of *The Sepoy Mutiny and the Revolt of 1857*[2] wherein the author relying on Metcalfe's edition and translation of the original Urdu text[3] of Munshi Jiwan Lal's Diary[4] has deemed it proper to denounce Bahadur Shah II as a 'traitor' and 'unfaithful to the cause of the Mutiny[5].' But now, when India is free and there are no British in the country to fetter Indian judgment, why should the Indian scholars 'blink the facts'[6]

[1] Referring to Dalhousie's annexationist policy the historian says, "It is hard to find fault with his intention, and his policy of annexation undoubtedly contributed to the political unification of India which was to serve as the foundation of Indian nationhood! (Sen, S. N.—*Eighteen Fifty-Seven*, p. 38).

[2] Majumdar, R. C.—*The Sepoy Mutiny and the Revolt of 1857*, p. 122.

[3], [4] See Chapter X *infra*, pp. 313-318.

[5] *Cf.* p. 318 *infra*.

[6] The British Government has turned the currents of Hindu-Muslim thought in the name of education and scientific history to communal consciousness and communalism. That the educated classes of Indians, as a result, became particularly communal-minded is evidenced by the *Vishwani* (विश्ववाणी) of Allahabad (1943). It says, '. . . . There is a profound distrust of each other these days in the minds of the Hindus and Musalmans. And it is deplorable that this district is particularly found in the educated classes'. This finds confirmation in a widely reported observation of Rev. E. C. Dewick of Nagpur :

> "There are schools and colleges in which the teachers actually inculcate communal feelings instead of

and endeavour to prove that the outbreak of 1857 was no more than a string of depredations of irresponsible sepoys uninspired by philosophy, traditions and nationalism? A modern historian's remark

---

trying to check them. Educational institutions avowedly run on a communal basis are a real danger to India as a whole; and under present conditions such institutions are (it may be unwittingly) increasing the difficulty of India's communal problem", *Statesman*, 1913.

That the movement of 1857 had been developing steadily for the past 50 years and could be traced back to the Battle of Plassey with a chain of outbreaks in 1806, 1824, 1844,1849 and with concentrated effect from the beginning of 1857 is the opinion of Arthur Magnin, (*La Revolte au Bengale en 1857 et 1858*, pp. 128-133), the Irish soldier who was in the East India Company's service in 1857. That the outbreak of that year was not unpremeditated and that the British were not unaware of it is the opinion of Metcalfe who says :

> "From both civil and military subordinate officers warnings were repeatedly given (1856-57) that some portentous event was brooding, but little credit was attached to them except by Sir John Lawrence. But even if the readiest credit had been given to every rumour, the Government of India was helpless to act. Its chief armour, offensive and defensive, was the Indian army, and that in Bengal was more or less disaffected. How far the Bombay and Madras armies were faithful was a matter of conjecture. The European soldiers were few and isolated. There were no railways and no ready means of communication. There was no possible move but to summon such native allies as the Government could trust, and to summon large drafts from England. What steps the East India Company may have taken to move the ministry at home to increase the European army and send out regiments can only be ascertained from unpublished records. The only course open to the Indian Government was to put a calm and bold face on the dangers which

that 'sporadic risings were mistaken for a deep-laid plot'[1] would amount to saying that the sporadic outbreaks of communal riots from 1920 to 1947 were mistaken for a deep-seated communalism and had nothing to do with 1947 when the Partition of India took place.

This reading of the character of the movement of 1857 reminds the writer of the reading which had been made by a mid-19th century French historian who said, 'The revolt of 1857 was a military movement; it was not a national rising'.[2] 'The year 1857', he continues, 'is conspicuous for that great outbreak of the storm which for a quarter of a century had ceaselessly menaced the existence of British power

---

threatened its existence and to await the course of events. . . . When the warnings were fulfilled in fact, it was found that the conspirators had chosen well their time and place. The season was the most deadly and trying to the European constitution, when the annual drafts of European troops had ceased, the time-expired, men had gone, and the small force left still more depleted by the exodus of the sick and delicate to the hills. The place selected for the outbreak was Meerut, some 40 miles only from the residence of the titular King of Delhi, and the first move was on to a fortified city with its magazines of powder and stands of arms and ammunition held by a native force only. There was, however, one calculation which had never entered into the plans of the conspirators, *viz.* that England would declare war against China and that a considerable European force should be sailing through the Indian Ocean within hailing distance of Calcutta. To this fortuitious circumstance under God's providence was due the early re-establishment of British authority in North-Western India (Metcalfe—T. N. N., pp. 20-21).

[1] *Statesman*, May 9, 1957.

[2] L. Martin, Ch.—*La Puissance Militaire des Anglais dans l'Inde* p. 226.

in India. And in that year our English neighbours were celebrating the centenary of the Battle of Plassey which had marked the rise of British power in India. The outbreak of 1857 was purely a military movement, and there was in it no dynamic and no directing force of patriotism which alone could make it a national movement. The question of patriotism could not arise in the case of Indians who for the past 600 years have had no national fatherland of their own. They had had no ties of common interest since they had been divided and split up, each community being indifferent to the sufferings of the other. As regards the alleged point of national or personal honour—which sometimes is said to have made them conscious of their inferiority and humiliation before the Europeans—the people who know the Hindus well tell us that this sentiment has no place in their minds and that they willingly consider this inferiority a law of nature; they think so little of complaining against it as against cholera . . . The people therefore have always been outside the sphere of such rising in India, for it cannot be denied that British rule was a great blessing to the people who had been always inured to the oppressive rule of the conquerors. . . . And the peace that they enjoyed under British rule they had never had under the preceding rulers'.[1] But this view is seriously misleading. Who does not know that the Hindus had continued throughout the period of 600 years mentioned by Martin to be patriotic and took pride in their motherland.[2] In this connection one may also note the opinion of

[1] L. Martin, Ch.—*La Puissance Militaire des Anglais dans l'Inde* p. 226.

[2] Timur and Nadir Shah's invasions may be studied carefully with a view to appraise Hindu patriotism

Charles Ball that the Hindus and Musalmans had a common sense of nationality, speaking a common language; and even the blind Emperor Shah Alam was looked up to in his weakness and decay as the centre of power, and his residence was also considered as the centre of nationality.[1] Describing the queen of Oudh's visit to Queen Victoria in 1853 the same author says, 'The queen of Oude wore a robe of gold tissue pendant from her shoulders which was borne by a Hindoo lady in waiting who alone was permitted to enter the carriage with her'.[2] This incident throws light on the high status and dignity that the Hindus had enjoyed in Oudh Durbar. Further Rev. Andrews has given an elaborate account of Hindu-Muslim unity during the reign of Bahadur Shah II[3] (1837-1857)

Looking back to a hundred years since 1857 the historian's eyes meet a different spectacle—evidence of communal harmony and of anti-British feeling in the country and particularly at the Mughul palace of Dehli, the Maratha palace of Brahmavarta at Kanpur and the Sahukari circles of Lakhnao. Amidst these centres volunteers and zealous patriots moved[4] about inspiring people with the spirit of freedom and rousing them to a war with the Firangi infidels.

Long is the list of the volunteers, patriots or revolutionary philosophers who moved about different places and were suspected by the British as seditionists.[5]

---

[1] Charles Ball—H.I.M., Vol. I, p. 453.

[2] *Idem,* p. 153.

[3] Andrews, C.F.—*Zakaullah of Delhi,* pp. 15-17.

[4] Cave-Browne—P.D., Vol I, p. 364.

[5] Malleson (*History of Indian Mutiny,* Vol. I, pp. 52-58) mentions some Wahabi maulvis namely Shah Muhammad

Charles Ball mentions one Maulvi Ahmad Ali of Patna and Rango Bapuji an agent of Nana Sahib as well as Maulvi Sikandar Ali Shah who is said to have 'arrived with some armed followers at Lucknow and preached war against the infidels'.[1] Maulvi Sikandar Ali Shah also distributed printed copies of proclamations and 'called upon the faithful as well as upon the Hindus to arise or be for ever fallen'. He was arrested by the British but not without a conflict in which he was wounded. Among other names of such 'seditious preachers', the top-most name was that of Maulvi Fazl Haq.[2] And it should be noted that although their call was mixed with religion, they called upon the Hindus and Musalmans alike to arise. Obviously religion then formed the road to union, and surely it served as the *feeder of nationalism*. The fact that the cries of *deen deen*[3] which characterized the opening stage of the War of 1857 were drowned subsequently in the tide of the hatred of the Firangi foreigner is a pointer to the true character and function of religion in those days.

Husain, Maulvi Ahmadullah, Wazirul-Haq, besides numerous leaders of the Patna rising of 3rd July 1857, the most notable being Pir Ali, and Lutf Ali. But Hunter has included the Shias also, saying 'While the more fanatical of the Musalmans have thus engaged in overt sedition, the whole Muhammadan community has been openly deliberating on their obligation to rebel'.

(Hunter—*The Indian Musalmans,* p. 10).

[1] Charles Ball—*History of the Indian Mutiny* I, p. 40.

[2] *Vide*, Appendix H.

[3] The ex-editor of the *Delhi Gazette* (p. 16) rejoices to say that even the war cry *Deen Deen* that was raised was a Muslim war cry. But the fact that the Muslim war cry was adopted by the Hindus shows the height of union, then reached, between the two communities.

Through his verses,[1] many of which express his personal grievances and were published a few years before the Revolution of 1857 Bahadur Shah expressed his hatred of the Firangi infidels, and his verses were commonly sung by his loyal subjects, Hindus as well as Musalmans.[2]

While the Press[3] readily echoed whatever he chose to assert, Bahadur Shah urged the sepoys to throw themselves in the war heart and soul.[4] In his proclamation which has been mentioned above,[5] he cursed the Firangis for their highly objectionable innovations under the cant of reform and he roused the Indian Princes to revolt also on account of the British refusal to acknowledge the right of adoption which had been enjoyed by the Indians from times immemorial in accordance with

---

[1] *Kulliyat-i Zafar* (Nawal Kishore Press), pp. 54, 55, 56, 57, 60, 61, 68, 71, 81, 105, 108. Also see the verses of Bahadur Shah selected by Amir Ahmad Alvi—*Bahadur Shah Zafar* (1st edition, p. 76, 2nd edition, pp. 125-126).

It should be noted that Bahadur Shah's language was figurative; as such he used peculiar synonyms for the English *e.g. ahl-i saumia, sitamgar, but, buto, kafir, yaron*—, none of which can be taken in the ordinary sense of '*ghazal*'. The royal author himself made this point clear in some of the verses wherein he stressed his old age and his ceaseless crying and weeping on account of his misfortunes and sufferings at the hands of the tyrants.

(*Idem*, pp. 2, 8, 25, 46, 68, 70, 72, 89).

[2] Zakaullah——T. U. A. I. S. P. 738.

[3] *Vide* (i) Mutiny Papers, Box 4-6, Vol. 4, No. 5.
(ii) *Pr. Tr. B.S.*, pp. 115-116.
(iii) *Sadiqul Akhbar*, 27th July 1857 (Poem of Hatred against the English).

[4] *Vide* Chapter III, p. 103, *infra*.

[5] Also see Charles Ball— I, pp. 301 ff

the Shastras. Similar was the spirit of Nana Sahib's propaganda against the British. But he did not throw his weight jointly with Bahadur Shah in the course of the latter's fight with the British. While Bahadur Shah was locked in the death-grapple with the British and when good many of the Indian troops from Lakhnao were going to Dehli *via* Kanpur in order to assist in the defence of Dehli, Nana Sahib followed them in person and persuaded them to return to Kanpur and assist his own force in attacking the European garrison.[1]

At the age of three in 1827 Nana Sahib had been adopted by the last Peshwa Baji Rao II; and for the next 24 years he lived at the Peshwa's palace of Brahmavarta. There he is said to have met Manikarnika better known as Lakshmi Bai, daughter of Moropant Tambe; she was 11 years older than Nana Sahib. She too was blessed by the Peshwa and remained in his palace until 1842 when she was married to Gangadhar Rao Sahib of Jhansi. After the marriage she left Brahmavarta for Jhansi where she became the Maharani of Jhansi and a popular idol of her devoted subjects. But her husband's untimely death left her a childless widow (1853). She adopted Damodar as her son. But the adoption was not recognized by the British Government and they annexed Jhansi. It would be absurd to say that the Rani of Jhansi still remained devoted to the British.

Nana Sahib left Brahmavarta after the Peshwa's death in 1851; he was victimised by the British two years before they had victimized the Rani of Jhansi. His adoptive father had enjoyed a pension of eight

[1] Holloway—*Essays on Indian Mutiny* p. 65.

lakhs which Nana Sahib now claimed as his right. But the British Government disappointed him and did not acknowledge his right. Nana Sahib sent Azimullah, his trusted counsellor, to London (1854) to plead his case with the Directors. Azimullah won as much appreciation in London as had done Raja Ram Mohan Roy, the ambassador of Akbar Shah, but failed in his mission. Then he went to meet the Russians in the Crimea. And it became the common talk in all the high circles of India including the Mughul palace of Dehli that the Russians would come over to India and uproot British power. It was reported that Bahadur Shah himself had sent an ambassador to Russia[1] as he had sent one also to Iran.[2] On his return to India Azimullah might not have advised Nana Sahib to work jointly with Bahadur Shah against the British. But Zakaullah says that an ambassador of Nana Sahib came to Dehli[3] and met Bahadur Shah; and Nana Sahib set to work openly against the British. Says Kaye:

> 'Nana Sahib and his counsellor Azimullah made joint tours of the country and visited Dehli, Ambala, Lakhnao and Kalpi in March-April 1857. . . . For months, for years indeed they had been spreading this network of intrigues all over the country. From one native court to another, from ont extremity to another of the great continent the agents of Nana Sahib had passed with overtures and invitations, discreetly, perhaps mysteriously, worded, to princes and chiefs

[1] Describing the plunder and confusion of 11th May 1857 Ghulam Abbas, the royal vakil said, "The inhabitants of the city generally thought that the Russians had come' (*Pr. Tr. B. S.* pp. 38-41).

[2] See p. 77n, *infra*.

[3] Zakaullah—T.U.A.S.I., p. 673.

of different races and religions, but most hopefully of all, to the Marathas. . . . There is nothing in my mind more clearly substantiated than the complicity of Nana Sahib in widespread intrigues before the outbreak of the Mutiny. . . The concurrent testimony of witness examined in parts of the country widely distant from each other takes his story altogether out of the regions of the conjectural.[1]

A detailed study of Nana Sahib and of the other heroes of the war of 1857 is outside the scope of this book which aims at presenting a correct picture of Bahadur Shah *vis-à vis* the British and the sepoys. Nor is it desired to build a comparison between Bahadur Shah and his contemporaries. But there is positive evidence[2] that Bahadur Shah was calling upon all the Indians to annihilate the Firangis.[3] And he also desired to organize a Confederacy of Indian Princes in whose favour he was prepared to abdicate his office and to whom he proposed to delegate his powers and rights as Emperor, provided they joined hands and lined with him in fighting and expelling the Firangis.[4] It is difficult, now to say accurately how this noble idea which surely involved a tremendous self-sacrifice on the part of Bahadur Shah originated. Did it originate with him, or with Azimullah and Nana Sahib, or with the sepoys at whose dictation he might have written his letters[5]? These are questions which call for further research. My study of the data has led me to the conclusion that Bahadur Shah himself conceived this idea and he made

[1] Kaye—*History of the Indian Mutiny,* I, pp. 424-425.

[2], [3] [4] See Chapters, V, pp. 167 ff. VII *infra,* pp. 196 ff. and P—L., p. 163. *Tel.* 539.

[5] *Vide* p. 195, *infra.*

a proposal to this effect, as has been mentioned by Munshi Jiwan Lal[1] and Cave-Browne.[2] Had the Indian Princes responded to him the British would have been expelled, and India would have been freed in 1857. In that case instead of being prepared as she actually was under the British rule of the succeeding century to be an arena of communalism with frequent outbreaks of communal riots and bloodshed and a final partition into Pakistan and Bharat, India would have remained peacefully united and undivided. But the Indian princes did not co-operate with Bahadur Shah.[3] And while the Maharaja of Patiala betrayed him delivering into British hands the secret and confidential letter[4] which Bahadur Shah had written to him, Maharana Saroop Singh[5] of Chittor firmly stood by the British and advised all the Rajwara chiefs not to deviate from the path of allegiance and loyalty to the British Government.[6]

Probably the above idea originated with Bahadur Shah for two cognate reasons: (i) he was primarily the people's king who had derived his powers from the joint support of the Hindus and Musalmans and he reigned throughout the eventful months (May to September 1857) as a constitutional monarch with the help of the two parties in the country, *i.e.* the army and the people. Unfortunately the stronger party *i.e.* the army ruthlessly exploited and damaged the interests of the weaker party, namely the

---

[1] Metcalfe T. N. N., p. 219.

[2] Cave-Browne, P. D., Vol. I, pp. 362-63-364.

[3] Cave-Browne P. D., Vol. I, p. 224.

[4] *Ibid.* Also P-L. p. 40. Tel. No. 8 of 27th May 1857.

[5],[6] Showers, C. L.—*A Missing Chapter of Indian Mutiny*, *Vide* Secret Correspondence relating to the crisis confided by Maharana Saroop Singh to Captain Showers, the Resident, pp. 200 ff.

people. Matters reached such a pitch that Bahadur Shah was compelled to act as the spokesman[1] of the weaker party against the relentless sepoys. As a result, he lost whatever little hope he had in the beginning of the liberation of the country and expulsion[2] of the Firangis. In utter desperateness he thought of making a proposal directly to the Indian Princes, believing that they had been enriched and inspired by the proud traditions of Mughul rule and Indian patriotism. (ii) Bahadur Shah was fully conscious of his personal responsibility for the war with the Firangis. But for his leadership the outbreak of the revolt in Mirath or in Dehli would have met with no better fate than that of the Vellore Mutiny of 1806. When in the course of the war he became apprehensive of his own defeat and of the enemy's ultimate victory he refused to open negotiations with the British although a powerful suggestion to this effect was made by Mirza Ilahi Bakhsh. On the contrary Bahadur Shah made immediately an effort to open negotiations with the Indian princes and broached his own idea.

How great was his responsibility for the war and how much he was conscious of it is also evidenced by the letters which Bahadur Shah wrote to his 40-year-old son Mirza Mughul, commander-in-chief of the Army[3]. His responsibility for the war is further evidenced by the testimony of his private Secretary Mukand Lal[4] and even by that of Major Abbot, commander of the 74th Native Infantry at Dehli who officially gave his considered opinion as follows:

---

[1] See Chapter VII *infra*, p. 214.

[2] *Idem*, pp. 197, 198, 201, 202 *infra*.

[3] *Idem*, pp. 209-217 *infra*.

[4] Appendix D. Also see Cave-Browne—P. D., Vol. I, pp. 362-363.

> 'From all I could glean, there is not the slightest doubt that this insurrection has been originated and matured in the palace of the King of Dehli, and that with his full knowledge and sanction, in the mad attempt to establish himself in the sovereignty of this country. It is well known that he has called on the neighbouring States to co-operate with him in thus trying to subvert the existing government'.[1]

Furthermore, Rotton, the British chaplain attending the British camp at Dehli, describes the efforts that Bahadur Shah had been making during the war to win over the Sikhs to his side. 'On the 2nd of July' says Rotton, 'a revelation was made through the fidelity of certain Sikhs whose regiment had recently come into camp. Unhappily an entire company of this regiment was composed of Poorbias while the main strength was Sikh. The Poorbias within the British camp had strong leanings and earnest longings for Dehli. "Down with the British rule!" was the secret wish of their treason-working hearts; *but before they could openly avow their treachery, they had to perform, by deception, an important mission which* THE KING OF DEHLI HAD ENTRUSTED TO THEIR EXECUTION. *This mission was to destroy the loyalty of the Sikhs, if possible, by offers of large bribes and by a train of subtle reasoning in which an appeal to the Divine Will formed a very prominent part.* Accordingly some leading men of the *Poorbia Company of the Sikh Regiment approached one of the leading men of the other companies and declared that "the Will of Heaven was to take away the Raj from the English and to give it over to the descendant of the*

---

[1] Cave-Browne—P. D., Vol. I, p. 364.

Great Mughul; and that it could be no benefit to them to continue. . . .in British service, as by so doing they would only incur the displeasure of Shah Bahadur Shah[1] *which would rest upon the Sikhs, and follow them from place to place, till destruction completely overtook and overwhelmed them.* If, however, on the other hand they made choice of the winning side the King would gladly enrol those of the Sikhs who were officers among his Colonels and Generals, and would give large pay to one and all."

'The Sikh having listened to the arguments of the mutinous Poorbias gave according to the Eastern custom, some evasive reply. He then made direct for the tent of his commanding officer to whom he disclosed the conspiracy; in consequence the ringleaders who were native officers, and I think three in number, were arrested forthwith. The remainder of the attained company were paid up and sent out of the camp, to the great satisfaction alike of Englishmen and of Sikhs'.[1]

Although this report of Rotton's has remained unconfirmed and may not be literally true for Bahadur Shah had no intriguing mind, yet the reference that it contains to the 'Divine Will determining the end and trend of human affairs' is characteristically Bahadur Shah-like. In one of his letters Greathed[2] also reports Bahadur Shah's firm belief in the Divine Will as decisive force in all human affairs.[3] Moreover Bahadur Shah was considered a saint; that is why he is called *Shah* Bahadur Shah. By virtue of his sainthood it

---

[1] Rotton—*Narrative of the Siege of Delhi*, pp. 113-115.

[2] Greathed's *Letters*—p. 102.

[3] The reader's attention is invited to this very point, among the salient features of Bahadur Shah's character; *vide* Chapter I, p. 63 *infra*.

was believed that his blessing and curse would be heard.[1]

The controversy regarding the correct name of the outbreak of 1857 may be set at rest by drawing upon the testimony of Charles Ball[2] and Malleson.[3] Impressed by the outbreak in Oudh, Charles Ball calls it 'a popular insurrection'. Says he, 'We had no longer any friends in Oude, and a Hindu confederacy acquired consistency under Raja Man Singh who at the first opportunity took the field before Lucknow with all the warlike classes of Oude ranged under his banner.[4] And 'Canning asked himself,' says Malleson,[5] 'whether the rising of 1857 could be only a military mutiny. He was definitely of the opinion that it had not originated merely in the unaided instincts of the soldiery. And he ceased to speak of the mutiny. He called it a rebellion'. He could not have called it War of Indian Independence or even an armed revolutionary movement aiming at the liberation of the country. Such a nomenclature on his part would have brought him into conflict with the Home Authorities; and it would have been inconsistent with the British national policy. Still, Canning went far enough when he said, 'I have no doubt that this rebellion had been promoted by Brahmans on religious pretences and by others for political motives. . . And among the causes of this rebellion an important cause was intemporized zeal of the English in India to assimilate all things to their own modes of thought. . . To this pass had the self-

---

[1] See Chapter I, *infra*, pp. 36. 63, 64.

[2] Charles Ball—*History of the Indian Mutiny*, Vol. I, p. 148 ff.

[3] Malleson—*History of Indian Mutiny*, p. 452.

[4] Charles Ball, *Op. cit.*

[5] Malleson, *Op. cit.*

assertion of the national character brought us'.[1] Canning had obviously in mind instances of serious violation of the fundamental principles of Indian religion and society under Dalhousie. This was not all. By his annexation of Oudh in 1856 Dalhousie had roused great discontent among the Hindus, for hundreds of Hindu zamindars of Oudh, who had grown rich and enjoyed prosperity under the benevolent rule of the kings of Oudh, now went overboard. 'As many as 3,500 jagirs of Hindu zamindars and Talukdars were seized by the British and a great commotion arose for there were then present in Oudh all kinds of disaffected elements—the Afridis, the Durukzyes of Khyber, the Beloochis of Kelat, the Waziris of the Sulaiman range, the malcontents of the Indian States and deserters from the British ranks'.[2]

A united Hindu-Muslim front—the fruit of the country-wide awakening of the latent spirit of Indian religion and community of interests—was an unavoidable outcome of the fangs of aggressive British nationalism referred to above. It cannot be denied that a national synthesis had been built up in medieval India that continued unshaken inspite of Aurangzeb down to 1857 and led to the great upsurge for Dehli and devotion to Bahadur Shah who was the *de jure* sovereign and the symbol of political unity. This was

[1] Malleson, *Op. cit.*

[2] Charles Ball (Vol. I, p. 248) explains this point saying, 'In Oude the Talookdaree system was almost universal. Nearly the whole country was parcelled out among great zamindars or Talookdars; and though under a Mahomedan government, those men were almost universally Hindoos. As native chiefs they had obtained great prescription, exercised great power and authority and were in fact the feudatories of the native government. They had their own forts and troops and guns'. (*Ibid*).

a reality which impressed Metcalfe who, rejecting the unilateral Muslim jihad, said, *'The probability is that it was a joint proclamation, the work of Hindus as well as of Mahomedan conspirators'.*[1] In fact this joint proclamation itself was the result of the great popularity that Bahadur Shah had been enjoying among the Hindus and Musalmans; and Metcalfe looked upon this as a symbol of Indian nationalism.[2] Another symbol was the 'Chapati Mystery' involving the circulation of chapatis from town to town and village to village irrespective of caste and creed among all the Musalmans and Hindus. 'How little was it thought that therein was hidden an Eastern symbol or portentous meaning. Five centuries before (1368 A.D.) the Chinese had by a similar plan organized and carried out a conspiracy by which the dynasty of their Mongol invaders was overthrown (and the Chinese to this day celebrate this under the name of the Festival of the Moon Loaves); and it now imported no less than the annihilation of the English race in India and restoration of the sovereignty of the house of Timur'.[3] So says the British chaplain Cave-Browne who attended the British camps during the War of 1857. Hunter confirmed this substantially when he spoke of the 'discontent against British rule then rife in India'.[4] That it had also spread to the Indian States is made clear by the *Delhi Gazette*. Describing the nature of the revolt in the States the editor observed, 'It

---

[1] Metcalfe—T. N. N., p. 9.

[2] Bahadur Shah looked upon both the communities as forming one nation; and his proclamation to the Hindu and Musalman chiefs opened with these words—'God, the Lord of the Nation' (Pr.Tr.B.S., p. 116).

[3] Cave-Browne—P.D., Vol. I, pp. 2, 3.

[4] Hunter—*The Indian Musalmans,* p. 147.

soon became clear that however sincere might be the goodwill of the princes themselves—Sindia, Holkar, Raja of Bharatpur, Rajas of Jheend and Patiala—no assistance was to be looked for from their subjects'. And the judges of the Military Tribunal which tried Bahadur Shah recalled feelingly Prince Jawan Bakht's bitter invectives against the Firangis and his rejoicings at the anticipation of murdering them.[1] And Mrs. Aldwell's evidence[2] too cannot be neglected. She said, 'I myself heard Muhammadan mothers asking their children to pray that the English should be destroyed root and branch'. Mukand Lal,[3] the Emperor's private secretary, said, 'Sitting at the door of the Royal Palace, Mughuls and others used to discuss the revolution openly. The subject of their talk was this: the sepoys would rebel soon; the army of Dehli would rise against the English'. And from some of the letters of the sepoys of Barrackpur intercepted by the English, Kaye elicited the following information, 'The second grenadier said, "The whole regiment is ready to join the King of Oudh." And Subadar Madar Khan, Sardar Khan and Ram Sahai said that in treachery no one could come up to the level of Firangi".[4]

Here it may be advantageous to recall what Maulvi Fazl Haq, a prisoner in the Andaman Islands, wrote feelingly about all this. His wording suggests the correct name for the Rising of 1857, that is 'Indian Revolution[5].'

---

[1] Pr. Tr. B. S., pp. 107, 158.

[2] Pr. Tr. B. S., pp. 97-99.

[3] *Op. cit.*, p. 101-102.

[4] Kaye—(i) *Indian Mutiny*, I, p. 429.

(ii) *History of Sepoy War in India*, 1857-58 p. 573. footnote.

[5] Appendix H.

CHAPTER I

CHARACTER OF BAHADUR SHAH II

Bahadur Shah II, the last Mughul Emperor of Dehli, commonly known by his pen-name Zafar, was the eldest son of Akbar Shah and his Rajput wife Lal Bai. Born in 1775/1253 in an age and atmosphere of mysticism he inherited from his father who was a sufi a mystic frame of mind which developed with his advance in years and his progress in the domain of knowledge and learning to such an extent that he became ultimately a sufi saint (*Qutb-i Alam*), and his memory is still cherished in sufi circles. A modern sufi scholar[1] who was connected with the Royal House and made a careful study of Bahadur Shah from the original sources holds a high opinion about him. He admires him among other things for his piety, his kingly demeanour, statesmanship, patriotism, conscientiousness and sincerity.

On the maternal side Bahadur Shah was related to the Hindus, his mother and grandmothers being of Hindu stock. Perhaps the most noteworthy trait which he inherited from them and his ancestors, particularly from Akbar the Great, was his national outlook

---

[1] *I.e.* Khwaja Hasan Nizami of Dehli (1878-1955). His father had joined the Liberation Army and fought in the last battle of the War of 1857 in front of the Jami' Masjid on 14th September and whose maternal grandfather Shah Ghulam Hasan, custodian of the Dargah of Hazrat Nizamu'ddin Auliya was a close friend of Bahadur Shah. On fleeing from the Fort in the morning of 20th September, Bahadur Shah had met him at the Dargah; to him he then spoke his mind. Hasan Nizami—G. D. A. (1919), p. 9; Abdullah Faruqi—A. G. H. G. (1940), pp. 22-25.

and kindness to the Hindus. He reposed great confidence in the Hindus and banked on Hindu-Muslim unity. And his diatribes against the Mullas tend to make his resemblance with Akbar the Great close.

Says he:

Kaho Mulla se kiya ham se rindon ko parhaega
Kih ham Lahol parh ke teri taqreer sunte hain
(Ask the Mulla how can he teach us—, probates?
We hear thy discourse while reciting *Lahol* (deprecating the same).

Bahadur Shah visited Hindu temples and idol-houses with a hallowed mark on his forehead and was welcomed by the idol worshippers who took him for a Brahman. Says he:

Butkhanon men jab gaya main khenchkar qashqa Zafar
Bol utha wuh but Brahman yeh nahin to kaun hai
(When after applying 'tika' I went into the idol-houses O Zafar! that IDOL burst saying, if he is not a Brahman who else can he be?)

Again,

Qashqa mathe pa hai zunnar gale men hai Zafar
Ban gaye ishq men us but ke Brahman sachmuch. (With the formal sandal mark on his forehead, Zafar wears round his neck the Brahmanic thread. Verily Bahadur Shah Zafar has become a Brahman-like figure out of his love for that IDOL.)

Bahadur Shah also abstained from taking beef.[1]

[1] Such was the habit of almost all the Mughul Emperors; it was particularly so with Bahadur Shah for he was a sufi. Sufism which primarily originates from the ascetic side of Prophet Muhammad's life and from Hazrat Ali enjoins

And on accepting leadership of the Telinga and Purbiya sepoys on 12th May 1857 he readily agreed to ban cow-slaughter in the city of Dehli and issued orders[1] accordingly. Later, on 28th July the ban on cow-slaughter was confirmed.[2] It was trumpeted forth in the city that whoever slaughtered a cow would be shot dead; and on 2nd August which was Bakar-'id, cow-slaughter was banned[3] a third time. This may be an evidence of the fact that Bahadur Shah had passed completely under the control of the Telingas and Purbiyas. But it would not be inexact to say that Bahadur Shah considered the ban on cow-slaughter during the war a necessary step in cementing Hindu-Muslim concord. And in this way Bahadur Shah acquired a force of character which enabled him to maintain communal harmony in Dehli during the most critical period of the war (May to September 1857), as will be explained later in this book.

Bahadur Shah observed[4] the Hindu festivals of Rakhi Bandan, Basant, Holi and Diwali ceremoniously in the royal court and granted[5] 'bakhshish' to the Hindu servants on the occasion of each festival. And he had such a high regard for the Hindus—a legacy which he had received directly from his forbears, notably Dara Shikoh—that he entrusted to their care even the performance of religious ceremonies like the *'dastarkhwan*

---

abstention of all kinds, particularly from beefs, a famous saying of Hazrat Ali to this effect being لحوم البقر داء و البانها دواء (Beeves are diseaseful while cows' milks are medicinal.) *Vide* Qummi, S. A.—S. B. Vol. II, 1352 A. H. Najaf, p. 507.

[1], [2], T.U.A.S.I. pp. 613, 687.

[3] *Vide* Metcalfe—T.N.N. p. 170 and *Bahadur Shah Ka Roz-namacha*, 1845-46-47.

[4],[5] *Delhi Urdu Akhbar*, 11th August 1851.

of Shah-i-Mardan Hazrat[1] Ali' and the 'niyaz' of Ghaus-i Azam. Among the numerous Hindus whom he honoured during his reign the following find particular mention in the Court Diary: Babu Suraj Narain Mukhtar of Banaras, Pandit Nand Kishore, Raja Bhola Nath, Kunwar Salag Ram, Raja Debi Singh, Gainda Mall,[2] Lala Shiv Lal, Jagjivan Das and Lala Mukand Lal. While Lala Mukand Lal being his private secretary enjoyed close access to him and was the constant recipient of royal favours, the remaining Hindus who occasionally visited his court, were awarded robes of honour. Zakaullah, who had seen Bahadur Shah with his own eyes and who being devoted to the British always discounted him, affirms that 'the memory of Bahadur Shah's goodness is cherished by the Hindus and Musalmans[3] alike'. Says he, 'It is still remembered that whenever the Hindus waited on him and complained against any of the Musalmans he warned the latter saying, 'If you, Musalmans! are to me like one eye, verily the Hindus are dear to me like another eye.[4] When during the 'mutiny' the mutineers harassed the Hindu mahajans and wealthy Musalmans, Bahadur Shah scolded them and said, 'Take away all my wealth and the ornaments of my wife for your own purposes but do not harass my subjects'. This sentence he reiterated three times.[5] And C. F. Andrews who wrote a life of Zakaullah says, 'Bahadur Shah was highly respected by the inhabitants of the royal city—Delhi. One of the survivors who had actually seen Bahadur Shah in his court told

[1] *Bahadur Shah ka Roz-namcha* April 22, 1847; *Dehli Urdu Akhbar* March 6, and May 13, 1856.

[2] *Op. cit.* Court Diary—entries ranging from 12th December, 1845 to 30th March, 1848.

[3],[4],[5] Zakaullah—T.U.A.S.I. p. 738.

me that he was dearly loved by Hindus and Musalmans alike for his good manners. His subjects loved him'. 'During the reign of Bahadur Shah', continues Andrews, 'there was a noticeable amalgamation of customs and usages among the Hindus and Musulmans . . . I have had more convincing and corroborative evidence about this specially friendly relationship between Hindus and Musalmans in old Delhi than I have had concerning any other factor. The information has come to me from both sides and has been practically the same. It was evidently a feature of the city of which the inhabitants themselves were proud. These older residents whom I approached whether Hindu or Musalman spoke of this fact with enthusiasm and contrasted it with the bitterness of modern times. It was quite common in those days for the two communities to join together in different religious festivals. Hindus would go to a Muslim festival and Musalmans would go to a Hindu festival. This had become a natural local custom . . . The Musalmans had great respect for certain Hindu ascetics. There are famous Mughul paintings representing the Emperor and his court visiting some such holy man. The Hindus on their side regularly flocked to pray for temporal benefits to the tomb of a Muslim saint. . . Hindus would quote Hafiz and other Persian poets both in their own Urdu writings and in their conversation . . . On Hindu feast days the children of Hindu households would always bring their offerings of food to their teachers in the mosque schools. They would invite their teachers to their families to share in their festivities, and such invitations were regularly accepted. Musalmans on their side spoke of the Hindu religious festivals with great courtesy and respect and were very particular to avoid any offence against Hindu customs. At their social functions such as marriages and the like presents were invariably sent to Hindu friends and they were asked to grace the wedding by their company. They would come to pay their respects to the bride and bridegroom and offer their presents in return. . . . The art of living peaceably with neighbours of a different religion had reached a very high level. . . . The Emperor Bahadur Shah was more punctilious in these matters right up to the end of his life. He would pass in procession with his royal elephants, decked in their cloth of gold and would take his seat afterwards at a special tower in the Fort from which he would watch the crowd beneath at the chief Hindu festivals as well as Muslim feasts. The crowds would recognise him and make their obeisance and thus much goodwill would be created. The Emperor on such occasions would give public recitations of his own verses and the people would loudly applaud'.[1]

Zaheer Dehlawi who was closely connected with the Royal Palace since his boyhood and who later became a courtier of Bahadur Shah, had seen him in different capacities. He tells us that[2] Bahadur Shah was yet in his teens when he became an athlete, an archer, a good shot, a master rider and a specialist in horses. As an athlete he would beat down eight adversaries at a time in athletic and gymnastic contests technically called *Alimad*. As an archer he would send out piercing arrows from bows with iron chains over a considerable distance through strong butts; and the strongest of bows in his hands, and on being used by him, was rendered so weak that it looked like a wrecked material (*kabada*). As a good shot he never

[1] Andrews, C. F.—*Life of Zakaullah* p. 13.

[2] Zaheer Dehlawi—D.G. pp. 18-23.

missed his aim and had the knack of shooting flying birds while riding on the back of an elephant. As a master rider he could not only manage and master the most wicked of horses but could make a horse, particularly one of his own choice called Damali, show itself off, sometimes trotting and sometimes galloping like a deer at will. As a specialist in horses he knew their breed and character to such an extent that he could tell their different stocks and families with precision as well as their hereditary qualities and the *carriere* of each horse. Later in life he became an architect[1]. an horticulturist[2] and a patron of arts[3] to boot. He

---

[1] Among the numerous buildings of those days the following which still exist in part are attributed to him: (i) a house of red stone in the Hayat Bakhsh garden of the Red Fort of Shahjahan; it goes under the name of Zafar Mahal; (ii) a marble balcony called Hira Mahal built in the said Red Fort in front of the Moti Mahal by the side of the Nahr-i Bihisht in 1842/1258; (iii) a well close to this balcony bearing an inscription from the pen of Bahadur Shah; *i.e.*

(O Zafar! this well by us is a memorial. Its water is sweet like sugar. No chronogram of it can be better than— 1256).

(iv) The palace of Zinat Mahal at the Lal Kuan street built in 1846/1262. Its gateway still bears an inscription from the pen of Bahadur Shah; *i.e.* (O Zafar! Zinat Mahal has constructed this palace which is unparalleled. The chronogram yielding the correct date of its construction is 1262).

(v) One of the Gateways of the Qutb shrine built in 1264 Hijra, A.D. 1847.

(vi) Palace of Taj Mahal Begum, wife of Bahadur Shah, inside Katra Khushhal Rai.

[2] *Dehli Urdu Akhbar;* 28th March and 13th June 1851.

[3] "Bahadur Shah was tolerably skilled in fine arts—music, manuscript illustration and miniature painting. . . ." (Andrews p. 13). *Vide Dehli Urdu Akhbar;* 6th February 1851

facing p. 42

SPECIMEN OF BAHADUR SHAH'S CALLIGRAPHY
(HOLY QURAN, III, 144)

Muhammad is no more than an Apostle; many were the Apostles that passed away before him. If he died or were slain, will ye then turn back on your heels? If any did turn back on his heels, not the least harm will he do to God.

This was written by Muhammad Abu Zafar Siraju'ddin Bahadur Shah, Badshah Ghazi.

facing p. 43

SPECIMEN OF BAHADUR SHAH'S CALLIGRAPHY
(HOLY QURAN; III, 144)
This was written by the slave of God,
Muhammad Abu Zafar Gorgani.

also invented a particular confectionary[1] which he made out of pungent pepper and bitter 'karela' vegetable. What was great still, was his gift of speech. Zaheer Dehlawi heard[2] that the audience were kept spell-bound by Bahadur Shah's speeches which were punctuated and interspersed with quotations and stories from the Palace life of Shah Alam's and Akbar Shah's times. Then he was a lover birds and had a special liking for doves and nightingales, one of these called Bulbul[3]-i Hazar Dastan being particularly mentioned by a contemporary writer[4]. The Bulbul-i Hazar Dastan—literally the nightingale of a thousand stories—delighted the Emperor by its ceaseless chirping in the garden as well as in the palace. It was to him something like the radio to a modern prince and lulled him to sleep in the night.

Regarding the manner and measure of his education practically no information is available beyond the names of his tutors[5]—Hafiz Muhammad Khalil, Hafiz Ibrahim and Saiyed Jalal'uddin Haider. While Hafiz Muhammad Khalil[6] was the head tutor (*ataliq*) who supervised his all-round training and culture, Hafiz Ibrahim taught him the Holy Quran as well as Arabic, Persian and Urdu; and Saiyed Jalal'uddin Haider taught him calligraphy.[7] Since he was a born poet Bahadur Shah took of his own accord to composing verses and learnt prosody. So much of

---

[1] Nasir Nazir—L. Q. E. J p. 7.

[2] Zaheer Dehlawi—D. G. p. 26.

[3], [4] Nasir Nazir—L. Q. E. J. p. 25.

[5] Zaheer Dehlawi—D. G. 19.

[6] Zakaullah the famous historian who knew Bahadur Shah personally was the grandson of Hafiz Muhammad Khalil.

[7] *Vide* facsimiles facing p. 43.

education he acquired during the most peaceful period of his life while his grandfather Shah Alam was yet alive. When Shah Alam died (1806/1221) Bahadur Shah was 32 years of age. By this time his character was formed. He possessed all the good qualities of his ancestors 'without sharing their vices'. He never tasted wine and abstained from all drugs including opium. Later, he only indulged in *hooka* and *pan* which have continued as the most innocent luxuries of princely life till the present day. His favourite pastime was cock-fighting and partridge-contest—a grotesque form of the more manly and dignified pastimes of the age of Babar and Akbar. But there was a silver lining : Bahadur Shah liked poetry and literature more than anything else and spent most of his time in cultivating his poetic and literary gifts. 'In the palace diary of later years there are glimpses of him spending whole days reading and writing, studying and composing verses in the Roshan Ara Garden[1]'. Charles Metcalfe who saw him about 1828 was impressed by his conduct and accomplishments.[2] "The Prince is a man of spare figure and stature, plainly apparelled', it was observed. But other Europeans—Emily Eden and Orlich—who had the opportunity of watching him did not appreciate his plain apparel. Some time after his accession to the throne he composed five diwans of mixed Urdu, Panjabi and Persian poetry, one of which running into 8000 verses was published in 1845/1262 at the Royal Press[3] in the Fort under the supervision of Hakim Ahsanullah; another was published in 1850/1266. His famous commentary on Shaikh Sa'di's *Gulistan* had been published

---

[1],[2] T. M. p. 73.

[3] *Tuhfatul Akhbar*, Bombay, 4th October, 1845.

seven years before at the same press. This was a masterly work[1] in which every verse of Shaikh Sa'di's was expounded by the royal commentator in mystical language (*'ilm-i tasawwuf*), thus giving evidence of his hold on sufi lore. His third and fourth diwans were published subsequently[2], but his fifth *diwan* never saw the light of day, and little is known about it beyond a few verses which have been passed on by word of mouth[3] from generation to generation among the highly cultured people of the East. The majority of his verses give a pen-picture of his mind, beliefs, temperament, habits and outlook towards life; but a select few contain the gospel of 1857 and direct the

---

[1] *Vide* Preface, p. xxvi.

[2] Nawalkishore Press, Lucknow.

[3] For instance,

چرخ نے آکر گھیرا ہے نیند گئی آرام گیا -
جی کا جانا ٹھہرا ہے - صبح گیا شام گیا -

Ill luck has invaded and besieged me; sleep is gone, comfort is gone. It is definite I shall die soon; may die next morning or evening.

(Mutiny Papers, Box 21.
Fair Copies of Collection 19)

On hearing this, and noticing that the Badshahi batteries were failing, some one composed sarcastically the following verse:

دمدمے میں دم نہیں خیر مانو جان کی
اے ظفر ٹھنڈی ہوی تلوار ہندوستان کی

'The batteries have no strength left; pray for the safety of life. O Zafar! the sword of India has become cold.

But the Emperor who had previously composed verses urging his Army to conquer London (*Vide* M. P. Box 19),

writer unmistakably to the conclusion that Bahadur Shah's object in accepting leadership of the sepoys was to wage the war of India's Liberation. In other words he wanted thereby to free himself and all the Indians from British thraldom (*QAID-I FARANG*)[1]. There is evidence to believe that Bahadur Shah's verses were sung about the streets by the old and young people of Dehli[2]. And it is rightly observed that a few plaintive *ghazals* of Bahadur Shah did much more to damage the British cause than all the combined guns of the mutineers[3]. And, it is these *ghazals* combined with many of his soul-stirring verses which have kept alive and verdant till today his memory in this sub-continent—India and Pakistan—as well as in Burma.

It is evident that Bahadur Shah considered himself virtually a prisoner[4] of the British; and for fear of their espionage which was very effective he could not give plain expression to his innermost thoughts. But he was upright, and was neither a liar, nor an intriguer. Says he:

---

and had made it a point thus to rouse their spirits, replied immediately, saying:

غازیوں میں بو رہے گی جب تلک ایمان کی
تب تلک لندن چلے گی تیغ ہندوستان کی

As long as the valiant soldiers will have in themselves (even) the smell of Faith, so long the sword of India will ply, reaching London.

(*Cf.* Sajjajn Lal—D. U. A. and F. S., p. 43).

[1] *Vide* p. 92 *infra.*

[2] Andrews—*Life of Zakaullah* p. 18.

[3] Spear, P.—T. M. p. 226.

[4] See Appendix, C.

اپنا ظفر ھمیشہ سے شیوہ ھے راستی
ھم تو کبھی پھٹکتے نہیں پاس جھوٹ کے

(O Zafar! our motto is always speaking truth;
we never even hear a lie.)

It is also evident[1] that Bahadur Shah was philanthropic, generous and charitable. Zakaullah tells us that he gave a fixed allowance on the 1st of every month unasked for to almost all the disabled persons known to him.[2] Instances are on record when he was compelled[3] to take loans[4] from the Hindu mahajans to be able to pay salaries to his servants and do the needful social work by awarding gifts to intending travellers, deserving poets and needy persons as well as to his courtiers.

The anonymous *Tarikh-i Bahadur Shahi* translated into English by Anderson which has been erroneously notified by the Asiatic Society[5] among the 'important

---

[1] *Vide* Bahadur Shah Zafar—*Diwans* I-IV.

[2] Zakaullah—T.H. ix-x. p. 346.

[3] This was the result of the cold war that had continued between Bahadur Shah and the British until 1857.

[4] This may appear paradoxical. But the Court Diary abounds in instances of these loans. Early in March 1847 he borrowed Rs. 1,500 from a mahajan Babu Suraj Narain and another sum of Rs. 4,000 from a Sahukar. Later a sum of Rs. 3,800 was borrowed from Kunwar Dhani Singh and Salag Ram and another of Rs. 20,000 from Hafiz Daud. Big sums were also borrowed from time to time from Mubarak-un Nisa, wife of Ochterlony as well as from Sahukars—Zorawar Chand, Daulat Ram, Gokal Singh, Chiranji Lal and Ghulam Ali.

Vide (i) *Sirajul Akhbar, Dehli* and *Ahsanul Akhbar,* Bombay, 22nd August, 1845, (ii) *Dehli Urdu Akhbar,* 21st January and 17th March 1851

[5] *Vide* the Asiatic Society publication—*Exhibition of books, documents and photographs relating to Indian Revolt.* 1857, p. 1.

publications on the Indian Revolt of 1857' dwells on the praiseworthy qualities of Bahadur Shah I. But it conjures up before the writer's eyes the corresponding qualities which Bahadur Shah II shared with his namesake, namely 'knowledge about various styles of letter-writing, strong belief in *taqdeer,* resignation to God's will, determination to seek the venue of the Almighty God's pleasure, accession to the throne in old age, filial devotion[1] and faithful obedience in spite of the father's displeasure to his commands,[2] and service to religious mendicants, ascetics, saints and men of piety'.

While the *Tarikh-i Bahadur Shahi* has in actual

[1], [2] It should be noted that Bahadur Shah I and Bahadur Shah II both lived patiently and in faithful obedience through the long reigns of their respective fathers; and each incurred his father's displeasure and was treated as a rebel but was finally absolved and reconciled. When Aurangzeb wanted to punish his son Bahadur Shah by throwing him into solitary confinement, the Shah of Iran wrote him a recommendatory letter saying, 'In what verse and what book of the holy traditions is it mentioned that you should confine a person who is the reciter of the tradition'? Aurangzeb asked the wise men about him for the answer to this question; no one could give a suitable answer. At last he told them to ask Bahadur Shah himself who immediately replied, 'It is incumbent on me to obey the command of my honourable father; he is a free agent.' Similar filial devotion on the part of Bahadur Shah II who had incurred his father's displeasure and had been disowned by him is attested by Charles Metcalfe who saw him as heir-apparent at the age of 53 in 1828. He observed, 'I must add that his conduct is in every respect highly creditable to him. He is undoubtedly the most respectable and most accomplished of princes, the most worthy of his Majesty's (Akbar II's) love; and although it is withheld from him I have never known him to deviate from the observance of proper respect and filial duty'. *Vide* (i) Anderson's *Tarikh-i Bahadur Shahi* (Asiatic Society collection p. 55). (ii) T.M p. 73.

fact nothing to do with Bahadur Shah II, there are a few other works[1] of his age written by Syed Ahmad Khan now commonly known as Sir Syed, by Muhammad Riza and Munshi Sada Sukh. Of all these Sir Syed's *Asbab-i Ghadr*[2]—an essay which he wrote in Urdu after the Mutiny—is the most notable.

In this Sir Syed has given a grotesque figure of Bahadur Shah saying,

> 'The ex-king had a fixed idea that he could transform himself into a fly or gnat, and that he could in this guise convey himself to other countries and learn what was going on there. Seriously, he firmly believed that he possessed the power of transformation'.

This has remained unconfirmed and is not borne out by the known facts of history. It only tends to confirm the common belief that while writing the *Asbab-i Ghadr,* Sir Syed was anxious to disqualify Bahadur Shah as a leader of the country and particularly of the Musalmans whom the British had held guilty of a conspiracy against British rule.

For similar reasons Zakaullah too spoke of Bahadur Shah 'in harsh terms for which he afterwards expressed sorrow'[3].

However Ghalib took a different view of things. He abstained from speaking ill of Bahadur Shah on any account though he suffered at the hands of the British and saved his own life with great difficulty. On one occasion he sang Bahadur Shah's praises saying,[4]

شہنشاہ سخن داں سخن سنج
کہ دارو نقد معنی گنج در گنج

[1], [2] Chapter X, *infra;* pp. 308-309.

[3] Andrews, C. F.—*Life of Zakaullah* p. 19.

[4] Ghalib—*Panj Ahang* MS. F. 70 a. *Cf. Kulliyat-i Nasr-i Ghalib* p. 79, Nawalkishore Press 1875/1292.

An Emperor who knows things; he is a weigher of words, a poet and a wise man who possesses treasures after treasures of the knowledge of Reality

خدا داں در کشور خدای
زہے درویشی وفرماں روای

'He is the man of God in the whole world. Admirable! he is a dervish and a king combined in one.

جہاں در خسروی ظل اللہ گفت
بدرویشی خرو خضرراہ گفت

(In the domain of kingship the world called him the Shadow of God; in the domain of poverty and austerity, wisdom gave him the epithet of KHIZR-I RAH—Guide of the Path)

سخن را تاج بخش سرفرازي
سراج الدین بہادر شاہ غازی

He is so exalted in the domain of poetry that he has become the bestower of crowns; he is SIRAJUDDIN BAHADUR SHAH GHAZI

خداوندا بدھرش جاوداں دار
جہانش بخش و دائم در جہاں دار

O God! maintain him always in this world. Grant him the world and make his reign perpetual!

On another occasion Ghalib paid a much richer tribute to Bahadur Shah. The following is but an abridgment of it[1].

[1] Ghalib—*Panj Ahang* MS. F. 70 a.

شاہ ما دارد بہم در رہروی
خرقہ پیر و تاج خسروی
شاہی و درویشی ایں جا بہم است
بادشاہ عہد قطب عالم است

'Our Shah possesses two great gifts—the mantellum of spiritual leadership and the diadem of sovereignty—which make him fit for the role that he is playing, namely the guidance of men. He is at once king and dervish; he is king of this age as well as the *Qutb-i Alam*—the highest sufi leader'[1].

Bahadur Shah had joined the Chishti order of sufism at an early age when he became a disciple of Shaikh Fakhru'ddin Chishti.

کیوں نہ تو سر بہ فلک کھینچے کہ فخر الدین نے
دی ہے دستار ترے سر پہ کھینچ کے باندھہ

(Why should you not raise your head to the sky for Fakhru'ddin has tied the turban tight on your head?)

On the death[2] of Fakhru'ddin Bahadur Shah swore *baiyat* (spiritual allegiance) to his successor Qutbu'ddin Chishti, and he remained sworn to the Chishti order till the end. He says:

بہادر شاہ میرا نام ہے مشہور عالم میں
ولیکن اے ظفر اُن کا گدائے رہ نشیں ہوں میں

---

[1] Ghalib—*Mihr-i Nimroz* pp. 259-267, Nawalkishore Press 1875/1292.

[2] 1784/1199.

(Bahadur Shah is my name, well-known throughout the world. But, O Zafar! I am a devotee at his threshold)

It was perhaps a legacy of the Chishti order with whom Bahadur Shah delighted to identify himself that he possessed a virtue which modern history has rarely recorded and which is found in saints only. It was this: Bahadur Shah had a soft corner in his heart, for all his dependants and servants. A person who once entered Bahadur Shah's service was never dismissed and was never in his bad books. He himself says:

ہم اُسکی بات کے قائل ہیں اے ظفر جس نے
بھلا کہا جسے منہ سے اُسے برا نہ کہا

(O Zafar! we have appreciation for that man who spoke not ill of the same person of whom he had once spoken well)

Bahadur Shah uniformly acted on this principle An illustration of this is afforded by his attitude towards Hakim Ahsanullah with whom he differed temperamentally.[1]

It should be noted that Hakim Ahsanullah was essentially a physician as the term *Hakim* suggests. He had been confirmed as court physician by Bahadur Shah, the fact being reported in the *Sirajul Akhbar*[2]. Hakim Ahsanullah's knowledge of ministerial functions and of practical politics was nil. Because he was shrewd and tactful he had wormed his way into royal favour. Since Mahbub Ali Khan the wazir had fallen ill and had become bed-ridden through dropsy on the eve of the Mutiny, Hakim Ahsanullah was allowed to officiate for him.

---

[1] *Vide* p. 53, footnote.

[2] *Sirajul Akhbar,* February 23 and May 17, 1840.

Evidently Bahadur Shah did not like Hakim Ahsanullah as wazir; he did not see eye to eye with him in political matters.[1] He did not accept Hakim Ahsanullah's advice regarding the 'mutineers' from the beginning. Immediately on their arrival from Mirath, Hakim Ahsanullah had advised Bahadur Shah to have nothing to do with them. Bahadur Shah did not act on this advice, and ultimately accepted the 'mutineers' leadership on his own responsibility (12th May 1857). Since then Bahadur Shah, considering his interests as identical with theirs, sincerely wished them victory and worked for the same whole-heartedly. But whenever the 'mutineers', suspecting Hakim Ahsanullah of pro-British trend, fell upon him and wanted to kill him, Bahadur Shah who did not want to see the destruction of a renowned scholar and courtier of his father's time saved him; and once he did so by throwing himself on his body which was the target of attacks.

Later it was proved that Hakim Ahsanullah was no less adverse to Bahadur Shah than Mirza Ilahi Bakhsh and Munshi Rajab Ali. Perhaps Bahadur Shah had said correctly:

راز دل جس سے کہا دوست سمجھ کر اپنا
اے ظفر ہم نے اسے جان کا دشمن دیکھا

(The person whom we considered a reliable

Says he figuratively:[1]

۱ میرے مزاج کے کیوں کر نہ ہو خلاف علاج
وہ دشمنوں سے رکھے ہے میرا طبیب اخلاص

Why should the treatment of my indisposition be not disagreeable; for my physician bears goodwill to (my) enemies? *Vide Kulliyat-i Zafar; Diwan-i chaharum*. p. 54.

friend and to whom we confided the secret of our heart, turned out a mortal enemy, O Zafar)

This feature of Bahadur Shah's character is typical. It may or may not be praiseworthy, but it has about it a simplicity and sweetness which endeared him even to some animals. Zaheer Dehlawi gives a reliable account of an elephant called Maula Bakhsh and a horse called Hamdam, in both of whom Bahadur Shah had inspired sincere love; both of these were his pets. They were so attached to him that they shared his feelings of joy and sorrow in their own way. When on 20th September 1857 Dehli was captured and the Red Fort was blown in and seized by the British, Maula Bakhsh as well as Hamdam declined to take food and drink. Seeing this the mahout who took a personal interest in Maula Bakhsh reported the matter to Saunders, the English officer then in charge of the royal stable. Saunders was amazed to hear it; and in order to test the matter he had a basketful of rich food placed before Maula Bakhsh which the latter threw away angrily to a distance, immediately at sight. Saunders was dismayed and said, 'This elephant is a rebel; he must be auctioned'. The mahout took the elephant to the mart where he was auctioned for a sum of Rs. 100/- to a grocer, other than whom no one dared make a bid. The auction over, the news was announced to the elephant by the mahout who said, 'O Maula Bakhsh! you had been all your life the Emperor's pet; now as ill-luck would have it you have been sold to a grocer under British orders'. On hearing this, the elephant shrieked and fell on the ground and expired. Zaheer Dehlawi relates that the fate of Hamdam was similar.[1]

It has been contended that 'Bahadur Shah's title of the Emperor of Hindustan was a mere hollow and mockery'[2]. But it is not known to many that theory and practice have very often differed in different climes and countries; nevertheless theory is not, and has never been, 'a mere hollow and mockery'; and surely it is not an altogether negligible thing. In the eyes of the British and according as they had made him, Bahadur Shah was a nonentity in practical politics but in theory he was still the Emperor, the *de jure* sovereign. This point was elucidated after the Mutiny by Dewar and Buckler[3] before whose logic Dodwell's[4] contention that the Company had enjoyed 'complete sovereignty' since 1813, or 1835 or 1844 fell to the ground. Buckler said, 'It seems clear that the king of Delhi could have no juristic obligation of obedience to a power which having ceased to recognize his paramount authority had neglected to exact from him any acknowledgment of formal dependence upon his late ceremonial subordinate. Bahadur Shah's relation to the British Government since 1844 was rather like that of the Merovingian to the mayor of the palace after his deposition by Pepin in A.D. 752. He had the right, but not the power. So long as the power remained firm in other hands, nothing could be done and the prescriptive right of *de facto* power would gradually assert itself. But until that process was complete, the legal rights were dormant, not extinct,

---

[1] Zaheer Dehlawi—D.G. pp. 24-26.
[2] Majumdar, R. C.—S.M.R. p. 116.
[3] T. M., p. 225.
[4] *Cambridge History of India* V, pp. 605 ff.

and were ready to be revived the moment they could be clothed with power . . . . . . The British had only 13 years of undisturbed possession before the storm broke out'. Buckler was criticised by Dodwell and Garrett. But their criticism is rebutted by Spear who observes: 'They (Dodwell and Garrett) seek to disprove the *de jure* Mughul claim by proving the *de facto* British power[1]. Spear does not accept their argument that 'the king of Delhi had surrendered his claims in the course of the negotiations for an increase in the royal stipend. And the plea that Raja Ram Mohan Roy offered to abandon all the royal claims to sovereignty in return for the doubling of the royal stipend is *ultra vires*. Raja Ram Mohan Roy had exceeded his limits, if he did so. Even in 1833 when in the words of Spear, 'a much smaller increase was granted on condition of such abandonment, Akbar Shah did not accept the condition. And because Akbar Shah did not accept the condition at all the offer was renewed to Bahadur Shah who too rejected it. But the British made a spurious announcement that 'Bahadur Shah actually accepted this condition in 1838.' Spear gives the right information when he says, 'But the negotiations eventually broke down in 1843 over the question of the manner of distributing the proposed increase. The king never drew the money, and so the surrender of rights never took place'[2]. Spear continues:

> 'Bahadur Shah waged war (against the British)......But he was no rebel against constituted authority[3]. He had broken no pledge, violated no treaty, committed no treachery; he had merely

[1], [2] Spear, T. M., pp. 225-226.
[3] *Op. cit.* p. 226.

exercised rights which Indian opinion had conceded to his ancestors through eleven generations. He should probably have been treated as a hostile ruler whose dominions might have been liable to annexation and whose person might be subject to detention. In fact the British were misguided enough to try him as a rebel, wise enough to treat him as a defeated prince and foolish enough to mingle indignities with their measures of precaution. Indian opinion never regarded him as a rebel, and always considered him to have been ill-used in his detention in Delhi and his exile in Rangoon. . . .'

In another connection Spear says:

'Bahadur Shah was a man of cultured and upright character. In the palace diary of later years there are glimpses of him spending whole days reading and writing, studying and composing verses in the Roshan Ara Garden . . . . Whether he could have developed the qualities of action we shall never know for he was denied all opportunity in his early years and the Mutiny experience came far too late. But as a philosopher prince he would have adorned any court. He would have made a dignified ruler of a minor German state under the Empire or an excellent constitutional king. Delhi in his time was a Weimer with Ghalib for its Goethe. His interests were primarily literary and aesthetic. He loved poetry and philosophy, gardens and nature in all its guises. Nearly every day of his life he went for excursion across the Jumna morning and evening; every monsoon found him established at

Mahrauli where he built a country palace. He patronized the Solona or Punkha festival, which was held each August towards the end of rains when he and his sons headed a procession to the shrine of the Qutb Sahib, the king on his elephant and his followers waving large fans. He enjoyed gardens and laid out at least two himself, one below the palace wall on the Jumna bank and one in Shahdera. He loved animals and had a special fondness for doves. He was religious without being fanatic. He was fond of visiting famous shrines and continued the Hindu custom of making disciples. The disciple accepted the spiritual guidance of the king and received a light red handkerchief as a symbol of his status. The practice had been begun by Akbar II and was encouraged by the Pirzadas of Delhi who were firm believers in the divine right of kings. But he was no bigot. He freely admitted Dr. Chunni Lal to the palace after his conversion to Christianity and rebuked those who criticised Dr. Chunni Lal's action. 'There was no cause for shame in what he had done' he said. . . . .

'Bahadur Shah was in fact the best, rather than the worst of the late Mughul kings of Delhi. The shadow of the Mutiny has darkened his fame and turned the philosopher-poet of fact into the scheming rebel of alleged history. But it should be remembered that Bahadur Shah was 82 years of age when the Mutiny broke out. For years travellers had been writing of his senility and weakness. The mutinous troops seized the palace and treated him so disrespectfully that he threatened to retire to the shrine of Qutb Sahib as a religious devotee. And those same critics denounced him as an arch-intriguer and conspirator, as one of the chief villains of the whole tragedy. These charges neutralize each other, and they are typical of a whole school of criticism of late Mughul Delhi. If the king kept up his palace he had too much money and his allowance must be cut down; if he lived within his income his establishment was squalid and should be abolished. If he maintained his dignity and the traditional etiquette, he was preposterous; if he was ready to give it up, there was no need to maintain him in the palace. If a prince was idle and dissolute, it was a proof of Mughul effeteness; if he showed any signs of character, he was a danger and not to be countenanced. If the *salateen* were given employment, they would be a danger to the State; their consequent enforced idleness and penury was a proof of their turpitude. To satisfy these critics Bahadur Shah should either have resisted the sepoys or fled from them. But no one has ever suggested how he could have done either. His own guard and most of his family had joined the mutineers. Was this octogenerian expected to rush out upon them, berserk, and to die resisting the restoration of the very authority he had always claimed for himself? Alternatively, where was he to fly? How was this young gallant to reach a non-existent British army in the height of a hot season? Perhaps he was to die alone in disguise like Sir John Metcalfe, to rest by day in caves and guide himself by stars at night until he reached a friendly British camp. And how friendly would it have proved?

'Bahadur Shah must be judged on the evidence of his own life, and not by the word of superficial travellers or of soldiers unbalanced by the strains of war, fatigue and racial passion'.[1] And, for similar reasons he cannot be judged even by the Spies' reports[2]; and cognizance should be taken of the pre-Mutiny appreciations of Bahadur Shah by Imam Bakhsh Sahbai and Sir Syed Ahmad Khan.

Imam Bakhsh Sahbai, a mid-19th century scholar and Professor of Persian at the Dehli College, was a contemporary of Akbar II[3] and Bahadur Shah II. Though he took no active part in the War of 1857, he was considered a rebel by the British and shot dead after the fall of Dehli. In high-flown Persian prose and poetry, he wrote a book entitled *Raiza-i Jawahir*[4] in appreciation of Bahadur Shah, an extract from which, translated into English by the writer, runs as follows:

> 'Hospitality and his (Bahadur Shah's) nature are interlocked like the waves and the sea. Greatness of his head is like the height of the sky.
>
> 'Bounty of his heart is like the showers falling from the clouds; and benevolence of his heart is effulgent like the sky.
>
> 'Effectiveness of the government has been possible through the aid of his severity.

[1] Spear—T.M. p. 72.

[2] *Vide* Appendix G.

[3] *Vide* Beale W.—*Miftahu-t Tawarikh*, pp. 594-595.

[4] Sahbai, Imam Bakhsh—*Raiza-i Jawahir*, Nizami Press, Kanpur, 1295 Hijra, pp. 19-23. Sir Syed Ahmad was highly impressed by this book; and incorporated some pieces from it in his own book—'*Asaru-s Sanadeed*', p. 23. Also see Abdul Haq—*Marhoom Dehli College*, p. 149.

'Bashfulness in his face is as clear as clarity itself in a mirror.

'Through his courtesy and kindness, ocean is like a bed of pearls; and through his charity mines are like gold in the treasury.

'Through his ceaseless pouring of money, waves of the sea are impatiently collecting pearls.

'His heart is such a vast receptacle of secrets that night blushes before it, (night being proverbially the time for secrets).

'On hearing from a distance of two-three stages the sound of his blessed army, victory assumes a receptionist's posture. And as soon as his dignified banners proceed, triumph gets ready to offer (him) fortune by way of a present.

'The body of the pen in his (Bahadur Shah's) hand has become a fountain of variegated topics.

'Compared to the beauty of his speech the rhythmical chirping of nightingale sounds like lamentations of the crow; and compared to the beauty of his calligraphy the handwriting of the master calligraphist looks like scrawls.

'Through his sword the administration of justice has reached culmination, and his resourceful mind is the well-head of equity and rectitude.

'In the course of war the arrows from the enemy are as ineffective as the eyes of a blind man. And the bow of Rustam, when pitted against his (Bahadur Shah's) worn-out bow, fails to pull its weight like the frail body of an invalid.

'The best kind of swords have rusted in the scabbards before his sword; his lasso in these days has completely outdone all other lassoes.

'He is such a warrior hero that Rustam has learnt the art of war from the meanest of his slaves; and he is such a man of fortune that Alexander has had the drums of victory made out of the leather of his (Bahadur Shah's) shoes.

'His royal bed-chamber he enjoys to such an extent that even a flower garden is put to shame; and through his luxuriant joys his private apartments have become the envy of orchards.

'The lustre of his sword brings destruction to the life of (his) enemies and the noise of thunder is drowned before the roaring of his war drums.

'In a battle with him the enemies are demoralized; and behaving like a hundred dislocated shooting stars, they flee for their lives and perish.

'His arrow penetrates to the other side of the sky more quickly than the bullet of a sigh.

'The height of his greatness is the summit of glory and his exalted majesty is a ladder to the roof of perfection.

'Through his noble generosity, the sky has attained its greatest height and ocean has acquired its weightiness through the laboratory of his bounty.'

'On account of his invitations (and encouragement) to those who are poor in intellect, the intellectual bankrupts have become great literary figures and are now anxiously searching their minds to produce virgin thoughts. Through the renown of his giving out ideas universally to all, poets are ceaselessly restless and anxious to bring forth unique thought.

'His physical strength is so great that the mere mention of lion's name gives him provocation.

Auspiciousness when attributed to him is enabled to embellish itself with the feathers of phoenix.

'He (Bahadur Shah) is such a wise emperor that in the height of his excellence when he halts, he places his foot on a summit. He holds a rank high like the sky, and through magnanimity dashes his horse in full glory on the face of the full moon.

'He enjoys the rank of an angel in such a degree that his royal shoulders bear the decoration mark of Divine grace.

'Should he strike terror into a marble stone, its veins would burst into sparks.

'On hearing the news of his (Bahadur Shah's) intended expedition, the lion loses his balance and flees and hides himself in a hare's hole.'

The above extract from Imam Sahbai's prose and poetry contains much exaggeration, and his appreciation cannot be taken literally. But he brings out some distinct features[1] of Bahadur Shah's character which were approved by Sir Syed Ahmad when, before the Rising of 1857 he paid him a rich tribute saying: 'In his (Bahadur Shah's) court of justice Noshirwan would be assigned a place befitting his lowest servant, and in his durbar Alexander would be given the grade of his meanest attendant. During his reign autumn is turned into spring; and thorns have become the envy of gardens. Evidently if I were to attempt an appreciation of this praiseworthy Emperor all the display of my genius in that line would certainly fall short of the

[1] *I.e.* his knowledge of Divinity and strong faith in Providence, his adherence to Law and gift of poetry besides his generosity, bravery and justice. (*Raiza-i Jawahir*, pp. 19-24).

mark. For this reason it is advisable in the very beginning to acknowledge my inability to cope with the task.

'The birth of this veritable guide and spiritual adviser, the refuge (*qibla*) of the righteous people, took place on Tuesday 28th Sha'banul Muazzam 1189 Hijra[1] towards sunset so that the world may know that after the coming into existence of this SELECT OF GOD—the Light of the Eyes of HOLY Men—the sun being ashamed, hid himself behind the curtain of bashfulness. *Abu Zafar* came to be the chronogram of his birth, the name Abu Zafar being an augury bespeaking his victory and triumph over his enemies. And his auspicious accession to the throne took place on Friday night 28th Jumada II,. 1253 Hijra.[2]

از نشه دولت بهادر شاهی - شد پرز طرب ایاغ دهلی

'Under the agreeable smell of the reign of Bahadur Shah the drinking vessel of Dehli became filled with the wine of pleasure.

بنشست به تخت دولت روز افزون -

نزهت بفزود ازو بباغ دهلی

'He mounted the throne of the day-to-day increasing dominion; and on account of him, pleasantness increased in the garden of Dehli.

تاریخ جلوس آں شه والا - آمد به لب خرد چراغ دهلی

'The date of the accession of that exalted and dignified Emperor was put into my mouth—*Khirad Chiragh Dehli*.

'May the Almighty God save this best of the great

[1] 24th October, 1775.

[2] 29th September, 1837.

kings—essence of the prominent and able-bodied rulers—till eternity! May the world continue to be enriched from the abundance of his justice through the intercession of the Prophet and his great descendants[1]'!

No less important than Sir Syed Ahmad's pre-Mutiny tribute is the post-Mutiny judgment of Sir John Lawrence.[2] Based largely on the 'documentary evidence produced at the trial' it bespeaks Bahadur Shah's faithfulness to the cause of the Mutiny as well as his energy, action and diligence which had resulted in the building up of 'the system in which the general Government was conducted; the raising of loans, military arrangements, the communications with foreign powers and neighbouring chiefs. . .[3]'. In other words the documentary evidence[4] studied by Sir John Lawrence testifies to Bahadur Shah's efforts at restoring order and discipline[5], building a government,[6], showing kindness to the sepoys[7], hearing and receiving complaints from all aggrieved persons[8] and readily consenting to punish the delinquent Mughul princes[9].

---

[1] Syed Ahmad, Sir—*Asaru-s Sanadeed,* 2nd edition, p. 23.

[2] *Press-List of the Mutiny Papers,* pp. ii-iii.

[3] *Ibid.*

[4] *E.g.* Mutiny Papers (i) Collection No. 2, Vol. 19. Nos. 1, 12, 23, 27, 29, 32, 37.

(ii) Box 60, Nos. 8-9. May 19, 1857; Box 69, July 22, 1857; Box 152, No. 6, June 10, 1857.

[5],[6] *Vide* Chapters VI and VII *infra.*

[7] That Bahadur Shah gave feasts and presents in cash to the sepoys is attested by Chunni Lal (*Pr. Tr. B. S.,* pp. 109-114).

[8] He was anxious to do justice to all classes and ranks of people; and with this object in view he personally received petitions from the aggrieved. Jiwan Lal attempted in vain to give this credit to Mahbub Ali Khan and Hakim Ahsanullah Khan (Metcalfe,—T. N. N., p. 110).

[9] Bahadur Shah never supported the Mughul Princes in

'However wrongly,' says Sir John Lawrence, 'he (Bahadur Shah) had assumed his position, it must be admitted that his orders were not unworthy of the situation[1]'. Of the numerous orders that he issued during the period of war (May—September 1857) none were found incongruous, impracticable or self-contradictory[2].

However, Bahadur Shah did not wield the sword during the war and killed no one though he visited the

---

connection with any complaint that happened to be filed against them. Jiwan Lal gives several instances which confirm this: "On 2nd July General Bakht Khan informed the King that if any of the Princes attempted to plunder the city, he would cut off their noses and ears. The King replied, 'You have full authority. Do whatever seems good unto you'. On 3rd July 'an order was issued whereby the Princes were relieved of all further duties connected with the army'. On 5th July when 'the King (Bahadur Shah) heard a complaint against Mirza Abu Bakr, he was very much displeased, and took away from him all military rank. And orders were issued for his arrest. Then the King ordered all the Princes to keep away from his levees. And he issued orders to all the sardars to note that he had disgraced the Princes and they were to be treated as ordinary persons if they were found committing any oppression. On 17th August General Bakht Khan complained to the King that the Princes had collected money from different bankers for the pay of the troops, but the troops had not received one pice. On hearing this, the King gave orders to Mirza Khizr to hand over all the money received to the General; and in future when money was requisitioned, it was to be paid to the General in the presence of the citizens.' (Metcalfe—T.N.N. pp. 133-198).

[1] *Press-List of the Mutiny Papers,* p. iii.

[2] *Vide* Mutiny Papers, Box 39, May 11; Box 35, January 13; Box 62, No. 30, May 17; Box 137, No. 2, May 18; Box 60, Nos. 8, 9, May 19; Box 152, No. 1, May 24; Box 131, June 2, 3, 4, Nos. 10, 11, 13, 16; Box 69, No. 41, July 22; Box 147, No. 1, June 5; Box 110, No. 174, June 6; Box 152, No. 5, June 9.

battlefield and frequently inspected the batteries. Perhaps he felt much too weak and had long been ailing. Perhaps his sufism deterred him, for sufism as interpreted by Ibn Khaldun 'trains the spirit and inner self of a devotee to such an extent that he obtains an insight into the higher regions beyond matter, thus perceiving what the average man with his material outlook cannot appreciate[1]'. Thus Bahadur Shah's character became a complex and was not estimated aright even by the writers who possessed first-hand information. One of them says, 'Bahadur Shah has lost the affection of his people, has quarrelsome temper and is not on good terms with his family and is constantly at variance with his ministers[2]'. Another says, 'Bahadur Shah is highly revered by all; all our servants (on seeing him) are in a state of profound veneration; the natives all look upon him as their rightful Lord;

---

[1] قال ابن خلدون فى اصول الصوفيه ومجاهداتهم ان هذه المجاهده والخلوة والذكر يتبعها غالبا كشف حجاب الحس والاطلاع على عوالم من امرالله ليس لصاحب الحس ادراك شى منها والروح من تلك العوالم

(Verily this training of the spirit, inner self and meditation removes very often the curtains of external matter and secures through divine blessings an insight into the higher regions which a man of the material outlook cannot perceive; he can have no idea at all of the spirit in those higher regions'.

Al-Mamun, Muhammad ar-Zinjani—

علم الروحيات الحديث

(*Modern Spiritualism*), p. 25 (Damascus, 1928).

[2] Orlich, Leopold von—*Travels in India*, Vol. II, pp. 20-21.

and so he is, I suppose'[1]. Another declares him a rebellious king and traitor to the British[2]. Another introduces him as a scheming rebel[3] and another depicts him as a simpleton[4]. Yet another denounces him as a Shia[5]. And Hakim Ahsanullah Khan[6] who knew him more than anyone else called him the Ibrahim Adham[7] of his age.

چو دارد فقروشاهی هر دو باهم -
تو اندش خواند ابراهیم ادهم
شهنشه بود ظفر سلطان عالم
که باشد عالم جان جان عالم
در اکلیل فرق سرفرازی
سراج الدین بهادر شاه غازی
خودش داود و دیوانش زبور است
زلحنش رشک ریزان کوه طور است

---

[1] Emily Eden——*Up the Country,* p. 97.

[2] (i) Metcalfe—T.N.N., p. 4.
(ii) Keith—*Delhi-1857,* p. 334.

[3] *Vide T.M.*—p. 72.

[4] *Spies' Letters.* Mutiny Papers, Box 15, Augsust 16, 1857.

[5] It is said that on hearing the charge that he was a Shia, Bahadur Shah wrote a book entitled *Dumghu-l Batil.* According to Hali, this book was written for Bahadur Shah by Ghalib. Anyway Bahadur Shah continued like the Shias to praise Hazrat Ali and the *Ahl-ibait*; and he composed devotional verses with touching references to the Tragedy of Karbala. He also observed Muharram, and ceremoniously held the *dastarkhwan* of Hazrat Ali.

[6] *Vide Roz-namcha Bahadur Shah,* MS. N.L.; last page.

[7] Ibrahim Adham or Ibrahim bin Adham was a king of

'Since he combines in his person poverty with sovereignty he (Bahadur Shah) may be called Ibrahim Adham of his age.

Zafar, the sultan of the world, is an emperor who is a world of souls and the soul of the world.

In the tiara of grandeur he is Siraju'ddin Bahadur Shah Ghazi. Himself he is like Daud[1] and his *diwan* is like Zabur[2]. Impressed by his intonation Mount Tauras is shedding tears.'

Like Hakim Ahsanullah Khan, Maulvi Fazl Haq also knew Bahadur Shah closely. Himself noted for his hatred of the English[3], the said Maulvi, commonly

---

Balkh whose dates are uncertain. He is said to have lived 110 years; and while the date of his birth is not known the dates of his death range between 776-783/160-166. He had renounced his kingdom and assumed the role of a dervish; he became a leading saint of his times, noted for his piety and probity.

(*Encyclopaedia of Islam,* Vol. II, p. 432).

[1] *I.e.* David.

[2] *I.e.* the Psalms of David.

[3] Out of the two odes of about 200 verses which Maulvi Fazl Haq composed in the island prison, several verses illustrate this point. Says he,

لم اقترف ذنباً سوى ان ليس لى

مع هؤلاء مودة و ولاء

'I did not commit any crime except this that I had no liking for them (Englishmen); nor was I friendly to them'.

فولاء هم كفر بنص محكم

ما فيه للمرء المحق مراء

'Showing affection to them amounts to infidelity according to the Quranic injunctions. No lover of truth can have any doubt about this.'

مقدمة الثورة الهنديه

(*Preamble to the Indian Revolution,* verses 109, 110).

known as Maulana Fazl Haq Khairabadi had found in Bahadur Shah a congenial soul. He supported him heartily in his war with the British. But when after the fall of Dehli he was seized and exiled as a life prisoner to the Andaman Islands, he was much embittered against Bahadur Shah and harped on his weaknesses[1]. But he did not consider him pro-British; nor had he known him as an intriguer.[2]

[1, 2] *Vide* Appendix, H.

Chapter II

BAHADUR SHAH II AND THE SEPOYS

It is said that Bahadur Shah was opposed[1] to the sepoys, and that he was a British subject[2]

[1] In his article 'Martyr or Traitor' published in the *Amrita Bazar Patrika* of November 28, 1956, Dr. R. C. Majumdar has declared Bahadur Shah a traitor saying, 'Bahadur Shah has not the least claim to be called a hero, a patriot or a martyr. The only epithet applicable to Bahadur Shah is traitor'. And in his lecture reported in the *Statesman* of 26th December, 1956 he says, 'Bahadur Shah was at heart opposed to the sepoys and devoted to the British.'

[2] The third charge brought against Bahadur Shah at the British tribunal which tried him was this....'He being a subject of the British Government in India and not regarding the duty of his allegiance, did at Delhi on the 11th May 1857...as a false traitor against the State proclaim and declare himself the reigning king and sovereign of India' ...(*Pr. Tr. B. S.* p. 223).

Saunders, officiating Commissioner and Agent to the Lt.-Governor was put the following question by the Judge Advocate:

Question—Can you give the Court any information as to the circumstances under which the kings of Delhi became subjects and pensioners of the British Government?

Answer—The city and fort having been evacuated by the Marattas the Emperor Shah Alam sent a message to General Lake applying for protection of the British Authorities, and on 14th September, the date since rendered more memorable by the successful assault in 1857, the British troops entered Delhi; from that day the kings of Delhi have become pensioned subjects of the British Government. The prisoner succeeded to the titular sovereignty of Delhi in 1837. He had no power whatever beyond the precincts

like them. But the sepoys—who bore names like Ganga Din, Mata Din, Ram Ghulam[1], Gulab Shah and Nihar Pandey—were for the most part unlettered, uncultured and greedy and quarrelsome and indulged in opium-eating[2] and even in drugs.[3] They were quarrelling among themselves, and one class was jealous of another. 'There is a jealousy', says Greathed 'between the old and new mutineers; the former are gorged with plunder and think they have done enough and wish to leave the hard work to the new arrivals but have no inclination to give them a share of the spoils'.[4] Regarding one of the sepoys of the Pandey class of the mutineers captured by the British, Greathed says that he was found in possession of eighty-seven gold mohurs[5]. Nasir Nazir, an eye-witness, says that some of the mutineers were seen at the goldsmiths' shops getting their gold and silver coins and bullion transformed into ornaments and small bars which they tied around their waist and thighs, carefully concealed under their clothes[6]. Presumably this wealth was

of his own palace; he had the power of conferring titles and dresses of honour upon his own immediate retainers but was prohibited from exercising that power upon any others. He and the heir-apparent alone were exempted from the jurisdiction of the Company's local courts but were under the orders of the Supreme Government (Pr. Tr. B. S. p. 146).

[1], [2], [3] *Vide* (i) Nasir Nazir,—L. Q. E. J., p. 73, Zaheer Dehlawi—D. G., pp. 86, 106.

(ii) Mutiny Papers Box 58, No. 17-24, May 15—August 13, 1857.

(iii) Photograph facing p. 72.

[4], [5] Greathed's *Letters*, pp. 46, 47.

[6] Nasir Nazir—*Lal Qile ki ek Jhalak*, p. 74.

facing p. 72

THE SEPOYS

acquired from the plunder[1] of the city of Dehli whose inhabitants had done the sepoys no harm and had been in the words of Greathed 'fervent and enthusiastic from the beginning to receive them'. According to an eye-witness[2] the whole area from the Lahori Gate of the Red Fort to the Lahori Gate of the city had been vacated by the people and all the premises therein were occupied by the sepoys numbering about a lakh by 26th May 1857. Bracketed with these[3] sepoys and judged from their point of view and in the light of their complaints and remarks, Bahadur Shah would

---

[1] These points are illustrated from the following order of Bahadur Shah dated 18th June 1857 issued to his sons:—'The illustrious and valiant Mirza Zaheeru'ddin Bahadur Mirza Mughul, and to Prince Mirza Khair Sultan Bahadur...Sons! 'Learn...not a day has passed since the arrival of the army and its taking up quarters in the city that petitions from the towns-people have not been submitted representing the excesses committed by numerous infantry sepoys, about whom there could be no suspicions of disguise and that orders have not been issued day after day to you, our sons, to take measures with the aid of a military force to suppress disorders. ...(*Pr. Tr. B. S.* p. 12) '...Learn that yesterday an order was passed under our own signature on a petition from the inhabitants...prohibiting acts of devastation...It is the business of the army to protect and not to desolate and plunder. The officers of the army will therefore immediately restrain their men from the commission of these improprieties so that our subjects may obtain immunity from the hardships complained of...(*Op. cit.* p. 10).

[2] Zaheer Dehlawi, p. 73.

[3] The character of the average sepoy in the words of Kaye 'was made up of inconsistencies...In his character qualities so adverse as to be apparently irreconcilable with each other met together and embraced. He was simple yet designing; credulous and easily deceived by others and yet obstinately tenacious of his own inbred convictions; now docile as a child and now hard and immovable in the stub-

appear no better, in fact worse. Hence the remark that 'the only epithet applicable to Bahadur Shah is traitor'.[1] Since a traitor is never a man of principles and is always extremely selfish and even depraved, the picture of Bahadur Shah that is conjured up before one's eyes is that of the most flagitious of mortals.

But it must be remembered that the sepoys who had revolted against the British in May 1857 were legally the subjects of Emperor Bahadur Shah who regarded them as his own children[2]. The East India Company was the wielder of *de facto* power while Emperor Bahadur Shah was the *de jure* sovereign. All his subjects in the city of Dehli and the country at large—in much greater degree outside Dehli than inside in the words of Sir Syed Ahmad[3]—'still considered him their Emperor and used for him the same high-sounding titles as had been used for Akbar the Great, Jahangir and Shahjahan', namely *Shahinshah* (emperor), *Zille Subhani* (Divine Shadow) and *Zillulah* (Shadow of God). In many of the petitions[4]

bornness of his manhood. Abstemious and yet self-indulgent, calm and yet impetuous, gentle and yet cruel, he was indolent even to langour in his daily life...' (*Kaye—Indian Mutiny I*, pp. 239-240).

[1] *Vide* (i) *Amrita Bazar Patrika*, November 28, 1956. (ii) S. M. R. p. 122.

[2] See *Pr. Tr. B. S.* pp. 31-32.

[3] Sir Syed Ahmed—*Asbab-i Ghadr*, p. 4.

[4] *Vide* No. 46 (*Pr. Tr. B. S.* pp. 31-32); No. 28 Petition of Jamna Das, Land-holder, resident of Muttra, dated 14th July 1857.

'To the King *Shelter of the World*' (Pr. Tr. B. S. p. 18).

No. 35 Petition of Karim Bakhsh alias Nathua

'To the King, *Divine and Merciful*'! (*Op. cit.* p. 23).

No. 42 Police Officers' Report of the Order having been

reproduced in the *Proceedings of the Trial of Bahadur Shah,* Bahadur Shah has been addressed as *'Your Divine Majesty;* Cherisher of the Poor; and he has used for himself the phrase *'Our Divine Person'* and for his court the term *'Darbar-i Khilafat'*[1]. The British wanted to deprive him of this honour in the same way as they had deprived him of all kinds of power, making him a nonentity in practical politics and administrative matters. Now they wanted to take his place as the *de jure* sovereign also. This was their naked policy of grab which the Indian mind did not appreciate. The Indians—Hindus and Musalmans—were not prepared to accept the divine right rule of the East India Company while they had accepted the divine right rule of Babur's dynasty for about 14 generations. They looked upon the British as 'usurpers' (trespassers)[2] as Muinu'ddin Hasan, a British pensioner, tells us in his narrative. Sir Syed Ahmad says, 'The Princes of India considered the Company's status no

carried into effect: 'To the King! *Nourisher of the Poor'* !

No. 39 Petition of Kasimu'ddin, Private of the 7th Company *'Your Divine Majesty'* Your slave was a private in the 7th Company . . . . (*Op. cit.* 27).

No. 58 Petition of Raja Nahar Singh of Ballabgarh: 'The king, Shelter of the World! *Dispenser of Justice'* ! (*Op. cit.* p. 44).

No. 59 Petition of Nahar Singh. 'To the King, *Lord of Mankind! Shelter of the World'* ! (*Op. cit.* p. 45).

No. 73 Petition of the Rajah of Ballabgarh dated 4th August 1857. 'To the King, *Vicar of God'* ! (*Op. cit. pp.* 53, 54, 56).

[1] *Pr. Tr. B. S.* p. 27, No. 56. Order under the seal of king different from that in the cypher.

[2] Metcalfe—T. N. N., p. 31.

higher than that of a wazir[1] of the Mughul Emperor.' Since neither of the two was prepared to give way and since the Company was aggressive and shrewd and on the look-out to oust the Mughul Emperor, virtually a war between the two continued.[2]

Unable to take offensive Bahadur Shah prepared himself for self-defence. He stuck to the legal aspect of the matter and banked on the traditions of Mughul rule, that is, a united national front against a foreign enemy. He felt interested in Britain's war with Russia[3] and

---

[1] Sir Syed Ahmad—*Asbab-i Ghadr,* p 4.

[2] Referring to this Metcalfe (p. 17) says, 'No inducement could make him (Bahadur Shah) leave his palace; not so much a fear of a revival of the Mahomedan power was entertained as that the king might become the rallying-point of a confederacy of native States.'

[3] '. . . . a sidi of the King who was in constant attendance at the palace, secretly urged a risaldar of 70th irregular cavalry to leave our service and to take service with the King, telling him . . . that before the hot weather was over, the Russians would come to India . . . The risaldar whose name is Everett . . . also informed me that about six months before, the king had sent an emissary to Russia.' (*Pr. Tr. B. S.* Evidence of T. Metcalfe, p. 122).

Says Hakim Ahsanullah, 'Bahadur Shah who was dissatisfied with the British Government, made anxious enquiries about the native army whenever any war took place but he took pleasure in hearing of the British defeats and reverses. He expected that any other ruler who might subvert British rule would treat him with greater respect and honour in consideration of the King's dynasty. In short he believed that his own prosperity would go in hand with the ruin of the British power (Pr. Tr. B. S. p. 250).

And Hakim Ahsanullah continues, 'I—believe information must have reached the King of the mutiny of some of the native regiments after the annexation of the Punjab...

Iran[1]; and to both these countries he sent messengers. But to Iran with whom there had been established close cultural relations since the time of Humayun he looked for active help. Says Hakim Ahsanullah, 'I never read the letter which was addressed by the King of Dehli to the King of Persia . . . I consider that he (the King of Dehli) must have asked for help in the shape of money and troops)'[2]. Bahadur Shah also looked to Providence for help and interested himself in the news which was occasionally available about the uprising of the sepoys in different parts of the country. His attempt made previously to establish contacts with the sepoys in British army had been foiled by the British Government. In spite of it Bahadur Shah kept himself informed about the army and their relations with the British Government and even about the trouble that was brewing in the country. News on all these heads, printed in the *Sirajul Akhbar,* the Court Paper, was eagerly read in the Royal palace. And Hakim Ahsanullah who was in touch with many other papers says, 'Bahadur Shah believed that the British Government really intended to change the religion of

---

and I doubt not but that the King learnt the fact with satisfaction...On hearing of the regiments' refusal to handle the new cartridges near Calcutta when the excitement spread extensively over the entire length and breadth of the country, Bahadur Shah remarked that he would in that case be placed in better circumstances inasmuch as a new dominant power would treat him with greater respect and consideration. (*Op. cit.* p. 251).

[1] The Teheran Gazette of 1856 reports that special letters were sent to the Mughul Court of Dehli by Nuri, the prime minister of Iran, together with a copy of the *jihadnawa* or war proclamation that the Shah of Iran had issued against Britain. See Appendix B.

[2] *Pr. Tr. B. S.* pp. 252 ff.

the people'. He also says, 'The sepoys were aiming at expelling the English and wanted to become masters of the country; and before the outbreak the sepoys all over the country had organized a conspiracy'.[1]

On Sunday, 10th May 1857, the sepoys commonly known as Telinga and Purbia rose in a body against the British at Mirath; and, securing arms by reckless killing and loot they came over to Dehli on Monday morning, 11th May, and called on the aged Emperor saying, 'O *Dharma Awtar* (Dharma Incarnate!) if you place your kind hand on our heads we shall secure you full-fledged kingship all over Hindustan.' At that moment Bahadur Shah acted shrewdly. On the one hand he looked askance at the mutineers and on the other hand he expressed great anxiety for the safety of the British officers—Douglas, Custodian of the Fort and Fraser the Commissioner. From this it has been inferred that Bahadur Shah was at heart opposed to the sepoys.[2] But the inference is untenable in view of the unfavourable and adverse circumstances—British surveillance—in which Bahadur Shah was then living. To the mutineers who had announced within the hearing of Douglas that they had killed all the British officers at Mirath and would do whatever they liked at Dehli, Bahadur Shah could not rashly commit himself. Yet he did not disappoint them. He said, 'I am a fakir and have neither a treasure nor an army. However, in your cause I would not hold my life dear, if necessary. I think your trouble which is due to some misunderstanding with the British will be remov-

[1] *Pr. Tr. B. S.* pp. 252 ff.

[2] (i) *Amrita Bazar Patrika,* Nov. 28, 1956.
(ii) S. M. R. p. 118.

ed if I intercede for you with the Resident who is expected here. Let me hear from him the root cause of the trouble'[1]. To be fair, it must be conceded that Bahadur Shah could then make no better reply, particularly also because he was habituated to study every new situation that arose before handling it. Says he,

کچھ ہی ہوجاے قدم پھر نہ ہٹے واں سے ظفر
پانؤں ہر کام میں تم سونچ کے اول ڈالو

(Whatever might come to pass, the step once taken must never recede. You should set your hand to any task that you choose to do after first seriously thinking over it)

Further he says:

آدمی کو چاہئے مردم شناسی اے ظفر
ہے یہ فرمودہ ہمارے حضرت تیمور کا

(Man must be able to scan the face of man, O Zafar! This is the saying of our ancestor, the revered Timur)

Again

نہیں ہے بے تامل خوب کوئی کام دنیا میں
ظفر کیجئے بھلائی یا برائی سونچ کر

(No work in this world should be attempted without thinking it out first. O Zafar! whether you do good or bad, you must think before you act).

Again

دیکھ تو روشنیٔ دیدۂ باطن سے ظفر
چشم ظاہر کی اُسے نور بصیرت سے نہ دیکھ

[1] This is based on a comparative study of Malleson, Munshi Jiwan Lal, Zaheer Dehlawi, and Nasir Nazir. The

(O Zafar! you should see things minutely in the light of the mind's eye. You must not see things superficially with the physical eye).

Again

ظفر کے منہ سے کب نکلی وہ بات
کہ جس کو صاحب ادراک پکڑے

(When did Zafar utter a word which a man of fine perception could bring as a charge against him?)

And again

جن کو کچھ پاس نہیں بات کا اپنی ہرگز
میرے نزدیک ظفر اُن کی ہے ہر بات خراب

(Those who do not abide by their word come to grief in everything that they attempt; this is my opinion, Zafar!)

These thoughts were flashing across his mind while Bahadur Shah was making a halting reply to the mutineers; hence the allegation that he was reluctant to accept their leadership and that on their approaching them he was taken by surprise.[1] From his own evidence in the Court it appears that while talking to him on their arrival from Mirath the mutineers had betrayed an air of cruelty and ruthless aggressiveness which alarmed Bahadur Shah and frightened him. He feared they would murder him too. Still, he wanted to support them against the British Government even at the cost of his own life. But he was not sure of the perseverence of the sepoys, if it came to a war to the knife with the

---

last two give eye-witness accounts. But Zaheer Dehlawi's is by far the best; it is more detailed and vivid.

[1] *Vide* Chapter V *infra*.

British. He thought that the sepoys would be reconciled to the British Government just as they had been after the Vellore Mutiny or the Barrackpur outbreak. This was exactly the point which Hakim Ahsanullah was dinning into his ears. But he did not see eye to eye with Hakim Ahsanullah in political matters; he had his differences[1] with him. However, he did not remonstrate with Hakim Ahsanullah and observed a discreet silence, of which advantage was taken by the latter. The same day in the afternoon the Hakim sent in the Emperor's name a message to the Lieutenant-Governor of Agra informing him of the situation. This message was considered by the Lieutenant-Governor as an ultimatum[2] from Bahadur Shah; he remarked that 'the King is shrewdly befooling us'.[3] He did not acknowledge the message and told the camel driver to go back without a reply. Then he sent that message with his own remarks to the Hindu ruling chiefs with the object of neutralizing them or inducing them to side with the British Government.[4]

---

[1] See Chapter I, pp. 52-53.

[2] This message was rightly treated by the Lieutenant-Governor of Agra as an ultimatum of war on the part of Bahadur Shah. Had it been merely an attempt on the part of Bahadur Shah to betray the sepoys, the Lieutenant-Governor could not have utilised it in rousing against Bahadur Shah the Rajput and Sikh rulers. On the contrary he would have been highly pleased with him and sent a favourable reply full of approbation.

[3] Zakaullah—T. U. A. S. I., p. 660.

[4] Kāmalu'ddin Haidar—*Tarikh-i Awadh* (1896), Vol. II, p. 439. Also see Chapter V *infra;* pp. 166, 168.

CHAPTER III

BAHADUR SHAH AND THE BRITISH

It is alleged[1] that Bahadur Shah was devoted[2] to the British[3]. But the allegation has arisen from certain postulates[4] of history dating from the time of Shah Alam, grandfather of Bahadur Shah. It has been assumed that Shah Alam had been devoted to the British and was praying for deliverance from Maratha hands. But it is forgotten that Madhaji Sindia, on becoming master[5] of Dehli in 1784, had acted as Shah

---

[1], [2], [3], *Amrita Bazar Patrika,* November 28, 1956 and S.M.R. p. 118).

[4] *Vide* (i) Francklin's *History of Shah Alam* (p. 196) announcing the dethronement of Shah Alam, termination of Mughul rule and that the Mahomedan power was dead and gone as early as 1737. And further when Lord Lake entered the city of Dehli he found the Mughul Emperor virtually a prisoner. Note also the letter drafted for George III of England by Prince Jawan Bakht Mirza Jahandar Shah whom the E. I. Company had, with the help of Nawab Wazir of Oudh, set up in Banaras with a view to exploit the situation in Dehli. This letter which was intended to invite British intervention in Dehli was drafted in 1724.

(ii) Metcalfe (T. N. N., p. 10) announcing that the British found him (Shah Alam) a puppet without a Court or a Treasury and as such they retained him . . . . . A considerable portion of the conquered territory was set aside to meet the stipends of the pensioned king . . . Dehli remained under the effective rule of Shah Alam . . . The king was to be absolute within his palace grounds and in the city . . .'

[5] Madhaji Sindia held the office of Amiru-l Umara which combined the post of wazir and commander-in-chief. Before

Alam's minister; and so did his successor[1] Daulat Rao Sindia (1794); he too submitted[2] to the authority of the Mughul Emperor and acknowledged himself as deputy of

---

Madhaji Sindia it had been held by Najibu'd-Dawla and Mirza Najaf Khan. On the death of Najaf Khan in 1782 it was contested by two rival candidates, Mirza Shafi and Afrasiyab Khan. In 1782 Mirza Shafi was killed and Afrasiyab Khan became the Amiru-l Umara. The following year when Afrasiyab Khan was also killed, Shah Alam appointed Madhaji Sindia as Amiru-l Umara and gave him two patents —one contained a firman appointing the Peshwa as *Vakil-i mutlaq, i.e.,* vicegerent of the Mughul Empire, and another vested in Madhaji Sindia command of the army as Deputy of the Peshwa—as a guarantee for the pay of the troops; the provinces of Dehli and Agra were assigned to him but they were made subject to a primary charge of Rs. 65,000 as a monthly payment for the household and personal expenses of the Emperor. This was called *peshkash* (persent or tribute). but not pension. *Vide* (i) Keene—*Madho Rao Sindia* p. 102. (ii) Francklin—*History of Shah Alam* p. 133.

[1] Daulat Rao was the nephew and adopted son of Madhaji Sindia.

[2] It should be noted that during the period of their ascendancy the Marathas had neither undermined Mughul rule, nor the position of Islam. They had contented themselves with taking one-fourth of the revenue without further interfering with the actual administration. As a result Shah Alam was satisfied with them. In his book *'The Indian Musalmans'* (p. 128) Hunter says, 'The Marathas left the Muhammadan Governors of Provinces untouched. They maintained the Muhammadan judges and law officers undisturbed. On the demise of a Musalman Governor a new ruler of the same religion was appointed. Indeed the confirmation of his hereditary successor was considered a matter of right upon payment of a present to the distant Maratha Court'. In these circumstances even the Ulama, when approached, did not advise the Musalmans to rise against the Marathas. On the contrary they permitted and even encouraged the Musalmans of all classes to co-operate with the Marathas (Hunter—*The Indian Musalmans*' p. 128).

the *Vakil-i-mutlaq*. Shah Alam did not like[1] the British. And in connection with the battle of Dehli then imminent (11th to 14th September 1803) between the Marathas and the British he announced, 'I will take the field against the English whose invariable custom it is, in whatever country they are allowed to reside under fixed stipulations, speedily to seize upon that country'[2]. But when after the battle Lake captured Dehli (1803), Shah Alam passed willy-nilly under British protection; and although they used polite language and treated him nicely, he was not satisfied. He had seen with his mind's eye that the new conquerors would not remain content with performing ministerial functions like the Marathas and that, on the contrary, they would endeavour to deprive him of his legal position and sovereignty and would ask him to vacate the Fort. In this connection he composed an elegy[3] in which he

---

[1] Among other reasons for Shah Alam's dislike for the British one was this. 'The British looked upon Madhaji Sindia as an independent prince and even advised him to assert his independence,' says Keene. 'If the British saw fit to regard him as an independent prince, he could not hinder them; indeed, such was their crude and ill-bred way of diplomatic action which he (Madhaji Sindia) might deplore but could not rectify'. (Keene—*Madho Rao Sindhia*, p. 105).

[2] Spear—T.M. p. 36.

[3] آفتاب از فلک امروز تباهی دیدی
باز فردا دهد ایزد سرو سرداري ما

'O Aftab! ('Aftab' being the pen-name of Shah Alam) to-day thou hast suffered ruin at the hands of Fate; to-morrow Providence will again give us our paramountcy'.

expressed a hope that one day he would recover his paramountcy. Shah Alam accepted no change in his status and felt offended at the idea of a crowned stipendiary—a position to which Lord Wellesley had wanted to reduce him. Shah Alam considered the British as successors to the ministerial office which had hitherto been held by the Marathas. He was not prepared to accept the British even as paymasters, much less as overlords. An incident soon occurred which clarified this point. When at the instance of Lord Wellesley, Lake demanded the amount of $5\frac{1}{2}$ lakh rupees which had been deposited with Shah Nawaz Khan the royal treasurer by Drugeon the French General of Daulat Rao Sindia before the battle of Dehli in order to prevent it falling into British hands, Shah Alam objected. He took the money and gave it away to the army in his own name, thus establishing his superiority in the eye of law and his own claim to the State money. Lord Wellesley acknowledged his mistake and ordered Lake to refund the money to the royal treasurer. Shortly after this occurred another incident which equally exposed Lord Wellesley. He communicated his desire to Shah Alam to vacate the fort and shift to a district in Bihar. Shah Alam flared up; and gripping his sword he said, 'This can never be. In spite of all I feel strong enough to live; and no one can bury a living person in the grave of his own choice.' And he had another grievance also against the British. He considered the *peshkash*[1] of $11\frac{1}{2}$ lakhs that

[1] The original word *peshkash* meaning present or tribute has been wrongly translated into English as pension. Not even 'civil list' will do as an equivalent (*Cf.* Magnin—*La Revolte au Bengale* p. 181) for pension or civil list is a periodical payment to a person in consideration of the

the British Government gave him as insufficient. His son and successor Akbar Shah also known as Akbar II inherited this grievance and demanded 30 lakhs. He secured the services of Ram Mohan Roy the Bengali leader and founder of the Brahmo Samaj, granted him the title of Raja and deputed him on his own behalf to London to plead his case before the authorities (1827). But nothing came of this and the Emperor's worst fears were roused by the British haggling and attaching strings to the proffered grant. So he reasserted his claim to Mughul supremacy and demanded for himself a rank higher than that of the Governor-general—a claim which he had already advanced two years after his accession to the throne[1]. Lord Minto had then disappointed him by describing British attitude to Mughul kingship 'as a complementary recognition of a nominal sovereignty'. Now Lord Amherst annoyed him saying, 'Your kingship is but nominal; it is merely out of courtesy that you are addressed as king'. And Amherst's successor Bentinck proceeded to put an end even to the legend of Mughul rule, by introducing[2] a new phrase—HUKM COMPANY

---

relinquishment of rights. But in this case there was no relinquishment of rights involved. On the contrary a *peshkash* was made out of the revenue of the country by the Company to its superior, namely Emperor Shah Alam. Note the literal meaning of *pesh-kash* as given by Richardson:—*Pesh-kash* is 'a magnificent present, such as is only presented to princes, great men, superiors or sometime to equals (particularly on receiving a great appointment), also tribute'.

[1] Metcalfe (T. N. N. p. 16) says, 'Intrigue followed upon intrigue, pretension upon pretension until in 1814 the Mogul claimed precedence of the Governor-General himself.'

[2] The regular phrase up till now used in all public announcements was *"Khalq Khuda Ki, Mulk Badshah Ka"*,

BAHADUR—in all public announcements. Furthermore, responsible British officers began to treat the Mughul Emperor with studied disrespect. When in 1831 Hawkins the Resident went into the palace to present a *nazr* to Emperor Akbar Shah, he declined to stand before him; and on reaching the queen's apartments he 'insisted on a chair to support his dignity. Then he refused dishes of sweetmeats from the heir-apparent and drove away in wrath gardeners who brought nosegays from the palace and turned back 'shuqqas' on the ground of disrespectful wording[1]. During the winter of 1832 when the Emperor had gone out of the Fort, Hawkins rode along with an English friend of his into the palace passing on horseback through the gates and Naqqarkhana (where according to custom they should have dismounted) into the Diwan-i Amm and the Diwan-i Khass in succession in spite of the protests of the royal chamberlain[2]. When on his return the Emperor heard of this incident, he burst saying, 'This is an affront unheard of in the whole annals of the house of Timur'[3]. With another Resident, Seton by name, Prince Mirza Jahangir, a son of the Emperor, had fallen out. He used to mock at him and nicknamed him LOOLOO.[4] One day while the Resident was going out of the Fort, Mirza Jahangir who stood at the roof of the Naqqarkhana with a rifle in

---

people belong to God; country belongs to the King. The third phrase which was now added meant "that order is that of the Company". But the sovereignty of the Mughul Emperor was still recognized; the Company asserted itself merely as the wielder of power.

[1] Spear, P—T.M. pp. 77-78.

[2],[3] *Op. cit.*

[4] Literally 'a bugbear'.

his hand shot[1] a bullet which hit the Resident's hat (1810). The aim miscarried and the Resident escaped. The British retaliated and their troops armed with guns and artillery entered the Fort, and order was given to open fire on the Lal Pardah—a term then used out of respect for the Diwan-i Khass. Two shots were fired in the air; and then Mirza Jahangir was made to leave the Fort. He was exiled to Allahabad where he remained till his death (1821). His dead body was then brought to, and buried, in Dehli. But the threatening attitude of the British continued; and they became guilty in the Emperor's eyes of five fresh affronts. *Firstly* Dehli was included in the North-Western Frontier Province and thus lost its old status in the empire. *Secondly* Akbar Shah's name was removed from the coins (1835). *Thirdly* the British Government deleted from the Governor-General's seal the term 'Fidwi Khass' (your special servant) and encouraged the Indian princes to do the same. *Fourthly* the British Government wanted to dispose of the great monuments of Mughul rule—the Agra Fort

---

[1] This event created a sensation in the Fort and the city. And a doggerel verse being composed was cited by the common people. It ran as follows :

Seton ko LOOLOO kiyun kaha Mirza?
Lal pardey se gola baj gaya Mirza.
Rajmanten bhi aien paltanen bhi aaeen
Lal pardey se gola baj gaya Mirza
Seton ko LOOLOO kiyun kaha Mirza?

(Nasir Nazir p. 38)

(O Mirza! why did you mock at Seton and nicknamed him Looloo? As a result guns were fired at the Lal Pardah. There came regiments as well as platoons; and guns were fired at the Lal Pardah, O Mirza; why did you nickname Seton as Looloo?)

Cf. Zakaullah—T.U.A.S.I., p. 369

and Taj Mahal; and rumours to this effect spread[1] everywhere. *Fifthly* the British Government declined to accept Mirza Nili, a favourite son of the Emperor, as heir-apparent. As a result a prince of the royal choice was set aside and Abu Zafar, another prince whom Akbar Shah had rejected, was recognized. Abu Zafar was raised to the throne in 1837 on the death of Akbar Shah.

Abu Zafar now became Emperor Abu Zafar Siraju'ddin Bahadur Shah with full consciousness of the British opposition to his dynastic interests and firm determination not to barter away his legal position as emperor for a paltry sum[2]. Shortly after his accession he renewed his father's demands and reminded the British Government of their promises made with the late Emperor. Lord Auckland then Governor-General insisted that as a pre-requisite to the fulfilment of the British promises Bahadur Shah must abandon all his rights and renounce his claims of all kinds on the Company. Bahadur Shah refused to do that and said angrily, 'If I am the son of my father I shall do what my father had done. I'll accept no condition imposed by the British'. Then the British Government discontinued the customary *nazr* which had been as a rule made by the Governor-General and the Indian princes to the Emperor on his birthday and festivals. Bahadur Shah resented this and complained that he had been thereby put to an annual loss of Rs. 10,000. But his protests went unheeded; and they debarred him further of the royal privilege of awarding khilats or robes of honour as well as of the privi-

[1] Ghalib—*Panj Ahang,* Ms. F. 80 (Yaqub Modak Collection).

[2] *Cf.* Metcalfe, C. T.—T.N.N. p. 18.

lege of mounting the throne and holding durbars. The Silver Throne which was as a rule placed in the Diwan-i Khass was removed from there and locked up in the underground cell whence, it may be noted, it was brought back on 12th May 1857. The Diwan-i Amm was also closed to be re-opened 13 years later after the outbreak of the War. All this was done about 1844 by Lord Ellenborough who also intended to deprive Bahadur Shah of his right to nominate his successor to the throne; and he desired him further to leave[1] the Fort and take his abode, instead, at Qutb. Dalhousie disapproved of the usual respect that was still shown in one form or another to the Mughul Emperor. It was ordered that 'the British officers were not bound to show respect to the King's cavalcade if they incidentally met it on the way.' It may be noted that Bahadur Shah's carriage was pulled as a rule by 16 horses while that of the queen Zinat Mahal Begum by 8 horses; and all along the way while her carriage moved, it was attended by drum-beaters who announced her by drum-beating.[2] All the passers-by used to stop in honour of the royal cavalcade and bowed.[3] Dalhousie disliked this too. As a result some British 'toadies' began to call her in mockery 'Danka Begum' *i.e.* 'Lady of Drum-beating'[4]. Another incident occurred; Bahadur Shah's sister-in-law Nawab Husaini

---

[1] Zakaullah, T. U. A. S. I., p. 370. *Cf.* Metcalfe, C. T—T. N. N., p. 18.

[2] Zakaullah—T. U. A. S. I. p. 383.

[3] *Cf.* Andrews, C. F. who says., 'The old traditional respect was shown to him and to the princes also. Whenever they appeared in public or entered the city, people riding on horseback at once dismounted and saluted'. (*Zakaullah of Delhi,* p. 27).

[4] *Vide* footnote No. 2.

facing p. 91

BAHADUR SHAH II AS A SUFI SAINT LECTURING TO HIS DISCIPLES

Begum, widow of his deceased brother Mirza Salim[1], advanced her claims on some gardens in the suburbs of Dehli. The gardens were in the possession of Bahadur Shah and were administered by him directly. She filed a suit in the Civil Court on the plea that the said gardens had been promised to her by her late husband in her marriage deed. The civil court decreed the case against Bahadur Shah arguing that the gardens lay outside his jurisdiction and that he had no right to administer any piece of land outside the Fort. An appeal made by Bahadur Shah to the Lieutenant-Governor of Agra was summarily dismissed. Bahadur Shah deplored this, saying,

قصۂ غم سے میرے خوش یہ ہوا وہ بے رحم
پھر کہانی نہ کوئی اوس نے ظفر اور سنی

(With the story of my sorrow that cruel man
was so delighted that no further statement
from me did he hear, O Zafar!)

Then he invoked God, saying,

اللہ ہی ہماری طرف ہے اے ظفر
کوئی اگر نہیں ہے ہماری طرف نہ ہو

(God alone is on our side, O Zafar!
Never mind if there is no one else on our side)

And he began to acquit himself as a sufi and to establish some contact with the sepoys of the Indo-British army by making them his disciples[2]. But the British Government objected to this. They

---

[1] Mirza Salim was the 7th out of the 9 sons of Akbar II, Abu Zafar Bahadur Shah being the eldest. (See Cons. No. 22, 18th December 1806; N.A.).

[2] *Pr. Tr. B. S.* Evidence of Hakim Ahsanullah. See photograph facing this page.

installed inside the Fort a body of Palace Guards headed by a British Military officer called Qiladar who reported every move of the Emperor and every incident of the Palace life to the Resident outside. Thus Bahadur Shah was in British bondage[1], the chains of which he longed to break. He never failed to assert himself whenever opportunity presented itself by raising his voice against British tyranny[2]. Whenever his subjects —Hindus and Musalmans—implored his help against British tyranny he fearlessly espoused their cause and even offered to sacrifice his life for their sake. Zaheer Dehlawi who was an eye-witness of such incidents gives a few instances. Says he, 'Once the British Government ordered the cowherds to take away their cows from the city and lodge them outside the inhabited area on the plea that the cowsheds inside the city were insanitary. The aggrieved cowherds came to the Emperor who immediately sided them saying, 'We shall live where our subjects live; we will share their discomfort'. Then he ordered his servants to pitch the

[1] *I.e. Qaid-i Farang.* See *Dehli Urdu Akhbar,* July 5, 1857.

[2] It was as a result of British tyranny that in the words of Metcalfe (T.N.N. p. 15) 'serious riots occurred'. It should be clearly noted that these were not communal riots, but risings of the Hindus and Musalmans against the British Government on a small scale. Says Metcalfe (p. 15): 'When serious riots occurred, as they frequently did, the people looked to the King for protection from the British authorities'. 'I am convinced' wrote the Assistant Resident on the occasion of these riots, 'that it would never have taken place if the people had not expected that the King would (as he did) protect them. It has its origin in the palace and if traced to its primary cause would be found to have arisen from the effect of the Resident's too delicate and submissive conduct; ideas of sovereign right ought, I think, to be checked.'

Royal tents in the sands by the riverside. This was reported to the British Resident who, fearing lest all the Hindus and Musalmans should walk out with the Emperor, implored him to cancel his order. Bahadur Shah did so on the condition that the British Government should cancel their own order and abstain in future from adopting any such measure against any class of his subjects. Before long, however another trouble arose. A group of workmen and labourers being this time the victim of British tyranny, they made a complaint to the Emperor who felt so embarrassed that he called the Resident and said, 'I warn you not to harass my subjects by uprooting them from their home. Do not force them to leave the city as long as I am here. After me, you may do whatever you like'[1].

All this was gall and wormwood to the British Government who began to treat him severely; and Bahadur Shah, feeling highly oppressed, exclaimed:

اے ظفر جو کچھه کئے هم نے زبر دستی مین کام
اونکے بدلے مل رهے هین زیردستی مین همین[2]

(O Zafar! now that we are weak, we are suffering from oppression for what we have done in the past)

Convinced of the high degree of respect and reverence shown to him by his subjects, since he moved about in a regular and illustrious course of virtue, the British Government considered it highly impolitic to use force against him. They fell back therefore on the only weapon in their armour—the rack[3] and propa-

---

[1] Zaheer Dehlawi—*D. G.* pp. 17-24; Zakaullah, p. 391.

[2] *Kulliyat-i Zafar* (Nawalkishore Press, p. 64.)

[3] 'But to my mind the position of the king was one of the most intolerable misery long ere the revolt broke out. His palace was in reality a house of bondage; he knew that the

ganda. That is, they harassed and embarrassed him beyond measure with the object of making him totally destitute of all shadow of influence. They wanted to announce to the world that Bahadur Shah was a king by courtesy and without the king-becoming graces—devotion, patience, courage and fortitude. They watched his movements jealously, banned his tours and contacts[1] of all kinds and disapproved of his leaving and entering the Fort at odd hours. They maintained a

---

few wretched prerogatives which were left to him as if a mockery of the departed power they represented, would be taken away from his successors; that they would be deprived of even the right to live in their own palace and would be exiled to some place outside the walls. We denied permission to his royal relatives to enter our service; we condemned them to a degrading existence, in poverty and debt inside the purlieus of their palace and then we reproached them with their laziness, meanness and sensuality. We shut the gates of military preferment upon them; we closed upon them the paths of every pursuit. We took from them every object of honourable ambition; and then our papers and our mess-rooms teemed with invectives against the lazy, slothful and sensuous princes of his house . . . .' (Russell—*My Diary in India* II, p. 51).

[1] (i) Says Metcalfe, 'When Bahadur Shah succeeded to Shah Akbar in 1837, an attempt was made, under instructions from the Governor-General, to obtain a formal renunciation of all claims upon the East India Company. The King who was an old man when he succeeded, refused to comply. Another proposal to remove the King to the Kutub (*Qutb*), was also indignantly rejected. A little later a Board was appointed to discuss and report on the course to be followed with regard to the retention of the Royal Family at Delhi. To this committee were nominated Shahzada Fakhru'ddin, heir-apparent to the King and the eldest of the nine princes, of whom the next in succession was Mirza Kobaish. Sir Henry Elliot, Mr. Thomason and Sir Thomas Metcalfe (Resident at Delhi) were the other members' (Metcalfe—T. N. N., p. 18).

(ii) *Dehli Urdu Akhbar*, July 5, 1857.

register of *Palace Intelligence* in English and prepared a kind of court diary called *Khulasa Akhbar*[1], each folio of which was divided into two parts—the *first* part giving news about Bahadur Shah, and the *second* about the local British officer who was given high-sounding titles and was always ceremoniously described as 'Mu'azzamu'd-Dawla, Sahib Kalan Agent Commissioner Bahadur; may his influence be perpetuated!' And while all the entries in the *second* part were set forth to the credit of the British officer concerned, those in the first part were designed to slight the Emperor and lower him in the estimation of his subjects. Folio 18 announces the poverty and bankruptcy of Bahadur Shah with the following remark from the Royal Vakil, 'The King is over head and ears in debt and does not possess even a pie'.

Folio 118 alludes to the chronic trouble and quarrel of Bahadur Shah with the British Government, particularly on two points: (i) While the Governor-General

[1] This is a Persian manuscript No. 128 dated April 20, 1849, now deposited in the National Archives. It should really be called *Khulasa-i Akhbar-i Atraf* (A Summary of the News of Districts) as is proved by internal evidence. I compared it with another Persian manuscript entitled *Akhbar-i Darbar-i Abul Muzaffar Siraju'ddin Muhammad Bahadur Shah Badshah-i Dehli* in the Naziriya Library of *Dehli.* It is a 14 month-long record of the last Mughul Emperor's day-to-day durbars (9th Rajab 1253, October 1837 to 29th Ramazan 1254, December 1838) and gives a genuine outline sketch of the orderly Palace life. Unlike it the *Khulasa Akhbar* embodies subtle British propaganda and is a pointer to the kind of relations that obtained between the British Government and the last Mughul Emperors—Shah Alam II and Akbar II. In spite of the pressure that the British Government brought to bear on him, Bahadur Shah II, son and successor of Akbar II, did not budge an inch from the stand that his two predecessors had taken.

insisted on paying their monthly allowances directly to the Mughul princes quite independently of Bahadur Shah, Bahadur Shah objected and protested strongly, saying: 'In this manner I shall lose all control over the house of Timur and on my own dependents'. (ii) The Governor-General refused to entertain further requests from Bahadur Shah regarding the recognition of Prince Jawan Bakht as heir-apparent.

Folio 154 shows that the British officers objected to Emperor Bahadur Shah's habit of returning at a late hour in the night. The Emperor's curt reply—*i.e.* 'I have come to know this; it will be seen in future'—is evidence of his displeasure and resentment.

Folio 105 opens with a reference to the Emperor's private talk with Hakim Ahsanullah and Mahbub Ali regarding his loans and increase in the *peshkash* and his express disapproval of all the affairs which might lead to his defamation. But a report, highly defamatory and scandalous, was immediately recorded in the *Khulasa Akhbar.* It may be recalled that the queen, Nawab Zinat Mahal Begum, the favourite wife of Bahadur Shah, owned a house at Lal Kuan street which he used to visit frequently. In the course of one visit (March-April, 1849) he attended a social function in that house and stopped accordingly for a period of 12 days. The queen entertained him in right royal manner spending for his sake a sum of Rs. 20,000. Thereupon it was reported that 'whoever entertained the King at his house would have to spend 1,500 rupees per day at the above rate'. Seeing this the sweeper of the house went to the Police Station and lodged a report 'that the King of Dehli was stopping in the premises of a housewife for the past 12 days and that it has been remarked in

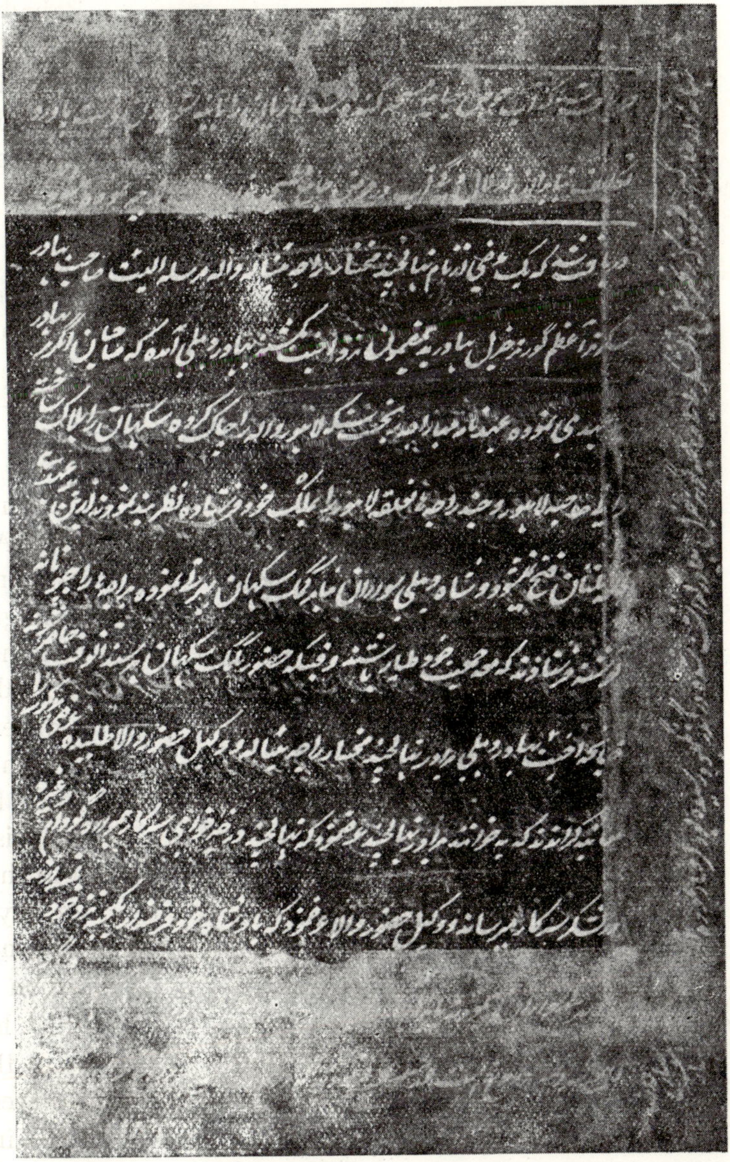

Folio 18, *Khulasa Akhbar* MS

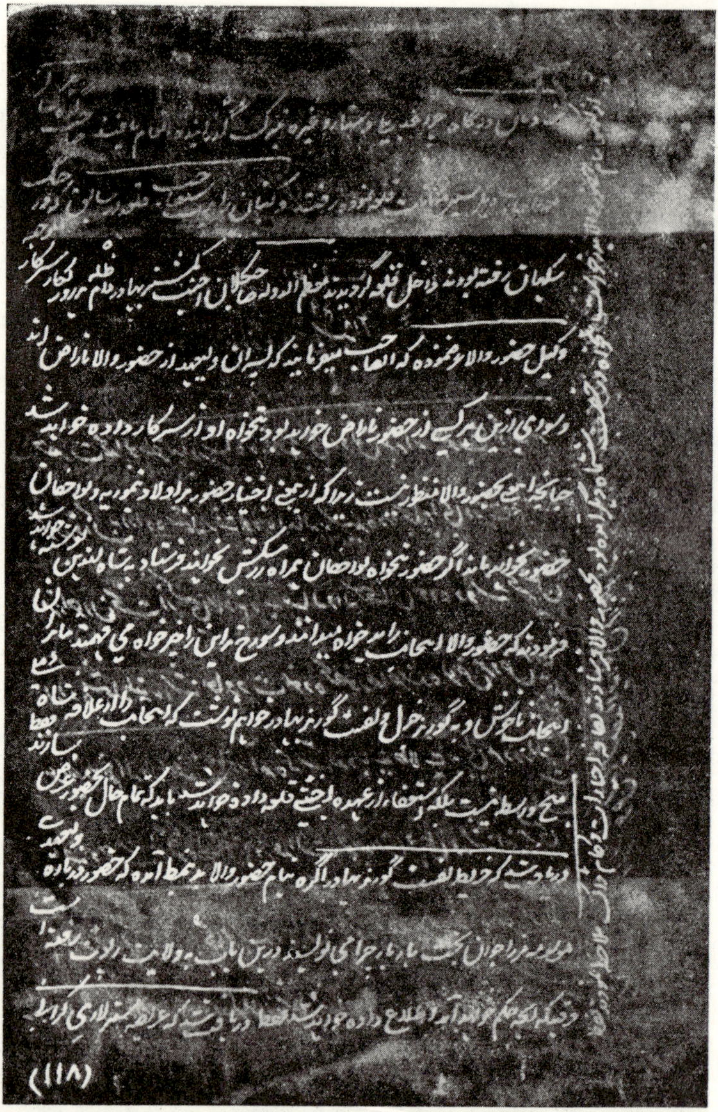

Folio 118, *Khulasa Akhbar* MS.

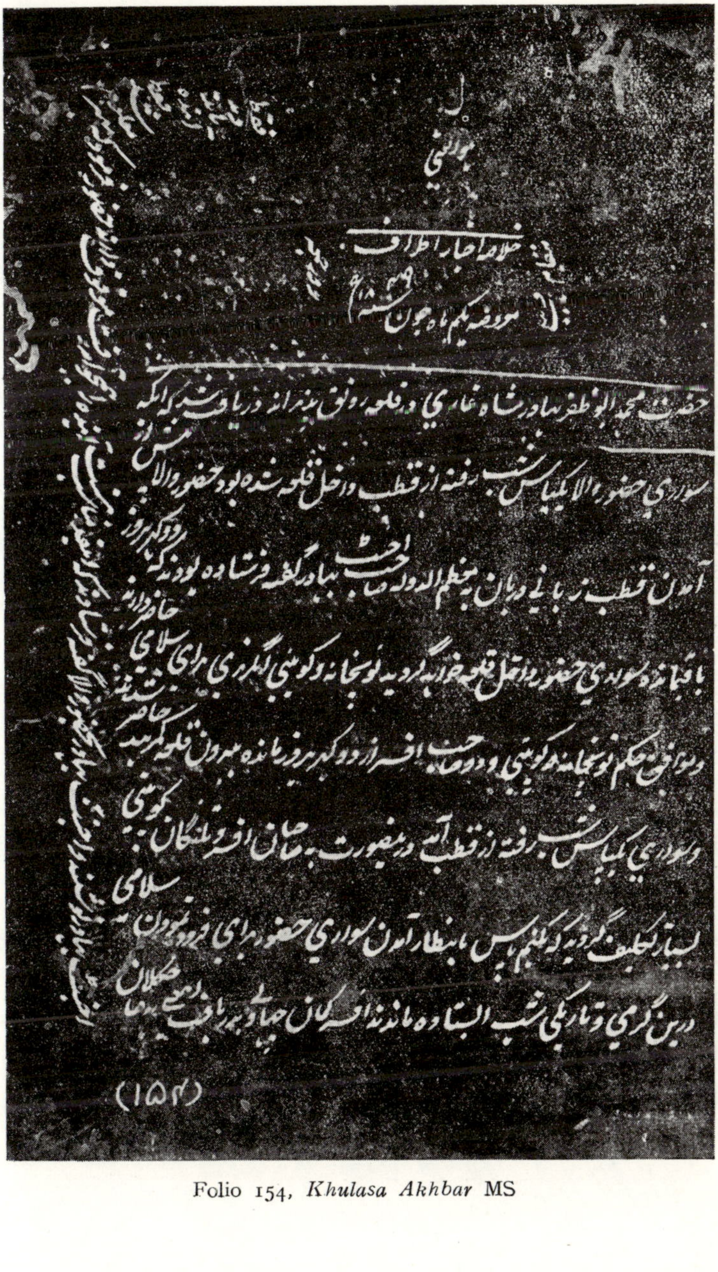

خلاصه اخبار اطراف

(۱۵۴)

Folio 154, *Khulasa Akhbar* MS

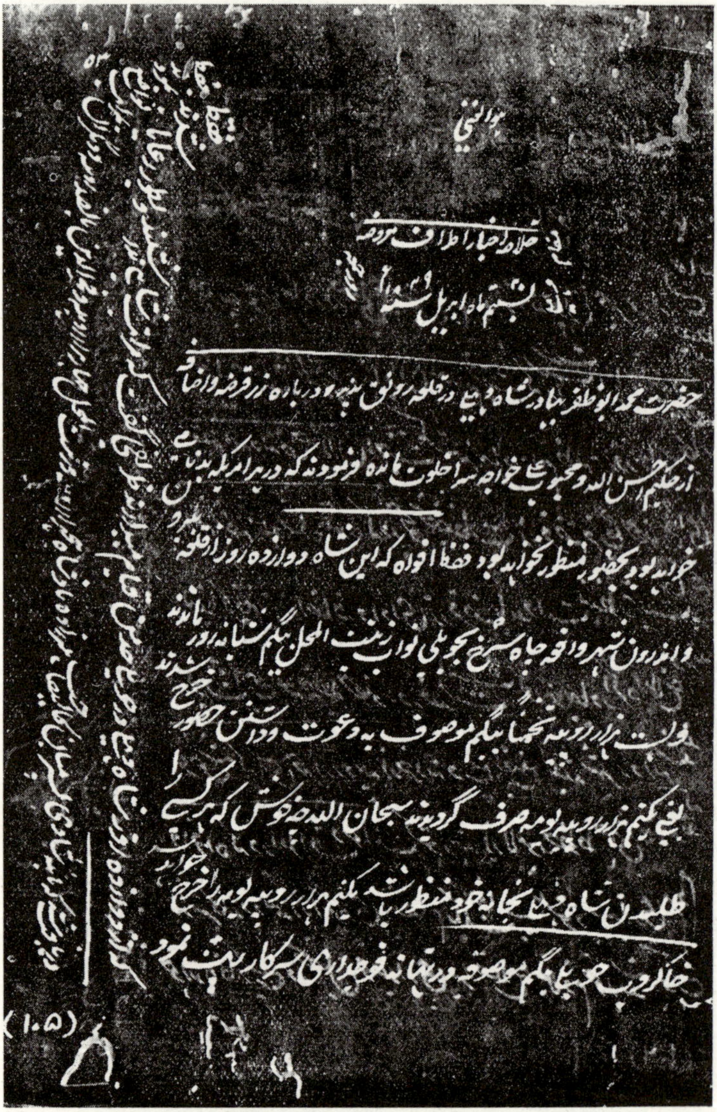

Folio 105, *Khulasa Akhbar* MS.

mockery that the King has ceased to be king and has lowered himself to the standard of an ordinary subject.[1]

This kind of campaign the British Government launched in 1849 and it continued unabated till 1857. In 1849 died prince Dara Bakht, the eldest son of Bahadur Shah; and the British Government hailed his death as marking the dawn of a new era. Says the *Delhi Gazette*: 'On Thursday morning departed this life Prince Dara Bakht, heir-apparent to the throne of Delhi, leaving Shahzada Fakhru'ddin as heir; and we have some reason to believe that all the right of the Royal House to the succession dies out, such having been guaranteed to him individually and to no other member of the family. We sincerely trust that such is the case and that our Government will now be in a position to adopt steps for making efficient arrangements for the dispersion . . . . of the family'.[2] In other words it was made public that after the death of Bahadur Shah the British Government would dispose of the throne as they liked; they might instal his son Fakhru'ddin, who had agreed to surrender all Mughul claims on the throne, and then proceed to adopt suitable measures to disintegrate the Royal House. In the same connection it was reported that Bahadur Shah was only a Shah, not Padshah.[3] Metcalfe attributed this report to the Indians, saying: 'The Indian newspapers have omitted the designation of Padshah when alluding to the King, styling him merely 'Shah'[4]. But the *Dehli Urdu Akhbar, Sadiqul Akhbar* and *Sirajul*

---

[1] See facsimiles facing p. 96.

[2] (i) *Delhi Gazette*—January 13. 1849.

(ii) Metcalfe.—T. N. N., p. 17.

[3], [4] 'Padshah', means 'Lord of Stability' (*Ain-i Akbari*. Blochmann, p. 4). 'Shah' is also a term for a sufi fakir.

Akhbar[1] continued down to 1857 to use the highest titles for him, *e.g. Hazrat Zille Subhani* (His Majesty the Shadow of God), *Khalifatu-r Rahmani* (Caliph of God), *Sahib Qirani* (Lord of the times). In its issue of 24th August 1857 the *Dehli Urdu Akhbar* gives evidence of the British propaganda saying, 'On the road to Lakhnao and in unfrequented thanas the British have posted placards stating, We are masters of Dehli and of all other places. Only a few renegades had joined hands to raise the revolt; they would soon be put to the rack. All the people and army are with us. All are supporters of our cause'[2]. Furthermore the British spread a net of intrigues in the city of Dehli and the Red Fort, employing an army of spies to bring down Bahadur Shah. With this object the spies collected and manipulated news about Bahadur Shah and his troops, and sent the same in the form of letters written on very small pieces of extremely thin paper and hidden in the shoes and sticks[3] of couriers every hour ceaselessly to the British camps at the Dehli Ridge and Ambala. One such letter says, 'The mutineers have begun to desert'[4]; another says, 'Mirza Mughul the commander-in-chief is favourably inclined towards the English'[5]; another says, 'The *Mujahideen* from Tonk are deserting the King'[6]; another says, 'The King has dismissed Mirza Mughul from the post of commander-in-chief'[7]; another says, 'The zamindars of certain villages have ceased to

[1] Mutiny Papers, collection No. 4-6, Vol. 4, No. 4-5 ff.

[2] *Idem,* Box 2, No. 24. *Dehli Urdu Akhbar,* August 24, 1857.

[3] *Cf.* p. 287, *infra.*

[4] Mutiny Papers Box 15, No. 6.

[5] Box 15, No. 7.

[6] Box 15, No. 10.

[7] Box 15, No. 13.

help the King and have decided to help the British'[1]; another says, 'The mutineers intended to kill Mirza Mughul the commander-in-chief as they had not received their pay but he saved himself by resigning his post'[2]; another says, 'The mutineers intend to appoint Prince Jawan Bakht as commander-in-chief'[3]; another says, 'The people of Dehli pray for the success of the English'[4]; another says, 'One hundred sepoys are stationed at every gate of the town. Mahbub Ali Khan is killed by the sepoys who used to trouble him in every matter since he was in league with the English'[5]; another says, 'Honoured Sir ! you ask me to request somebody to deliver the gate[6] to you. God willing I am trying my best to do this at the cost of my life or liberty, and I have hope in a person of success in this matter. But if you send a small number of troops and the news of their arrival spread over the town, undoubtedly the object will be attained. Prince Muhammad Azeem who belongs to my tribe is the commander-in-chief. If he likes he can do, God willing. I shall show, as I do, great courage. They (mutineers) come to fight with great reluctance and get ready after repeated calls. The inhabitants of the town are living towards the Dehli gate. All the people will be pleased with you and will be on your side'[7]; another says, 'In yesterday's fight-

[1] Box 15, No. 14

[2] Box 16, No. 6.

[3] Box 16, No. 16.

[4] Box 16, No. 23.

[5] Box 16, No. 34.

[6] Box 15, No. 14, Aug. 18, 1857.

This should be read along with the story of the gomashtas in Appendix G. It would appear that General Reed or his assistants had engaged the two gomashtas 'Futteh Muhammad and Boolakie Doss Bunniah' to induce some one in the Palace to deliver the gate.

[7] Box 15, Letter received on June 20, 1857.

ing also 2 or 3 regiments went to fight but did not take part in it and fled. The King asked them the reason for their not fighting to which they replied that only the new-comers fight'[1]. Another says, 'This morning Mirza Ilahi Bakhsh sent for me and communicated the purport of a talk that he had the preceding night with Zinat Mahal Begum. She suggested that Maulvi Rajab Ali and Maulvi Mazhar Ali be invited; she would pay them the travelling allowance and would be responsible for their personal safety and that through their mediation a settlement be made. She is quite willing to accept British terms'[2]. Another says, 'Mirza Mughul wants to kill the King. The King is very angry with the army. He does not come out of the palace[3]. Another says, 'Yesterday when a hundred or two hundred Telingas were deserting the camp, the King seized their weapons and said, 'I do not mind; those who want to go may go; those who want to remain, may remain. I can't stand in the way. I had not called you; I do not care. These arms the Army should take away, else when the English come I shall give to them'[4]. Another says, 'The Princes had prepared a certain paper containing certain names of the inhabitants from whom they wanted to raise money; and the money was being realized accordingly when the King came to know this. He intervened and demanded the paper. On seeing it he became highly indignant. He cast an angry look at the Princes and tore the paper saying, 'We do not want to raise money in this manner'.[5] Another says, 'To-day being Monday I went into the King's Army. I found

---

[1] Box 15, letter received on 25th June 1857.

[2] Box 16, *Letters of spies to English officials.*

[3] Box 15, *Idem.*

[4] *Ibid.*

[5] *Ibid.*

the troops extremely discontented; every sepoy defies his immediate officer and does not obey him. He says, 'If I do not get my pay I shall not remain here'[1].

These are but a specimen of the spies' reports[2] which were intended to lower and degrade Bahadur Shah and to finish him by making him a laughing-stock. When these reports reached the ears of Greathed, Reed, Rotton, Barnes, Keith, Kaye and Muir at the British camps they rated them highly and utilized them in writing news letters to their relations in England. Says Muir, 'For sometime I have been pressed to give the family an account of our experience during the Mutiny of 1857 .... I was led to look over the half-dozen volumes of Mutiny records which I kept up in 1857 when in charge of the Intelligence Department. It dawned upon me that these same old neglected books containing as they do the result of my daily correspondence with the officers of the Company throughout our beleagured districts and still more the often hourly record of reports taken at the mouth of the messengers and spies might have a special interest and value not only for the family but for others desiring to consult them[3]'. And Norman, a co-worker of Keith says, 'Many reports of the advance of the British troops came to us from the city of misfortunes to the mutineers—such as failure of percussion-caps, a want of ammunition or of deser-

[1] Box 15, *Ibid.*

[2] For further instances of the network of the spies' reports woven with the above-mentioned object the reader's attention is invited to the *Delhi News* reproduced in Chapter IX and to the Appendix G of this book. The British Intelligence Department which had been in the words of Kaye 'wisely organised' at these war camps functioned through the said network. (Cf. Muir—R.I.D., I, pp. 1-3).

[3] Muir—*Records of the Intelligence Department*. Vol. I, p. 2.

tion by mutineers from the city. These stories were grossly exaggerated by our informants but they did raise the spirits of our Force'[1]. A compendium of the reports and stories of this kind is found in the diaries of Munshi Jiwan Lal and Muinu'ddin Hasan, edited by Metcalfe[2]. On the basis of all these—and whoever will read these will form a high opinion of British character, military knowledge and bravery,—it has been contended that Bahadur Shah was 'devoted to the British' and even 'in league with the British'[3], that 'he was unfaithful to the cause of the Mutiny'[4]; that 'he had opened negotiations with the English as early as June 1857[5] with a design to betray his army', that 'he was bereft of courage'[6] and that 'he has the least claim to be called a hero or patriot and that the only epithet applicable to Bahadur Shah was 'traitor''[7]. But almost all these reports are found in direct conflict with Bahadur Shah's own thoughts and ideas as expressed *in* his poems and embodied *in* his firmans, shuqqas and proclamations, *in* his system of government, *in* his earnest prayers to God for victory, *in* his despatches to the Army officers and sepoys, *in* his affectionate but thoughtful correspondence with his son Zaheer'd-din Mirza Mughul, *in* his anti-British verses[8] and *in* the contemporary newspapers—the *Sirajul Akhbar*[9], *Sadiqul Akhbar* and *Dehli Urdu Akhbar*. It follows that, while

---

[1] Young Keith.—*Delhi-1857*, p. xiv.

[2] See Chapter X *infra, pp.* 313-319.

[3] and [4] Majumdar, R. C.—*The Sepoy Mutiny and the Revolt of* 1857. Book III, Chapter I, pp. 116 ff.

[5] Sen, S. N.—*Eighteen Fifty-seven*, pp. 94-95.

[6] *Op. cit.*, p. 70.

[7] *Amrita Bazar Patrika*, November 28, 1956.

[8] *Vide* Appendix C.

[9] *Sirajul Akhbar* (Pr. Tr. B. S., pp. 88-90).

he doted on his Hindu-Muslim subjects and did not dislike the Christians and individual Englishmen[1], Bahadur Shah was opposed to the East India Company's claim to paramountcy[2] and to the Englishmen as a class enjoying the highest and most lucrative offices in the State[3]. Francis Godlieu Quins commonly known by his pen-name Frasoo, the contemporary Urdu-Persian poet of European stock, elucidates this point, saying[4]:

مسلمان جہادی ھندوان ھمه -
جمع ھر سه گشتند از آن کہه و مه

'The Musalmans, *mujahideen* and the Hindus—each of the three classes having revolted, all of them high as well as low came together.

بہادر شاه طلبید آن ھر سه را
قسم خورده آورد بر مدعا

'Bahadur Shah called all the above three classes of people to a personal interview, and having taken an oath explained his object.

ھندوان قسم رام و گنگا خورند
مسلمان قران بر سر نہند

[1] The reference to 'harbouring English fugitives and helping them to escape' (S. M. R., p. 118) might serve to illustrate this point. But the given incident, which is the only one of its kind, does not show that Bahadur Shah had adopted or pursued such a policy during the War (May-September 1857).

[2] Appendix C

[3] *Ibid*. Also see. (i) Bahadur Shah's Proclamation in the *Friend of India,* October 7, 1858.

(ii) The Azamgarh Proclamation, pp. 248-250 *infra*.

[4] Frasoo—*Fath Nama Angrezi,* MS. 129, Patna, Verses 513-516.

> 'He asked that the Hindus should swear by Ram and the Ganges and that the Musalmans should swear, each placing a copy of the Holy Quran on his head.'

And Pandit Kanhiya Lal would have us believe that Bahadur Shah was aware of the preconcerted date of a general rising of the army in the country. That is, the idea of a simultaneous rising of all the Indian troops had been broached to the Mughul Emperor by Wajid Ali Shah, the ex-king of Lakhnao immediately after his deposition in 1856[1]. In one of her letters Nur Zaman Begum, a devoted wife of Wajid Ali Shah, speaking highly of the forbearance shown by her royal husband under British oppression[2] uses a language which, read in the light of Wajid Ali Shah's sentiments[3] and expressions, would tend to confirm[4] the point at issue. But Bahadur Shah never dreamed of an outbreak at Mirath, nor did he expect the arrival of the mutineers in Dehli. He was rightly alarmed when on 11th May he heard of the murder of the Europeans at Mirath and of the arrival of the murderers at Dehli. This will be further discussed in a succeeding chapter[5]. Here the reader's attention is invited to the solemn occasion of *'Id* which fell on 2nd August 1857. Bahadur Shah then earnestly prayed to Allah, composing a quatrain[6] which is translated by the writer as follows:

---

[1] Kanhiya Lal, Pandit—*Mahariba-i Azeem,* pp. 7-8.

[2] Wajid Ali Shah—*Tarikh-i Nur,* MS. 122, Bankipur, F. 31 b.

[3] *Idem,* F. 3.

[4] This point needs further research, which I hope to continue, if circumstances permit.

[5] *Vide* Chapter V *infra.*

[6] *Vide* p. 245 *infra,* footnote 3.

'O Allah ! May the enemy troops be all killed ; may the Gurkhas, whitemen, Gujars and Englishmen be all killed !

'We shall recognise this day as the day of *'Id-i Qurban* (Festival of Sacrifice) only when, O Zafar! your murderer be put to the sword to-day'.[1]

The royal prayer was seconded by the Emperor's loyal follower Munshi Ghulam Muhammad Ali Mushtaq who immediately composed some quatrains in tune with the royal quatrain. Three of these were published in the *Sadiqul Akhbar* and the translation is given below.

'May the *'Id* be welcome to Your Majesty every year; may the blood-shedding dagger remain weltering in the life-blood of the enemy!

'May the infidels be killed and may victory be welcome to you, O Zafar! May no trace of an Englishman remain on the face of the earth!

Again

'The army of victory and conquest came with great eclat the moment the name of Zafar came up from the heart to the tongue.

'Your Majesty! may you enjoy to-day *'Id* after *'Id* and joy after joy! Accept congratulations Your Majesty! for the enemy has come under the sword.[2]

---

[1], [2] For facsimiles, see the adjoining page.

Vide Sadiqul Akhbar of 3rd August 1857. (Mutiny Papers, Collection No. 4-6, vol. 4, No. 5).

Chapter IV

BAHADUR SHAH AND THE BRITISH (*continued*)

The ground already covered in the preceding chapter is here surveyed in the light of the records[1] which show that the settlement made between Shah Alam and Wellesley in 1803-4 had resulted in the establishment of an *imperium in imperio* and the position of the Governor-General *vis-à-vis* the Mughul Emperor was that of a vassal. It was laid down that for the maintenance of the Royal Family certain territories should be set apart—territories which had been ceded to the East India Company under the treaty of Surjeeanjungaum and lay on the right bank of the Jumna and to the north-west of the village Kaboolpur as shown in Colebrooke's map;[2] that the revenue of these territories be collected and justice administered in the name of the Emperor Shah Alam who would appoint functionaries to see to the collection of the revenues; that justice be administered in Dehli as well as in the said territories according to Muslim law and that no sentences of the criminal courts involving capital punishments could be carried out without the

---

[1], [2] (i) Secret Consultation No. 302, 29th November, 1804.

Secret Consultation Nos. 218, 219, 227, 230, 31st January, 1805.

Secret Consultation No. 188, 28th March, 1805.

(ii) Kays, J. W.—*The Life and Correspondence of Charles, Lord Metcalfe,* Vol. I, pp. 218-219, 221.

(iii) Secret Consultation No. 422, 20th June, 1805.

approval of the Emperor to whom all proceedings of the criminal courts must be reported and that sentences of mutilation should be commuted; to meet the requirements of the Royal Family the East India Company should pay to the Emperor a monthly sum of Rs. 90,000 which might be raised to one lac rupees should the revenues of the assigned territories increase; and another sum of Rs. 10,000 should be paid annually to the Emperor for purposes of the celebration in the Palace of the chief Hindu-Muslim festivals according to old usage. Finally it was laid down that the 'Government did not desire to oppose those outward forms of sovereignty to which His Majesty had long been accustomed'.

After the death of Shah Alam (1806) his eldest son Mirza Akbar ascended the throne and assumed the title—Abu Nasr Mu'inu'ddin Muhammad Akbar Shah *Sani* Badshah. He became commonly known as Akbar *Sani* or Akbar II. Under the special orders of the Governor-General a royal salute of 82 guns—signifying the number of years His late Majesty Shah Alam had lived—was fired from the ramparts of Fort William and at all the military stations in Bengal as well as in the Presidencies of Madras and Bombay. The East India Company expressed their belief that the credit and reputation of the British Government had advanced, their interests were promoted and their character was elevated in the estimation of the States and people of India by their continuing to manifest towards the Royal Family the same respect and attention as they had promised to Shah Alam[1]. But in spite of this acknowledgment on the part of the Company they were not considerate to the son and

[1] Secret Consultation No. 23, 18th December 1806.

successor of Shah Alam. None was more conscious of this than Akbar II himself. In the very first letter[1] that he wrote after his accession to the Governor-General acknowledging his congratulatory address[2] he opened his mind and said, 'It must be known to you that since our accession to the Throne the expenses and disbursements of the Royal Household have become more numerous while the receipts have continued the same as they were before. The arrangements for the establishments of the Princes, the Ladies of the Royal Family and ministers of Court are consequently suspended. Our sacred mind is confident therefore that in consideration of these circumstances you will now in a more satisfactory manner than ever fulfil the promises which were given to His late Majesty with respect to a further augmentation of the sources of His Majesty's convenience and comfort. Considering our Royal favour towards you to be daily increasing continue to transmit addresses to the Royal Presence'.[3]

By virtue of his position as the *de jure* emperor, Akbar II, afterwards, sent his two representatives Shah Haji and Raja Sher Mal to Calcutta (1808) on a mission to invest the Governor-General Lord Minto with a *khila't* or robe of honour; and the Shah Haji mission—as it became subsequently known—claimed a right to confer on behalf of the Emperor khilats, also on the Indian ruling chiefs. But Lord Minto felt that 'such a performance on the part of Shah Haji was calculated to represent the exercise of imperial authority on the part of His Majesty Akbar Shah, and

---

[1], [2] Pol. Cons. No. 98, 12th February 1807.

[3] Pol. Cons. No. 1, 1st January 1807.

to manifest to all the States of Asia a public acknowledgment of vassalage and submission on the part of the British Government to the Throne of Dehli'.[1] He rejected the offer; and as a result while the Shah Haji mission failed, beginning was made of a sharp and ceaseless conflict between the Company and the Mughul Emperor. A careful study of the records shows that the fault was of the East India Company's alone. They honoured the name of the Mughul Emperor and kept alive his reputation as the Sovereign of India as long as it served their purpose. As soon as they found that their power had been well established they began to look upon the Emperor as a burden and resolved to overthrow him and the Mughul Royal House at the earliest opportune moment. It would appear that they had made a gross mistake in supposing that the sovereignty of the Mughul Emperor had never been recognised by the Marathas.[2]

Though strong and uncompromising in matters of principle[3]—his own legal sovereignty and vassalage of

[1] Political Letters to the Court of Directors, 1st August 1809; Pol. Cons. No. 103, of 13th March, 1809.

[2] *Cf.* Spear—*Twilight of the Mughuls,* p. 44.

[3] These principles Akbar II had inherited from his royal father and he rightly claimed legal sovereignty as invested in him. The Company which was now anxious to deprive him of all kinds of sovereignty was bound to fall out with him. They conveniently ignored the fact that Shah Ālam had never accepted protection under the British Crown. In fact he had accepted the friendship of the East India Company and considered the Governor-General as 'a son and servant'. This was a legacy which Akbar II had received from Shah Alam; and he uniformly addressed the Governor-General as his 'son' and even as 'servant' (Pol. Cons. No. 45, 30th June 1810; Pol. Cons. No. 3, 17th June 1809; Pol. Cons. No. 60; 14th July, 1810. Also see pp. 111, 112 *infra.*)

the East India Company—Akbar II was prepared to yield in small matters. Early in January 1810 he agreed[1] to the proposal of the British Government to appoint Abu Zafar, his eldest son, as Heir-Apparent. In his letter of 16th January 1810 the Resident of Dehli informed Lord Minto of 'this happy event' saying, 'I have the honour to acquaint you that His Majesty the King of Dehli was pleased this day being the day of Muhammadan festival of Bakar-'id to elevate his eldest son Prince Abu Zafar to the dignity of Heir-Apparent and invest His Royal Highness with the *khila't* adapted to the occasion. The ceremony was performed in full Durbar in the presence of the whole of the Royal Family and of all the Natives of rank now at Dehli as also in that of the Hon'ble Mr. Elphinstone, the Envoy to the Court of Kabul and the gentlemen of his suite. At the conclusion of the ceremony the King according to the established etiquette withdrew, leaving the Heir-Apparent to

[1] It should be remembered that prior to the Emperor's agreeing to the British proposal to appoint Prince Abu Zafar Heir-Apparent he had been supporting the candidature of his third son Mirza Jahangir. Now he withdrew his support from the latter and agreed to the dispersal of his party, that is the removal of the Guard of Honour which had been attending him and urged by which he had shot Seton as described in the preceding chapter. Referring to this incident the Court of Directors said in their letter of 4th September 1811 addressed to the Governor-General, 'The contumacious behaviour of Mirza Jahangir afforded the opportunity and suggested the expediency of re-occupying the Palace Gates by British troops; the execution of that measure having been opposed by the Prince at the head of his turbulent followers an affray ensued which terminated in the loss of some lives on the side of the Prince and seizure of his person'.

[*Political Letters from the Court of Directors,* 4th September 1811, also dated 14th May 1812.]

receive the usual compliments and nazrs on the occasion of His Royal Highness's elevation. I am persuaded that the elevation of the Prince will be attended with effects of the most salutary and beneficial nature. To the inhabitants of the city of Dehli as is already evident—the arrangement is highly satisfactory; the mild character and conciliating conduct of His Royal Highness having justly rendered him a favourite with all ranks and descriptions of people'.[1]

Three months after this the Emperor sent to Lord Minto a *shuqqa* of goodwill which ran as follows: 'We have received your Lordship's letter and have been made acquainted with the further particulars which were entrusted to the verbal communications of Mr. Seton. The good government of the country in general and the great expenses attending it were already known to our royal mind. But the establishment of order within the Districts of Hurreeana and Bhowany and in the vicinity of Dehli which has now been effected under your Lordship's orders by Mr. Seton is a good work and furnishes to the world an example worthy of imitation. The addition to the *peshkash* which your Lordship's loyalty has led you to transmit through Mr. Seton has been accepted.

'With regard to what your Lordship has stated in your address on the subject of the present *peshkash*[2] being double the amount of that which was paid in the time of the Maratta chiefs, Faithful servant! inasmuch as our Royal favour and regard are far greater towards the British Government than towards

[1] Pol. Cons. No. 4, 6th February 1810.

[2] For the term *peshkash* see pp. 85, 86n, *supra*. It has been wrongly translated as stipend in the English rendering of Akbar II's *shuqqa* in question. *Cf*. Majumdar, J. K.—*Raja Ram Mohan Roy and the Last Moghuls, p. 132.*

others, we always entertained a confident expectation that the British Government would pay us a larger *peshkash*. We are in every respect pleased with your Lordship's loyalty and attachment, and we repose the greatest confidence in your sincerity. While we have such a loyal servant as your Lordship we can have no cares or apprehensions since we are satisfied that your Lordship will always direct your attention to whatever is calculated to elevate ease and happiness'.[1]

It was an irony of fate that while Akbar II was expressing his great appreciation of the British Government and paying a rich tribute to Lord Minto, the latter was drafting his Minute of 1809 wherein he observed, 'The King bent on his unattainable purpose but destitute of power to attempt it openly and too feeble even to avow it, stoops to every little artifice, engages in every petty intrigue and is drawn into all the oblique and disingenuous courses which the ladies of his palace or councillors equally feminine can suggest or recommend to him. An opening is furnished for such practices by the liberal courtesy with which the exterior observances due to the real sovereignty of his ancestors are, most properly, extended to his nominal title; and under cover of the formal homage which a tenderness for his personal feelings alone prompts us to render him, he seeks to advance a silent and gradual claim to the substantial attributes of greatness'.[2]

Akbar II was depressed but did not lose heart. Being unable to fight the British power he made a fresh effort to make a friendly approach; and with a view

---

[1] This *shuqqa* was received by Lord Minto on 26th January 1810. *Vide* Pol. Cons. No. 60, 14th July 1810.

[2] *Vide* Majumdar, J. K.—*Raja Ram Mohan Roy and the Last Moghuls,* p. xliv.

to settling the fundamental issues of the conflict by means of a one-man deputation he engaged a Hindu nobleman Pran Kishan by name and conferred on him the title of Raja. In 1811 he sent him on a special private mission to the Governor-General at Calcutta without making any reference to the British Resident at Dehli. But the British Government considered it *ultra vires* on the part of the Emperor and raised a hue and cry; ultimately they disgraced Pran Kishan and had him divested of his title.[1] This incident was mentioned in a letter dated 30th September 1814 of the Court of Directors to the Governor-General under the heading of *'Clandestine deputation of Pran Kishan from the King of Delhi to the Governor-General'*. An extract from it runs as follows: 'In expressing our concern at the clandestine deputation of Baboo Pran Kishan from the King of Delhi and at the tenor of his credentials and letters which accompanied that deputation, we have to signify our approbation of the measures which were adopted on that occasion and of the instructions issued to the Resident at Delhi of the 22nd July and 20th September 1811. Our despatches noted in the margin[2] have already conveyed to you our approbation of the resistance you have uniformly opposed to His Majesty's pretensions, and our opinion in regard to the relations subsisting between His Majesty and the British Government'.[3]

---

[1] 'Lord Minto . . . . publicly deprived Pran Kishan of his seal' (Spear, p. 45).

[2] 17th August 1808; 28th June 1809; 15th September 1809; 4th September 1811.

[3] Political Letters from the Court of Directors, 30th September 1814; (ii) Pol. Cons. No. 20, 6th January 1816; (iii) Pol. Cons. No. 22, 6th January 1816.

Akbar II was so provoked that when subsequently Hastings, the successor of Minto in the Governor-Generalship of India, wanted to meet him he insisted that *'Hastings should appear as a subject and present the usual nazrs'*.[1] Hastings refused to come to Dehli and meet the Emperor except on a footing of equality; and he is reported to have observed, 'The King tried a variety of modifications as to the particular form in which his suzerainty over the Company's territories was to be asserted; but at length after Mr. Metcalfe's assuring him that the more or the less of the distinctions to be shown to me could have no effect where my resistance was to the admission of any foreign supremacy over our dominions, His Majesty at length gave up the hope of a meeting. This procedure on my part was dictated not more by the tenure of the recent Act of Parliament which declares the sovereignty of the Company's possession to be in the British Crown, than by a clear conviction of our impolicy in keeping up the notion of a paramountship in the King of Delhi'.[2]

Evidently the British Government now determined to kill at all costs the Mughul Emperor's belief in his paramountcy and the vassalage of the East India Company. Before long Hastings encouraged the Nawab Wazir of Oudh to shake off all allegiance to the

---

[1] 'The Mughul (emperor) might not treat the Governor-General as a subject in Calcutta; but what was to happen when the Governor-General visited the Mughul in his palace? The question arose when Lord Hastings proceeded up-country to direct operations in the Gurkha War. Akbar insisted that Hastings should appear as a subject and present the usual nazrs'. (Spear—p. 45). *Vide Delhi Residency and Agency*, pp. 343-344.

[2] Majumdar, J. K.—*Raja Ram Mohan Roy and the Last Moghuls*, p. xlv.

'effete' Mughul Emperor and to set up as an independent king. The Nawab Wazir was prompt in acting; but when he announced his kingship it was highly resented by Akbar II.[1] This was not all. Hastings also conferred a *khila't* on Faiz Muhammad Khan, son and successor of the Chief of Kanonah.[2] Furthermore he prevented the Raja of Jaipur from having his *tika* ceremony performed by the Mughul Emperor,[3] and discontinued the presentation of *nazr* which the Governor-General and the Commander-in-chief used to make to the Emperor on the occasion of festivals.[4] A change was also made in the form and style of the epistolary communication. When in 1819 Colebrooke was appointed Resident at Dehli the news was communicated by the Governor-General without designating himself in the letter as *Fidwi* Akbar Shah or Vassal of Emperor Akbar. The old seal bearing the above inscription was discarded; it was substituted by another seal which the Governor-General had been using for his correspondence with the Princes of Western Asia. And henceforth all epistolary communication between him and the Emperor was suspended for some time.[5]

Akbar II looked forward to the termination of

---

[1] Hastings—*Summary of the Administration of the Indian Government* (1824), p. 104.

[2] and [3] (i) Secret Consultation No 14, 18th November 1814.
(ii) Secret Consultation No. 20, 18th November 1814.
(ii) Secret Consultation No. 33, 24th January 1815.

[4] Political Letter of the Governor-General in council to the Court of Directors, dated 14th September 1825.

[5] (i) Political consultation No. 68, 21st September 1827.
(ii) Political Letter to the Court of Directors, 25th June 1844.

Hastings' period of office; and to his successor Amherst he is known to have made some advances. A meeting between the two was consequently arranged, and took place most ceremoniously. 'His Lordship proceeded to the Palace in the morning of 17th March 1827 to visit His Majesty. When the Governor-General's *sawaree* reached the inner gate called Naqqarkhana the Resident and several gentlemen of His Lordship's suite alighted from their elephants according to custom and proceeded on foot while the Governor-General was carried in his *Tonjohn* to the steps of the Diwan-i Khass. The King came into the Darbar-i Amm from the Toshakhana at the same moment that the Governor-General entered at the opposite side, and meeting His Lordship in front of the throne embraced and welcomed him in the most cordial manner. His Majesty then ascended the Peacock Throne and the Governor-General took his seat in a chair in front of it on the right and sat at right angles to His Majesty, the Resident and other officers present as well as the chief personages of the Court, all standing. No nazrs were presented. After a short conversation consisting entirely of expressions of a complimentary and congratulatory nature the King took a handsome string of pearls and emeralds from his neck and placed it around that of Lord Amherst, His Lordship rising to receive the Royal gift. *'Itr* (perfume) was then given by the King; and His Majesty descending from the Throne took the Governor-General by the arm and led him to the door of the Tasbeehkhana where His Lordship took leave. Salutes of 19 guns were fired from His Majesty's Artillery Park both upon the entry and departure of the Governor-General. On the 22nd the gentlemen of His Lordship's staff and suite, 20 in number, were introduced to the King by the

Resident. Each presented the usual *nazr* and received a *khila't*. On the 24th the Emperor paid a return visit to the Residency. There he took his seat on the Peacock Throne which had previously been placed in the principal room of the Residency for the purpose and the Governor-General sat on a state chair to the right, every other person standing. Then presents were brought for His Majesty consisting of 101 trays of jewels, shawls and cloths of various kinds, two elephants richly caparisoned and six horses with costly trappings. The Governor-General then rose and presented the *'itr dan* (perfume box) to His Majesty, after which His Majesty signified his intention of taking leave and was accompanied by Lord Amherst to the *Hawadar* (open conveyance of the Emperor) in the veranda'.[1]

On 26th[2] the Governor-General was visited by the Heir-Apparent Mirza Abu Zafar and eight of the Emperor's sons. 'His Royal Highness was conducted to the Residency by Sir Charles Metcalfe and met at the head of the steps by the Governor-General. The Prince sat in a state chair on His Lordship's right and the other sons of His Majesty were seated below His Royal Highness according to their ages. Presents consisting of 51 trays, one elephant and three horses, were given to the Heir-Apparent and 21, 15 and 13 trays with horses, to each of the junior Princes. The following day the Governor-General returned the Heir-Apparent's visit at the Qudsia Bagh and was received with the same honours as had been shown to His Royal Highness.[3]

---

[1] *Delhi Residency and Agency*, Chapter X, p. 337.

[2] 26th March 1827.

[3] *Op. cit.* p. 339.

This was a meeting between Mughul Royalty and the Head of the British Government on a footing of equality which Akbar II disapproved. In the course of a letter[1] to the Resident he said, 'Providence at length favoured me with a visit from Lord Amherst, which I hailed with feelings of the fullest confidence and delight at the prospect which it afforded of securing to me the fulfilment of the pledges that had been given me and the realization of all my desires. I accordingly did everything in my power to please His Lordship and showed him every kindness that I could possibly manifest explaining at the same time the engagements of the British Government with me and making a full disclosure of my wishes to him.[2] His Lordship, however, evinced as little disposition as others to redeem those engagements or to execute the provisions contained in the regulations of Government; and not confining himself to this, he had recourse to the novel procedure of setting aside the ceremonial and forms of address (*adab-o alqab*) observed by his predecessors, thus lowering me even in respect of the style of correspondence adopted towards me—a thing that I could have least expected'.[3]

As a result, no further meetings took place between the Mughul Emperor and the Governor-General; and Bentinck[4] and after him Auckland[5] failed to have a

---

[1] Political Consultation No. 68, 21st September 1827.

[2] This was the essence of the *Paper of Requests* delivered by Akbar II to the Governor-General on 1st March 1827 (Political Proceedings, No. 6; 15th June 1827).

[3] Pol. Cons. No. 5; 13th January 1832.

[4] (i) *Records of Delhi Residency and Agency,* 1807-1857, pp. 343-344.
(ii) Pol. Cons. No. 6, 13th January 1832.
(iii) 'Concession having proved as useless as resistance, Akbar II refused to meet Bentinck in 1831' (Spear)

[5] See p. 132 *infra*.

meeting even though each desired one. Convinced that there was something fundamentally wrong with the responsible British officers in India, Akbar II now resolved to send Raja Ram Mohan Roy as his envoy to the British authorities in London with a personal letter from him addressed to his Britannic Majesty George IV. Thus an appeal was made primarily to the King of England but ultimately to the whole civilized world. And Raja Ram Mohan Roy who was expected to prosecute before different tribunals the Mughul Emperor's claims arising from certain provisions of the treaty of 1803[1] was charged to exhibit to the world instances of the violation of pledges on the part of the East India Company. The letter[2] which Raja Ram Mohan Roy carried and which he is said to have under the Emperor's order drafted in Persian and translated into English[3]—comprised 18 paragraphs. Out of these, 15 paragraphs which contained important points are given below to the exclusion of the first three which were merely complimentary.

To

His Majesty the King of the British Empire

Sire! My Brother!

4. I hasten to specify the wrongs of which I complain and to substantiate my allegations by the necessary proofs. In brief then I beg to recall Your Majesty's attention to the accompanying Articles of

---

[1] This treaty was finally confirmed and communicated to Shah Alam in 1805.

[2] Pol. Procgs. No. 20, 13th March 1829.

[3] (i) Banerji, B.—*Raja Ram Mohan Roy's Mission to England,* pp. 3-4.

(ii) Majumdar, J. K.—*Raja Ram Mohan Roy and the Last Moghuls,* pp. 196 ff.

convention which were transmitted to my August Father from the Governor-General in Council in conformity with the promise made by Lord Lake and which were duly recognized on both sides as expressive of the mutual obligations of the contracting parties, but of which the first and most important clause is now injuriously evaded.

5. That Article provides that 'all the mahals to the west of the Jumna situated between the west and north of Mauza Kabilpoor shall be considered the crown lands of His Majesty'. The second article provides that 'the management of these mahals shall be continued according to custom in the hands of the Resident'; but in proof that the entire revenues were to be placed at the Royal disposal it is expressly provided in the third article that 'for His Majesty's satisfaction the royal Mutasaddis (civil officers) shall attend at the Cutchery to keep accounts of the receipts and disbursements and report the same to His Majesty'. The memorandum referred to in the 7th article specifies a minimum of monthly stipends for the King and the Royal Household and that article provides that the sums so specified shall be paid monthly from the Public Treasury whether the whole of the amount is or is not collected from the Khalsa lands'. The English article to which I solicit Your Majesty's special attention contains the important provision that 'should the collections from the above mahals increase in consequence of extending cultivation and the improved condition of the ryots—a proportioned augmentation will take place in the King's *peshkash* or Revenue'; and finally to show that the royal stipend was to consist not of the net but of the gross produce without any deduction, the Eleventh article provides that the

'expense of the Troops, Police Corps etc. employed in the Khalsa shall be defrayed by the Hon. Company'. What could be more clear and explicit than these provisions? What words could have more strictly guarded against the possibility of perversion or misapprehension? Yet the first and important part has been since rendered a dead letter as if neither honour nor justice demanded their fulfilment.

6. In the recent communications which I have had with your Majesty's late representative in India Lord Amherst on this subject, there is the admission that 'it was the original intention of Government to have assigned certain Mahals to the west of the Jumna for the support of His Majesty and the Royal Family' but it is added, 'The plan was never from unavoidable causes carried completely into effect'. It now seems to be tacitly inferred that therefore it ought not ever to be carried into effect. To me and my family, to my immediate dependents and to the numerous individuals who cannot refuse their disinterested sympathy to my fallen House it does not appear clearly to follow because an act of justice has hitherto been denied that it could never be performed; nor when we consider what British power and influence have accomplished, can we bring ourselves to believe that any causes would have proved unavoidable if a disposition really favourable to the accomplishment of the object had existed. The assertion, however, that the plan was never carried completely into effect is essentially erroneous; for while the revenues of the assigned Mahals did not exceed the minimum of the Royal stipends and allowances the Royal Mutasaddis were allowed to attend at the Cutchery in conformity with the third stipulation for the express purpose of keeping

accounts of the receipts and disbursements and reporting the same to my August Father and to myself. The right and title of the Royal Family to the entire revenues of the Mahals were thus for a length of time distinctly and unequivocally acknowledged by the concession to the Royal Mutasaddis of the power of supervision and report, but when these revenues materially exceeded the minimum of the Royal stipends, then it was that it became inconvenient to carry the plan completely into effect, and the Royal Mutasaddis were in consequence directed to withdraw their attendance at the Cutchery. In like manner the practice of submitting by the Resident for my Royal decision the proceedings in cases where capital punishment was adjudged by the Criminal Court has also long since been discontinued in neglect of the provision contained in the 6th article of the agreement.

7. Even in the communication above stated insult in point of form was added to injustice. All the Governors-General who have preceded Lord Amherst in the government of the British territories in India have thought it no degradation to themselves to address me or my August Father in the style that custom has accorded to Royalty. Lord Amherst, however, thought proper to reduce me in the form of communication to the footing of an equal and thereby to rob me even of the cheap gratification of the usual ceremonies of address so as to humble me as far as possible in the eyes of all ranks of people.

8. Before however these derogatory steps were adopted, repeated, solemn, and public recognitions of the claims of my Royal Family to the revenues of the assigned Mahals had been recorded in the code of Regulations and Laws enacted by the Governor-General

in Council for the civil government of the territories under the Presidency of Fort William in Bengal. Thus at section 4th of Regulation XI of 1804 it is clearly expressed that 'the revenues of the territory on the right bank of the Jumna are assigned to His Majesty Shah Alam'; and precisely the same language is repeated at sections 22nd and 35th of the same Regulation, at section 3rd of Regulation VI of 1805 and at sections 2nd and 4th of the Regulation VIII of the same year. At sections 1st and 2nd of Regulation X of 1807, and at section 1st of Regulation XI of the same year, the language is similar although more general, for in these 'the territory assigned for the support of the Royal Family at Dehli' is mentioned without specifying its locality as in the former instances, the very absence of this specification marking its notoriety and the distinctness of the purpose to which the revenues of that territory were exclusively applicable. These declarations cannot be disavowed, retracted or misapprehended. They are embodied in the code of Regulations by which this branch of the British Indian Empire is governed, and they incontrovertably demonstrate that for a series of years the plan was carried completely into effect and the right of my family to the revenues of the districts in question was clearly and undisguisedly admitted.

9. Even the minimum of the Royal stipends was at one time arbitrarily and unjustly curtailed of several items, contrary to the express provisions contained in the stipulations and without the consent of the contracting party whose rights were thereby violated, having been obtained or even sought. It was in this way that one of the items amounting to 10,000 rupees for support of the Heir-Apparent was reduced to

7,000; a second of 5,000 rupees for Mirza Ezad Bakhsh to 2,000 and a third amounting to Sicca Rs. 2,500 for Shah Nawaz Khan, a connection of His Majesty, was entirely resumed at his death and his family thus left destitute. To crown these acts it has been pretended that an augmentation to the *peshkash* made in the year 1809 amounting after several previous deductions only to Sicca Rs. 13,200 per mensem was granted by way of commutation for the Royal claims on the improved revenues of the Khalsa lands though so far was such an agreement from receiving my sanction that the increase was only communicated to me as a resolution taken by the Government without the slightest reference to the pretended equivalent.

10. The original articles of agreement are either binding or they are not. If they are binding then any alteration or commutation of any part of the Royal income made by one party without the consent of the other to whom it is injurious, must be null and void. If they are not binding this must be either because they were never entered into, which cannot be affirmed or because some subsequent voluntary arrangement between the two contracting parties has superseded their obligation. But no arrangement tending to supersede the original articles of agreement has ever been voluntarily recognized by my Royal predecessor or myself and therefore the numerous and unauthorized deviations from the provisions which they contain constitute a series of direct and systematic violations of truth, honour and justice.

11. A relation of the particulars connected with this pretended increase of Sicca Rs. 13,200 per mensem will show to Your Majesty how little real was the value of the alleged concession. When the gross and

palpable infringements by the local authorities on the stipulations entered into with Lord Wellesley's Government were brought to the notice of Lord Minto in the year 1809 and the Royal claims on the then improved revenues of the Khalsa Mahals set forth, that nobleman virtually admitted the wrongs that had been inflicted. And the total sum of the Royal stipends including the allowances on the Princes and Princesses and every contingency which after several deductions then amounted to only Sicca Rs. 86,000 was raised to one lakh, the real augmentation being however considerably less in amount than this apparent one. By Lord Wellesley's agreement the allowance to the Royal Family[1] was paid under the following heads:

His Majesty's personal allowance	Rs.	60,000
Presents at 7 festivals[2] Rs. 10,000 each	,,	5,833
The Heir-Apparent	,,	10,000
His jageer in the Doab ...	,,	3,000
Princes and Princesses ...	,,	10,000
Mirza Ezad Bakhsh—personal allowance	,,	2,000
Mirza Ezad Bakhsh—by his jagir in the Doab ...	,,	1,000
Shah Nawaz Khan ...	,,	2,500
Total monthly allowance ...	,,	94,333

so that the stipend established by Lord Minto in 1809 then considered as providing an increase of allowance

[1] Secret Letter to the Court of Directors, dated 2nd June 1805.

[2] *I.e.* the *Jashn* (anniversary of the accession); the two Ids; Nauroz; Basant; Holi; Ramazan. (See Sec. Cons. No. 316, 20th June 1805).

to the extent of Rs. 13,200 per mensem as above stated and also alleged to be in satisfaction of the terms of the treaty in fact added no more than the paltry sum of Rs. 5,667 to the original minimum provision. But even this augmentation was granted arbitrarily without any reference to the amount actually due by stipulation and without any consent being asked or obtained; and it was moreover accompanied by an insulting intimation that the 'sovereignty I possess is only nominal and that the Governor-General's recognition of it is merely 'complimentary'. Does the complimentary recognition of a nominal sovereignty authorize or justify the arbitrary infringement of direct and positive obligations or denude myself and family of the common rights of men and society? Because the Governor-General in Council condescends to recognize in me an empty title, is it therefore that the solemn faith of the British nation and Government may be wantonly broken? Do I become less entitled to the performance of the contract that has been entered into with my family because my ancestors were great and powerful and I am feeble and helpless, held down by those who make my weakness and degradation the excuse for their injustice? I cherish the confident persuasion that Your Majesty will not sanction the principle that in my case a National contract ought not or need not to be fulfilled because I am powerless to enforce its obligations. What king or subject will avow such a principle except in India and to the injured and unhappy House of Timur?

12. I have now briefly explained to Your Majesty the wrongs I have suffered and the rights which I demand. *I claim the entire revenues whatever they may be of the Mahals* originally assigned for the

support of the Royal Family, unjustly alienated from the rightful owner and appropriated to themselves by the Hon. Company. I claim restitution of the sums of which the Royal Family have been deprived in past years, and I claim your Majesty's guarantee for the rigid fulfilment in future of the Articles of Convention by which a minimum is fixed for the Royal *peshkash*. by which the gross revenues of the Mahals to the west of the Jumna are assigned to the Royal Family should they exceed that minimum, and by which the means and opportunity of obtaining a perfect knowledge of the actual revenues of those Mahals are stipulated rights. I am not unaware of the practical evil that is likely to result according to the known principles of human nature, by imposing upon one party all the toil of superintendence and all the expense of improvement and bestowing upon another all the fruits of his labour and sacrifices. I am therefore willing to submit to any reasonable compromise of my rights either by assuming for a fit compensation all the trouble and outlay attending the Government, police, and cultivation of the territory in question or by receiving a fixed monthly sum in lieu of all further claims. In the latter case the present gross annual revenues of the Mahals would form a proper standard and if they do not fall short of 30 lakhs I hereby offer to commute all my prospective claims under the articles of convention for that yearly stipend.

14. It behoves me to satisfy your Majesty that the concession of my undoubted rights may be rendered perfectly consistent with sound policy and a just regard to the safety and permanence of the British rule in India. The largeness of the sum I have mentioned considered by itself—without any reference to the

numerous regular and increasing demands upon my exhausted treasury—might seem to indicate a wish to accumulate money for some concealed hostile purpose: I utterly disavow every such object and as alike dishonourable to the race from which I have sprung and inconsistent with the open course which I have ever pursued. Some of my ancestors have fallen victims of the disloyalty of others, but they never betrayed those who confided in their honour; and in imitation of their noble examples while I have not hesitated and will still continue to complain of the injustice I have suffered and vindicate the rights that belong to me, I will not disgrace them and myself by secret machinations against a Power which I dare not combat in the open field. As a complete security against any such attempt I will cheerfully agree not to retain more than 12 lakhs of rupees in my treasury at any time, to invest the surplus, should there be any, in the loans opened by the British Government; and to forfeit to the Hon. Company any sum found in my possession in excess of that amount, not so invested. If any other check can be suggested which shall not subject me to a degrading inquisition in all the minutiae of my expenditure I shall willingly accede to it.

15. But to a Prince of Your Majesty's enlarged and magnanimous views it will be obvious that the most just and generous policy must also be the most wise and provident. For on what firmer bases can the duty and tranquillity of the subjects of a distant and conquered country be founded or the confidence of the surrounding States naturally jealous of their independence be established than on the irresistible evidence continually presented to them of good faith and moderation displayed in the strict observance of

engagements even if burdensome and although spontaneously entered into with one bereft of the power of dictating terms or of effectually resenting their violation.

16. Should on the other hand a conspicuous example subsist of broken compact on the part of your Majesty's Vicegerents towards me, because no longer in a condition to vindicate my rights by an appeal to arms—if contempt and indignity be measured out to the representative of a once mighty monarchy in proportion as he is powerless to enforce respect, Your Majesty's acquired subjects, once amongst those of my ancestors, now with anxious fears observing the conduct of their new rulers, the neighbouring Princes who have beheld with alarm the progress of Your Majesty's arms nay the whole civilized world, will assuredly sympathise with my griefs and look on my oppressors with the feelings and wishes which their conduct must infallibly inspire.

17. If I had any doubt of the justice of my claims I might still rest them on an appeal to your Majesty's known generosity. I might remind your Majesty of the time when my ancestors ruled supreme over these countries where their wretched descendant and sole representative of their dynasty is compelled to drag on a dependent existence in a dilapidated palace exposed to the contempt or receiving the sympathy of the different classes of society both Europeans and Asiatics who resort to Dehli with means utterly inadequate to support the dignity even of a nominal sovereignty or to afford a scanty subsistence to the numerous branches of his family who look to him as their only stay. But I will not condescend to accept and your Majesty will disdain to confer as a

favour that which is due as a right. I rest my cause on your Majesty's high-minded sense of honour and justice. I cannot permit myself to suppose that your Majesty will lend a deaf ear to my complaints. I address by this letter not only your Majesty but the world at large and I anticipate the plaudits which present and future ages will bestow on your Majesty's benevolent and enlightened sympathy with the unworthy representative of once great and illustrious though now fallen House of Timur.

18. To your Majesty what need I say more'.[1]

This letter speaks for itself and needs no comment beyond the fact that it failed to produce the desired effect. The Court of Directors agreed to offer an increment of a monthly sum of Rs. 25,000, subject to certain conditions which the Emperor declined. But subsequently under the increasing pressure of financial needs he intimated his acceptance. He also drew up a *razinama* to this effect when asked by the British Government to do so. But he required that the increment should be made available to him from the date the intentions of the British Government became known to him. The British Government referred this requisition of the Emperor to the Court of Directors and pending their orders wanted to give the increment from the date of communication on which the royal consent had been expressed. They also requested the Emperor to send in a list of the names of those among whom the grant in question might be distributed. The Emperor sent in the list and said, 'Raja Ram Mohan Roy Bahadur confiding in my promises and favour undertook the distant journey to

[1] (i) Political Consultatiion No. 20, 13th March 1829.
(ii) Pol. Cons. No. 25, 8th May 1837.

England and fell a sacrifice. Other zealous servants such as Raja Sohan Lal and others were promised rewards and salaries . . . . The fulfilment of my promise is just and proper. And independently of my promise and without reference to the increase, the family of a man who has sacrificed his life in the service of his master ought to be maintained by that master—specially Rao Radha Prasad and Rao Rama Prasad—sons of the late Raja Ram Mohan Roy—who are my devoted servants and have likewise received a promise of remuneration. Moreover for the space of two years past Rao Radha Prasad has been in attendance at the royal threshold in the hope of realizing the promised remuneration and salary on account of his father's devotion. . . . Justice demands that Your Lordship should first consider the fulfilment of my promise and engagements, due attention to which will add to Your Lordship's renown. . . .'[1]

The British Government paid no heed to all this, nor did they approve of the Emperor's list. On the contrary they submitted their own list in which the Emperor found that neither he himself nor his sons and princesses were to have a pie, not to speak of the sons of Raja Ram Mohan Roy. Seeing this he was so disgusted that he refused to accept the increase and asked for the return of the *Razinama* saying, 'Under such circumstances I am unwilling to accept the increase or execute a *Razinama* and I shall hereafter make known my reasons for the same'.[2] Before this despatch, he had already written[3] to the Governor-General in Council to reconsider their decision. That

---

[1] *Idem.*

[2] Political Consultation No. 25, 8th May 1837.

[3] Political Consultation No. 22, 16th October 1834.

too produced no effect. So the matters remained where they were. And while the British Government was still unwilling to untie their purse and had not paid a single pie out of their promised increment, the aged Emperor was claimed by the Angel of Death. He died[1] at the age of 82 on 28th September 1837.

His successor Abul Muzaffar Siraju'ddin Bahadur Shah showed an equal amount of recalcitrance and obstinacy. The following *five* documents give positive evidence of his determination not to recede an inch beyond the stand taken by his royal father. *Firstly* he refused to meet Lord Auckland on 'a footing of perfect equality' and sent a *shuqqa* addressed to the Agent to the Governor-General saying, 'His Majesty has received your petition stating that a letter has been received from Mr. Secretary Macnaghten signifying the Right Hon'ble Governor-General's wish on visiting Dehli to have an interview with His Majesty provided it be on terms of equality. And that after his Lordship shall have visited the Palace, His Majesty shall return the visit at His Lordship's quarters. That the custom of nazrs and *khila't* and the interchange of presents etc. be dispensed with and that no form and ceremony inconsistent with the rank and dignity of His Lordship shall be expected.

'His Majesty has long cherished the pleasing hope which God be praised is about to be realized. What Sir C. T. Metcalfe Baronet deemed proper and carried into effect in the time of his late Majesty is as well known as the noon-day sun. You are likewise His Majesty's well-wisher.

'The usages of our Royal House are these, that whatever may have been heretofore established by the

[1] Political Consultation No. 66, 16th October 1837.

officers of the British Government are readily and with pleasure observed and no innovation or change is allowed to take place. And with regard to the Form and Ceremony to be observed at the meeting and on the occasion of the embracing between the Governor-General and His Majesty it is evident that the true affection is not dependent on public forms but the same etiquette which was observed in the interview between Lord Amherst and His late Majesty through the counsel and advice of Sir C. T. Metcalfe Baronet will be observed on the present occasion of His Lordship's arrival in Dehli without any deviation whatsoever; more than this cannot be conceded'.[1]

As a result the proposed meeting did not take place; and Auckland and Bahadur Shah never met. Bahadur Shah also declined to accept the conditions attached by the British Government to the aforesaid increment. Intimating this fact to the Court of Directors the Governor-General said, 'From the documents now sent your Hon'ble Court will learn that the King of Dehli has declined to accept the addition of three lakhs per annum to the stipend of the family on the conditions annexed to the grant by your orders'.[2]

Secondly Bahadur Shah despatched a *shuqqa* to the address of the Agent to the Governor-General N. W. P. saying,

'I have received your petition enclosing a letter from the Honourable the Lieutenant-Governor of the N. W. P. in reply to a communication from me respect-

---

[1] This was received by Lord Auckland on 5th February 1838. *Vide* (i) Political Consultation No. 122, 9th May 1838, (ii) Political Consultation No. 122, 9th May 1838.

[2] Pol. Letter to the Court of Directors, 8th February 1839.

ing the increased amount of the *peshkash* . . . . . stating that in the lifetime of His late Majesty the Supreme Government had signified that the Hon'ble the Court of Directors had been pleased to make an increase of 3 lakhs of rupees annually to the established *peshkash* of His Majesty on condition that His Majesty would give up all further claims and execute a deed of renunciation of every claim on his part. That the distribution of the increase among the royal dependants and relatives should be made solely under the orders of the Government and that some portion of the amount shall be assigned either monthly or yearly for the repairs of the Palace ... and I have fully comprehended their contents.

'You are aware that before the British authority came into this country communications from His Excellency Lord Lake the commander-in-chief and the most noble the Marquis of Wellesley the Governor-General had been received by His Majesty Shah Alam assuring His Majesty that no want of attention should ever take place on any occasion wherein the honour, dignity and happiness of the Royal House might be concerned. It is true that hitherto such has been the case, and on the part of their late Majesties also the pleasure and approbation of the Government have on all occasions been held in view. For instance in the 48th year of His Majesty Shah Alam's reign a monthly sum of 6000 rupees was added to the Royal *peshkash* for the benefit of the *salateen* and the *nazirat* and other departments of the Palace... and 14000 rupees on the 16th of the month of Jamadiool Awwal in the 3rd year of his late Majesty's reign corresponding with the Ist of January 1809, agreeably to Mr. Seton's communication, without any agreement having been entered into, and

His Majesty was pleased to consider it as a preliminary to future advantages of a superior nature—but as regards the present increase, deeds of acquittance and renunciation of all future claims are required from me —which is a matter of much surprise specially as I have on every occasion sought to please Government and have never acted contrary to their wishes nor have any intention of doing so now. *How then can I agree to the proposed demand*? I am uninformed as to the nature and extent of the claims alluded to and it is but just and proper for me to be made acquainted with them. Formerly during their late Majesties' lifetime no agreements of renouncing claims were required on the increase of their *peshkash*. But the present demand for such documents requires attention and reflection.

'The allotment of the present augmented amount with the approbation of Government is agreeable to me, but with reference to the list prepared during the lifetime of his late Majesty I have to observe that I was then Heir-Apparent and 100 rupees was allotted to each of my sons and 500 to those of His Majesty; but now that by the decree of Providence and the goodwill of the Government I am placed on the throne of my ancestors my sons are entitled from their present rank to similar considerations. I therefore trust that on the assignment taking place, their rights and those of my other dependants will be had in remembrance. You are acquainted with the whole of my affairs from the beginning to the present time and are my friend and well-wisher and will no doubt make such arrangements as will be advantageous in removing my pecuniary embarrassments. The repairs, etc. of the Palace which you have mentioned were commenced upon from the day of my accession; and please God, they will be continued. It is necessary that you forward a translation of this *shuqqa* for the information of the Right Hon'ble the Governor-General.[1]

Thirdly Bahadur Shah despatched a *shuqqa* to the address of the Agent to the Governor-General saying,

'I have received your petition in reply to my *shuqqa* and have fully comprehended its contents. The substance of which is briefly this, that if it be my wish to receive the increased amount I must execute an engagement clearly disavowing all further claims and intimate my willingness to allow the distribution of the augmentation to be made by the Government and to accede to their wishes with respect to the repairs of the Palace.

'You are aware that the goodwill of the Government towards this House is known throughout the world and no occasion has occurred wherein His Majesty has ever conducted himself contrary to the approbation and pleasure of the Government; considering this, therefore, the execution of a deed disavowing all further claims would be peculiarly improper because God Almighty has in every way blessed the Government with Power and Freedom of will. They are the refuge of the world; independent of this the affairs of the Royal House have been from first to last dependent upon you in your character of agent and will so continue. The execution of a deed of the nature required is therefore under such circumstances unbecoming. But the proposition of the Government relative to the allotment of the increased amount with due regard and attention to myself and to

[1] This *shuqqa* was received by (i) the Agent to the Governor-General on 26th March 1838. (ii) Pol. Cons., No. 13, 26th September, 1838. *Vide* (i) Pol. Cons. No. 12, 26th September 1838, (iii) Pol. Cons. No. 15, 31st December 1834.

the dignity of my descendants and connections is agreeable to me. The repairs of the Palace commenced upon from the day of my accession to the throne are in progress and will be continued, and the expense thereof will be defrayed by me.

'You will please to forward a copy and translation of this *shuqqa'*.[1]

Fourthly Bahadur Shah despatched a *shuqqa* dated 7th June 1838 to the address of the Agent to the Governor-General saying,

'Your petition under date 26th May has been submitted for our consideration. It is written therein that the Right Hon'ble the Governor-General from motives of friendship is desirous of complying with all our wishes as far as they may be consistent with propriety. But that his Lordship is unable to give any reply to our objections on different points connected with the proposed augmentation to the Royal *peshkash* such as the payment of the Princes' salaries, the repairs of the Palace etc. until we may execute a deed under our hand and seal renouncing all claims upon the British Government.

Now the first question is relative to the nature of the deed required from us, for it is by no means plain to what particular matters it refers whether to former, present or future claims; the terms used in your petition now under acknowledgment are *Ladawa mutlaq*. (لادعوی مطلق). This is capable of being rendered into various interpretations; we therefore request you will

[1] It was received at the Governor-General's office on 25th April 1838. *Vide* Pol. Consultation No 13, 26th September 1838.

give the Persian designation for that particular kind of deed required of us; we can then distinctly reply to your former communication.'

Fifthly Bahadur Shah despatched a *shuqqa* dated Ist August 1838 to the address of the Agent to the Governor-General saying,

'We have received and fully comprehended your petition together with a translation of a letter from the Hon'ble the Court of Directors to the address of the Right Hon'ble the Governor-General in Council under date the 13th February 1833.

'In the 3rd para it is stated that the increase to the former *peshkash* has been assigned for the benefit of His Majesty and the Descendants of the Royal House of Timur now living, the *peshkash* amounting in the aggregate to 15,00,000 of rupees annually. In the letter of the Government it is stated that the increase is made for His Majesty and the members of the Timur family; and in the list of the distribution of the above increase submitted to His late Majesty, no provision was therein made for His Majesty's privy purse although in the above letter the stipendiary increase is stated to be made for His Majesty and the Descendants of the Timur family. It is surprising that no portion of the increase is allotted for His Majesty's personal use in the list of distribution.

'In the 4th paragraph it is distinctly stated that His Majesty must consider the present increase as in lieu of all claims of every description which he may suppose himself to possess against the British Government. We require you to reflect, how such a deed of acquittance can be granted. It is an established custom with Sovereigns in mutual amity at all times

facing p. 258

THE PEOPLE'S WAR IN DEHLI

ment.[1] This shows that Bahadur Shah was aiming at releasing completely the problem of succession to the throne from the control of the Company's Government.

[1] See the above Persian text and its English translation, (2nd piece).

Chapter V

CONFRONTING A FORMIDABLE SITUATION

(11th May 1857)

In the preceding chapter half a century of Mughul twilight has been followed under the searchlight of the Records wherein the reader has seen by glimpses the cold war between Akbar II and after him Bahadur Shah II on the one side and the British Authorities on the other. This cold war was transformed into hot war shortly after the arrival of the Mirath mutineers in Dehli on 11th May 1857. But this transformation took place on account of the circumstances over which Bahadur Shah had no control. And since after the four months of war (May-September 1857) he stated in his defence[1] before the military commission or tribunal which tried him that he had no intimation on the subject of the Mutiny previous to the day of the outbreak, that the mutineers had made him a prisoner and that he was coerced to do whatever they required —it has been contended that Bahadur Shah played no independent role in the war of 1857.[2] But the defence of a prisoner under trial is almost always prepared with the object of defeating the prosecution, and the defence of Bahadur Shah was no exception. He was a prisoner and a victim of defeatist mentality who did not assert his rights of *de jure* sovereignty and the vassalage of the East India Company before the military tribunal. His life had been guaranteed conditionally by General Wilson;

[1] *Pr. Tr. B. S.*, p. 138.

[2] Majumdar, R. C.—*The Sepoy Mutiny and The Revolt of 1857*, pp. 116 ff.

and whatever might be the truth about it, Bahadur Shah was treated by the military tribunal as the arch-culprit, and his mental distress during the 42-day-long trial[1] (January 27—March 9, 1858) was like that of a criminal awaiting his conviction. Consequently he was anxious to dissociate himself from the mutineers; he disowned all their doings. In fact Bahadur Shah's fears of the mutineers on the one hand and of the British on the other neutralize themselves; and it would be unscientific to draw conclusions from his defence. Yet almost all English writers have made the written defence put in by Bahadur Shah the basis of their studies on the subject; and a modern historian drawing upon Malleson says, 'There can hardly be any doubt that when after a great delay and wavering Bahadur Shah at last accepted the title of emperor of Hindustan he assumed the responsibility of the position which had been forced upon him. It is more than probable that the old man left to himself would have shrunk from the position'[2]. But such an observation betrays complete ignorance of the 50-year-long cold war that had preceded the uprising of 1857. It is true that in the course of his letter[3] to George IV of England, Akbar II had promised not to have recourse to arms[4] for the redress of his grievances; but now the times had changed. Bahadur Shah had become more conscious of British tyranny and considered himself a prisoner of the British as is evident from his verses composed a few years before the Mutiny.[5] Mukand Lal the Emperor's private secretary and Hakim Ahsanullah

---

[1] Appendix A, p. 321 *infra*.

[2] Majumdar, R. C.—S. M. R., p. 118.

[3], [4] *Vide* p. 128, *supra*.

[5] *Vide* Appendix C.

Khan, his physician, explained the situation in the course of their evidence before the military tribunal during Bahadur Shah's trial. Says Mukand Lal, 'The King of Dehli has for some two years been disaffected against the (British) Government and was disposed not to respect his obligations to the English. The particulars are as follows:—When Mirza Haidar Shikoh and Mirza Murad, sons of Mirza Khan Bakhsh son of Mirza Sulaiman Shikoh came here from Lakhnao they in concert with Hasan Askari arranged and suggested to the King that he should have a letter prepared and despatched to the King of Persia. This letter they suggested should represent that the English had made the King a prisoner and had put a stop to all those marks of respect to which as King he was entitled and had suspended the appointment of any heir-apparent. It was further to represent that his wishes in reference to the appointment of any particular son as heir-apparent were not attended to. Under these circumstances the letter was to request that such an understanding might be established that mutual interchanges of visits and letters might be the result. Sidi Qambar who was one of the King's special armed retainers, was presented with Rs. 100 through Mahbub Ali Khan for the expenses of his journey and was despatched in the direction of Persia with a letter that had been prepared in the King's private secretariat. After this Mirza Haidar and his brother returned to Lakhnao, and having despatched his brother Mirza Najaf, a distant relation of the King, with Mirza Bulaqi son of Mirza Musharrafu'ddin son of Mirza Agha Jan to Persia reported the same to the King in writing. It is now about three years since some infantry soldiers stationed at Dehli became the disciples of the King through Mirza Ali whose duty it was to receive and present all petitions and through Hamid Khan Jamadar: and on that occasion the King gave each of them a document detailing the names and order of those who had preceded him in the direct line, disciples to each other, himself included together with a napkin dyed pink as an emblem of his blessing. The Agent of the Lieutenant-Governor hearing of this occurrence enquired regarding it and for the future prohibited the King's making any more the men of the army his disciples. It may be said that from that day a sort of understanding was established between the army and the King. *Some 20 days before the commencement of the late rebellion intelligence was received here that the troops at Mirath were about breaking out in open mutiny but it had not been heard that they were to come here. When the troopers arrived they first came under the Palace windows and told the King that they had come to him after killing all the English at Mirath and that they would slay immediately those that were here; and they further said that they would for the future consider the Prisoner their King and that now there was not one Englishman left in all India*—all had been slain. *They further said that the whole army would obey the King's orders. The King said that if they had a disposition to come, they should prepare themselves for all the consequences and if they were so prepared they were at liberty to come and take the management of matters into their hands.* While these disturbances were going on these traitors got into the city; the special armed retainers joined them and Qadir Dad Khan a resident of Kabul slew the Resident Mr. Fraser while some of the infantry soldiers with others of the King's retainers went to the apartments of the Commandant of the Palace Guards and slew him there. After that the English were killed all about the city wherever they were met with. The same day proclamation was made by beat of drum throughout the city that God was the Ruler of the World and Bahadur Shah was Sovereign of the country and had the supreme authority'.[1]

Like Mukand Lal, Hakim Ahsanullah Khan also emphasized that in order to vent his anger against the British Bahadur Shah was prepared to go to extremes. He was prepared even to change his religion and adopt the Shia cult if it pleased the Shah of Iran to help him against the British. Says Hakim Ahsanullah, 'Since the time when during the administration of Lord Ellenborough the *nazr* which used to be presented to the King of Dehli on the part of the Governor-General was discontinued the King was always very much aggrieved. At first he wrote on the matter to England and he always afterwards used to complain against the order and to express his dissatisfaction thereat. Subsequently the king was very much grieved in consequence of the Government not having acceded to his wish that his youngest son Mirza Jawan Bakht might be recognized as heir-apparent. Sometime afterwards the King sent Mirza Haidar, his nephew, to the King of Persia. I enquired from Mirza Ali Bakht who was a great friend of Mirza Najaf whether the latter had carried any letter from the King of Dehli to the Sultan of Persia. He replied in the affirmative and described the contents to be to the effect that the King of Dehli had adopted the Shia creed and the King of Persia should help him. Moreover in that letter the King of Dehli described his miserable and helpless condition . . . Then Sidi Qambar was sent by the King to Mirza Najaf to obtain a reply to his previous communications. ...From the conversation of the King it appears that

[1] *Pr. Tr. B. S.*, pp. 101-102.

Mirza Jawan Bakht

when war[1] was going on in Bushire he had strong hopes of receiving aid from Persia in the shape of money and troops, and during that period he used constantly to make enquiries regarding the events which were occurring in that quarter. During the period of war with Persia some of the princes used to observe that if the Emperor of Russia were to aid the Persians the English would be defeated and the Persians would become masters of India; and the King himself agreed to this opinion'[2]. Furthermore Hakim Ahsanullah Khan hinted that Bahadur Shah was not unware of the

---

[1] Three years after the arrival of Lord Canning in India (1856) broke out the Anglo-Persian War. Says Sewell, 'That nation had for years been in the habit of treating the representatives of England with growing contempt. In 1855 this conduct had become so marked that the British Commissioner at Teheran was compelled to leave the city. And at the commencement of the year 1856 the Persian Government had committed a wanton outrage by the seizure of Herat from the Afghan, Esa Khan. Accordingly Lord Canning declared war on November 1st. Early in December the troops landed 12 miles south of Bushire in the Persian Gulf, and an action ensued between the British and the enemy who had marched down to prevent a landing. The British army marched on Bushire, and fleet also advanced thither and commenced bombarding the town. A breach was easily effected and the town surrendered. In January 1857 a treaty of friendly alliance was signed between Amir Dost Muhammad of Kabul and the British Government; and thus strengthened, the British were able to inflict a defeat on the aggressive Persian troops in the battle of the Khooshab (7th February, 1857). In April 1857 the British captured Mahamreh which was followed by a Treaty of Peace guaranteeing that Persian troops should be for ever wthdrawn from Herat and Afghanistan and that the English Commissioner should be treated with all distinction at Teheran'.

[1] Sewell, R.—*Analytical History of India,* pp. 263-264.

[2] *Pr. Tr. B. S.*—pp. 161-163.

large-scale preparations that the sepoys had made for the Mutiny. He said, 'I believe information must have reached the King of the mutiny of some of the native regiments after the annexation of the Panjab and I doubt not that the King learnt the fact with satisfaction. On hearing of the regiments refusing to handle the new cartridges near Calcutta when the excitement spread extensively over the entire length and breadth of the country Bahadur Shah remarked that he would in that case be placed in better circumstances inasmuch as a new dominant power would treat him with greater respect and consideration. Dissatisfied with the British Government, Bahadur Shah made anxious enquiries about the native army whenever any war took place but he took pleasure in hearing of the British defeats and reverses. And when it was known that the discussion about the cartridges was spreading, it was remarked that *whereas the matter touched the religion of the people the excitement would spread extensively over the entire length and breadth of the country and the native army would desert the British Government and thus their rule would be put to an end. The King remarked that he would in that case be placed in better circumstances inasmuch as a new dominant Power would treat him with greater respect and consideration. In short Bahadur Shah believed that his own prosperity would go hand in hand with the ruin of the British Power*'[1]. Hakim Ahsanullah Khan also hinted that Bahadur Shah was hostile to the English not only on his own account but also on account of the people of India since he believed that the British Government wanted to change the religion of the people. 'The sepoys were aiming at expelling the English and at

[1] *Pr. Tr. B. S.* pp. 163-164.

becoming masters of the country; and before the outbreak at Mirath they had organized a conspiracy all over the country. The 38th Native Infantry otherwise known as Volunteer Regiment of Dehli said that before the breaking out of the mutiny they had leagued with the troops at Mirath and that the latter had corresponded with the troops in all other places so that from every cantonment troops would arrive at Dehli'.[1]

Then Hakim Ahsanullah Khan described the events of 11th May saying, 'On the morning of 16th Ramazan 11th May at about 7 o' clock A.M. a Hindu sepoy of the 38th Regiment of Native Infantry came up to the door of the Diwan-i Khass in the Palace and said to some of the door-keepers that happened to be on the spot that the native army at Mirath had mutinied against the State and were now on the point of entering Dehli; that he and the rest of them would no longer serve the Company but would fight for their faith. My house is in the Palace and close by the Diwan-i Khass; and I was immediately informed by one of the Musalman door-keepers of what the 38th sepoy had said. I had hardly received this information when the King of Dehli sent for me. I went to him immediately and the King said, 'Look, the cavalry are coming by the road of the Zer-jharoka (ground immediately under the lattices of the Palace). I looked and saw about 15 or 20 of the Company's Regular Cavalry, then about 150 yards distant. They were dressed most of them in uniform but a few had Hindustani clothes on. I immediately suggested to the King to have the gate fastened by which entrance to the Palace from the Zer-jharoka is obtained; and this had scarcely been done when 5 or 6 sawars came up to the closed gate which leads directly

[1] *Op. cit.*, p. 165.

under the Musamman Burj Palace where the King has his own private residence in close contiguity with the apartments of the queens and other secluded females of the establishment. The sawars commenced calling out, '*Dohai, Badshah*! (Help, O King!) we pray for assistance in our fight for the faith.' The King hearing this made no response, nor did he even show himself to the men beneath; but told Ghulam Abbas who was also present to go to Captain Douglas commandant of the Palace Guards and apprise him of the arrival of the sawars and request him to do whatever might be necessary in the case. The King then returned to his inner apartments and I went to the Diwan-i Khass and almost immediately Ghulam Abbas returned accompanied by Captain Douglas. The latter instantly went to the balcony overlooking the Zer-jharoka where the cavalry still remained and said to them, 'Go away from this place: this is the King's Palace; your presence here is an annoyance to the King'. On this the cavalry went off in the direction of the Rajghat Gate which gives an entrance to the city immediately to the south of the Palace. The King on hearing that Captain Douglas had come went out and met him in the open space between his private residence and the Diwan-i Khass when Captain Douglas said to him, 'Don't be alarmed, the disturbance shall be put down at once. I will have the men apprehended'. He was going off apparently for this purpose and requested that the gate under the Musamman Burj which I had closed might be opened to enable him to go and speak to the cavalry for the purpose of reasoning with them. The King said: 'You have neither pistols, nor guns, nor soldiery with you; your going among these men would be indiscreet'. So Captain Douglas went off to his own apartment. Shortly after Pran Jamadar, a servant of Captain Douglas, came and said that Captain Douglas wished that I and Ghulam Abbas would go to him. We accordingly went and Captain Douglas said to us, 'I have sprained my foot. There was another gentleman with him whom I did not recognize; he was lying down on a couch and had a sabre wound on his right arm. Captain Douglas said, 'Send two palanquins with bearers immediately that the English ladies here may be taken to the Queen and placed under her protection'. And just at this time Mr. Simon Fraser, the Commissioner, came into the room and said, "Get from the King two guns with artillery and place them at the gateway underneath us." On this Mr. Fraser came down from Captain Douglas' apartment above the gateway accompanied by myself and Ghulam Abbas. I and Ghulam Abbas went straight to the King to deliver the above message. With the King's permission we immediately sent the palanquins for the ladies and also gave instructions about the guns; but shortly after this, information reached us that the Cavalry had entered the Palace enclosure by the Lahore gate where Mr. Fraser wished the guns placed and over which Captain Douglas had his residence: it was also told us that they had killed Mr. Fraser and had gone up to Captain Douglas to kill him. This was instantly confirmed by the return of the *palki* bearers who told us that they had witnessed Mr. Fraser's murder, that his body was in the gateway and that the troopers had ascended the upper building for the purpose of murdering those who were there. The King on hearing this gave orders for all the gates of the Palace to be closed; but answer was given that the Infantry, *viz.* some of the 38th Native Infantry who were on guard at the Palace would not allow of such being done. After the lapse of some time the cavalry to the number of about 50 rode up to the Diwan-i Khass, dismounted and picketed their horses in the adjoining garden. The infantry—I am not sure of what regiments, but I think of all the three Dehli regiments—also came into the Palace enclosures and laid down their beddings in any of the Palace buildings that they could lay their hands on. The infantry from Mirath did not reach Dehli till about 2 p.m. of that day; they did not reach Dehli in a body but came straggling in; and as they arrived they joined the infantry of the Dehli regiments in spreading their beddings over all parts of the Palace enclosures. There was no regular Court that day; but the King came out some 3 or 4 times to the Diwan-i Khass where the mutineers were lying about all over the palace: and the rebel troopers came flocking into the Palace the whole day and even after the night had set in. The 54th came in the evening and went off at once to occupy the Salimgarh Fort where they, on the next day, fixed guns which they had brought out of the magazine for the purpose of checking any advance of the European troops from Mirath. For three days constant alarms, and specially at nights, were given that the Europeans were coming when the bugles sounded and mutineers got under arms'.[1] Hakim Ahsanullah Khan continued, 'The King was surprised to see that the troops had come to him. I also wondered at the circumstance because nothing had happened immediately before their arrival which might have led us to expect them though when the discussion about the cartridges first became known it was believed that it would cause some mischief. On the same day (11th May on which the troops arrived) I represented to the King that nothing good could be expected from them. And I addressed a letter to the Lieutenant-Governor of Agra on the part of the

[1] *Pr. Tr. B. S.*, p. 94.

King informing him of the arrival of the troops and representing the King's inability to take any measures against them and begging for help in the shape of European troops'.[1]

The evidence of Hakim Ahsanullah Khan being incomplete in many parts it is hereby completed by that of Ghulam Abbas the royal vakil who said, 'Before 10 o'clock Captain Douglas and all other European officers were killed. Immediately after this two companies of infantry which were on guard at the Palace gates followed by the rebel cavalry that had come from Mirath marched into the courtyard of the Diwan-i Khass and commenced firing their muskets, carbines and pistols in the air, at the same time making a great noise. The King hearing the noise came out; and standing at the door of the Diwan-i Khass told his immediate attendants to direct the troops to discontinue the noise they were making and to call the Indian officers forward that they might explain the object of such proceedings. On this, the noise was quelled and the officers of the cavalry came forward, mounted as they were and explained that they had been required to bite the cartridges the use of which deprives the Hindu and Musalmans of their religion as the cartridges were greased with beef and pork fat, that they killed the Europeans at Mirath and had come to claim his protection. The King replied, 'I did not call for you; you have acted very wickedly. However the troopers in large numbers came into the Diwan-i Khass and said, 'Unless you, the King, join us we are dead men and we must in that case just do what we can for ourselves.' The King then seated himself in a chair and the soldiery—officers and all—came forward one by one and bowed their heads

[1] *Idem,* p. 164.

before him, asking him to place his hand on them. The King did so. After a little while he went to his own apartments and the troopers picketing their horses in the courtyard took up their quarters and spread their bedding in the Diwan-i Khass and placed guards all about the Palace. After sunset I went home. On coming to the Palace next morning I learned that the guns the reports of which I had heard at 10 or 11 o'clock the night before, had been fired by the Dehli native battery as a salute to the King[3], I then came to the Diwan-i Khass where I met Hakim Ahsanullah whom I asked whether the King had decided on any measure to put down the disturbance. He told me that the King had despatched a letter on the subject by camel express to the Lieutenant-Governor at Agra; and about 15 days later I again asked him if any answer had been received. He said that the camel rider had returned without a receipt or reply but said he had delivered the letter and was told a reply would be sent afterwards[1]'. Zakaullah reproduces the Lieutenant-Governor's reaction to the said letter saying, 'On hearing the contents the Lieutenant-Governor remarked: "Himself he (Bahadur Shah) has become Badshah, and now he writes this to us[2]". It follows that the Lieutenant-Governor treated the letter in question as an ultimatum, else he would have immediately sent a grateful reply. Far from it, in the words of the author of the *Qaisaru-t Tawarikh* 'he sent the same letter of Bahadur Shah to the Ruling Chiefs of Rajasthan'[3]. It should also be noted that the above letter had been sent to Agra by Hakim Ahsanullah Khan in the afternoon of 11th May and

[1] *Pr. T. B. S.*, p. 28.

[2] Zakaullah—T. U. A. S. I., p. 660.

[3] Kamalu'ddin Haldar—*Qaisaru-t Tawarikh* or *Tarikh-i Awadh*, Vol. II, p. 439.

it was in the following night that Bahadur Shah accepted the mutineers' request.

In the course of his account of 11th May Zaheer Dehlawi writes, 'When crossing the Jumna the mutinous troops came to the Fort and stood underneath the Jharoka; the Emperor ordered Hakim Ahsanullah to enquire of them the particulars. 'We have decided', said they, 'that all of us should act unitedly on one specified day and time to raise the standard of rebellion. Your Majesty should place your hand on our heads and do justice.' 'Listen brethren!' replied Bahadur Shah, 'Who calls me "king"? I am a retired fakir. Why have you come here? I have neither a treasure nor an army. I can do only one thing for you. I can mediate between you and the English, the Resident is coming to see me, Let me hear from him the fact of the matter.'

Of all the above witnesses Mukand Lal and Hakim Ahsanullah Khan were the most important; and both gave a clear account in unequivocal terms of Bahadur Shah's hostility to the English and of his desperate efforts to secure allies in his war with the Company. Bahadur Shah was not an enemy of individual Englishmen and did his utmost to save Douglas and Fraser and other unarmed Europeans—men as well as women; but he was at war with the East India Company. His psychology of war and his ways and methods of war differed completely from those of the mutineers as is evident from his letters still extant[2]. He was not a simpleton as the British Government or some of the mutineers blinded by their mad fury and lust for indiscriminate bloodshed appear to have

[1] Zaheer Dehlawi—*Dastan-i Ghadr*, p. 50.

[2] *Pr. Tr. B. S.*, p. 134.

supposed.[1] He was the owner of a newspaper[2] and was in touch with the leading newspapers of Dehli and had diaries[3] written at the Court giving all kinds of events local as well as provincial and foreign. Undoubtedly he was alive to the situation and was fully aware of the mutineers' grievances against the British and shared the common belief that the death knell of British rule would be sounded shortly[4]. He was also aware, as Hakim Ahsanullah Khan hinted, of the sepoys' concerted efforts at raising a rebellion[5]. But he was not prepared for and certainly did not like the sudden arrival in Dehli of the mutineers from Mirath; therein he perceived a great blunder on their part. Obviously he stood at a vantage ground compared to the average sepoy and he realized that in striking the blow rashly at Mirath and then leaving behind the task of finishing the enemy incomplete, their coming over to Dehli was the greatest and most unpardonable blunder on the part of a handful of mutineers from Mirath. Malleson who was a contemporary, graphically describes what Bahadur Shah had, in fact, already realized or visualized[6]. He says, 'The story of the events of the

---

[1] Majumdar, R. C.—*Sepoy Mutiny and Revolt of 1857*, p. 116 ff. Book III, Chapter I.

[2] *Sirajul Akhbar.*

[3] (i) Pr. Tr. B. S., p. 93; (ii) *Khulasa Akhbar*, MS. N. A. I., No. 128; (iii) *Roz-namcha Bahadur Shah.*

[4] Pr. Tr. B. S., p. 164.

[5] *Ibid.*

[6] Detailed information to this effect is given by Pandit Kanhiya Lal in his book *Tarikh-i Baghawat-i Hînd,* also called *Maharaba-i Azeem,* Vol. II, pp. 7-8. See Chapter III, p. 104 *supra*.

It is a fact attested by all the historians that Mirath remained under British control throughout the period of war. In fact it formed the shelter of the Europeans—men and women—who were hunted down in Dehli; and there was a

10th May at Mirath and of the 11th at Dehli came as a surprise to the revolters all over India because the astute men who had fomented the ill-feeling against the British which by this time had become pretty general had laid down as a cardinal principle that there were to be no isolated outbreaks, that the explosion should take place on the same day all over the Bengal Presidency and they had fixed upon Sunday the 31st May as the day of the general rising. But the chief conspirators had to employ a large number of instruments. The rashness of premature action of a single instrument may destroy the best laid plot. The heads of the conspiracy had corrupted the 3rd Native cavalry and the 20th Regiment N. I.[1] and had formed their committees in these regiments. But at a critical conjuncture these latter had been unable to restrain the rank and file of the regiments from premature action. Excited to fever pitch, 85 men of 3rd L. C.[2] had with the sympathy of their comrades refused to receive the proffered cartridges. Brought to trial for the offence, they had been condemned, sentenced and lodged in jail. This sentence had been too great a stimulus to

---

constant danger on 11th May, 1857 of some European troops moving down from Mirath in pursuit of the mutineers. (Sewell—*Analytical History of India,* pp. 266-267). On 14th May Chunni Lal reported that four men coming from Mirath told the soldiery at Dehli that European troops were coming from Mirath in their pursuit (*Pr. Tr. B. S.,* p. 110). For some inexplicable reason these much-talked-about European troops of Mirath did not come down to Dehli till the close of May. According to Sewell (p. 267) when Anson the commander-designate died of cholera on 27th May, 1857, his place was taken by Sir Henry Barnard. Sir Henry Barnard was joined at Dehli by a body of troops from Mirath under Wilson on 7th June, 1857.

[1] *I.e.* Native Infantry.

[2] Light Company.

the passions of the troopers to allow them to await patiently the day fixed upon. They saw that the English were unsuspicious and they believed that the plot, so far as Mirath was concerned, might, by a prompt rising be brought to a successful issue. In that events proved them to be right. But they had lost sight of the fact that by acting solely for their own hand they were imperilling the great principle which had been impressed upon them by their committees and with it the general success aimed at by their chiefs. This premature action proved ultimately as fortunate for the English as disastrous to the cause of revolt. A blow which struck simultaneously all over India might have been irresistible lost more than half its power when delivered piecemeal and at intervals[1]'. At another place Malleson reports that 'Canning highly rejoiced to hear that the mutinous troops from Mirath had gone over to Dehli. He had great faith in the power of the Commander-in-chief to retake the imperial city. Past history affords good reason for that belief. In September 1803 the troops of Sindhia had not offered the semblance of a resistance to the small army of General Lake. In the wars of the earlier Mughuls with the representatives of the dynasties which they supplanted, Dehli had never offered any but the slightest resistance to the army which had been victorious in the field. Even the conviction prevalent at Calcutta, especially in military circles, was that the mutineers had played the British game by rushing into a walled city where they would be as rats in a trap'[2].

Bahadur Shah who knew all this confronted a formidable situation on the arrival of the mutineers from Mirath. He thought of reconciling the mutineers to the

---

[1] Malleson—*The Indian Mutiny of 1857*, pp. 87-88.

[2] *Op. cit.*, p. 92.

British Authorities and at the same time prepared himself for the worst by despatching the much-talked-about letter which amounted to an ultimatum to Agra.[1] Then he waited for the Dehli regiments to decide and determine their attitude; and it was subsequent to their joining the Mirath mutineers in the afternoon that he accepted the joint leadership of all at night.[2] That in spite of all the follies of the Mirath mutineers Bahadur Shah sympathised with them and 'cherished a hearty disposition to show them every favour and kindness and directed them to take up their quarters in Salimgarh[3] and called them 'his children'[4] speaks volumes for his patriotism, and balance of mind. Since he had fully realized the urgent need of restoring order he lost no time to impress upon the mutinous soldiery the importance of stopping at once all plunder and robbery in the city. But the mutineers who took full advantage of the Emperor's name and of the protection that he offered to them did not share with him the responsibility for restoration of order and maintenance of peace. Driven by their erratic fears and irrational suspicions verging on insanity they continued to smell an Englishman in every quarter and in every private house and dwelling which they on that plea looted unscrupulously. Says Chunni Lal, 'The cavalry and infantry hearing that some Europeans with their wives had gone into the Magazine brought 2 guns from Darya Ganj and loading them with stones fired them at the gates, the Europeans within returning the fire from several pieces with grape. Subsequently the

---

[1] *Vide* Chapter II, p. 81 *supra*.

[2] Tr. B. S., p. 105 and *Tr. of Ex-King of Delhi*, p. 220.

[3] *Op. cit.*, p. 108.

[4] *Idem*, p. 134.

Magazine blew up when several men of the city were killed and many of the houses in the neighbourhood destroyed. The European men and women who had been in the Magazine fled in the direction of the river. They were however pursued by the cavalry and killed. Three sergeants and two women were brought prisoners to the King. One of the sergeants begged the King's protection for himself and fellow-prisoners saying that otherwise they would be killed by the mutineers. The King had them placed in the Tasbeeh Khana. Then the infantry mutineers attacked the house of Salig Ram, the treasurer, but were unable to force its massive gates till midnight when they made an entrance and in conjunction with the Mahomedans of the city plundered the place of all the property it contained. Some sergeants were taking away two guns from the cantonments but the cavalry came up with them and brought the guns back. There was a salute of 21 guns fired under the Palace, and all night throughout the city the greatest uneasiness and tumult continued to prevail in consequence of the plunder, pillage and burning of houses'[1].

---

[1] *Idem*, pp. 108-109

CHAPTER VI

GRAPPLING WITH TERRIBLE PROBLEMS

(12th May 1857)

At least 350 out of about 10,000 Mutiny Papers in the National Archives dealing with the War of 1857 in Dehli and over 200 documents[1] given in the *Proceedings of the Trial of Bahadur Shah* bring into relief the terrible problems with which Emperor Bahadur Shah grappled from the beginning to the end of the long drawn-out drama of the War, every day bringing in

[1] These documents were studied and reviewed by Major Harriott, the Judge Advocate-General in connection with his survey of Emperor Bahadur Shah's role in the Mutiny and War of 1857. And he said, 'If I have not succeeded in tracing to the King himself a foreknowledge of the leading events that were to take place on Monday, the 11th May, I trust it has been made obvious that the secret was in possession of some influential inmates of the palace. The babbling garrulity of Prince Jawan Bakht sufficiently indicates this, for such is his joy at the anticipation of murdering the English that he is unable to restrain his expressions of it. My chief object has been to render clear what I believe to be the truth, *viz.*, that the conspiracy from the very commencement was not confined to the sepoys and did not even originate with them but had its ramifications throughout the palace and city. We have evidence that the mutineers of the 11th and 20th Regiments of Native Infantry before the Magazine was exploded, proceeded to attack and escalade it, and it is then for the first time that we find the King through his troops acting in open alliance with these traitors. From that moment there is no further disguise and no attempt at concealment. Fairly launched into the stream of sedition he is hurried onward by the swollen flood.' (*Pr. Tr. B. S.*, p. 145).

a fresh set of problems—control of the lawless elements in the city and among the mutineers[1], maintenance of

[1] Their numbers, according to different accounts, range from 4,000 (*Friend of India*, August 27, 1857) to 50,000 (Muir—R. I. D., 1, p. 535) and 60,000 (Metcalfe, T N N, pp. 179 and 181).

It should be noted that the terms 'mutineers', 'rebels' and 'traitors' were used by the British. Mirza Mughul was angry with Jiwan Lal for his using such terms as these (Metcalfe, T. N. N., 179). Mirza Mughul meant to say that the sepoys whom the British called mutineers and rebels became patriots on joining the standard of Emperor Bahadur Shah. And there is positive evidence that the Emperor looked upon them as patriots and wanted them to behave as patriots; and he rebuked them and expressed his displeasure and anger whenever he noticed that their conduct was unpatriotic. In one of his letters to Mirza Mughul he said, "It is the business of the Army to protect and not to desolate and plunder. The Officers of the Army will therefore immediately restrain their men from the commission of these improprieties; and further as the intelligence of the approach of the enemies was false, these lawless soldiery should not now be kept in the old Fort but on the contrary entrenchments should be constructed for them at the distance of 5 or 6 miles, and they should be stationed there so that OUR SUBJECTS MAY OBTAIN IMMUNITY from the hardships complained of, and that at the same time a barrier may be raised against the approach of the enemy troops. You will immediately take steps to arrange this matter and will allow no neglect to occur in reference to it. Be assured of our kindness". (In pencil in the King's handwriting, to give the order greater force: *Make arrangements quickly*. (*Pr. Tr., B. S.*, No. 8, 18th June, 1857, p. 8).

He also wrote the following letters :

(i) To

Mirza Mughul,

Son,—The illustrious and valiant Mirza Mughul Bahadur. Learn, that orders have day after day been issued to the Officers of the Cavalry to vacate the Garden and they have

the Army and shortage of supplies, restoration of

---

till now done nothing but make excuses and promises. Definite orders are therefore now issued to the intent that you, our Son, will summon the Officers and will tell them that *if they consider themselves the servants of the State* they will not go to the Batteries tomorrow, but will leave the Garden and remove their quarters to Keetur's (Englishman's) house situated under the Palace where there is abundance of accommodation and ample shelter of trees. What they urge in reply you will submit for our consideration. (No. 17, *Pr. Tr. B. S.*, dated 26th June, 1857, p. 9).

Order under the autograph cypher of the King in pencil, dated 27th June, 1857.

(ii) To

Mirza Mughul and Mirza Khair Sultan.

Sons,—The illustrious and valiant Mirza Zaheeru'ddin, otherwise Mirza Mughul Bahadur and Mirza Khair Sultan Bahadur. Learn, that your petition regarding the proceedings of four or five ill-conducted men, who assuming as a disguise, the appearance and dress of soldiers of the Native Infantry of the Company have gone about plundering the inhabitants of the City and have now left for the country, and representing the detriment to the Government which must ensue, in consequence, and further requesting permission to take measures for suppressing such practices and for capturing the men alluded to, has been perused. It is a matter of some surprise that from the lawless doings of but four or five men so much plunder and devastation in the City and so much ruination of the people generally should result; and that on their capture alone the establishment of order should be expected to depend; for not a day has elapsed since the arrival of the Army and its taking up quarters in the City that petitions from the townspeople have not been submitted representing the excesses committed by numerous Infantry Sepoys, about whom there could be no suspicion of disguise and that orders have not been issued, day after day, to you, our Sons, to take measures with the aid of a Military force to suppress these disorders. Considering all this, it seems now altogether unlikely that order can be secured while the Army remains in the City. How-

peace and order in the city and its protection against

ever, you, our Sons, are nevertheless directed to send to our glorious presence some one able to recognize the vagabonds alluded to, that he may be sent accompanied by horsemen and footmen of our own Royal Levies with a mandate to the Chief Police Officer of the city, and his subordinates to arrest and forward without delay to our presence those whom he may point out, and if any villainy or instigation to plunder shall be proved against those who may be thus apprehended they will receive punishments adequate to their guilt. But you, our Sons, are directed to take all proper steps to prevent the men of the Army from plundering and desolating the City. In every case of an offence of these kinds being proved or where a man may be found in the private residence of any of the inhabitants, the Officers will award punishment to the offender so that these evils may be suppressed. Be assured of our kindness. *Pr. Tr. B. S.*, No. 18, p. 9.

Autograph Order by the King, in pencil dated 4th July, 1857: Mirza Mughul Bahadur will lay strict injunctions on the Officers of the 9th Regiment Native Infantry, to refrain from the spoliation complained of. (*Pr. Tr. B. S.*, No. 24, p. 11).

Order of the King dated 16th July, 1857 in reference to the petition from Ratan Chand, Superintendent of the Royal Gardens.

(iii) To

Mirza Mughul,

Son,—The illustrious and valiant Mirza Zaheeru'ddin otherwise Mirza Mughul Bahadur! Learn,—that we are informed by a petition from Ratan Chand, Superintendent of the Sahibabad Garden . . . that the Troopers of the Cavalry, come from Jodhpur, have picqueted their horses in front of the shops and have taken possession of a number of them; that some of the shop-keepers have in consequence vacated their shops and gone away and those of the tenants who remain are ready to do the same. Under these circumstances loss to our personal Revenue must ensue. You, our son, are therefore directed to cause these Troopers to remove from their present location and to assign them some other

the British attacks; suppression of plunder and robbery; revival of the administrative system[1] includ-

place to stay in, so that this cause of loss to our Revenue may be checked. Be assured of our kindness. (*Pr. Tr. B. S.*, No. 29, p. 14).

Autograph order by the King, in pencil in answer to the petition of Sheo Diyal and Shadi Ram merchants, dated 17th July 1857.

Mirza Mughul will provide for the protection of the petitioners. (*Pr. Tr. B. S.*, No. 39, p. 15).

Order under the autograph special cypher of the King, in pencil, dated 17th July, 1857.

(iv) To
Mirza Mughul,

Son,—The illustrious and valiant Zaheeru'ddin otherwise Mirza Mughul Bahadur! Learn, that on perusal of the petition of Syed Husain Ali Khan, Police Officer of Pahar Ganj regarding the wounding of a Jamadar and some Policemen by the violent hands of the Goojars of Aliganj, Mallanji Hasangarh and Alapur, a special order was sent to you with the said petition in original. Today on perusal of a representation from the Police Officer of Mahrowli we learn that the same Goojars are now engaged in highway robbery and in plundering the country. The suppression of such disorders is of the utmost moment and, you are directed, therefore, immediately to send out one Company of Infantry and 50 Troopers to capture the Goojars in question with the Chief Men of their Villages. If they are captured they shall receive the punishment due to their misdeeds, and complete order will ensue. Be assured of our kindness. (*Pr. Tr. B. S.*, No. 31, p. 15).

[1] The old administrative institutions had not died out. Almost all were kept alive under the nominal rule of the East India Company. They began to function with the restoration of order on 12th May and the following days. Reference might here be made to the Civil, Military and Artillery departments, besides the Revenue and Pay departments mentioned in the Mutiny Papers, (Box 57, Nos. 539 and 541) and in documents 11, 41, 43, 47 of the *Proceedings of the Trial of Bahadur Shah.*

ing the civil, criminal and revenue courts and the machinery for the regular collection of revenues; recruitment of new soldiers; securing arms and gunpowder as well as funds to meet the salary bills of the Army and the Palace staff, maintenance of the Royal house in the midst of scarcity caused by the suspension of the *peshkash* and the prosecution of war in order to expel the English from the country. These problems were terrible enough to have scared away a sprightly and powerful despot. But Bahadur Shah the octogenarian was not frightened and did not slink away.

On 12th May, 1857 he took his seat on the Silver Throne in the Diwan-i Khass and held a durbar after it had been discontinued for the past 15 years[1]. The Army Officers presented nazrs and promised allegiance; then at their request high commands in the Army were given to the Princes[2]. This done, a feast was given under Royal orders to the whole Army who were supplied with confectionary, and the Army Officers received in addition a present in money. The Emperor then ordered the grocers Ram Sahai and Dilwani Mal to provide (at his expense[3]) for the Army

---

[1] The Silver Throne had been removed from the Diwan-i Khass into the vault below and had been lying there since 1842. It was brought back to the Diwan-i Khass on 12th May, 1857. See Chapter III, p. 90, *supra*.

[2] Mirza Mughul, who was the eldest and as it appears from the *Roz-namcha Bahadur Shah,* MS. N. L., about 40 years of age, was appointed Commander-in-chief. Mirza Kochak Sultan, Mirza Khair Sultan and Mirza Mendhu were appointed colonels of Infantry; and Mirza Abu Bakr, the youngest prince and a grandson of the Emperor, was appointed colonel of a regiment of cavalry. (Metcalfe—T. N. N., pp. 85-87. *Pr. Tr. B. S.,* pp. 30, 94).

[3] The bracket is mine. Until a satisfactory arrangement

500 rupees worth of meal, pulse and gram daily. And he appointed Muniru'ddin Khan, ex-thanadar of Pahar Ganj, Governor (*subadar*) and Kotwal of the city and charged him to prevent plunder. A few cases of plunder in the Churiwalan street being brought to his notice, the Emperor sent for the officers of the infantry regiments and directed them to place one regiment at the Dehli Gate, one under the Palace windows and one in Darya Ganj; and he said, 'I do not like that my subjects should be plundered'. When, shortly after, he heard of another case of plunder in the Nagar-Seth street he ordered Mirza Mughul to take a company of infantry and adopt measures so as to stop plunder completely in all parts of the city. Mirza Mughul went to the principal police stations seated on an elephant and had it proclaimed that every individual convicted of plunder would be punished with the loss of nose and ears and that the shopkeepers who did not open their shops and refused to supply necessaries of food to the Army, would be confined and imprisoned. Not content with this, later in the day the Emperor himself went in state mounted on an elephant with Prince Jawan Bakht in the hind seat through the Chandni Chowk street. The Royal procession was accompanied by two regiments of Telinga infantry and some guns; and the Telingas shouted '*Bahadur Shah ki jai*'[1]. The Emperor spoke to the shopkeepers kindly, promised them peace and order and directed them to open their shops and resume their business and supply the Army the necessaries of food. Afterwards letters were despatched to the rulers of Patiala,

---

was made, the Emperor considered the sepoys his guests and fed them. This is evident from the text of the documents.

[1] Zakaullah—T. U. A. S. I., p. 662.

Jhajjar, Ballabgarh, Bahadurgarh and Alwar asking them to come over to Dehli to join the 'patriotic' Army and 'to repel any attack upon the city by the English[1]'.

The above account presents before our eyes one of the most memorable scenes of the drama of the War in Dehli. An Indian Emperor highly popular among the Hindus and Musalmans has staked his life and the lives of all dear to him on the face of the earth by accepting leadership of the national or *quasi*-national Indian troops whom he calls *his own Army;* and in order to expel the English from the country he solicits help from the Indian Rajas and Ruling Chiefs. And without waiting for their reply he proceeds to grapple with the problems before him. He is seated on the throne of his great ancestors in full glory but without an atom of their powers. His position is like that of a constitutional monarch without a constitution, all physical powers having supposedly rested with the Army who are sorely lacking in discipline.[2] He wants to awaken in them the spirit of patriotism by building a liaison between them and the people; and he wants also to secure their co-operation in building a normal life in the city. With the help of some of their leaders and the highly accomplished Maulvi Fazl Haq[3] as the director, he improvises a system of administration and a constitution based on the principles of democracy. An executive committee or Administration Court of

[1] The above account is based on the Mutiny Papers Box 39, May 11, December 7, 1857 and the *Narrative* of Chunni Lal the news-writer and the evidence of Mukand Lal, Private Secretary of the Emperor. (*Pr. Tr. B. S.*, pp. 101-102, 107-114).

[2] This is evident from the numerous complaints made to the Emperor by the people. *Vide Pr. Tr. B. S.*, pp. 5-26.

[3] *Vide* (i) Appendix H (ii) For. Pol. Cons. 13th May 1859, N. A.

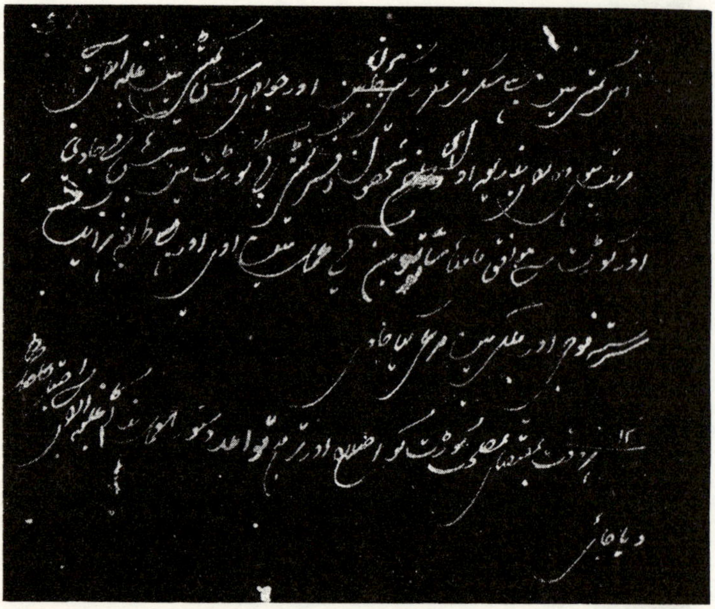

M.P., N.A.; Box 57, Nos. 539-541

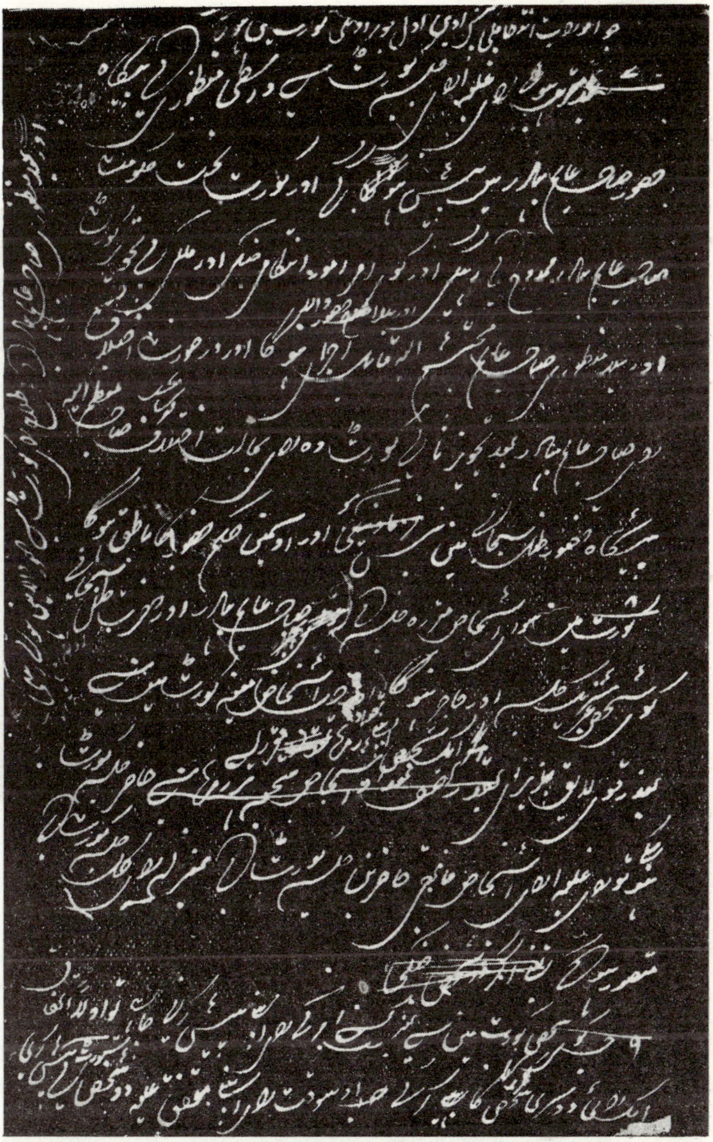

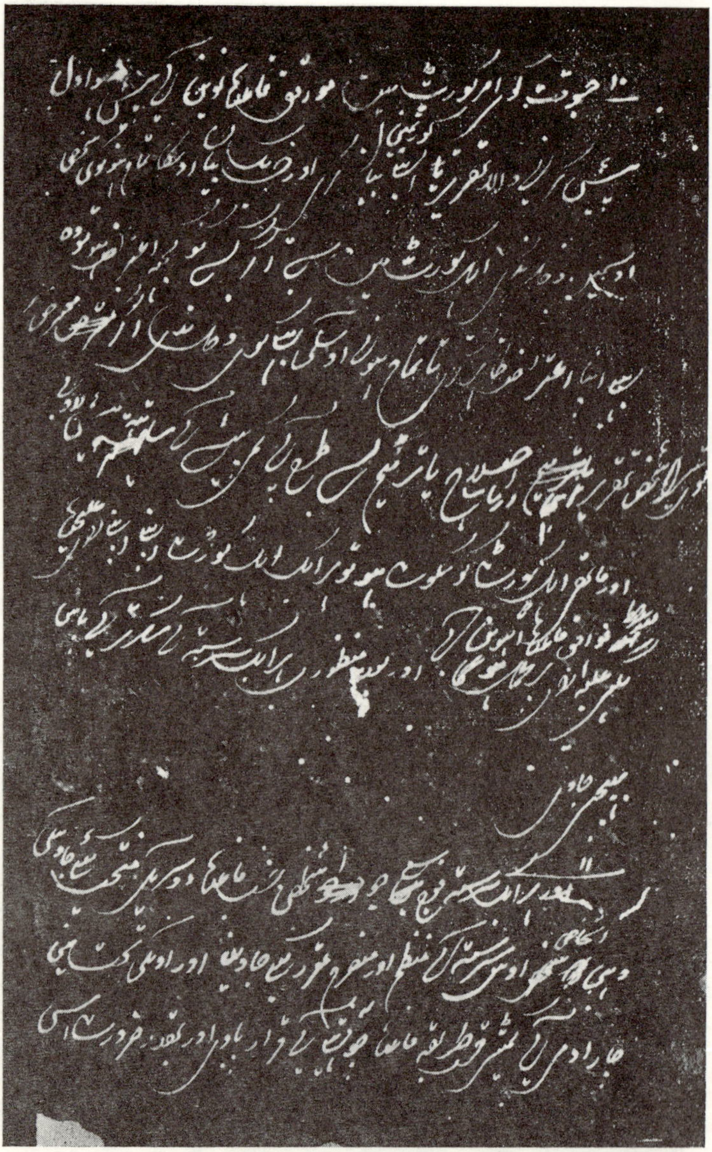

Facing Pages 183—187

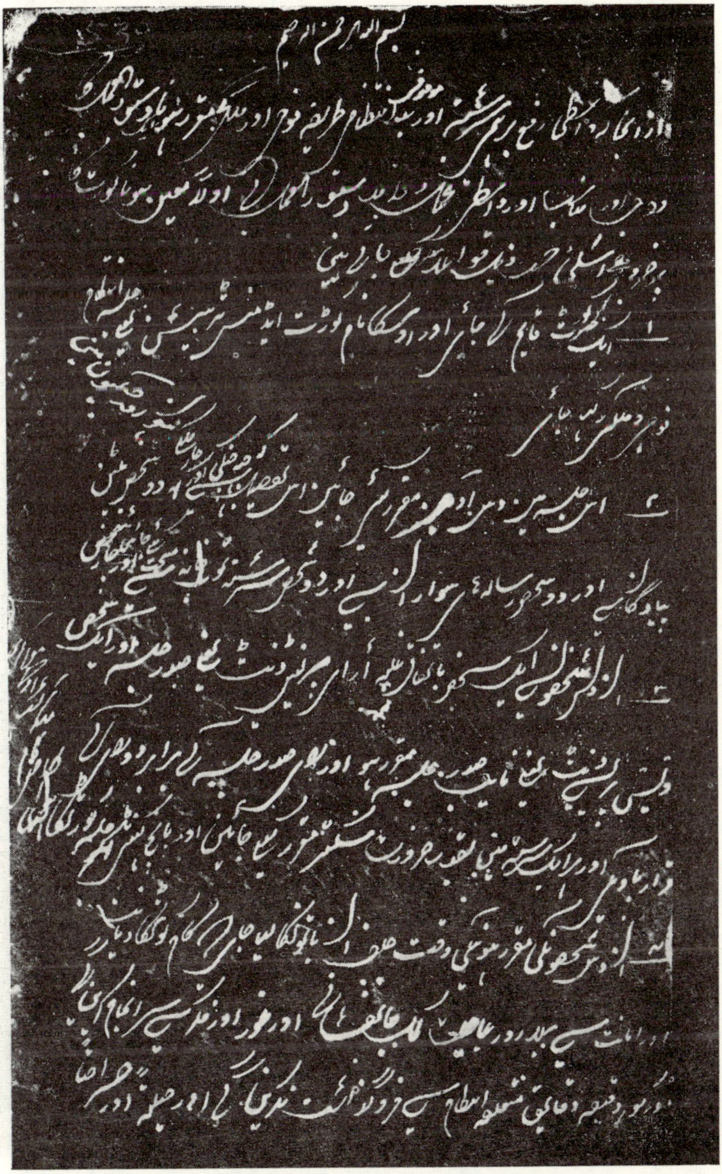

بسم الله الرحمن الرحیم

Administration Court also called *Ahl-i Shoora*
(*Sirajul Akhbar*)

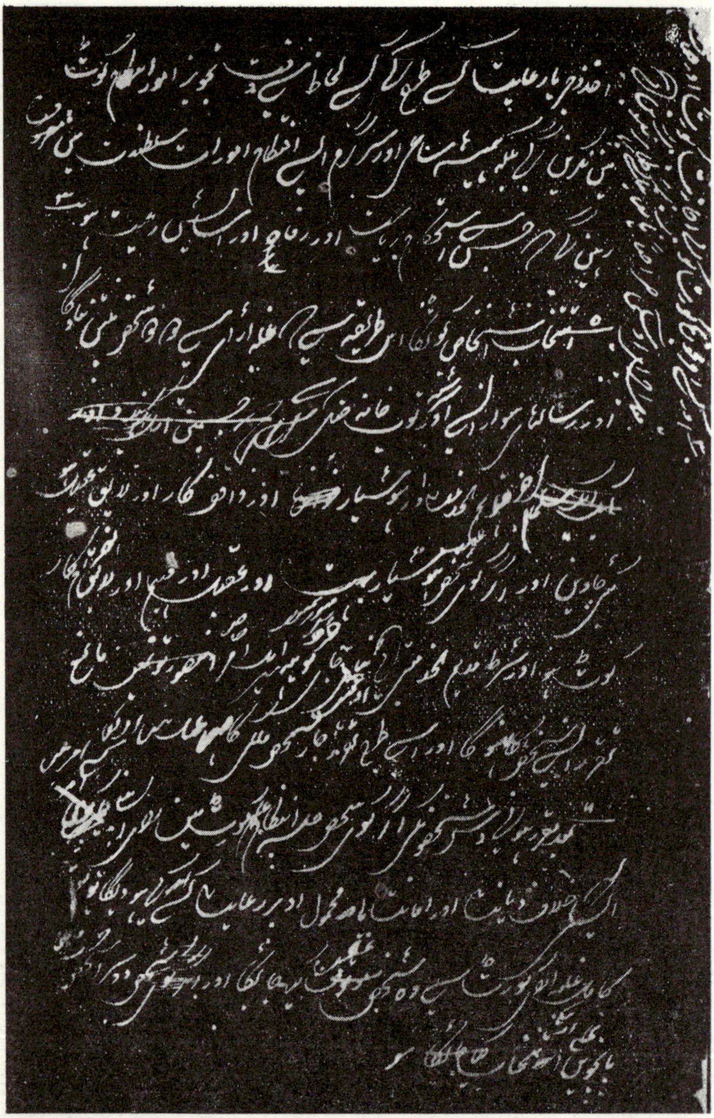

ten members from the civil and military department of government is formed; and it is laid down:

'Whereas to avoid disorder in the sections of administration of the military and civil departments it is absolutely necessary to form a constitution, and whereas to work out the constitution it is necessary first to appoint a Court[1] the following regulations are hereby laid down:

(i) A court should be established and named Administration Court, that is a Court to administer military and civil affairs.

(ii) This Court should consist of ten members—6 military and 4 civil. Of the military members two should be selected from the infantry platoons, two from the cavalry and two from the artillery.

(iii) Out of these ten men, one should be appointed President (*Sadr-i Jalsa*) and another Vice-President (*Naib Sadr-i Jalsa* by a unanimous majority of votes. In ever department there should be appointed secretaries according to need. The quorum for the Court meeting should be five whereby work should be done satisfactorily.

(iv) At the time of the appointment of these ten

[1] This Court has been called the Court of Mutineers. Spear (p. 206) puts its formation in the month of July. But it was surely a part of the Constitution (*Dastoor-ul Amal-i Saltanat*) which according to Zakaullah (T. U. A. S. I., p. 687), Maulvi Fazl Haq had drawn up for the government of Bahadur Shah.

Muinu'ddin says that the period between the 11th and 25th May was occupied in restoring order and discipline in the city—a task which could never have been performed without a constitution. *Cf.* Metcalfe—T.N.N., p. 61.

men they should take an oath that they would do court work with honesty, sincerity, great industry and with deep thought and care; and that they will not neglect even the slightest detail in matters administrative and that they would not covertly or overtly have resort to taking and seizing, or to partiality of any kind and in any manner or at the time of dealing with matters of administration in the Court. On the contrary they will always keep themselves engaged in and apply themselves attentively and diligently to executing the State matters whereby the State should obtain security and the people should enjoy peace and repose; and that they would not divulge any item of the Court work under consideration before its enforcement plainly or by allusion without the permission of the Court and *Sahib Alam*.

(v) Election of the Court members should be in this manner: by the majority of votes two men should be elected from the infantry platoon, two from the cavalry troops and two from the artillery; such men must possess a long record of service and must be clever and well-versed, able and intelligent. Should any person be highly clever, intelligent and learned and an adept in the administration of the Court work but lacking long service, this latter disqualification in that case will not obstruct the appointment of such a person. And in the same way will be appointed four civil members.

(vi) After ten members have been appointed, if any member gave his vote before the full

Court regarding any matter in such a manner as to be against honesty and sincerity or calculated as partial to anyone, then that member will be removed from the Court by the definite majority of votes; and another person will be elected in his place according to regulation *five*.

All the items of administration to be considered should be first treated in the Court and after the approval of *Sahib Alam* the decision of the Court should be communicated to His Majesty (*Huzur i Wala*)

(vii) After the programme has been drawn by the majority of votes it will be submitted for approval to *Sahib Alam Bahadur* and the Court will remain under the control of the alluded *Sahib Alam Bahadur*. And no matter of administration whether military or civil will be executed without the sanction of the Court and the approval of the *Sahib Alam* and without the information of the same being given to His Majesty (*Huzur-i Wala*). In the event of a difference of opinions and after being re-considered by the Court, the same matter—the difference still continuing—will be sent up through the *Sahib Alam* to His Majesty the Shadow of God (*Huzur Zille Subhani*). The order given thereupon by His Majesty (*Huzur*) will be final.

(viii) In the Court none, barring the *Sahib Alam Bahadur* and His Majesty the Shadow of God (*Huzur Zille Subhani*) who will be entitled to be present, no non-member will be present, nor will he join the meeting.

When out of the specified number of the Court

members, anyone for some valid and acceptable reason be unable to attend the court meeting, then the votes of the remaining members of the Court will be tantamount to the vote of the Court in full strength.

(ix) Should a member of the Court desire to express his opinion regarding any matter, he would first secure the consent of another member; then he may make the proposal of the same as a matter already agreed upon by two members.

(x) When an item is to be considered in the Court according to Regulation *nine,* then the proposer should first speak in the Court meeting. No one will interrupt his speech until he has finished it. If a member of the Court has any objection to make regarding it, he should explain it and no one will interrupt him either, until he has finished speaking. Should a third man make a speech amending or adding or subtracting from the objection, and if the remaining members of the Court observe silence regarding it, then every member of the Court should write out his opinion separately. After consulting Regulation *eight,* decision will be arrived at by the majority.

(xi) Those who from every section of the military are elected according to Regulation *two,* should be appointed managers and administrators of that section. Under their control should work a committee of 4 men according to Regulation *four* : in that committee secretaries should be appointed according to need. And whichever proposal is formally put up in that committee by the majority of votes that proposal will be presented to the Court by those very officers of that Committee. It should be executed by the Court according to Regulation *seven.* The same process should be adopted in every military and civil section.

(xii) At any time according to the demand of the occasion right should be vested in the Court to make amendments by majority of votes in this constitution[1].

Since the above document is undated and since it contains the ambiguous terms *'Court'* and *'Sahib Alam'*, it has been assumed[2] that it was created after the arrival of Bakht Khan. But the above-mentioned court was an *administration court,* not an ordinary court as the term 'court' was commonly understood among the soldiers in those days. Says the Emperor in the course of a letter dated 8th July 1857 to his son Mirza Mughul,

> Son! you the light of our eyes, already know that a very small balance of cash remains in our Treasury: that there is no immediate prospect of revenue from any quarter and that the little money that remains must of necessity be very soon expended. You are directed to call together during the day or to-night all the officers of the Regiments which first arrived, in order that they may deliberate and decide on means to be adopted for raising funds to meet the daily necessary and emergent expenses. *A meeting of this kind in the language of the Soldiery is called a 'Court*[3]*'.*

In the light of this information the assumption that the

---

[1] (i) Mutiny Papers, Box 57, Nos. 539-541.

(ii) Translated by the writer from the original Urdu text. *Vide* facsimile of the document facing p. 187.

[2] Spear—T. M., p. 206.

[3] *Pr. Tr. B. S.*, p. 40.

said Administration Court was created after the arrival of Bakht Khan falls to the ground and the nature of the court in question becomes intelligible as being a court of *administration* ruling and linking together all the branches of the administrative system like a modern cabinet and not merely a military council or a meeting of soldiers organised for the purpose of raising funds. As for the term *'Sahib Alam'*[1] it should be noted that there are some letters of the *mujahideen* wherein Mirza Mughul has been clearly addressed as *'Sahib Alam'*[2]. And there are many documents in the *Proceedings of the Trial of Bahadur Shah* which envisage a constitution much before the arrival of Bakht Khan and show that Mirza Mughul had been performing the role of a *Sahib Alam* without brandishing the title[3].

---

[1],[2] 'Muhammad Bakht Khan' says Spear, 'was nominated Governor-General (the title was Sahib Alam) and a Court known as the Administrative Court or Court of Mutineers was created after his arrival' (T. M., p. 206). But there is no connection between the terms 'Governor-General' and *'Sahib Alam'*. Bakht Khan was called 'General' or 'Lord Governor-General' but not *'Sahib Alam'* which was the title or honorific used for Mirza Mughul, as is seen in the letters addressed to him by the *Mujahideen* in fair number (Mutiny Papers, Box 65, No. 32, 37, 39). Since the *Mujahideen* had come to Dehli about the same time as did Bakht Khan (and many of them came in his company), they could not have used his title (if *'Sahib Alam'* had been his title) for his rival Mirza Mughul. Further Prof. Spear implies that General Bakht Khan created the Administration Court after his arrival in July. This is untenable, for Bakht Khan knew nothing about administrations or constitutions. It is true that he liked to maintain a constitution and to abide by law but he had no knack of making or drawing a constitution. This work Emperor Bahadur Shah and Maulvi Fazl Haq could do very well.

[3] For instance, documents No. 2 dated 14th May; No. 4

An undated document No. 15 arranged under the head of Loan exhibits the role that Mirza Mughul continued to play even after the arrival of Bakht Khan[1]. Similar is the case with the documents Nos. 19, 22, 23, 25, 27, 28 and 33 of 12th, 17th, 19th July and 1st, 2nd, 4th and 23rd August respectively arranged under the head of Military[2]. All kinds of petitions addressed to the Emperor including one from Bakht Khan himself were sent down by the Emperor with his own remarks to Mirza Mughul for disposal. Another document numbered 39, dated 9th September, brings into relief the position of Mirza Mughul as officer in charge of the commissariat arrangements and the distribution of pay to the troops, and depicts him as the 'vicar' of the Emperor[3]. And a document No. 35 of 23rd August gives a 'petition' of Bakht Khan addressed to Mirza Mughul, Commander-in-chief Bahadur; it runs as follows :

---

dated 24th May; No. 13 dated 18th June; No. 15 dated 20th June; No. 17 dated 26th June; Nos. 24 and 25 dated 4th July; No. 26 dated 11th July; Nos. 29, 30, 31 and 32 undated; No. 33 of 18th July; No. 36 of 22nd July; No. 38 of 24th July; No. 40 of 25th July; No. 43 of 30th July; No. 48 of 18th August and the undated documents numbered 50, 52, 53 and 54 (*Pr. Tr. B. S.*, pp. 4-40). Also see documents numbered 1, 4, 5, 8, 10 and 13 dated 8th July, 15th July, 28th July, 29th July, 6th August, and 27th August respectively arranged under the head of Loan (*Pr. Tr. B. S.*, pp. 41-47). *Vide* document No. 1 dated 1st June 1857; No. 2 dated 22nd June; No. 3 dated 9th July; No. 4 dated 10th July; No. 5 dated 12th July; No. 6 dated 13th July and the undated documents numbered 7 and 8, arranged under the head of Pay (*Pr. Tr. B. S.*, pp. 50-51).

[1] *Idem*, p. 46.

[2] *Idem*, pp. 57, 58, 59, 60, 62.

[3] *Idem*, p. 64.

Petition from Muhammad Bakht Khan dated 23rd August 1857

To

Mirza Moghal—the Lord of Gifts, etc., Mirza Muhammad Zaheeru'ddin, Commander-in-chief Sahib Bahadur.

'The order directing me to send one officer from each corps of infantry, Cavalry, etc., to meet as members of the Court arranged by Your Highness's wish has been received. I sent for the Commissioned Officers in question, and explained to them the necessity for their attendance at your Court at 10 A.M. to-morrow. They have all willingly and heartily agreed to attend, as they have been directed. They urge, however, that their baggage has just now been laden; but that after reaching Palam, they will return, and will with hearty pleasure attend the Court in question. This petition is submitted for your information. Petition of the slave Muhammad Bakht Khan, Lord Governor-General, attested with the seal of Muhammad Bakht Khan, Commander-in-chief of the Army'.

Note on the face—'The purpose of the petition has been learned'.[1]

In this 'petition' Bakht Khan has addressed Mirza Mughul as Commander-in-chief and has subscribed himself as Commander-in-chief and Lord Governor-General, but not as *Sahib Alam.*

All these documents combine to show that a constitution (*Dastur-ul Amal-i Saltanat*) had been enforced much before the arrival of Bakht Khan and that Mirza Mughul had been acting as *de facto Sahib Alam.* And the elements of that constitution are traceable in the administration that obtained during the months of May and June 1857. Probably after the arrival of Bakht Khan in July some amendments were made since meetings of the Court became frequent and regular. Or as the *Delhi News* suggests the old Administration Court became unpopular and the Army formed an independent Court consisting of the delegates

---

[1] *Pr. Tr. B. S.*, p. 63.

from every company and every troop in Dehli[1]. But the branches, if any, shot up as time advanced from the parent body namely the War-State mechanism the Emperor had set to work in the middle of May with a vast secretariat in the Red Fort and sub-offices in the city. Thanas[2] were established in different parts of the city, and so were the revenue,[3] civil and criminal courts of justice[4] as well as the Court of General Supervision[5] and even hospitals[6] and news-papers.[7] Every thana was daily inspected[8] and reports were sent regularly through proper channels to the Royal Court. Price lists[9] giving standard prices fixed by a tariff board passed through different thanas, and were then sent out for circulation in the city at stated intervals. As a result profiteering was stopped. Jiwan Lal gives only one example of a defaulter, saying: 'The shop of Jamna Das was

[1] *Delhi News*— 9th September, 1857.

[2] Mutiny Papers, N. A., Box 157, No. 2, June 16, 1857; 158, No. 2, June 1, 1857.

[3] *Idem,* Box 189, No. 6, 28th June, 1857; Box 171, August 19, 1857.

[4] *Idem,* Box 69, No. 41, 22nd July, 1857.

[5] *Idem,* Box 69, No. 1.

[6] *Idem,* Box 137, No. 7, also No. 8 dated 14th July 1857 which contains a statement of the daily allowances and wages of the employees in the Hospital.

[7] *Pr. Tr. B. S.,* p. 9. Order under the King's Seal dated 29th June, 1857.

[8] There is a document of 13th June 1857 stating that the thanas in the city were inspected and a report made about the diary of each thana. *Vide* Mutiny Papers, N.A. Box 61, Nos. 16-17. Also see (i) Box 194, Nos. 13-14 of 23rd and 31st July, 1857; (ii) Box 135, Nos. 149-153 which give daily reports of the Thanas of the Turkoman gate, as well as of those of Guzar Dareeba and of other quarters of the city.

[9] *Idem,* Box 131, No. 71, August 6, 1857; No. 83, August 11; No. 90, August 14; No. 95, August 15, 1857 and Box 131, No. 126, 12th September, 1857.

plundered because he sold *atta* at a high price'[1]. All matters, great and small, were recorded in the registers of the different offices, for instance the death of a gunner,[2] the burial of a dead body[3] of a *mujahid,* remittance to a camel driver of Re. 1 in advance[4]; the payment of wages to the coolies, each coolie being paid 10 annas[5]; the theft of a sepoy's gold bangle[6]; a list of the water-suppliers sent to the various trenches from the Kotwali[7] and a list containing the names[8] of all the Hindus and Musalmans in the Emperor's service besides a list of the Army officers who took part in the Mutiny as well as the names[9] of all the functionaries at the Kotwali and different thanas and an alphabetical list of all the mutineers[10] with their parentage, caste and residence. There are also files of all kinds of petitions received at the Royal Court as well as of the official communications and circulars under the name *parwana.* Gauri Shankar, Brigadier-Major, sent to the office of Diwan Jwala Nath three parwanas asking him to approve and return the same.[11] A separate court

[1] Metcalfe—T. N. N., p. 121.

[2], [3] *Idem,* Box 65 Nos. 16-18, 2nd August, 1857 and Box 135, No. 158, August 31, 1857 and No. 202, 2nd September, 1857.

[4] *Idem,* Box 135, No. 9, 3rd June, 1857.

[5] *Idem,* Box 131, No. 101, August 22 1857.

[6] *Idem,* Box 131, No. 41, 5th July, 1857.

[7] *Idem,* Box 194, No. 9 12th July, 1857.

[8] Mutiny Papers, N. A., Miscellaneous Box 28. Altogether there are 633 names, the majority of which are Hindus.

[9] *Idem,* File N. 117.

[10] *Idem.* There is a big chart of 43 lines, each line with an average of 18 names, containing in all, about 800 names. The Hindus form the majority.

[11] Mutiny Papers, N. A.—Box 135, No. 202, 2nd September, 1857.

facing p. 193

MIRZA MUGHUL

with a secretariat functioned under Mirza Mughul subject to the Emperor's orders which were issued frequently on sundry topics.[1] Mirza Mughul also wrote letters[2] to his Royal father with filial feeling and affection, and received immediate replies[3] containing directives for war and advice in all matters concerned. In his capacity as commander-in-chief Mirza Mughul worked as a liaison officer between the civil and military departments and formed a link between the brigadiers, colonels, artillerymen, warriors and police officers on the one hand and the amirs, mahajans, merchants and local chiefs on the other. He was a very busy officer[4] under whose care functioned the aforesaid Administration Court. Under his personal supervision there was also a ceaseless flow of official correspondence—missives, directives, parwanas, financial and technical reports and credit-letters and receipts. And he kept the Emperor informed about every detail.[5] Almost in the same way the functionaries of lower grades and even ordinary men[6] wrote letters to the Emperor, each in his individual capacity, and occasionally made some suggestions, which the latter acknowledged. Particularly worthy of mention here is the order issued from the Court of Justice to the Chief Police Officer of the city

[1] *Pr. Tr. B. S.*, pp. 8-9, order under the autograph cypher of the King in pencil, dated 20th June, 1857.

[2] and [3] *Idem*, p. 13, Nos. 23 and 27. Petition of Mirza Mughul, dated 11th July, 1857.

[4], [5] Mutiny Papers, N. A., Box 131, No. 126, September 12, 1857.

[6] (i) Petition of Mathra Das and Salig Ram, *Pr. Tr. B. S.*, p. 15, August 23, 1857.

(ii) Petition of Gauri Shankar Shukul. *Idem*, No. 3, p. 52.

(iii) Petition of Nabi Bakhsh, No. 14, p. 46.

giving instructions as to the procedure to be followed in submitting cases, besides a similar document illustrating the functioning of the Civil Court. There is yet another document with interesting references to the letters written by Bhao Singh Naib Kotwal to (i) Col. Khizr Sultan[1], (ii) the thanadars of the different Police Stations, (iii) Lala Gulab Rai and Mehr Chand, mahajans[2], (iv) Hakim Ahsanullah Khan and Faizullah Khan Kotwal[3], (vi) Jamadar Shihabu'ddin[4], (vii) Bakhshi Mirza Fazil Beg and even to the Emperor[5]. Another document gives contents of the papers sent by Khwaja Khairiyat Ali, an accountant of the Commander-in-Chief's office, to Col. Khizr Sultan announcing the programme of the Commander-in-Chief's tours and that he was at the moment in the trenches with his army[6].

These documents impressed Sir John Lawrence who observed, 'The papers referring to the *system of the King's government* exhibit in a remarkable manner the active personal share which the king himself took in the conduct of affairs. . . . it must be admitted that his orders were not unworthy of the situation. He did make an effort to preserve order in the city, to repress rapine and murder in the villages, to check malversation and to restrain the excesses of the soldiery'.[7]

---

[1], [2], [3], [4] and [5] Mutiny Papers, N. A., Box 131; Nos. 1, 5, 14, 25, 30, 33, 34, 39-40, dated May 8 to September 12. 1857.

[6] Mutiny Papers N. A., Box 135, No. 216, September 8, 1857.

[7] *Press-List of the Mutiny Papers*, pp. ii-iii.
Also see Chapter I, p. 66, *supra*.

Chapter VII

FIGHTING TO EXPEL THE ENGLISH

(13th May—1st July 1857)

Almost all the problems with which Emperor Bahadur Shah was grappling were interconnected, one depending upon the other for its solution. But the problem to expel the English headed them all and was the all-embracing one. Shortly after accepting the leadership of the sepoys on 12th May, he had sent letters to the Indian Princes asking them to join him in the war.[1] When he obtained no response and came to know that the Chiefs of Patiala[2] and Jind[3] and other Indian Princes[4]

[1] *Vide* pp. 181-182, *supra*.

[2] According to Jiwan Lal the Maharaja of Patiala had joined the English with his army; and the mutinous sepoys coming from Ambala were attacked by the Patiala troops. Their weapons were taken from them and men despoiled (Metcalfe T. N. N. p. 97). Then Jiwan Lal says: 'About 200 men arrived from Lahore and Firozpur to join the mutineers. They came unarmed and many wounded. They were full of complaints that they had been attacked by the Maharaja of Patiala when they were sitting unarmed and unclothed on the ground and had fled' (*Idem*, p. 105). In his entry of May 21, Jiwan Lal also says that the Maharaja of Patiala had tried to gain over to his cause two regiments of he Purbias who had promised to extinguish the fire of mutiny among their relatives serving in the regiments which had mutinied at Meerut' (*Idem*, p. 99).

[3] 'A carter reported,' says Jiwan Lal, 'that the forces of the Maharaja of Patiala and of the Raja of Jind, and the English were to be seen between Ambala and Delhi; also that heavy artillery was seen on the road drawn by elephants' (Metcalfe—T. N. N., p. 114).

[4] 'News was received that both Jaipur and Patiala were

were actively helping the English, he concentrated on the defence of Dehli and the territory directly under his rule[1]; this too could not remain safe from the enemies unless they were completely driven out of Mirath. The Emperor lost no time in urging his Army to make an attack and expel the English from that city.[2] But the Army was sorely lacking in discipline and allegiance. 'The King' says Muinu'ddin Hasan, 'repeatedly urged an attack upon Meerut but the mutineers delayed, first on one pretext, then upon another'[3]. The Emperor thought he could not make them march without supplying the sinews of war[4], without removing the disorders from the city and without freeing it completely from pillage and plunder. To this end he now turned his thoughts and energies; and the success he attained was noticed by Muinu'ddin Hasan who observed, 'The period between 11th and 25th May was occupied in restoring order and discipline in the city'[5]. Similar is the information given by the Dehli newspapers—*Sirajul Akhbar*[6], *Dehli Urdu*

---

taking precautions to prevent the mutineers from remaining in their territories. (*Idem*, p. 99).

[1] The territory directly under Bahadur Shah's rule besides Dehli proper extended to Rohtak in the north-west, Riwari to the south-west, Mathura and Palwal to the south and Ghaziabad to the east.

[2], [3] (i) Metcalfe—T. N. N., 61. (ii) *Dehli Urdu Akhbar*, May 31, 1857; p. 4. Mutiny Papers. Collection No. 2, Vol. 19; No. 22.

[4] A few sepoys coming from Firozpur and Ambala expressed their readiness and desire to go to Mirath provided they were given the sinews of war—arms and provisions (*rasad*). (*Dehli Urdu Akhbar*, May 31, 1857, p. 3).

[5] Metcalfe—T. N. N., p. 61.

[6] Mutiny Papers, Box No. 1, Vol. 13, No. 24.

Akhbar[1], *Zafar Akhbar*[2] and the *Sadiqul Akhbar*[3] which continued their publications throughout the period of war, thus testifying to the order and discipline in the city and territory of Dehli. The *Sirajul Akhbar* mentions pointedly how the *Emperor*[4] charged Mirza Mughul and others to maintain peace and order. According to almost all contemporary evidence the Emperor remained extremely busy all these days (11th—25th May) with sundry affairs but he was ceaselessly intent on creating favourable circumstances and conditions which might enable him to send the Army towards Mirath to expel the English[5]. Viewed from this standpoint all the details of the Royal

---

[1] *Idem*, Box No. 4-6, Vol. 4, No. 6.

[2] *Idem*, Box No. 2, Vol. 19, No. 34.

[3] *Idem*, Box No. 2, Vol. 19, No. 27.

[4] Emperor or *Huzur-i wala* (Mutiny Papers, Box 57, No. 539-541) is one among many other forms of address used for Bahadur Shah, for example *Shanshah-i Hind* or Emperor of India; (*Vide Sadiqul Akhbar* p. 4; July 27, 1857, Box 4-6, Vol 4); *Zille Subhani* (Shadow of God); *Khalifatur Rahmani* (Caliph of God); *Farogh-i Khandan-i Aalishan-i Gorgani* (the height of the exalted dynasty of Timur), *Chiragh-i Dudman-i najdat nishan-i Sahibqirani* (the light of the Family of the Lord of Times whose emblem is valour). *Vide Dehli Urdu Akhbar*, May 31, 1857. Deliberately ignoring all this the British writers have used for Bahadur Shah the term 'King'. I have used the term Emperor as found in the *Sadiqul Akhbar* mentioned above.

[5] The *Dehli Urdu Akhbar* of 21st June, 1857, reproduces an authentic letter of an earlier date which stresses the great need of an attack on Mirath to expel the English. It says, 'In Mirath there are only 300 white soldiers. If the victorious troops march on Mirath they will be readily supported by the inhabitants of Mirath who are waiting for them to come'. (*Dehli Urdu Akhbar*, Box 2, Vol. 19; No. 25, June 21, 1857). The same suggestion is also reported in another issue of the *Dehli Urdu Akhbar* (Box 2, Vol. 19; No. 28, July 12, 1857).

activities and day-to-day programmes which appear bewildering and incongruous at first sight, become intelligible. On 13th May the Emperor called Mirza Muniru'ddin governor and kotwal of the city to account for his failure to procure necessaries of food for the Army and ordered him to make immediate arrangements. Later, on hearing a report of the outbreak of disorder and pillage in the Cantonment, Sabzi Mandi and Pahar Ganj areas, he ordered him to proceed with the 38 Regiment N.I. in that direction to prevent plunder and restore order. And he personally attended to the needs of the Army and awarded all the regiments Rs. 400 each; and summoning the grain dealers he ordered them to regulate the rates and open their granaries and commence selling the grain in the market. In order to protect the grain dealers and grocers he appointed 200 sepoys with headquarters in Darya Ganj and they were told off to different streets in the city to look after the maintenance of law and order. Then the Princes—Mirza Mughul, Mirza Khair Sultan and a few others—were ordered to proceed severally with two guns each to the Kashmiri, Lahori and Dehli gates to preserve peace[1]. A wazir, Hamid Ali Khan by name, being accused by the sepoys of concealing some Englishmen in his house, the Emperor had the vezir's house searched, but no Englishman was found. Hamid Ali Khan who had been imprisoned and whose property had been looted on this account was released, and the property restored. It was then proclaimed under Royal orders that those in whose houses Europeans were found would be dealt with as

[1] *Vide* copies of the Newspapers written by Chunni Lal, news-writer from 11th to 20th May, 1857 (*Pr. Tr. B. S.*, pp. 107-112).

offenders. In connection with the Emperor's attempts to restore law and order it is also mentioned that two watermen who had stolen some butter from a shop in the Lal Kuan street were arrested; and two notorious characters Gami Khan and Sarfaraz Khan besides a few men accused of plunder in the Teliwara and Sabzimandi zone were apprehended. An attempt was also made by the Emperor to raise an army in the hope of finding the new recruits comparatively more submissive and ready to carry out his orders and march against the English at Mirath[1]. According to Chunni Lal it was proclaimed by the Kotwal that all such persons who wished to take service should come forward bringing their own arms[2].

On 14th May the Emperor appointed Maulvi Sadru'ddin Khan judge of the Civil and Criminal Courts. 'And an order was written' says Chunni Lal, 'to the address of Raja Ram Singh, Ruler of Jaipur, directing his early attendance at the Royal Court together with his army; and orders were also issued in writing to Nawab Abdur Rahman Khan of Jhajjar, Bahadur Jang Khan of Dadri, Akbar Ali Khan of

[1] In his entry of 18th May Chunni Lal tells us that orders were issued to Hasan Ali Khan of Jhajjar to raise troops, cavalry and infantry (Pr. Tr. B. S. p. 113). And the reason for this new recruitment is also found in a remark of Jiwan Lal. Referring to the kind of bravery shown by many of the mutineers, Jiwan Lal says, 'In the absence of the English they were as lions, but on hearing of their (English) approach they sought places of refuge like rats in the presence of a cat' (Metcalfe—T. N. N., p. 102). And the *Dehli Urdu Akhbar* reports that some of the mutineers had become extremely rich and it gives details to illustrate how they were trying still to increase their wealth (Mutiny Papers, Collection No. 2, Vol. 19; No. 22; May 31, 1857).

[2] *Pr. Tr. B. S.*, p. 111.

Patowdi, Raja Nahar Singh of Ballabgarh, Hasan Ali Khan of Dojana and Nawab Ahmad Ali Khan of Farrukhnagar, desiring them all to attend the Royal Court[1]. Subsequently news being received that the Gujars of Chandrawal—the allies of the British—were every night plundering the shops in Sabzimandi, Teliwara and Rajpur, Mirza Abu Bakr was ordered to pursue the said Gujars. Mirza Abu Bakr went immediately to Chandrawal and laid it waste but the culprits had made their escape. The following day *i.e.* 15th May a *shuqqa* was again sent to the Raja of Jaipur soliciting his attendance at the Royal Court; similarly *shuqqas* were also sent to the chiefs of Jhajjar and Ballabgarh. Then arrangements were made for bringing money from the Rohtak treasury as well as for the enlistment of 400 foot-soldiers and one regiment of cavalry at the rate of a monthly salary of Rs. 5 for the foot-soldier and Rs. 20 for each trooper. Then Mirza Muniru'ddin, the kotwal and governor of the city who had never given satisfaction by his work and who was in fact a British spy[2], was dismissed; he was superseded as kotwal by one Qazi Faizullah Khan and the post of governor of the city was abolished. The same day when it was reported that the sepoys were in the habit of patrolling the streets and lanes with drawn swords which frightened the inhabitants and shopkeepers, the Emperor ordered that no one should go about the city with a drawn sword. And with a view to further control the soldiery he ordered the commandant of the Jhajjar cavalry to take up his quarters in the Mahtab Bagh. Then news having reached him about the arrival of

[1] *Ibid.*

[2] Metcalfe—T. N. N., pp. 27-31.

14 boats laden with edibles belonging to Ramjidas Gurwala, the Emperor ordered Dilwani Mall who had been previously appointed to arrange for the supplies, to have the cargo of the said boats landed and to bring it along'.[1]

In pursuit of his efforts to expel the English beyond the eastern bank of the Jumna and to deprive them of their allies the Gujars, the Emperor sent an order on 16th May to Walidad Khan of Malagarh,[2] drawing his attention to the 'anarchy that prevailed on the eastern side of the Jumna' and charged him to suppress it. Then he considered a petition of the shopkeepers of the Lahori gate to the effect that Kashi Nath, the thanadar of their locality demanded a bribe of Rs. 1,000, else, he said, he would send them as prisoners to the Kotwali. Qazi Faizullah was directed to place the said Thanadar under arrest.[3]

On 17th May in an attempt to rouse the sepoys to fight the English before it was too late, the Emperor went to inspect the fortifications of Salimgarh and assured the soldiers that he was associated with them in a common cause. Then he arranged for the recruitment of new troops, and looked into the administration of villages. In the words of Chunni Lal, 'the landholders of the Nadholi having attended, the Emperor told them to keep up a proper management in Nadholi, failing which they would be expatriated'[4].

Some time back the Emperor had sent two messengers to bring news about the English position in Mirath. Now they returned from Mirath and reported that about 1000 European soldiers with some English-

---

[1] *Pr. Tr. B. S.*, pp. 111 ff.

[2] District Bulandshahr, I. G. IX. p. 50.

[3] *Ibid.*

[4] *Ibid.*

men, women and children were collected there in the Sadr Bazar and had erected fortifications on the Suraj Kund on which they had mounted guns, drawn by elephants. They further represented that the Gujars were committing highway robberies all along the road from Mirath to Salimpur and had maltreated them too[1]. On hearing this the Emperor was so disconcerted that he thought of making a fresh attempt at securing the co-operation of the Indian Princes and with their help to organize an assault on the English at Mirath. In the words of Chunni Lal, 'several missives were written and despatched by two, three or four troopers each, directing early and immediate attendance, to Maharaja Narendra Singh of Patiala, Raja Ram Singh of Jaipur, the Raja of Alwar, and the Rajas of Jodhpur, Kotah, Bundi, etc'[2]. At the same time the Emperor charged Hasan Ali Khan of Dojana to raise new troops, cavalry and infantry[3]. And he also made an attempt to raise funds. A list of the leading merchants of the city was prepared and they were required to provide collectively 5 lakhs of rupees to meet the daily expenses of the troops, amounting to 2,500 rupees'[4]. He achieved no success. But he did not lose heart. He ordered Mirza Mughul to proceed with a strong force towards Mirath to attack any English force assembled there[5], and had also two companies of infantry stationed at the Jumna bridge[6]. But Mirza Mughul was not a warrior. Although the Emperor had placed at his disposal 4 guns and 4 regi-

[1] *Pr. Tr. B. S.*, pp. 112-13.

[2] *Idem*, p. 113.

[3] *Ibid.*

[4] *Ibid.*

[5] Metcalfe—T. N. N., p. 99.

[6] *Pr. Tr. B. S.*, p. 113.

ments of infantry and cavalry and charged him positively 'to blow up the British entrenchments at Mirath , he hesitated and requested that Mirza Aminu'ddin Khan, Mirza Ziyau'ddin Khan and Hasan Ali Khan, and other great chiefs holding extensive territories might be sent with him; in that case he promised to exterminate the English[1]. When these amirs who were present made no response and remained silent, the Emperor ordered his grandson Mirza Abu Bakr who was a raw youth in his teens to start with the force[2]. Mirza Abu Bakr obeyed and prepared himself to conduct the expedition. The Emperor ordered Mahbub Ali Khan and Hakim Ahsanullah Khan to provide funds for it[3].

Muinu'ddin Hasan tells us the story of Mirza Abu Bakr's expedition saying, 'At last under pressure from the King, Mirza Abu Bakr as commander-in-chief started with a force on the 25th of May to attack the English at the Hindan River. The force consisted of Cavalry and of Field and Horse Artillery. The battle began with artillery fire. The Commander-in-chief mounted on to the roof of a house near the River Hindan close to a bridge across the river and watched the battle. From time to time he sent messages to his artillery to tell them of the havoc their fire was creating in the English ranks. Near the bridge he placed a battery which carried on an exchange of fire with the English which became like a conversation of question and answer. Presently a shell burst near the battery, covering the gunner with dust. The Commander-in-chief, experiencing for the first time in his life the effects of a bursting shell, hastily descended

[1] *Idem*, p. 114.
[2] *Ibid.*
[3] *Ibid.*

from the roof of the house, mounted his horse, and galloped off with his escort of sowars far into the rear of the position, not heeding the cries of his troops. A general stampede then took place[1]'.

From the spies' reports it appears that in the course of five days (24th to 29th May, 1857) the Badshahi troops who had been sent across the Hindan to make an attack on the 1700 Englishmen—'entrenched at Mirath, shooting every black person who passed by'[2],—went as far as Salimpur. Then they 'created a disturbance and returned on the pretence that no arrangements had been made for *rasad* (provisions) for them[3]. Information was also received that a small force of Europeans was encamped on the banks of the Hindan intending to guard the bridge. Troops were ordered out to engage the Europeans[4]. Towards evening news was received that there had been a fight with the English at the Hindan. It transpired that the artillery of the mutineers had been taken and the gunners had fled. The firing of the English had been so good that many of the rebels covered with dust had gone to hell; many like birds borne on the wing had fled back to the city. Report said that there had been a fight at close quarters with swords in which the English were victorious. Many wounded men with sword and gunshot wounds had been brought into the city in doolies (covered stretchers) during the night. The Dehli Hindus who had suffered much at the hands of the mutineers since their arrival in the city expressed their joy that these wicked men, like decapitated fowls, with

---

[1] Metcalfe—T. N. N., pp. 61-62.

[2] *Delhi News,* File No. 15, Nos. 120-146. Dated 24th May, 1857.

[3], [4] Metcalfe—T. N. N., pp. 107-108.

bloody wounds had now themselves been tossed hither and thither and had lost all their manhood and bravery. The King ordered reserves to be sent to the assistance of the mutineers. Mirza Abu Bakr who had commanded, arrived and boasted to the King of his bravery in the fight. The King was much perplexed; all night he sat, surrounded by his advisers and those who adorned his court, taking counsel and discussing the turn that affairs had taken'[1]. This took place on 30th May. 'On 31st May', the reports continue, 'bodies of cavalry arrived from the Hindan, and impressed every man of every class high and low on whom they could lay hands for transport service. The city was in great uproar. Many rose to resist such oppression by force of arms. The Subadars of the infantry came to the King and represented that a great many Mahomedans had fallen in yesterday's engagement, claiming that they had fallen in jihad. It was admitted that as soon as the rebels received a volley from the English they lost heart and began to return to the city'[2].

This was the first defeat of the Badshahi Army at the hands of the English. It had serious repurcussions, and in fact sealed the fate of the war. Bahadur Shah had read the situation correctly when he, foreseeing the advance of the British across the Hindan had pressed his Army to take time by the forelock and attack them before they were prepared, and to expel them completely from Mirath. He was sorely disappointed by the Army officers including Mirza Mughul[3]. It fell to the lot of a boy commander—Mirza Abu Bakr—to lead the army and fight the

---

[1], [2] *Ibid.*

[3] *Vide*, pp. 202-203, *supra.*

first battle of the War of 1857 in Dehli. Mirza Abu Bakr had never seen any battle before. He was struck with terror on seeing the shells burst, killing hundreds of his men; he was stunned at the sight of bloodshed. His flight which was a foregone conclusion could have been easily avoided, not by sending reinforcements as the Emperor did, but by going into the battlefield personally. The Emperor's presence alone would have set the matters right. Even his death in the battlefield would have been a redeeming feature; it would have saved the Royal house from the charge of cowardice.

According to Zaheer Dehlawi the battle of the Hindan was not an aggressive battle; it was a defensive one. While the sepoys in the Badshahi Army were enjoying themselves and had become lax for want of regular parade and military exercises and were completely unaware of the British preparations in the Mirath region and on the eastern side of Jumna whence they never dreamed of a British attack, one fine morning it was suddenly announced that the British troops had crossed the Hindan and were alvancing into Ghaziu'ddin Nagar. Panic seized them and everybody in the Fort and Palace. The Emperor felt more afflicted and embarrassed than anybody else; he had realized the crisis. Unable to find any man to lead the troops in that critical moment, he was compelled to ask his own grandson Mirza Abu Bakr to take the lead. The helter-skelter[1]

[1] Shri Nigam charges Bahadur Shah with destroying his own army, and says 'The defeated Indian troops returned to Delhi. At that time the river Jumna was crossed by a boat bridge. When Bahadur Shah learnt about the defeat of the Indian force he ordered the boat bridge to be destroyed just when the troops were crossing it. Hundreds of troops

that followed has been described by Zaheer Dehlawi[1] and others[2].

That Bahadur Shah had foreseen the British aggression is also borne out by the statement of Forrest to the effect that General Anson and Sir John Lawrence had been concerting measures[3] to make an attack upon Dehli. Previously the British had secured promises of help from the Rajas of Patiala and Jind. By 23rd May their plan of operations was complete. A British army consisting of 300 Europeans, 1000 Indian troops and 22 field guns were to march from Ambala and Karnal *via* Baghpat where they were to join Hewitt's troops from Mirath; then the united forces were to advance upon Dehli'[4]. But the sudden death of Anson at Karnal (25th May) spoilt the British plan and the attack was postponed and did not come off until 27th May. Then the Mirath contingent under Brigadier Wilson joined at Baghpat the troops headed by Barnard, the successor of Anson. At daybreak on

---

were thus drowned and their guns fell into the hands of the British'. Nigam, N. K.—*Delhi 1857*, pp. 72-73.

It is dangerous to draw hasty conclusions, the above incident like many others in the diaries of that momentous period of war is not given in an intelligible form. The *diaries* comprise scattered and disconnected notes which unless substantiated by other sources in detail cannot be relied upon. Muinu'ddin Hasan's statement from which the above inference has been drawn is not confirmed by Jiwan Lal; nor is it borne out by Zaheer Dehlawi who gives an eye-witness account of the wounded soldiers returning from the battle of the Hindan. And both state that the sepoys who were defeated in the battle returned to the city, though they were hungry, thirsty and vexed'.

[1], [2] (i) Zaheer Dehlawi—D. G., pp. 86-88 and (ii) Metcalfe—T. N. N., pp. 61-62 and 109.

[3], [4] Forrest, G. W.—H. I. M., I, pp. 64-70.

30th May, Wilson's contingent reached Ghaziu'ddin Nagar, a village about a mile on the left bank of the Hindan and nine miles from the city of Dehli. Now the Badshahi troops who had been already sent by the Emperor under the command of Mirza Abu Bakr had taken their position on a ridge on the opposite bank of the Hindan. As soon as they saw the enemy approach they opened fire so vigorously that it impressed Cave-Browne[1]. But it was ultimately silenced by the heavy British guns, and the Badshahi troops retreated leaving behind their guns. However, they returned the following day, 31st May. Again they opened fire from the ridge where they had again taken up a good position. An artillery duel began and continued for two hours at the end of which the British troops made an advance and the Badshahi troops retired though they continued their fire and managed this time to carry away their guns.

Great reactions followed the defeats of the Hindan and Ghaziu'ddin Nagar. The confidence which on 12th May, 1857 the Emperor[2] had inspired in the minds of the inhabitants[3] was shaken; and the hopes of order, discipline and prosperity, which had dawned, receded. Complaints arose about the difficulty of getting provisions into the city owing to the shops being closed. 'Under the King's orders soldiers were stationed in the bazar to keep the shops open', says Jiwan Lal[4]. A letter was received from the Raja of Ballabgarh saying

[1] Cave-Browne—P. D. I., p. 312.

[2] *Dehli Urdu Akhbar*, 31st May, 1857. Mutiny Papers, collection No. 2, Vol. 19; No. 22.

[3] *Vide* pp. 181; 191-194 *supra* and the *Sirajul Akhbar*, Mutiny Papers, Box No. 1, Vol 13, No. 8 (May 9-15, 1857) and No. 9 (May 16-22, 1857).

[4] Metcalfe—T. N. N., p. 110.

that 'he had imprisoned 11 soldiers, found deserting to their homes with gold mohurs to the value of 2,000 rupees[1]. In these circumstances the Emperor wrote the following letter to his son, Mirza Mughul :

'My son! be it known—when the sepoys foot and horse came to me in the beginning, I told them plainly that I possess neither army nor wherewithal to help them but that I would NOT HOLD MY LIFE DEAR IF MY LIFE WERE OF ANY USE TO THEM. When I said this all of them became happy and contented; and they promised to lay down their lives in the attempt to carry out my orders and in showing me allegiance. Thereupon I advised them that their first task was to supervise the Magazine and Treasury so well that both these things should later prove assets to them as well as to me. Afterwards they frequented the Diwan-i Khass, the Diwan-i Amm, the Mahtab Bagh and other places inside the Fort and put up and stayed there as they liked. With the object of giving them all possible comfort—knowing that they were ignorant and unacquainted with the Court Etiquette —I prohibited my servants from intercepting them. Although I had given no word to supply them wherewithal, I went out of my way to the extent of borrowing money so that due salary may be given to everyone of the sepoys, infantry and cavalry. Many a time I gave warnings that they must not plunder the city and must in no circumstance exercise high-handedness over the inhabitants but my warnings have produced no effect.

'By now ten[2] days have passed but the sepoys continue to indulge in their old vicious habits. True,

[1] Metcalfe—T. N. N., p. 110.

[2] The number 'ten' is rather idiomatic than mathematical. (*Pr. Tr. B. S.*, p. 134).

the sepoy regiments have withdrawn from the Diwan-i Khass and the Diwan-i Amm, but *they are not carrying out my orders*[1]. I had ordered them that they should encamp outside the city, that no one from the infantry and cavalry should go about in the city wearing arms and that no one should oppress and exploit the inhabitants of the city. But I find that one regiment is residing at the Dehli gate, a second at the Ajmeri gate and a third at the Lahori gate right inside the city walls. And I find they have plundered some of the bazars outright; they carry on their plunder by day and by night. On the false pretence that an Englishman is lurking inside, they dash into the people's private dwellings and plunder them; they break open the locks and take away the shutters and doors and they plunder the goods in the interior most shamelessly. Although it is an accepted old convention that the cities and towns which fall into the hands of aggressors before the commencement of aggression and bloodshed remain exempt from plunder, yet these sepoys do not care to observe this time-honoured convention. Even Chingiz Khan and Nadir Shah who became notorious for their tyranny used to give amnesty to those cities and towns which had surrendered without making resistance.

'Moreover these sepoys threaten my servants and the inhabitants of the city and harass them. Although I ordered—and have ordered repeatedly—that the

[1] The phrase—*'they are not carrying out my orders'*—has a close bearing upon Muinu'ddin Hasan's statement previously quoted, *i.e.* 'The King repeatedly urged an attack upon Meerut but the mutineers delayed, first upon one pretext, then upon another' (Metcalfe—T. N. N., p. 61). This lends strength to the conclusion that the given letter was written on the eve of, or probably after, the battle of the Hindan.

sepoy Infantry must vacate the Farrashkhana quarter and although I have similarly ordered the cavalry to vacate the Mahtab Bagh, yet they have not given up possession of those places. These are the most exalted places into which no one—not even a Nadir Shah, an Ahmad Shah or a Governor-General—has ever come, riding on horseback.

'Furthermore the sepoys requested me in the beginning that I might allow the princes to hold high commands in the army, and they promised them complete obedience and allegiance; I did according as they desired that the princes—now army commanders should be given khilats so that they should look grand and worthy of the military offices and posts of responsibility and trust they held. They insisted upon my doing this much for them whereby, they contended, they would feel honoured and would enjoy recognition and esteem. They all insisted that all the European prisoners should be killed at once; even this was done to meet their wishes and demands. The same day a circular order bearing my royal seal was issued announcing that civil courts had been opened in the city; but the inhabitants took no notice of this.

'Apart from all this it is worth noting that whenever a high and responsible officer of the British Government came into the Fort, he dismounted from his horse at the gate of the Diwan-i Amm whence he proceeded on foot. But these sepoys come riding on horseback and dash into the Diwankhana and Jilokhana while they are underdressed and wear no turbans on their heads. They do not know how to pay homage and how to observe etiquette at the court. While attending the durbar the sepoy officers pay no heed to their dress; they use topis as headgear instead of turbans and keep their swords hanging about. Not even the British officers did so during the period of British rule.

'These sepoys have spoilt and wasted all the material of the Magazine and they have squandered the amounts of money in the Treasury. Then they clamoured for increment in their daily allowance; that too was granted. Although they have got the increment more than their numbers warranted, yet they lay severe hands on the shopkeepers and oppress them in different ways; they take edibles from them but do not pay the price.

'As for the condition outside the city it should be noted that these sepoys do not proceed to the countryside to look after the functioning of the government machinery. Consequently hundreds of people are killed and thousands robbed.

'As for the administration of the city it should be noted that our men and functionaries are not sufficient in number to be able to cope with the administrative problems of all the districts; no tahsildars and no police officers are available. No one from the sepoy infantry and cavalry ever go to the countryside in which case there might have been a hope of improvement in administration.

'In these circumstances it has become tremendously difficult to maintain transit of goods and provisions and to keep open the commissariat; and it is now almost impossible to collect revenue.

'As an unavoidable result of all this, chaos in the city and country has become imminent. And to crown all the sepoys accuse the royal servants saying, 'They are hostile to us'. Then they imperiously and haughtily demand of them their own daily allowance. In compliance with my personal orders these servants of mine show kindness to them and are even meek to them; they humour them and show them every indulgence. In spite of all this the sepoys are not happy.

'THIS BEING THE TRUE STATE OF AFFAIRS HOW CAN ONE POSSIBLY SUPPOSE THAT THESE SEPOYS DESIRE IMPROVEMENT AND WELFARE OF THIS COUNTRY OR THAT THEY WANT TO SHOW ALLEGIANCE TO OUR AUTHORITY?

'There is still another point which demands consideration. In the treasury there is no money left. As for the mahajans and merchants of the city, so much have they been fleeced and ruined that they are not in a position to advance further loan. On the horns of this dilemma how and for how long can payment of the sepoys' daily allowance continue, and what will be the plight if and when one day the supply of food from the countryside being cut off the commissariat is closed down and the sepoys' allowance is discontinued?

'OVER AND ABOVE THIS THE FUN IS THAT WHILE THE SEPOYS THEMSELVES COMMIT MISCHIEF AND THE MISDEEDS WHICH ENTAIL ALL KINDS OF EVILS, THEY THROW THE BLAME ON AND ACCUSE THE ROYAL SERVANTS. THIS IS A SITUATION WHICH BRINGS TO MIND THE PROVERB—THE THIEF PLAYS THE POLICEMAN.

'The sum and substance is that when the army is in this bad, dirty, untidy state, my kingship will obviously go to dogs and will be ruined. My destitution and helplessness having so aggravated and reached such a pitch, I have made it a point to spend the rest of my life in undisturbed devotion to God, bidding goodbye to kingship which abounds in unending troubles and disasters. I have resolved to go first to the shrine of Khwaja Sahib whence after making proper arrangements I should leave for Mecca.

'It should also be noted that when the sepoys had arrived from Mirath then the royal servants and the inhabitants of the city made no resistance whatsoever. They did them no harm, nor did they do anything adverse to them and detrimental to their interests. So in no way do the inhabitants of the city deserve ill of the sepoys; in no way can, fairly speaking, the lives, honour and property of the inhabitants be imperilled and destroyed. NOW ON BEHALF OF MY SUBJECTS AND PLAYING THE ROLE OF THEIR SPOKESMAN I CALL UPON THE SEPOYS TO REALIZE THE SITUATION THAT HAS RESULTED. I ask the sepoys to think why we should continue to participate in their doings and why we should make our sons their partners and helpers.

'The oppression and tyranny which the sepoys are now exercising and inflicting call for serious thinking on our part. I consider THAT OPPRESSION AND TYRANNY DEROGATORY TO MY KINGSHIP. I consider this a derogation that being a king I should ally myself with these sepoys and approve of their killing and plundering the innocent inhabitants of the city. Here is a point worth considering: on the one hand there should be love and friendship and goodwill between myself as king and my subjects and on the other hand *my army* should commit such misdeeds as not even the enemy forces would commit; and yet the said army should consider their misdeeds an act of merit. HAD THESE SEPOYS ACQUITTED THEMSELVES WISELY AND WELL, PROTECTING THE

SUBJECTS AND LOOKING AFTER THEIR INTERESTS, IDENTIFYING THEMSELVES WITH THE ROYAL SERVANTS AND THUS WINNING THE ROYAL FAVOUR, THEY WOULD HAVE IN THAT CASE EARNED MY APPRECIATION AND ADMIRATION. We had entertained hopes that by discharging their duties and responsibilities in this manner the sepoys would promote and help the maintenance of peace.

'My son! you should summon the infantry and cavalry officers and explain fully all these points to them and make them understand the same. If they really desire to serve and promote the interests of my empire they should give a written bond and agreement, the draft of which will be forwarded to them. In order to give them assurance we will also on our part write a bond. They must give up their excesses and indulgence in oppression and high-handedness, and they must not commit the misdeeds which they have been committing up till now. Let the infantry troops carry away their tents from the city and out of the city this very day. If anyone of the sepoys will be found killing or plundering any of the inhabitants his guilt being proved he will be awarded such condign punishment as should serve as a deterrent to others; others must know that by committing such misdeeds they cannot escape punishment.

'This done, one regiment or several should, armed with royal orders, proceed into the country to put an end to tumult and disorder; they should be employed in maintaining peace. These regiments must proceed to the work thus assigned to them with a light heart and without murmuring. Imprudently and audaciously they must not make unreasonable requests for acquiring control of the Magazine and Commissariat. The regiments thus told off would be entitled to return when and if it were fully ascertained that the English troops had closed on them. In that case they would be free to fight in whatever manner and according to whatever plan they liked. The sepoy army must decide and fix the strength of the troops necessary to be allocated to different places; they should determine how the troops should be distributed. Need will arise for keeping some inside the city but it is not necessary for the present. The city and country alike are being ruined while the sepoy army does not care to help maintain order at all outside.

'There is still another point which along with other points you should bring home to the sepoys and impress upon them. It is this. If the sepoys will not strive cheerfully and with sincerity to achieve and accomplish these wishes of their king and if they will not exert themselves wholeheartedly to execute his plans and instructions then we shall betake ourselves to the Khwaja Sahib and sit up there as a fakir. In that case no one should raise objection to our doing so; and then the sepoys themselves should become masters of the city, fort and country. No one of the kings and no one of the war-mongers of history has through the ages oppressed a person who has surrendered and sued for peace. To such a person all kings and conquerors have given free choice and option to adopt and pursue his own way.

'You should speak to the sepoys and tell them that out of the two stipulations mentioned above *they must accept one,* and the same should be inserted in their petition which must be signed, sealed and confirmed by their officers. That petition you should forward to us.

'My son! you must not take this lightly. On account of old age and feebleness I cannot bear all the loads on my shoulders. It is not a child's play to rule a people and at the same time to keep an army under control[1]'.

From the internal evidence of this letter which is undated it appears that it was written either on the eve, or after the battles, of the Hindan and Ghaziu'd din Nagar. The probability is that it was written in the midst of the reactions which had followed the defeat and flight of the Badshahi Army. It was then that Bahadur Shah felt terribly disgusted with the undesirable elements in his Army almost in the same way as a father feels disgusted with his unworthy sons. Then it was that he sent for his sons and grandsons—Mirza Mughul, Mirza Abu Bakr and Mirza Abdullah and 'expressed his anger at their sympathy with the sepoys, warning them that one day they would be hanged as soon as the English entered the city'. 'My fate', he said, 'may be thus expressed:

> *'Kafan pahan kar zindagi ke aiyyam kisi bagh men guzar doonga'.*
>
> (For the rest of my life I shall live in the seclusion of some garden clothed in my winding-sheet)[2]

And it was about this[3] time that Bahadur Shah had heard the news of the preparations in the British Camp for an assault on the city of Dehli. Says Jiwan Lal, 'It was reported that 9 regiments of British infantry, 3 regiments of cavalry with field batteries and siege train had arrived at Alipur'. On hearing this in the durbar of 3rd June, the Emperor discussed with

---

[1] Translated by the writer from the original Urdu text. *Vide Zakaullah*—T.U.A.S.I., pp. 691-695. *Cf. Proceedings of the Trial of Bahadur Shah,* pp. 134-135 or *Trial of the ex-King of Delhi,* pp. 201-204.

[2] Metcalfe—T. N. N., p. 111.

[3] 3rd June, 1857.

the Army chiefs their chances of defending the city. 'The mutineer chiefs', continues Jiwan Lal, 'declared their ability to defend the city. The King inquired at what points it was proposed to oppose the English. The places stated were Dhirajki Pahari, Kenghur[1] Purtosa[2] near the garden of Mahaldar; also at Salimpur. The forces to be collected at each spot were to be specified, and an early attack on the city was anticipated'.[3]

At all events the above letter is a positive evidence of Bahadur Shah's sincerity of purpose. While it shows that good many of the sepoys and perhaps some of the officers had been disobedient and had been misbehaving, it absolves the Emperor from all responsibility for the consequences. This letter also shows how morally strong Bahadur Shah was in the midst of troubles and afflictions; not only was he conscientious but also possessed a wakeful and resourceful mind. He was by no means apathetic or indifferent to the problems of war and administration; he was intent upon all these. And he was hopeful amidst failures, and was ready to evolve new plans to meet a rapidly aggravating situation. Where robust and youthful commanders would have shuddered and paled, fled or committed suicide, the aged Bahadur Shah stuck to his guns, knowing the value of persistence, tenacity as well as of life. However, he did not hesitate to express his displeasure, on noticing instances of the shameful conduct of the sepoys, and held out threats to quit the Fort, to renounce the world and to commit suicide. But these threats were really intended to work out a psychological change in the Sepoys and to make them zealous in war; these were intended to give the delin-

[1], [2] These names are not in their original forms.

[3] Metcalfe—T. N. N., p. 112.

quents in the Army a fresh chance to start with a clean slate by atoning for the past and by promising under a written bond to remain loyal to the State and to the cause of the Mutiny till the end. The threats were noble and the motives behind these threats were nobler still. The threats were a picture of a desperate and agitated mind, but the constructive suggestions which attended them reflected also a mind which was at once thoughtful, legal and constitutional.

The victorious British troops had halted after the battle of Ghaziu'ddin Nagar. They were reinforced on the 1st of June by a battalion of the Gurkhas commanded by Major Reid. On 7th June they advanced; and crossing the Jumna at Baghpat reached their headquarters at Alipur. Then it was resolved to proceed to Dehli without delay. But news spread in the British Camp that the Royal Army was preparing to oppose the British advance and had with this object occupied a strongly fortified position at Badli-ki-Serai. Says Forrest, 'The position which the rebels had chosen was admirably formed by nature for withstanding the march of an attacking force, and was capable of being made strong. They held a large enclosed building with a strong gate called the Serai (resting-place of travellers) of Badli. It stood on the left of the road and the camp was grouped about it. About a hundred and fifty yards in front of the serai on a small natural elevation, the enemy had made a sandbag battery of four heavy guns and an 8-inch howitzer. To the right of the Serai was a small village whose mud walls and enclosures and gardens offered a strong cover for infantry. The ground on either side of the road was intersected with water-cuts and generally swampy, while nearly parallel to the road on the right, at the distance of about a mile, ran the canal, spanned by numerous bridges'.[1] The British troops crossed the canal at midnight, and at daybreak an artillery duel began. But the royal artillery proved much superior. Thereupon the 75th regiment of the British troops made a desperate attack upon the Royal Army and defeated them completely. The sepoys fled leaving their guns behind, and their camp fell into the hands of the British who pursued them. The victors then seized Badli-ki-Serai and occupied the whole area and suburbs of Sabzi Mandi including Hindu Rao's House.[2]

It was in the course of preparation for this battle that the Emperor was approached on 3rd June 1857 to declare jihad on the English[3]; and immediately in the words of Jiwan Lal, 'all the remaining bungalows were destroyed and fired. Ghaziu'ddin Nukur, the zamindar of Poonah[4] and Satgaon[5], issued notification that no supplies were to be given to the English; every straggler from the English Army was to be murdered, if caught, the village obeying these instructions to be held hereafter rent free. Other zamindars took similar action, showing their hatred of the English and sympathy with the King'. Great hopes were built in the Dehli circles on the results of the forthcoming battle; and confidence having returned 'a meeting of the bankers was held under the orders of the King and one lakh of rupees was subscribed and a promise was given of a second lakh payable in 4 days[6]. Then the Royal Army erected two batteries in front of the Serai; they had also fixed there several heavy guns to sweep the whole of the

[1] Forrest, G. W.—H. I. M., pp. 72-73.

[2] *Idem,* p. 77. *Vide* Map of the War of 1857 in Delhi.

[3] Metcalfe—T. N. N., p 113.

[4], [5] Names of parganas in the vicinity of Dehli.

[6] Metcalfe—T. N. N., p. 113.

open ground; and to give effect to their guns they placed at intervals large gumlas (earthen jars)[1] painted white to enable them more accurately to mark the distances and to regulate the elevation of their guns'.[2] On 6th June news having reached the Royal Camp that the English would enter the city that night, the Emperor had the ramparts of the city lined with soldiery. Hakim Ahsanullah Khan was ordered to serve out rations. One hundred maund of *atta* and *dal* were taken from Dwalli Baniyah. The city kotwal was ordered to have ample provisions ready, and 24 guns were sent to the front to oppose the English advance; and all the approaches to the city including the bridges were destroyed.[3] The Emperor was doing everything in his power to encourage the Army to fight well. According to Jiwan Lal's entry of 7th June 'orders were issued through the police that each sweetmeat seller was instantly to prepare twelve rupees' worth of sweetmeats to be sent out to the victorious troops to reward them for their bravery, seventy sowars from Alipur having reported that they had defeated the English force and pursued it for six miles'.[4] Jiwan Lal further says that sixteen carts of provision for the English forces having been seized by the Gujars, the carts were taken to the King and were plundered by the city Musalmans under the King's orders.[5] Furthermore, he says, 'A sowar arrived from Badli Serai to inform the King that the mutineers would engage the English that day at midday and that the English had sent spies into the camp of the mutineers in the disguise of 4th Native Infantry who were acting as the King's bodyguard. A

---

[1], [2] *Vide* (i) Map of the War of 1857 in Dehli, (ii) Cave-Browne—*The Punjab and Delhi* in 1857, Vol. I, p. 318.

[3] Metcalfe—T. N. N., p. 115.

[4], [5] *Idem,* p. 116.

fight had ensued and the English had taken possession of the camp of the mutineers. Heavy firing continued all day till 4 P.M. Seventeen guns fell into the hands of the English who advanced as far as Mubarak Bagh on the road to Sabzi Mandi; and the mutineers retired to the city leaving the countryside into the hands of the English. Only Mahommedans were killed in this fight, and no Hindus. Ammunition and supplies were constantly despatched in the direction of the battlefield. The city people poured volleys of abuse upon the mutineers who were seen returning to the city, accusing them of cowardice'.[1]

Like the defeats at the Hindan and Ghaziu'ddin Nagar the defeat of the Royal Arms at Badli-ki-Serai created a panic in the city; many shops were closed. In his entry of 10th June Jiwan Lal says, 'The King issued a proclamation for the forcible opening of all the shops in the city'.[2] He was extremely perplexed; and in the course of his diligent search for a man who might be brave enough to attack the English before they attacked the city, he made a choice of General Samad Khan and called him to a private interview. According to the information of Jiwan Lal, 'General Samad Khan agreed to attack the English if placed in command of the King's troops. The King ordered his appointment as commander-in-chief with the presentation of the usual *khila't*. A proclamation was issued to the army to muster and advance under the generalship of Samad Khan when victory would be their reward. About 10 o'clock a force of 1,800 Sepoys and 12-horse guns issued from the Lahore Gate and Kashmiri Gate. On reaching the English position Samad Khan communicated with the English to say that he had been sent

[1] *Idem*, pp. 117-118.

[2] *Ibid*.

by the Raja of Jhajjar to join the English force. This feint did not succeed, and an order was issued to attack. About 100 English were killed; the English then pushed forward their artillery. The General came under fire, and immediately retreated leaving several fieldpieces behind him. The force retreated through the Kashmiri Gate into the city. Artillery fire was then opened from the Kashmiri Gate bastions. The whole force by the evening returned within the city walls. The heads of the Europeans killed in the fight were cut off and paraded through the city'.[1]

It was after their victory in the battle of Badli-ki-Serai reported on 8th June by Forrest and on 9th by Jiwan Lal that the British were able to establish their camp at the Ridge—a long series of rocky hills ranging from the banks of the Jumna about two and a half miles above the city of Dehli and extending an equal distance, closing below a large stone building called Hindu Rao's house adjacent to the Grand Trunk Road. Rising 60 feet above the level of the city with an average distance of a mile from the city walls, this Ridge served the English well both as a place of defence and a vantage point for offence.[2] And Hindu Rao's house in the possession of the British was the keypoint of their position. The Royal Army wanted to capture it. And with this object in view they made several sorties, on the 9th, 10th, 11th and 12th June 1857 but were always repulsed. The sortie of 12th June aimed furthermore at the capture of the Metcalfe House which lay close to the river, but was equally a failure. In the course of the next few days the English set about planning to take the city by a *coup de main;* but before their plans were mature the Royal Army made another

[1] Metcalfe—T. N. N., p. 119.

[2] *Vide* Forrest—H. I. M., I., p. 78.

attack on the Hindu Rao house on 17th June. They were repulsed after a hard and close fight, which became known as the battle of the 'Idgah mound which lay on the right of Hindu Rao's house. Here the Royal Army had intended to construct a battery but were prevented from doing so by the British. Here too, a bitter fight took place comprising a hot musketry fire under the joint command of Major Tombs and Major Reid.

After two days another sortie was reported. Says Forrest, 'On the 19th secret notice of a sortie having been received, the picquets were reinforced and in the afternoon threatened the whole of our position, whilst a large body filed unobserved through the gardens and suburbs to our right. About sunrise some flying sowars announced that the enemy were about to attack our rear. The infantry were employed guarding the picquets from the attack in front, and only some few troops were in camp. Twelve guns and some four or five hundred cavalry under Brigadier Grant were quickly collected and sent forward to meet them. They found the enemy strongly supported by infantry posted in wall gardens, against which our artillery could make but little impression. Their guns poured forth a quick and well-directed fire, and the infantry from the gardens shot down our artillerymen and horses. As long as it was light, the steady fire of our guns and the dashing charges of the cavalry succeeded in keeping the rebels in check. But in the dusk of the evening their superior numbers began to tell, and they very nearly succeeded in turning our flank, and for some time two guns were in great jeopardy. All was now in confusion, and the darkness of the night began to increase the disorder when the infantry came up, dashed forward, and cutting a lane through the rebels, rescued the guns.

The firing on both sides gradually ceased, and our infantry being much too weak in numbers to attack the enemy's extended line, our troops returned to camp about 8.30 P.M. At daybreak our troops again advanced to attack the enemy, but found only a strong picquet which was easily driven back, and we captured a gun and two waggons which they had left the night previous. The force had scarcely returned to camp when the enemy again made their appearance, pushed on their guns and opened fire. Our troops promptly turned out in force and the enemy quickly dispersed'.[1]

Forrest's confessions regarding the superior artillery and firing of the Badshahi Army finds confirmation in the diary of Jiwan Lal who testifies to the high ability of Quli Khan, an artilleryman in Badshahi service, saying: 'Quli Khan distinguished himself by his exertions keeping up a constant fire from the bastions at the English; the whole city was full of his praises. The King cheered by the prowess of this man, ordered one hundred maunds of gunpowder to be prepared. Saltpetre and charcoal were purchased'.[2] The same day the English established a battery in full view of the Kashmiri Gate and opened fire on it. But the fire of the Badshahi artillery confounded the English so much that they lost all courage and were disheartened!

It appears from Jiwan Lal's account of 12th June that the Emperor now took stock of the situation; and finding that his Army had made no progress 'expressed anger at the apathy of the mutineers who were making no serious attempt to drive off the English; he (King) chided the chief at not having gained a single victory'[3]

[1] Forrest, G. W.—H. I. M., I., pp. 89-92.

[2] Metcalfe—T. N. N., p. 120.

[3] (i) Metcalfe—T. N. N., p 120.
(ii) D. N. 20th June, 1857.

'The following day (13th June) the whole force was mustered including the sappers and miners, and the King's Bodyguard, and marched out of the Kashmiri Gate to give battle to the English. (Some time later) a sowar arrived from the battlefield and reported that the Sepoys had reached the Kaband and came under the artillery fire of the English. The mutineers having lost twenty cavalry and sixty sepoys by the fire, the whole force was retreating, the regiments reported as having set the example being the mutineers from Umballa'.[1] On 14th June about 3 P.M. '6,000 sepoys with 12 guns marched out of the city. A fight ensued, in which loss occurred on both sides. Reserves were sent up. Heavy artillery fire lasted the whole night. Early in the morning on 15th June seven canon balls fell in the King's Palace. Ten thousand mutineers were let out of the city at midnight to attack the English camp. Many fell on both sides but the troops could make no headway against the heavy fire of the English and returned in great disorder to the city'. On the 16th again a fight took place between the Sepoys and the English. It was indecisive as usual; many were killed.[2] On the 17th 'an order was issued to Qazi Faizullah Beg to prepare provisions for the troops that were about to attack the English. Forty cannonballs were picked up this day, fired from the English Camp. Many persons were killed by them. It was reported to the King (in the Durbar) that three batteries had been constructed—at Dir Chuki Hill and also on the 'Idgah—and that they (mutineers) intended to attack the English. Later on in the day the English attacked the 'Idgah battery and drove the mutineers out of it, capturing two guns'.[3]

---

[1] Metcalfe—T. N. N., p. 121.

[2] *Idem* p. 123.

[3] *Ibid.*

On the 18th reinforcements came to the Royal Army from Nasirabad. On the 19th the officers of the Nasirabad troops attended the Royal durbar and made special preparations for an attack on the English Camp. The attack materialized on 20th June. A severe engagement followed, in which many were killed.[1]

Every day the usual fighting took place ending indecisively in an artillery duel. The 23rd of June was a special day, being the centenary of Plassey and the first day of the month of Zilqada for the Musalmans and the festival of Jatra for the Hindus. On this day took place the battle of Sabzi Mandi whence the Royal Army advanced to the rear of Hindu Rao's house, 'and made such a vigorous attack on a British Battery commanded by Major Reid that Major Reid could not help paying them a tribute: "No men could have fought better. They charged the Rifles, the Guides, and my own men again and again; and at one time I thought I must have lost the day. The cannonade from the city, and the heavy guns which they had brought out raged fast and furious, and completely enfiladed the whole of my position. Thousands were brought against my mere handful of men, but I knew the importance of my position and was determined to do my utmost to hold it till reinforcements arrived',[2] observed Major Reid. 'After a while', says Forrest, 'the reinforcements came, and an attempt was made from the Mound Battery to drive the rebels from the Sabzi Mandi, which with its narrow lanes, mud walls, enclosures and flat-roofed houses offered good cover to infantry; and from wall and roof the enemy poured forth a stream of fire on the advancing troops. The men fell fast, stricken by the bullets of the foe and the

[1] Metcalfe—T. N. N., p. 124.

[2] Forrest, G. W.—H. I. M., Vol. I, p. 94

fierce rays of the sun. Thrice were the streets cleared, but when the soldiers tried to force the houses, the enemy returned from every lane and renewed their murderous fire. "The mass then got into the Sabzi Mandi and gardens on our right and made repeated attacks on the rear of Hindu Rao's house and on the mound. Our fellows followed them three times into the Sabzi Mandi, but they got into houses and closed the doors on themselves; and when our troops withdrew, came out again and fired away." Through the whole of the hot tropical day did the battle rage, and it was not until evening had closed that the enemy returned into the city having lost over a thousand men'.[1]

The battle ended in British victory, and Sabzi Mandi was now in their possession; and they fortified it so well connecting it by a line of breastworks and picquets with the Ridge that further attacks by the Royal Army on the rear of the British Camp were rendered impossible.

The following day (24th June) General Chamberlain, commander of the British siege train in the Panjab, arrived at the Ridge to fill the post of Adjutant-General of the British Army. And his arrival was followed by that of the reinforcements from the Panjab. About the same time (1st and 2nd July) reinforcements also came to the Royal Army.

---

[1] *Idem*, p. 95.

CHAPTER VIII

UNABLE TO DRIVE THE ENGLISH FROM THE RIDGE

(2nd July-25th August 1857)

The given period (2nd July-25th August) presents a momentous scene in the drama of the war of 1857 in which the most important actor is General Bakht Khan. Bakht Khan or Bakhtawar Khan being his sobriquet, his name was Muhammad Bakhsh, his father's name being Abdullah Khan. He hailed from Sultanpur[1] and had sprung on the paternal side from the Rohila stock of Ghulam Qadir Rohila and on the maternal side from the Oudh family of Nawab Shujau'd-Dawla[2]. Jiwan Lal reports his descent twice over. The first report says: 'The General pointed out that he was the descendant of the same family as the King of Dehli and asked the King to satisfy himself that this was true'.[3] The second report says, 'Bakht Khan represented that he was a native of Sultanpur in Lakhnao and related to the royal family of Oude and requested that the truth of his statements might be inquired into'.[4] Regarding his antecedents only this much is

[1] Sultanpur—a town in Oudh 34 miles south of Ajodhya was the scene of an outbreak of revolt caused by the 13th Bengal irregular cavalry on Tuesday morning, 9th June 1857 (Ball, C.—H. I. M., I, p. 247)

[2] Najmul Ghani—*Akhbaru's Sanadid* II, 35; *Ajkal*, Dehli; August 1957, pp. 97-102.

[3] and [4] Metcalfe—T. N. N., pp. 134, 146. Without mentioning his authority Cooper says, 'Bakht Khan came from a family of Hindu extraction but was converted under temptation of territorial acquisition'. (Cooper—*Crisis in the Punjab*, p. 201). This is not correct.

known that he had served the East India Company as the chief Indian officer of a field battery of the artillery at Jalalabad in the First Afghan War. On his return from Afghanistan he was made Subadar of the Artillery at Nimuch whence he came over to Bareilly after the outbreak of the Mutiny. There he helped Khan Bahadur Khan, grandson of Hafiz Rahmat Khan, the last independent ruler of Rohilkhand, rise to eminence as Nawab Nazim under the Mughul Emperor Bahadur Shah. According to Forrest, Bakht Khan then assumed the title of Brigadier and drove every evening in the carriage of the murdered Brigadier (Sibbald) escorted by a large staff.[1] Afterwards he proceeded to Rampur, Moradabad and Rajabpur *en route* to Dehli which he reached on 2nd July, with a formidable reinforcement[2], for the Royal Army.' 'On the 1st and 2nd July', says Forrest, 'the Rohilcund mutineers arrived at Delhi marching across the bridge of boats within full view of the spectators from our Camp posted on the Ridge. They consisted of four regiments of infantry, one of cavalry, a horse battery and two post guns, and were commanded by one Bakht Khan, an old subadar of artillery. He was well-known to many officers of that arm in camp. They described him as a big fat man, obsequious, fond of the society of Europeans, and very intelligent[3]'.

The aged Emperor who needed badly a general,

---

[1] Forrest—H. I. M., III p. 309

[2] Forrest—H.I.M.. I p. 96. It appears that a large number of the *mujahideen* accompanied Bakht Khan from Rampur, Moradabad and Rajabpur in the vicinity of Amroha where he had halted in the course of his journey to Dehli. *Vide* (i) Najmul Ghani—*Akhbaru-s Sanadid* II, pp. 36 ff; (ii) Zaheer Dehlawi—D. G. p. 97.

[3] Forrest—H. I. M.,—I, pp. 96-97

able to build discipline in his army, welcomed Bakht Khan and 'grasped his hand in token of friendship'; and considering him the right man he appointed him commander-in-chief[1] and also awarded him a personal distinction by calling him *farzand* (honoured son). Mirza Mughul who had hitherto been the commander-in-chief and whose authority had been uncontrolled in all matters relating to the Army was made Adjutant-General[2]. It is said Mirza Mughul did not like this change; and in course of time frictions arose between the two contestants. But a minor friction[3] of 17th July apart, which was removed on a personal intervention from the Emperor, the two appear to have worked amicably till the end of the period when Bakht Khan's hold over the military and civil administration of which he had been put in charge began to shake[4], and complaints against him began to arise. Referring to the good effect of Bahadur Shah's intervention, Major Harriott the Judge Advocate-General remarked, 'I think this is conclusive of the three[5] conspiring, consulting and agreeing together[6]'.

[1] 'A shield, a sword, and the title of General were bestowed on Mahammed Bakht Khan, and he was appointed commander-in-chief of the whole of the forces' (Metcalfe—T. N. N., p. 134).

[2] *Ibid.*

[3] and [6] *Pr. Tr. B. S.*, p. 149.

[4] If Jiwan Lal be credited Bakht Khan's powers were restricted on 15th July 1857. *Vide* Metcalfe T. N. N., p. 152. It is reported that under pressure from the Army officers the Emperor then appointed three Generals of Division: 'Mirza Mughul and officers were summoned by the King and ordered to select three Generals of Division, placing eight regiments of infantry and two of cavalry under each. Under these circumstances the Bareilly Brigade alone remained under General Bakht Khan (*Idem,* p. 152).

[5] *I.e.* the Emperor, Mirza Mughul and Bakht Khan.

At the time of Bakht Khan's arrival the British position was weak, even critical. The numbers of the white-skinned troops who alone could be relied upon was small; their base of operations was unsafe; their camp was not immune against diseases, and treachery was not unknown. They were still on the defensive, anxious to conserve their energies and avoid unnecessary loss of lives. The untimely death of General Anson, who had been commander-in-chief at the time of the outbreak of the Mutiny at Karnal[3] while he was intending to proceed to Dehli on 24th May 1857 followed by that of his successor Sir Henry Barnard on 5th July 1857, both falling victim to cholera, combined with the precarious health of Reed the next incumbent of the post, had tended to create a bad omen. And 12 days after Barnard's death, Reed had to proceed (17th July 1857) on sick leave, passing the command of the British army to General Wilson. Referring to the difficult position of the new General, Cooper observes, 'There is, we believe, no parallel in the annals of warfare to the position of Major-General Wilson when he assumed command of the indomitable little band before Delhi on 20th July, the numerical force at his command (exclusive of small bodies of cavalry and artillery) consisting of only about 2,200 Europeans and 1,500 natives, in all 3,700 bayonets while the enemy were literally numberless, in perfect preparation behind strong defences and perfectly equipped'.[1] Cooper may well have added that Bakht Khan, the new Commander-in-chief of the Royal Army, was an experienced general, capable of inspiring the sepoys with confidence and of giving them a lead in fighting. Knowing that Bakht

[1] Cooper——*Crisis in the Punjab*, p. 183

Khan was aware of their weaknesses the British officers were impressed by him; and their writers have spoken highly of him though sarcastically[1] also. They described him as a clever man of large body with a height of 5 feet 10 inches and a chest, 44 inches round, possessing varied experiences of 40-year-long service under the East India Company[2]. But Bakht Khan—literally lord of good fortune—was not favoured by luck; he was luckless as Zakaullah calls him sarcastically[3]. And it was a herculean task which Bakht Khan on his appointment as Commander-in-chief of the Royal Army was called upon to perform—building discipline in the Army, restoring peace in the city, stopping plunder and oppression of the inhabitants, making new regulations and executing new plans, and finally driving the English from the Ridge. Bakht Khan applied himself strenuously to this task; but while he succeeded to some extent in improving discipline in the Army and also in restoring peace in the city he failed completely in driving the English from the Ridge.

The troopers who had been occupying the exalted places like the Diwan-i Khass and the Royal gardens were made to withdraw from these as well as to vacate the crowded parts of the city whence they had been accustomed to collect money through plunder and illicit means. Now they encamped in protected places[4] out-

---

[1] Keith has given a caricature of Bakht Khan with sarcastic remarks. *Vide* Keith—*Delhi-1857*, p. 178.

[2] Cooper—*Crisis in the Punjab*, p. 201

[3] Zakaullah calls Bakht Khan, Kambakht Khan, *i.e.* chief of the luckless.

[4] The Bareilly troops were lodged in Kalan Mahal; some were lodged in Salimgarh and Hammam Kothi and so on. Bakht Khan himself was posted along with some troops

side, and were called to the parade every morning at a fixed hour. After the parade which used to be held frequently from the Ajmere gate right up to the Dehli gate and sometimes at other places, Bakht Khan spoke to them kindly and comforted them; and a special message from the Emperor was announced to every regiment to the effect that 'each man who went out to the battlefield and each man who distinguished himself would receive a grant of 5 bighas of land and receive honorary posts'[1]. After the parade General Bakht Khan rode to the Magazine and examined the Park of Artillery. Thus he satisfied himself daily as to the efficiency of the army as well as that of arms. Good reports about these having reached the Indians on the other side, some of them in the British Camp are reported to have rallied to the Emperor. So did, for instance, good many Sikhs who joined the Royal Army according to Jiwan Lal[2]. Moreover the troops applied themselves under the Emperor's orders to helping the collection of revenues. When Walidad Khan, Collector of Revenues, sought aid from the Emperor to realise his revenue. 'Bakht Khan was ordered to despatch immediately troops to bring the defaulting tenants to their senses[3]'. On another occasion, according to reports, 50 sepoys were enlisted and sent to assist Walidad Khan in collecting revenue[4]: orders were also issued to the Chief of Rewari to collect the revenue and pay the amount into the treasury[5].

---

under his charge outside the city. (Metcalfe—T. N. N., pp. 134-135).

[1] Metcalfe—T. N. N., p. 142.

[2] *Idem,* pp. 168, 183.

[3] *Idem,* p. 145.

[4] *Idem,* p. 157.

[5] *Idem,* p. 147.

The attempts of the English officers to collect revenue for themselves from Baghpat were foiled[1], and collections of revenue from Farrukhnagar and other places were made[2]. In the city a vigorous search about spies and suspicious characters was instituted, and many places of secret communications and supplies to the British were stopped. Some butchers caught red-handed carrying meat to the British camp were decapitated[3]. Similarly an attempt to carry provisions for Englishmen was intercepted by Bakht Khan personally; twenty carts loaded with provisions sent by the Maharaja of Patiala to the British Camp were captured[4]. Jiwan Lal himself was arrested and exposed. He was charged with sending news to the British and with causing Brahmins to pray for the restoration of the English and for the defeat of the King. He was also accused of treason and held guilty for calling the Sepoys 'faithless traitors[5]'. Furthermore regular payments for the royal servants were arranged[6]; and the Emperor, at least for some time, was relieved from worries about the payment of salaries to the Army[7]. In a word there was an all-round improvement; and Bahadur Shah's position was better than before, and his prestige was exalted. Before the arrival of Bakht Khan the Royal Palace used to be thronged by undesirable people and

---

[1] *Idem,* p. 156.

[2] *Idem,* p. 174.

[3] *Idem,* pp. 143-144.

[4] Metcalfe—T. N. N., pp. 137-138.

[5] *Idem,* p. 179.

[6] *Idem,* p. 136.

[7] On his arrival Bakht Khan had paid the Army six months' pay in advance. He reported also that he had treasure to the extent of 4 lakhs. He declared he would not trouble the King for assistance. *Vide* Metcalfe—T. N. N., p. 135.

the Emperor was assailed by loud cries and addressed sometimes disrespectfully[1]. Now not only was all this stopped but Bahadur Shah asserted himself in right royal manner. He embellished the Diwan-i Khass and restored its dignity having excluded all armed men from it. Youths without turbans were also excluded from the royal levees[2]. All loose practices not in agreement with the Court etiquette were tabooed 'as being both distasteful and disrespectful to the King[3]'. Once Bakht himself had to apologize when he, forgetting the convention of Court, whispered something after the durbar into the Emperor's ear. The Princes at once objected and openly charged the General with bad manners. The General apologized, and after flattery from him the matter was dropped'[4]. The Emperor was looked up to for support and guidance by the patriotic amirs and princes abroad. He was looked up to, for instance, by some eminent deputationists from Lakhnao and Kanpur who sought his approbation on announcing that they had killed all the English in their respective cities[5]. The victory of Agra being reported, a triumphal poem was composed and formally presented to the Emperor, celebrating his victory over the English[6]. And whenever the Emperor noticed the slightest apathy on the part of the Army—officers or sepoys—he showed temper and censured them in strong words. One day on being told that 'in consequence of the heavy rains the troops had found the country flooded and had

---

[1] Metcalfe—T. N. N., p. 87.

[2] *Idem,* p. 140.

[3] *Ibid.*

[4] *Idem,* p. 161.

[5] *Idem,* p. 148.

[6] *Idem,* p. 150.

returned, Bahadur Shah became very angry and said, 'You will never capture the Ridge[1]'. Then he summoned all his officers to the Diwan-i Amm and addressed them saying, 'All the treasure that you brought me you have expended; the Royal Treasury is empty and without a pice. I hear that day by day the soldiers are leaving for their homes. I have no hopes of becoming victorious. My desire is that you all leave the city and go to some other central point. If you do not, I'll take such steps as seem most advisable'[2]. Later when about 6,000 *mujahideen* from Nasirabad and Tonk desired permission to come to Dehli, Bahadur Shah prevented them, saying: 'There are 60,000 men at Dehli and they have not yet driven the English from the Ridge. What can your 6,000 do[3]'? And when Bakht Khan complained that soldiers no longer obeyed his orders, Bahadur Shah said angrily, 'Tell them to leave the city[4]'. Then he called the Army officers and said, "It is intolerable that the residents in the city should be harassed and threatened by the soldiers who had come to the city with the avowed object of destroying the English and not their own countrymen. These soldiers are always boasting that they are going out of the safety afforded by the fortifications to destroy the English, and yet they are always returning to the city. It is quite clear to me that the English will ultimately recapture the city and will kill me[5]". On hearing this the officers seemed impressed; they besought him to put his hand on their

---

[1] *Metcalfe*—T. N. N., p. 178.

[2] *Idem*, p. 177.

[3] *Idem*, p. 179.

[4] *Ibid*.

[5] *Idem*, p. 180.

heads for without doubt they would be victorious. There were about 150 officers present; and as they passed before him he placed his hand on the head of each man. Then His Majesty uttered a prayer and said, "Go with haste and be victorious on the Ridge". This done the King rose, and after they had gone he entered the fort of Salimgarh and ordered them to fire the shells from the batteries'[1]. Then he ordered pay[2] to be distributed to the soldiers and made it a point to interview every man of note in the army. Like other officers Bakht Khan too was encouraged by the words and expressions of Bahadur Shah. He informed him that the officers had gone out with an escort of 400 cavalry and the local zamindars to make themselves acquainted with the various positions they were to occupy; then he said feelingly, 'Now I shall be victorious; if God wills I shall prosper. My plan is to attack the English at Alipur'.

On his arrival in Dehli Bakht Khan had created a stir in the British ranks, and the British plans of action for 3rd July were altered. These were to take the city by means of a *coup de main* when on the given day three assaulting columns with a large infantry reserve were to advance on the city: 'one column was to effect an entrance by blowing in the iron grating of the canal near the Kabul Gate; another column was to enter the

---

[1] Metcalfe—T. N. N., p. 181.

[2] Both the statements—the distribution of pay by the Emperor and Bakht Khan's giving the force 6 months' pay in advance—come from the same source (Metcalfe—T. N. N., pp. 134, 181). They appear self-contradictory and cannot be reconciled unless the diarist meant to convey that Bakht Khan had paid a few troopers only, leaving the rest of the Army to be paid by the Emperor.

Kashmiri Gate after it had been blown in; a third was to escalade the side and endeavour to effect an entrance in that direction'. But on hearing of Bakht Khan's arrival and his plans of assault on 3rd July the British dropped their own plan of assault. They feared that unless they fortified themselves in self-defence, the surprise on the part of Bakht Khan might be complete. General Chamberlain then commanding the British troops had been impressed by the vigilance of the *Badshahi* Army 'who were not by any means shut up or unable to send out patrols and picquets'.[1] 'On the afternoon of 3rd July', says Forrest, 'large bodies of the insurgents moved into the gardens and suburbs on our right, and all our troops were turned out to meet the expected attack. But instead of attacking our picquets, the rebels moved rapidly upon Alipur, one march in our rear, and compelled a squadron of the Punjab cavalry to fall back. The fire of their guns was heard in camp, and soon after 2 A.M. a force marched to overtake or to intercept them. It was commanded by Major Coke, and consisted of about three hundred horse, eight hundred foot and twelve guns. At first it was impossible to determine whether the rebels were pushing forward to Karnal or returning to Delhi. About sunrise, however, Major Coke "found the enemy were retiring to the city, but spread all over the country. On crossing the canal, a considerable body with guns were seen at a village about a mile from the bridge, where I at once proceeded to attack them. After a few rounds from their guns, they carried them off in the direction of the city before we could get up to them which they were enabled to do as they were on a road; whereas we had to advance over the open country

[1] Forrest—H. I. M., I, p. 97.

which was in many places a swamp through which the guns and troops could make their way with difficulty. A number of the enemy sought refuge in a village where they were killed. The rest fled in all directions, followed by the Guides Cavalry who sabred many. It was, however, useless to attempt any further pursuit for the heat was great and the European soldiers were exhausted. Major Coke therefore returned to the banks of the canal and rested his men under the shade of the trees. By some misconception his artillery returned to camp. While his men were resting, a fresh force from Delhi attacked them and we beat them back and pursued them for a considerable distance; but seeing that there was a large force collecting behind them, I withdrew the infantry and took up a position that commanded the bridge; and as I expected they were bringing up guns, I sent into camp for artillery. Before the guns arrived, however, the enemy made a second attack with considerable loss. Soon after, the artillery and cavalry came up and followed the enemy who again dispersed and fled in all directions''. Our men returned completely exhausted by the heat; indeed many of the 61st sank down beneath the trees, and elephants had to be sent from camp to carry them in. The enemy took off their guns and returned to camp, having lost about a hundred men. Major Coke was at the time severely criticised for the comparative failure of the action. I am dissatisfied, wrote Hodson, with the day's work inasmuch as more might have been done, and what was done is only satisfactory as a proof of the ease with which Anglo-Saxons can thrash Asiatics at any odds[1]''.

It should be noted that the Indian sources— Muinu'ddin's and Jiwan Lal's diaries, the spies' reports

[1] Forrest—H. I. M., I, pp. 99-100.

and Maulvi Zakaullah and Zaheer Dehlawi's works—give no details of the military operations like the above; nor are the Mutiny Papers worth much. We are therefore compelled to borrow the story of military operations from the English sources. From the Mutiny Papers we get only this much of information that on 3rd July 1857 Khwaja Khairiayat Ali, a *munshi* in the office of General Bakht Khan, wrote to the Emperor requesting that the 18th Regiment which was under orders to march to Alipur might be replaced by some other regiment. The Emperor left this to the discretion of Bakht Khan[1].

Regarding the action on 9th July too, the information given by the Mutiny Papers is scanty, *i.e.* 'the trenches at Sabzi Mandi were seized from the English along with two guns, and two gunners—Sarfaraz Khan and Muhammad Khan—deserted the English camp'. According to Jiwan Lal, General Bakht Khan attacked the English camp with 10,000 men—both cavalry and infantry—besides a large number of the *mujahideen*. 'Fighting took place at the Chowni Bastion. General Bakht Khan captured Tis Hazari[2] from the English and then charged with cavalry into the English lines, cutting down a large number of officers and soldiers. Part of the English camp was being plundered when the gunners turned the fieldpieces upon the sepoys and shot them down wounding and killing a great number. The sepoys then retreated to the city having seized 20 horses, 70 camels and much valuable property besides 13 cavalrymen and 20 infantry soldiers who were taken prisoner. The heads of the English

[1] Box 199, No. 112. M. P., N. A.

[2] Tis Hazari—now known as Tis Hazari Maidan—still exists outside the Mori Gate. But it is fast disappearing under the new scheme for habitation and building purposes.

killed in action were presented as trophy to the Emperor who was much pleased and gave a reward of 100 rupees each to those who had killed them'[1] This account is on the whole borne out by the English writers—Forrest, Ball, Cooper, Keith and Sidgwick, who testify indirectly to the gallantry and rapid movements of the 'insurgents' without mentioning their leader, Bakht Khan. The English writers also tell us that in the midst of an unceasing rain of artillery fire from the ramparts of the city on the English batteries and Sabzi Mandi pickets, sprang a body of cavalry out of the Kabul and Lahore gates at 9 A.M. on the 9th of July. Their numbers increased as they proceeded towards the British camp at which they suddenly fell about 11 A.M. The British Carabineers bolted and were pursued by the invaders who were engaged by a division of the British army headed by Major Tombs and Hills. In the course of the hand-to-hand fighting that followed, Hills was wounded. Then the invaders made an appeal to the Indian gunners in the British Camp saying, 'Get your guns ready and come away with us to Dehli'. But the gunners did not respond. They shouted for Major Olpherts' European troop, whose guns were unlimbered in their rear to fire at them. They fled but managed to carry off some horses and killed several camp-followers who fell into their hands. This action which had lasted the whole day continued in the midst of torrential rains. In a contemporary letter of 11th July it is described as 'a day of the "most hard fighting"; and although the said

[1] In Jiwan Lal's narrative (Metcalfe—T. N. N., p. 145) of the above action there is no continuity of thought and the chain of events is broken more than once. I have built a connected account without altering his meaning (M. H.)

letter speaks magniloquently of the success of the British arms, the writer could not help acknowledging, at least indirectly, that the coup of 9th July had been well devised by the invaders. Subsequently the British called a court of inquiry to sift the circumstances attending their defeat, but nothing came to light beyond the fact that there was treachery on the part of their own picket of the 9th irregulars. The finding of the Court of Inquiry was that 'the enemy deceived every body by advancing as friends and pretending they were the 9th. When Hodgson of the Guide Corps rode up and asked who they were, the men quietly said, ''We are the 9th Irregulars; go and bring up the rest of your regiment; the enemy is in front''. Thus they walked slowly to the bridge leading out of the British Camp, then made a rush and bolted. It was a bold thing to do, but resulted in nothing'[1].

Of the next action of 14th July, Jiwan Lal takes no notice. But the English writers give a rich account saying, 'On the morning of the 14th July the mutineers moved out of the city and attacked our batteries at Hindoo Rao's House and picket in the Subzee Mundee suburb. Our troops remained on the defensive until 3 P.M. maintaining their position against a force, believed to consist of 20 regiments of infantry, a large body of cavalry and several fieldpieces and supported by a fire of heavy artillery from the walls. At 3 o'clock a column was formed under the command of Brigadier Showers; Major Reid with the troops from Hindoo Rao's picket co-operating on the left. This service was gallantly performed and the enemy driven in confusion'[2].

---

[1] Ball, C—H.I.M., I, pp. 480-481.

[2] *Idem*, p. 483.

It appears that the objective of the Royal Army's attack on 14th July as on the 9th was to get at 'one of the British batteries close by'; but they failed on both occasions. Seeing this, a British soldier who had participated in the fight on 14th July remarked, 'Their (Sepoys') cavalry, I knew, could not do much and their infantry I did not care for. Had the enemy had one particle of pluck and rushed in at us, not one of us would have lived to tell the tale; as it was they came so close that they pelted us with stones. At 2 o'clock we had a general advance and drove the enemy like so many sheep into the city. We all got up within 200 yards of the walls and were much punished by the grapeshot again'[1].

Regarding the action of 18th July Jiwan Lal is extremely sketchy. He says, 'The rebel forces from Nasirabad and Dehli engaged the English; the fighting continued for some time. The English were overpowered and retreated leaving their guns on the field of battle'[2]. But the English writers as usual deluge us with details. Space forbids to have anything more than a bare summary from their writings. Reid, on relinquishing command of the Dehli field force on 17th July, said, 'The enemy scarcely allowed a day to pass without an attack or demonstration upon some part of the British position. Thus from the 17th to 31st the troops were kept in a state of incessant activity. And a letter of 27th July conveyed the following, 'The Pandies are dispirited at finding so little advantage follows their efforts against our position'[3]. On 30th July General Wilson wrote to Colvin, Lieutenant-Governor of the N. W. Provinces, 'The enemy are very

[1] Ball, C.,—H. I. M., pp. 483-484.

[2] Metcalfe—T. N. N., p. 154.

[3] Ball, C.,—H. I. M., p. 486.

facing p. 245

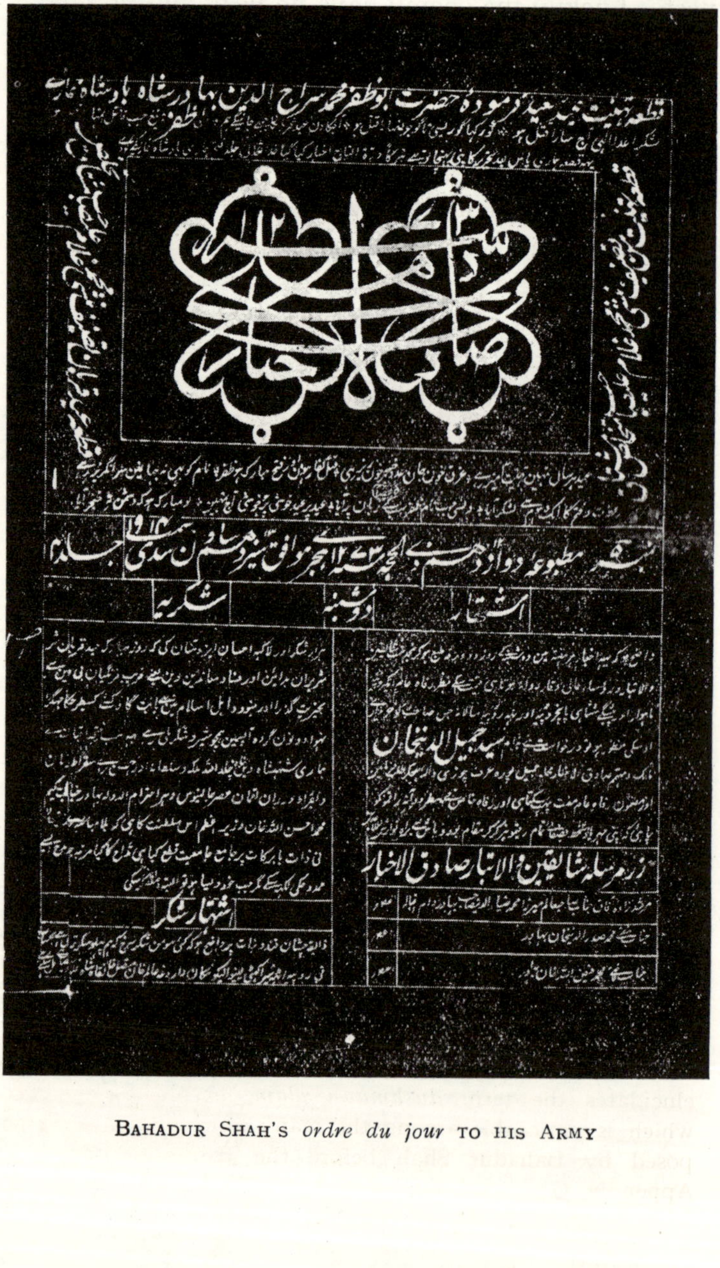

قطعہ تہنیت عید فرمودۂ حضرت ابوظفر محمد سراج الدین بہادر شاہ بادشاہ غازی

اشتہار | دوشنبہ | شکریہ

سید جمیل الدین خان

صادق الاخبار

Bahadur Shah's *ordre du jour* to his Army

numerous and may possibly break through our entrenchments and overwhelm us; but the force will die at their post. Luckily the enemy have no head and no method, and we hear dissensions are breaking out amongst them. Reinforcements are coming up under Nicholson. If we can hold on till they arrive, we shall be secure'[1].

On the 1st of August while Jiwan Lal says that the English with a battery of six guns had attacked the Sepoys and were beaten back, Forrest describing it as the Bakar-'id day emphasizes the joint fight put in by the Hindus and Musalmans[2]. According to Jiwan Lal the Bakar-'id festival fell on 2nd August when Bahadur Shah recited some verses[3] that he had com-

---

[1] Ball, C—H.I.M., I. P. 487.

[2] Forrest (I, p. 113)reproduces the spirit of Hindu-Muslim zeal saying. 'The Jami' Masjid rang with the prayers of the faithful; and Brahmin priests stimulated the fanaticisim of the followers of Vishnu.'

[3] لشکر اعدا الہی آج سارا قتل ہو۔
گور کھا گورے سے تا گوجر نصاری قتل ہو
آج کا دن عید قربان کا جب ہی جانینگے ہم
اے ظفر تہ تیغ جب قاتل تمہارا قتل ہو۔

'O God! May the whole army of the enemy be killed to-day! May the Englishmen along with their allies—the Gurkhas, Goras and Gujars be killed! We shall recognize this day as the 'Id day only when to-day, O Zafar! your murderer (Englishman) be killed.' For the facsimile of the document containing these verses see p. facing 245. It should be noted that the term *qatil* (murderer) used in the above quatrain is neither accidental nor poetic. It has a background, and elucidates the term *dushman-i alam* (enemy of the world) which is noticeable among the many anti-British verses composed by Bahadur Shah before the Rising of 1857. *Vide* Appendix C.

posed encouraging the sepoys to fight and fight to the end. A few days before this, the ulama had proclaimed a jihad[1] against the British. Keith says, 'The King caused a proclamation to be made that 14,000 fanatics and 8 regiments are on their way from Peshawar and will arrive in two days, and it enjoins all who wish to take part in a holy war to join this body'[2]. In the words of Forrest, 'Again and again the (Hindu-Muslim) assailants rallied and rushed upon the breastworks but the steady volleys stopped their charge. All that August night the battle raged, the batteries from 4 bastions poured forth without ceasing their shot and shell'[3]. The fight continued the succeeding day till past noon; then the valiant Hindu-Muslim soldiers retired. The Sammy House where some crucial fighting took place was the silent witness of this fiercest scene in the long-drawn-out drama of the war. The result created a great depression in their ranks; they were literally sickening. Forrest rejoices to note that 'the tide had begun to turn; the British were fast becoming the besiegers and not the besieged'[4]. Five days later exploded 'accidentally'[5] the powder manufactory at the Churiwalan street. There is a conspiracy of writers about the term 'accidentally'[6] used in this connection. But it appears that the explosion was brought about through some device of the British spies. All the same the sepoys kept on fighting the whole of this day. And

---

[1] *Sadiqul Akhbar* of July 27, 1857. Mutiny Papers, Box No. 4-6.

[2] Keith—*Delhi-1857*, p. 173.

[3] Forrest—H.I.M., I., p. 113.

[4] *Idem*, p. 114.

[5] *Ibid.*

[6] According to a British spy, 'A spark from a *hooqa* was the accidental cause of explosion' (*Delhi News*, August 8 1857)

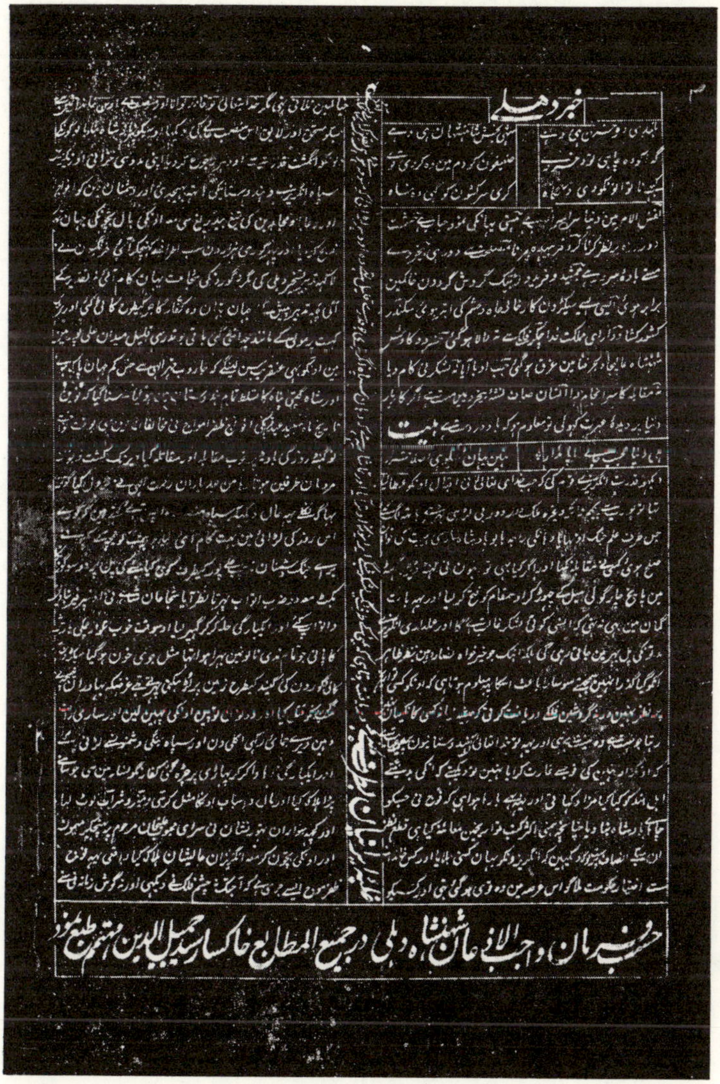
خبر دہلی

حسب فرمان واجب الاذعان شہنشاہ دہلی در جمیع المطابع خاکسار سید جمیل الدین مہتمم طبع نمود

ANNOUNCEMENT OF A TERRIBLE ASSAULT MADE BY THE BADSHAHI ARMY ON THE BAKAR-'ID DAY
(*Sadiqul Akhbar*
published under orders of
the Emperor of Dehli in
the Jami'ul Matabi's Press
by Saiyed Jamilu'ddin)

they seized the Ludlow Castle'[1]. The Emperor finding himself unable to drive the English from the Ridge reproached the troops for not carrying the Ridge. They replied that neither artillery nor cavalry could mount the Ridge and that they were consequently helpless and could not take it'[2].

On 14th August at last the long-expected reinforcements under Nicholson arrived at the Ridge but they had to wait for the necessary ammunition and siege train—a movable column to suppress the Mutiny wherever it might appear—which took another ten days to come. This period Hodson utilised in making successful raids through rapid movements over a wide area from Dehli to Hansi and Jind. In this manner the English avoided pitched fighting and battles. This is the meaning behind Jiwan Lal's following remark: 'The King received a report that the Army had gone out to fight but the English did not care to engage. It became an artillery duel'[3].

On 21st August—just after a month when the Emperor had issued orders to General Bakht Khan to attack the English vigorously and simultaneously at Sabzimandi, Alipur, Mubarak Bagh and at other points so as to ensure their total discomfiture[4]—appeared a silver lining. Reviewing the work done by General Bakht Khan and his troops since their arrival, Bahadur Shah felt that a word of commendation and approbation from him might prove more useful than mere criticism,

---

[1] The Ludlow Castle was seized from the Badshahi army by the British on 8th September 1857, not earlier. Greathed's report that the King's troops were driven out of the Ludlow Castle on 23rd July or 12th August is not correct. *Vide* Greathed, p. 230 and Forrest, I, p. 127.

[2] Keith—*Delhi-1857*, p. 172.

[3] Metcalfe—T. N. N., p. 156.

[4] *Idem*, p. 160.

rebuke and disparagement. Hence he issued a *shuqqa* to the officers of the Bareilly force praising them for their bravery and directing them to present themselves at the Royal Court[1]. He appreciated the progress that had been made in different spheres, pointing out the defects that had remained, and promised rewards in case of his victory. Then he stressed that the candidates to be recruited in the Royal service, particularly in the Army, must be carefully scrutinized[2]. Some of the Sikhs also were praised for their move in the right direction. Prince Khizr Khan wrote to them a letter stating that the Emperor was highly pleased with them. He praised them and advised them to send six companies to Shamgarh[3]. The Sikh officers replied that their soldiers had gone to the trenches at Teliwara. This done the Emperor set his hands to preparing a proclamation which he issued on 25th August—the day of the Najafgarh battle.

The said proclamation was a threefold appeal to (i) the Zamindars, (ii) the Sepoys and (iii) the Artisans. Addressing the Zamindars he said, 'It is evident that the British Government in making the zamindari settlements have imposed exorbitant *jammas* and have disgraced and ruined several zamindars by putting up their estates to public auction for arrears of rent insomuch that on the institution of a suit by a common ryot—a maid servant or a slave—the respectable zamindars are summoned in court, arrested, put in jail

[1] Mutiny Paper, Box 199, No. 300.

[2] It appears that Zinat Mahal Begum was also interested in this matter. The Mutiny Papers contain a letter from her, disapproving the recruitment of worthless men made by Nawab Vilayat Ali Khan in the regiment. But the *ecriture* is not very clear, and the wording of the letter is not intact. *Vide* Box 191; 18th August, 1857.

[3] Box 152, No. 35, 23rd August, 1857.

and disgraced. In litigations regarding zamindaries the immense value of stamps and other unnecessary expenses of the civil courts which are pregnant with all sorts of crooked dealings and the practice of allowing a case to hang on for years are all calculated to impoverish the litigants. Besides this the coffers of the zamindars are annually taxed with subscriptions for schools, hospitals and roads etc. Such extortions will have no manner of existence in the Badshahi Government, but on the contrary the *jammas* will be light, the dignity and honour of the zamindars safe and every zamindar will have absolute rule in his own zamindari'[1]. (ii) Then addressing the Sepoys the Emperor said, 'Indians in the Military Service, after having devoted the greater part of their lives attained to the post of Subadar of 60 or 70 rupees per mensem; and those in the Civil Services obtained the post of *Sadr-i Ala* with a jagir or present. But under the Badshahi Government like the posts of Colonel, General and Commander-in-chief which the English enjoy at present,

[1] In the course of its comment on this Proclamation the *Friend of India* (which also gave its English translation) says, 'The declaration that the land-tax is oppressive and ought to be lowered was only to be expected . . . The promise that every zamindar should be absolute on his domain was natural from one who knew what we did not know that the feudal aristocracy was still strong . . . .

'The King calls the subscriptions 'extortions' and describes . . . . their popular estimation. The utter hatred in which stamps were held was perhaps more generally known. It was perceived even by Europeans that they were a breach of that great social contract on which socialistic society is founded. The Ruler is to enjoy boundless luxury . . . But in return he is to do justice, swift stern justice between man and man without favour and without price. It is this feeling more than actual hardship which produces the bitter hatred of our courts by every class of native society'. (*Friend of India,* 7th October, 1858).

the corresponding posts of Pansadi, Panjhazari, Hafthazari and Sipahsalari will be given to the Indians in the Military Service; and like the posts of Collector, Magistrate, Judge, Sadr Judge, Secretary and Governor which the European Civil Service servants now hold, the corresponding posts of Wazir, Qazi, Safeer, Suba, Nazim and Diwan etc. with salaries of lacs of rupees will be given to the Indians of the Civil Service together with jagirs, khilats and inams and influence'[1]. (iii) Then addressing the Artisans he said, 'It is evident that the Europeans by the introduction of the English articles into India have thrown the weavers, cotton dressers, carpenters, blacksmiths and shoemakers etc. out of employ and have engrossed their occupations so that every description of native artisans has been reduced to beggary. But under Badshahi Government the native artisans will exclusively be employed in the services of the Badshah, the rajas and the rich; and this will no doubt ensure their prosperity'[2].

---

[1] 'The next complaint that natives under British sovereignty do not rise is simply the enunciation of truth . . . It is admitted by Europeans as much as by natives, and plan after plan to amend the grievance has broken down. The attempt to remove it by new offices and increased salaries is merely a palliative. What natives want is not salaries but power; and according to the European line of thought they always misuse power; power they cannot have. The *Sadr-i Ala* as the King implies is very well paid but he has no influence and no presents'. (Comments from the *Friend of India*, 7th October, 1858.)

[2] 'The new class of artisans prospers but the old one of Manufacturers has undoubtedly been eaten up by Manchester and Sheffield . . .

'With regard to the traders the King can find no grievance except the customs; so he promises boldly an impossibility—the carriage of all merchandise at State expense'. (*Ibid*).

In the course of its comment on this Proclamation the *Friend of India* says: "This is the most invaluable contribution to the history of the rebellion'.

One day before this Proclamation was issued, *i.e.* in the morning of 24th August a big attack was organised by the Royal[1] Army. 'The Mutineers' as the British writers call them, 'started with 18 guns with a view to put off British communication with the Punjab and prevent the arrival of the said siege train. But they were pursued by Nicholson who overtook them towards the close of the day near the Najafgarh canal'. 'The enemy position,' says an English report, 'extended for about 3,000 yards with their left occupying a village near a bridge over the canal and their right on a hillock and a serai. Nicholson at once decided to attack this hillock and the serai. Under cover of the guns the infantry advanced in line and after storming the hillock changed front and bore down on the enemy's right. The mutineers gave way but a party held out in a village in rear and slipped off in the night[2].

This was the battle[3] of Najafgarh of which a graphic account is given by Nicholson himself in the course of a letter to his adjutant-general. He emphasizes the dangers that he and his troops encountered saying, 'The troops are likewise entitled to credit for the cheerfulness with which they bore the hardships they were exposed to; they marched at daybreak and had to cross

---

[1] *I.e.* 'Badshahi'—a term commonly noted in the Urdu and Persian records.

[2] Sidgwick, F. R.—I. M., p. 72.

[3] Since it was a mere surprise and there was no pitched fighting, it would be perhaps better to call it 'action' instead of 'battle'. *Vide* Map of the War of 1857 in Dehli facing p. 251.

two difficult swamps before their arrival at Nangloo[1]; and as it would not have been prudent to take the baggage across the ford at Baprowla[2] they were obliged after 14 hours' marching and fighting to bivouac on the field without food or covering of any kind[3]'.

---

[1] Nangloo was a village about 9 miles from Bahadurgarh on the road from Dehli to Najafgarh.

[2] Baprowla or Bassrowla was a village along the Najafgarh jheel or canal.

[3] Ball, C—H. I. M., I., p. 495.

CHAPTER IX

FALL OF DEHLI

(26th August—20th September 1857)

For the disaster of Najafgarh which marks the epilogue of the drama of the war, and in the words of Zaheer Dehlawi 'the beginning of the complete demoralization of the Purbiyas'[1] the Emperor held Bakht Khan responsible[2]; Bakht Khan had at a critical moment withheld support from Sudhari Singh also called Sirdhara Singh, commander of the Nimuch troops[3]. Relating the circumstances that had led to the said disaster, Zaheer Dehlawi says, 'All the Generals had agreed to proceed from Dehli to Najafgarh considering it a fit place to intercept the arrival of the British siege train from Firozpur, and they also intended to proceed *via* Bahadurgarh to make an attack

---

[1] Zaheer Dehlawi—D. G., p. 105.

[2] Gauri Shankar, a British spy, says, 'The King is very displeased with General Bakht Khan and accuses him of destroying the brave Neemuch Brigade by failing to render timely support. He is not to show his face and is abused'. (*Dehli News,* August 28, 1857). Jiwan Lal says, 'One Tsree Bing from the Nimuch Camp related (to the King) how the English first captured two guns which he with great bravery, afterwards, retook with the assistance of certain landholders. He accused the Bareilly troops of quarrelling with the Nimuch force, and returning to Dehli without co-operating with them. He prevailed upon the King to give him the command of five hundred cavalry and four companies from each regiment to attack the English with'. (Metcalfe—T. N. N., p. 209).

[3] *Delhi News,* August 28, 1857.

on the British Camp in the rear. One day Bakht Khan started from Dehli and marched with his troops along the road to Najafgarh. On arriving near the Najafgarh canal he chose a particular site and encamped. The following day Ghaus Khan[1] and Sudhari Singh started and marched with their troops likewise along the same road. They found Bakht Khan camping on this side of the canal and suggested that he should advance and encamp across the canal. Bakht Khan did not accept the suggestion and continued his encampment on the site he had already chosen. Ghaus Khan and Sudhari Singh proceeded to cross the canal. They had hardly pitched their camp when they were overtaken by torrential rains and were at the same time subjected to heavy bombardment from the British guns. Great was the loss of lives and ammunition that the Nimuch troops suffered; and it was with great difficulty that Ghaus Khan and Sudhari Singh made their way back to Dehli with a small number of the soldiers who had survived. Bakht Khan now came back to Dehli[2].

From the spies' reports it appears that General Ghaus Khan had not accompanied his Brigade to Najafgarh and that the Nimuch troops defeated in the

[1] Zaheer Dehlawi (p. 104) has erroneously put Ghaus Khan along with Sidhari Singh as being present in the battlefield of Najafgarh. In fact, he was not in the action. On arriving afterwards in the Durbar when he was informed about the disaster, he disclaimed all knowledge of any engagement with his troops, saying that he had received no information and doubted the truth of what he had heard. On being assured that his troops had been defeated, he asked for reinforcements. One regiment of Sikhs and four of cavalry were placed under his command. The force marched, but after going a short distance met the defeated force returning. so covering their retreat, they returned to camp.' (Metcalfe —T.N.N., p. 208).

[2] Zaheer Dehlawi—D. G., p. 104.

said battle were then under the command of General Sudhari Singh[1] only. Writing on 26th August Turab Ali, a British spy, says, 'To-day is Wednesday. Early this morning intelligence was received of the total defeat of the Neemuch Division. It appears that in order to evince their bravery the troops made a march of 13 *koss*, crossed the Najafgarh Bridge (leaving the Division under General Bakht Khan in their rear) and attacked the British force under General Nicholson. At the commencement of the battle, the bridge was destroyed and thus the retreat of the mutineers was entirely cut off. They were doomed to destruction. Their guns, ammunition, baggage etc. all fell into the hands of the British. It is reported that the three Regiments of Infantry fought separately. They exhausted all their ammunition. General Bakht Khan with his Division could not join in the attack, nor advance to the rescue. The cavalry made their escape; most of them have reached Dehli. The destruction of the Najafgarh Bridge has entirely prevented the return of the rest to Dehli. It is confidently reported that all the Neemuch Division are destroyed'[2]. In a supplementary letter of 27th August, Turab Ali says, 'After receiving intelligence of the defeat of the Neemuch Brigade at the instance of Bakht Khan, the personal troops of the King also turned out to the attack, *viz.* Khassabardars, the Bachhera Regiment (horse and foot) of Hakeem Abdul Haq etc. etc. The conflict was maintained till evening. About forty men of the King's levies were killed and wounded'[3]. Turab Ali's reports are supported by those of Rajab Ali and Jiwan Lal. Rajab Ali says, 'General Nicholson returned triumphantly at 5 P.M. on 26th August. The battlefield was at Nunglee, a village one mile from Najafgarh

[1], [2], [3] *Delhi News,* File No. 124, August 260. 1857.

on the Dehli road on the other side of the Najafgarh bridge. The British troops were drawn on the Najafgarh side. The rebels had taken up a position on either side of the Bridge with a strong picquet at the Bridge and the main body in the rear. General Bakht Khan was at Palam, three *koss* from the scene of action and seven *koss* from Dehli. When he heard of the total defeat of the rebels under General Sirdhara Singh he struck his camp and made hot haste for Dehli. The discomfited troops of General Sirdhara Singh followed precipitately in his rear'[1]. Jiwan Lal says, 'The King sat in the Hall of Public Audience. A trooper named Ashraf Khan entered the Hall; and, saluting His Majesty, proceeded to relate how the Bareilly Brigade being encamped at Palam (*Elipalam*), the Nimuch Brigade unexpectedly arrived. General Bakht Khan held a consultation with the officer commanding the Nimuch force. He advised him to halt there (as the English force was only a short distance off) and join forces with him, proposing to make a joint attack the next day. The Brigade of the Nimuch force would not agree to this plan, but pushed on to Bakghara[2], intending to encamp there for the day and rest his men. While the camp was being pitched, and the men had piled their arms, and many had taken off their belts and accoutrements, they were suddenly attacked by the English from two directions with a heavy fire of artillery and musketry. Taken unawares, the sepoys bolted, leaving twelve guns and their ammunition. The loss, Ashraf Khan went on to say, was a thousand killed and wounded. The King on hearing this news was greatly disheartened'[3]. All this finds confirmation in the

[1] *Delhi News,* File No. 124, August 26, 1857.

[2] *I.e.,* Bapraula. *Vide* p. 252 *suprsa* footnote.

[3] Metcalfe—T.N.N., pp. 207-208.

account given by Forrest to the effect that the news of the Badshahi troops having reached the British head-quarters at the Ridge, General Wilson sent a British column under the command of Nicholson to intercept them. Nicholson arrived on the Bahadurgarh road in the morning of 25th August and learnt that the Badshahi troops had been at Palam the previous day and would be reaching Najafgarh in the afternoon. 'He left the Bahadurgarh road and planned to intercept them at Najafgarh before nightfall. He crossed the Najafgarh canal near the village of Basrowla[1]; and finding the said troops spread out over a distance of two miles between the Najafgarh canal and the Nunglee village with thirteen guns placed strategically in an old Serai and near the canal bridge, Nicholson fell on them unawares and surprised them so completely that they fled pell-mell towards the bridge leaving behind their guns. Nicholson then made an attack upon the Serai and seized it as well as the village'.[2]

In connection with his report that the King was disheartened on hearing the sad news of Najafgarh, Jiwan Lal says, 'The King regarded the information as very serious. He summoned the following persons to his Council Room—Mirza Mughul[3], Mirza Koaish[4], Mirza Khair Sultan, Mirza Abu Bakr, Mirza Abdullah and Mirza Abu Nasr. After consultation His Majesty directed a force to be sent off at once under the command of Captain Walidad Khan to take the English Camp'[5]. The Emperor was given to understand that all the British forces had at the moment gone out[6]. From

[1] *I.e.* Bapraula. *Vide* p. 252 *supra,* footnote.

[2] Forrest—S.L.D.S.P., I., pp. 359 ff.

[3], [4] Mogul' and 'Koash' are the incorrect forms of Mughul and Koaish. I have not used the incorrect forms.

[5] Metcalfe—T.N.N., p. 208.

[6] According to Rotton (N. S. D., p. 209) the Nimuch

the account given by Keith it appears that all the reactionary elements rallied to the Emperor, and an army of the people of Dehli—even women[1] and unarmed men—marched to make an attack on the British Camp; they risked their lives in the attempt to take the English batteries. But they failed completely amidst a great slaughter that followed[2]. This army was also joined by Mirza Mughul who started simultaneously with his men to attack the British Camp; but returned, in the words of Jiwan Lal, 'without making an attack with the loss of seventeen men killed[3]. The guns which Mirza Mughul had mounted in different batteries kept up an incessant fire all day from the Mithai Bridge under the command of Mirza Koaish and from Kishanganj under the command of Mirza Abdullah'.[4]

Evidently the war in Dehli had now become the People's War. The people of Dehli proper as well as of the villages were helping the Royal[5] *cum* Nationalist troops, looking upon them as the Army of Liberation. In his report of 27th August Gauri Shankar, a British spy says, 'The people of the village of Nunglee gave great assistance to the rebels and fought side by side with the sepoys. There was a great attack on the (English) Batteries yesterday. Mirza Mughul took out

troops had ascribed their defeat to the '*whole* English army turning out to the attack made against them'.

[1] Referring to these women Charles Ball (H. I. M., vol. I., p. 504) quoting a contemporary letter says, '. . . It must be fresh in your memory that when the mutineers came out of the city for a grand attack upon our camp, while Nicholson's force was at Nujufghur, they were followed by crowds of these very women.'

[2] Keith—*Delhi-1857;* pp. 243-244.

[3] Metcalfe—T.N.N., p. 208. [4] *Idem,* p. 209.

[5] *I.e.* the personal troops of the Emperor.

THE PEOPLE'S WAR IN DEHLI

all his Division. The Nasirabad regiments also turned out. There were several Shahzadas present with all the personal troops of the King and the contingents of Nawab Aminu'ddin Khan and Taju'ddin Khan and other nobles of the city. About fifty of them were wounded or killed; and one of the Shahzadas, Ghulam Mustafa, was wounded. There were not sufficient doolies for the wounded, and at last they were carried in, on the crossed muskets of their comrades. The city people are much terrified at the utter defeat of the Neemuch troops and the Army gets more and more dispirited. They have now no hopes of victory. General Bakht Khan's Division, however, is still confident and hopeful'[1]. According to another report General Bakht Khan reassembled the fugitives of the Nimuch Brigade and intended to march out again to Najafgarh[2]. Writing on 28th August Turab Ali says, 'Yesterday[3] two regiments of Infantry with some ammunition left Dehli for Najafgarh. Shahzada Muhammad Azeem has returned from Hansi and has joined the King's personal forces. About 20,000 of the country people have got together and have diligently spread reports that they have recovered the twelve guns captured from the Neemuch Brigade and have taken seven of the British guns besides. Yesterday the Neemuch and Bareilly Brigades again started for Najafgarh with eight guns. The cavalry were to start at midnight or early this morning. The infantry and guns have undoubtedly started as the writer further saw them off. Ever since Maulvi Fazl Haq arrived in this city from Alwar, he is unceasingly employed in stirring up the army and the

---

[1] *Delhi News*—27th August, 1857.

[2] *Delhi News*—August 28; Gauri Shankar, a British spy being the reporter.

[3] *I.e.* 27th August, 1857.

city people against the British. It is likely that an attack on the British batteries will be made to-day. The Shahzadas now turn out in these sorties at the instigation of Maulvi Fazl Haq and usually take their stand on the Sabzi Mandi Bridge[1]. While Turab Ali gave the above report Gauri Shankar, another British spy, writing on the same day said, 'Bakht Khan wishes to make a second attempt to reach Najafgarh but he proposes this time to go round by Gurhee Harsaroo and Gurgaon. The Najafgarh zamindars promise to give him all the assistance, and some zamindars of Panipat and Sonipat are also with him. Bahadur Ali Khan of Bahadurgarh is endeavouring to raise the country and he sends a messenger to Bakht Khan assuring him that the country is on his side. Some Sikhs (also) have been instructed to go to the Punjab to endeavour to raise Manjha (?) in revolt. In the village of Sahni, district Rohtak, Risaldar Khan has collected a large body of insurgent Ranghars. In village Tosham, district Harreeana, there is another body of insurgents and the sowars go off to join them; and many troopers on leave and pensioners of the Government have also collected at this spot where they say there are 20,000 rebellious zamindars. Their object is to plunder Hisar. These *risings of the country population* are more to be dreaded than a military revolt. To-day the city Brigade under the command of Mirza Mughul went out to the batteries at Kishanganj and Qudsia Bagh. In to-day's Durbar the zamindars of Nunglee came to complain that they had been punished for assisting the King's forces. Their villages had been totally destroyed. The King sent them to General Bakht Khan'[2].

---

[1] *Delhi News,* August 28, 1857, Turab Ali being the reporter.

[2] *Idem,* Gauri Shankar being the reporter.

The aforesaid report about Maulvi Fazl Haq's anti-British views and activities which give a clue to his attempts at jihad is reflected in his own writings[1]. But a hidden feature in the picture which the spies could not notice lay in the fact that Fazl Haq shared his views with Emperor Bahadur Shah. On account of his weakness; old age, sainthood and sufism Bahadur Shah could not speak out like Fazl Haq, but he seized every opportunity that presented itself to encourage the Army. Writing on 2nd September from the city of Dehli, a British spy says, 'Yesterday Heera Singh, Brigade Major of the Neemuch force had an audience with the King. The King spoke encouragingly to him and directed him to reorganize the Brigade; and although he could not give such guns as had been lost, he (King) would replace them to the best of his ability. The King has promised to give siege guns. He also bestowed 2,000 rupees upon Heera Singh to make new camp equipage'[2]. As a result an atmosphere of devotion was created; and to this effect some volunteers wrote[3] to the Emperor, and the Princes also expressed their readiness to go to Panipat[4]

[1] *Vide* Appendix. H.

[2] *Delhi News,* File 129, September 2, 1857.

[3] *Vide* Appendix. F.

[4] *Joint Petition of Mirza Mughul, Mirza Abdul Hasan, Shah Bakhtawar and Mirza Khair Sultan, sons of the King.*

TO

NO DATE.

THE KING! SHELTER OF THE WORLD!

RESPECTFULLY PRAYETH,—That four Regiments of Infantry, two of Cavalry, and twelve Guns of Horse and Foot Artillery, according to the detail below, with a full supply of ammunition, other necessaries of war and some treasure, may be speedily made over to your slaves in order that they may proceed to Paneeput, and may there, through

in order to intercept the British siege train. In the same spirit Mirza Mughul wrote a letter assuring the Emperor on his own behalf and also on behalf of others of the common resolve to fight till the end.

'Your Exalted Majesty' said he, 'may keep your mind free from the dread of the enemy. Your slave has personally been staying in the batteries with the Troops for two days; and where the batteries of the infidels were, there they are still. They have made no advance. If their batteries had advanced considerably, they must have come into the city. The whole Army is prepared to slay the infidels, and an attack is about being made immediately. Through Your Majesty's prestige the batteries will be speedily taken. And as some of the soldiers come into Your Majesty's presence and report what they have heard and not what they have seen, pray do not believe their statements; but be fully assured that so long as there is life in the frames of your slaves, no harm shall reach Your Majesty. Let it be known that matters are in the dispensation of God. Your slave is

---

Your Majesty's auspices and by God's blessing, obtain immediate and complete victory and at once return to the Royal presence. This day has been fixed for our departure.

74th Regiment of Native Infantry			...	1
38th	Ditto	Ditto	...	1
54th	Ditto	Ditto	...	1
20th	Ditto	Ditto	...	1
Volunteers	...	...	...	400 Men
Corps of Gwalior Cavalry			...	1
Corps of Regular Cavalry			...	1
24-Pounder Guns		...	...	4
Howitzer and Mortar		...	...	2
Companies of Militia		...	...	2
Jhajjar Cavalry		...	...	100 Troopers

Petition attested with seals of Mirza Sultan Zaheeru'ddin, Commander-in-Chief Bahadur; Mirza Muhammad Abdul Hasan, Colonel of the 20th Regiment of Native Infantry; Shah Bakhtawar, son of the king, Abu Zafar, and Mirza Khair Sultan Bahadur.

Autograph order by the King in Pencil.

The departure of you, our sons, is exceedingly right and

not neglectful. Let it be known to Your Majesty that he stays personally in the batteries[1]!

But Mirza Mughul was not far-sighted; he did not know that the fall of Dehli was not far off. The British had made active preparations for a big assault on the city of Dehli while the morale of the Badshahi Army which was never very high had lowered appreciably since the disaster of Najafgarh. In its ranks differences, always deep-rooted, had leapt to the surface. Fath Muhammad the British spy says, 'The Nasirabad and Neemuch Brigades are supporters of Mirza Mughul and the Bareilly Brigade is devoted to the King. The officers of the Bareilly force and Mirza Mughul are bitter enemies. Every brigade is clamorous; they are actually in want of food. There is not a silver in the Treasury. The Bareilly troops talk of returning to Bareilly. The Bareilly Officers after holding a separate meeting went to the King. Some of the cavalry said they had gone to ask for the dismissal of Mirza Mughul or for leave to go to Bareilly; and if both these requests were refused, they would commit some violence'[2]. What the Emperor did to pacify the Bareilly troops is not known. The spies'

---

proper; but first get a petition from the Officers of the Regiments expressing their willingness to accompany you, and lay it before us, that we may have assurance on this point.

(*Pr. Tr. B. S.* No. 41, p. 65 and Tr. E. K. D., pp. 91-92).

It should be noted that Zahoru'ddin is wrong; the correct word given in the Persian original is Zaheeru'ddin; (M.H.).

[1] This letter is undated according to the *Proceedings of the Trial of Bahadur Shah* (No. 47, p. 68). But the context shows that it was written, after the disaster of Najafgarh, in the opening days of the month of September.

[2] *Delhi News,* File 131; September 1, 1857.

reports are incomplete, but they emphasize the split in the Badshahi Army saying, 'Each cavalry is now split up into 'Thokes'—confideracies comprising those who are residents of a particular tract of the country. For instance, Hansi fellows form one 'Thoke', the Kalanor men another 'Thoke', and so on through the whole body. No one agrees with the other'[1]. Matters aggravated as days advanced. Perhaps the enemy[2] hand was working secretly in their midst setting them all by the ears and making them all quarrel with their own king as they actually did, demanding their pay under threats of plundering the Palace and the City. 'I have 40,000 rupees which you are welcome to take' said the Emperor in an attempt to pacify the quarrelsome heads. Then he added, 'There are 101 gold mohurs which were recently presented to me by the Subadar of Bareilly, you might have them too'[3]. When he found the Army Officers still dissatisfied, he offered all the jewels of the Zenana; and rising from his chair he threw before them the embroidered cushion on which he had been sitting

---

[1] *Ibid.*

[2] Read carefully the following quotation from Keith will give an insight. It is suggestive enough. Writing on 14th June, 1857, he says, 'We still continue to occupy our old position on the Ridge, and the enemy occasionally make faint efforts to dislodge us . . . But it is annoying to think that there seems little prospect now of our entering Delhi until the Sikh corps join us or until the Bhurtpore or Jeypore or other contingents make their appearance; or until there is such a decided schism in Delhi as to show that the two parties are pitted one against the other. News of a reliable nature came yesterday to Greathed to the effect that the Hindoos were becoming disgusted, finding they were being made complete dupes by the Mahomedans who wish to make a religious war of it.'

Keith—*Delhi-1857*, p. 60.

[3] *Delhi News*, September 5, 1857.

and bid them take that[1]. Then he went into his private apartments, and brought out jewelry and gave them to the officers saying, 'Take this and forget your hunger'[2]. There was such a clear note of sincerity in his word and deed that the hearts of the unprincipled[3] and unyielding soldiers now melted and they were heard to say, 'We cannot accept of your Crown jewels, but we are satisfied that you are willing to give your life and property to sustain us'[4]. Thereupon the Emperor gave away 40,000 rupees and promised to pay the balance within fifteen days; and he made arrangements to raise a loan.[5]

---

[1] *Ibid.*

[2] Metcalfe—T.N.N., p. 207.

[3] On 11th May, 1857 the Emperor had said plainly to the 'mutineers', 'I am a fakir and possess no treasure.' *Vide* (i) p. 169 *supra;* (ii) Zaheer Dehlawi—D. G., p. 50.

[4] Metcalfe—T.N.N., p. 207.

[5] Writing on 2nd September, 1857 a British spy says, 'The writer went to the Palace hearing that the Officers had all gone there to demand an issue of pay. A crowd of 500 men of all ranks was collected round the Diwan-i Khass. Mirza Mughul, Mirza Abu Bakr and Mirza Khair Sultan Shahzadas were surrounded by the crowd. The soldiers shouted out that Ahsnullah Khan Hakeem alone prevented their receiving their pay. They clamoured for his death and for the imprisonment of the Shahzadas and avowed their intention of dividing the City into allotments and extorting their pay by force. They were most fierce and insolent in their demands. Mirza Mughul, in fear of his life, sent for Mirza Ilahi Bakhsh who succeeded in appeasing them and took them before the King. The King declared he had no pay to give them. The troops rejoined that in that case they would plunder both the Palace and the City and massacre all the Court. Upon this the King rose and threw down the *cassoolee* on which he usually sits in the Durbar and gave orders that all the property of the Court, the horses, elephants, caparisons and even the ornaments of his Begums

This was decidedly a pathetic and heart-rending scene in the drama of the war, staged in the course of a few days following the disaster of Najafgarh; but it was not the last[1]. The Emperor pulled himself together and

should be immediately made over to them; and then turning his face towards Mecca he burst into tears exclaiming that he was well punished for his sins. . . Hearing these passionate cries, the whole Court and the Begums were moved to tears, and even the soldiery were ashamed of their violence, excusing themselves on the ground of the extreme distress and hunger to which they were reduced. Mirza Mughul brought out 40,000 rupees and begged them to take that sum as an instalment. The influential men of the city hearing of this scene repaired to the Palace and agreed among themselves to raise 1,50,000 rupees; and should more be required the Begums were to furnish the excess until the English should arrive. The King and the citizens have no escape from the clutches of the tyrants . . . There was a grand consultation which lasted till midnight at the house of Mufti Sadru'ddin, and a deputation has gone this morning to wait on the King.

On 3rd September Munshi Agha Jan and Waris Ali agreed to pay 10,000 rupees each. They yielded only when the soldiers beating their swords, threatened to pour holes in their bodies. Munshi Agha Jan stood out bravely calling upon them so as to kill him, but his relations could not bear the sight of seeing him tortured. . . . The ambassadors from Lucknow and Bareilly are much surprised and terrified at the state of affairs in Delhi. They now know the prospects of the King's cause; and perhaps will not be so anxious to obtain grants from the King'.

(*Delhi News,* 2nd September
Turab Ali, the British spy, being
the reporter)

[1] Writing on 3rd, 4th and 7th September the British spies reported similar scenes and said, 'The Army now think of nothing but of their pay and how to get food. . . . Bakht Khan's troops say if they do not get pay in a day or two they will bolt. On 6th September 'the Gwalior sowars and Bareilly officers went to the Durbar and asked for pay with a great deal of insolence. The King replied, 'I have been

Providence enabled him to endure the worst afflictions that have ever befallen a crowned head. He continued to perform his usual duties. 'The King', says a British spy, 'exercises the affairs of the Country and Revenue[1] which he will administer himself'. In addition he adopted new measures to collect money to be able to pay the promised balance to the Army[2]; he also

---

wearing mourning ever since you came here and have been always ready to expire; you would better kill me'

(*Delhi News*—6th September, 1857

from the pen of Turab Ali, the British spy).

Writing on 4th September Jiwan Lal says, 'Certain officers of the Nasirabad camp gave His Majesty a great deal of annoyance last night regarding their pay. In consequence of this the King ordered all the silver goods to be made over to them, saying 'Sell them, and divide the proceeds among yourselves for pay'. The officers were still dissatisfied. (Metcalfe—T.N.N., p. 219).

[1] *Delhi News*, 2nd September, 1857.

[2] 'His Majesty' says Jiwan Lal, 'sent a written order to General Bakht Khan to pay the troops to the amount of 26,000 rupees.' (Metcalfe—T. N. N., p 221). It should be recalled that on his arrival in Dehli (*vide* p. 235 *Supra*) Bakht Khan had promised to relieve the Emperor of all anxieties for the payment of the Army since he had brought from Bareilly a sum of 400,000 rupees. But General Bakht Khan now disappointed the Emperor.

Then at the instance of the Emperor 'Mir Said Ali Khan, Hakim Abdul Haq, Mirza Ilahi Bakhsh and Salig Ram the Treasurer met and consulted on the ways and means of paying the Army.' (*Idem*, p. 222).

On September 7 Mir Said Ali Khan, Diwan Mukand Lal Badru'ddin Khan, Hakim Abdul Haq with his sons, and Nawab Quli Khan were all arrested and put in the Palace Guard-room by order of the Military Court till money was forthcoming. They pleaded that they were making arrangements to raise the money. On September 8, the Emperor summoned the Military Court and made them release the honourable prisoners. They agreed to 'raise money by a self-imposed tax throughout the city for the pay of the

encouraged frequent sittings of the Military Court[1] and referred to it certain problems, and concerted measures with Bakht Khan to meet the British assault[2]. Writing on 4th, 5th and 7th September 1857, Jiwan Lal says, 'The King held a council to-day[3] in which the position of affairs was considered. General Bakht Khan reported that the English siege train had arrived and they were erecting breaching batteries opposite the Kashmiri Gate. The King inquired, 'What arrangements are you making for meeting the English fire? If you cannot oppose them you had better open the gates of the city at once'. The General said, 'I am removing the Magazine outside the city, and I propose to meet the English fire with forty guns for which I am constructing batteries'. The General further said that he had arranged to employ 2,000 cavalry to cut off all commissariat supplies from the English camp. The King inquired what stock of gunpowder there was; and an urgent letter was sent off to the Nawab of Farrukhabad to send without delay 2,000 maunds of sulphur. Then orders were sent to the police to appoint a 'Punch' every day to fix the prices of food. The police had also caused the attend-

---

Army'. (Metcalfe—T. N. N., p. 225). On the same day the Emperor ordered the Police 'to collect three months' rent from every shop and dwelling-house for the pay of the Sepoys. Then he ordered the arrest of the Princes who had misappropriated the money collected for the pay of the sepoys' (*Idem,* p. 226).

On September 9 when the Sepoys had resumed fighting the Emperor sent them 60 maunds of sweetmeats and 24 rupees. (*Idem,* p. 227). On September 12, he sent 5,000 rupees to the gunpowder factory for the manufacture of gunpowder. (*Idem,* p. 228). Then 200 men were enlisted to collect the revenue from Loharu.

[1] Metcalfe—T. N. N., pp. 214, 225, 226.

[2] *Idem,* p. 222.

[3] *I.e.* September 5, 1857.

ance of every jeweller. They were informed that the citizens must raise eight lakhs of rupees immediately for the pay of troops. After giving these orders the King directed Mirza Mughul to exercise due diligence in the realization of the money and notify the Royal orders by beat of drum throughout the city. In consequence of this step being taken the Military Council decided to attack the English next day, and it was proclaimed that every citizen, Hindu or Mahomedan, who assisted in the attack, should share in the plunder and whoever made prisoners of the Gurkhas, Sikhs[1] or the English would be handsomely rewarded'. Previously Jiwan Lal says, 'Autograph letters were despatched to the Rajas of Jaipur, Jodhpur, Bikaner and Alwar that the King was in want of troops and was desirous of annihilating the English; but inasmuch as he had no reliable person to organize and administer the very important affairs of the empire at this juncture, he wished to form a Confederacy of States; and if the States he now addressed with these letters would combine for the purpose, he would willingly resign the imperial power into their hands'[2].

By 5th September the British siege train and ammunition convoy had arrived safely at the Ridge, as was reported by Bakht Khan who complained:

---

[1] While the majority of the Sikhs were with the British, a small number were certainly with the Emperor. In his letter to G. C. Barnes, Commissioner and Superintendent, Cis-Sutlej States, Ambala, Rajab Ali. Meer Munshi to the British Commander-in-Chief, says, 'I have the honour to inform you that yesterday I sent a man to Delhi in order to persuade all the Sikhs in the rebel army there to come over to the English Camp.' (*Delhi News,* File 133, September 6, 1857). Also see Metcalfe—T. N. N., p. 208.

[2] Metcalfe—T. N. N., pp. 219-220.

'For days I have been saying that a force must be sent out to intercept the siege train at Panipat[1] but no attention was paid. The siege train has arrived, and now we are in a plight and the population are in a state of great alarm'[2].

The Emperor made no reply. Perhaps he recalled how Bakht Khan himself had brought about the destruction of the Nimuch troops through self-obsession. He also recalled that Bakht Khan had been untrue to his word. On his arrival in Dehli on 2nd July he had declared that he had brought treasure to the extent of four lakhs and that he would not trouble the Emperor for any assistance[3]. But he had since then held tight the strings of his purse and had in a way encouraged the insolent demands of the Army officers for pay. And himself too, he pressed the Emperor for paying the Bareilly troops[4]. Says Jiwan Lal, 'General Bakht Khan made a complaint that whereas, the King's servants and other troops had received wages, the Bareilly force, on which the brunt of the fighting fell, had received nothing; that all his men were in consequence discontented. The King replied I have already caused one lakh of rupees to be distributed; the treasury is empty. How many lakhs of rupees have passed through your hands? Why have you not paid your men with some of the money?'.[5] Bakht Khan on whom the Emperor had counted so much from the beginning and whom he had called *farzand,*[6] now

---

[1] The Princes had expressed their readiness to go to Panipat for this very purpose. *Vide* p. 261 and footnote *supra.*

[2] *Delhi News,* 6th September, 1857.

[3] Metcalfe—T. N. N., p. 135.

[4] *Idem,* p. 223.

[5] *Idem,* p. 224.

[6] *Vide* p. 231 *supra.*

stood exposed. He could make no reply. The Emperor was wroth but he kept his head cool and continued to urge his troops to fight the English to the last. Says a British spy, 'The king inspected and approved seven rocket guns and ordered them to be placed in position to commence firing rockets'[1]. To-day the force inside the City was paraded outside, and each Regiment was accoutred for fighting and they were told that this was not the time for fighting but they must die at their posts'[2]. Further the Emperor ordered conscription; and it was proclaimed in the streets of the City of Dehli that 'every adult whether Hindu or Musalman in the King's service or out of his service, a resident of the city or visitor, should go out and attack the English. All plunder after the victory except arms and ammunition is to belong to the captors. Let everyone strive his best, as his eternal and temporal interests depend upon his exertions. Whosoever wilfully neglects his duty will be considered an enemy of the Government'. Afterwards a parade was held, and a slip of paper containing the Proclamation was put into the hands of every soldier. The matter is kept as secret as possible. And a munshi of the Kotwali is now going the rounds of the city accompanied by the crier explaining the order to all concerned[3]. This proclamation was announced by beat of drum under the joint orders of the Emperor and Mirza Mughul[4]. And again it was proclaimed that 'every man should fight as they were of one body and one life. Every Hindu and Musalman has been sworn by oaths, the most binding upon his

---

[1] *Dehli News,* 6th September, 1857.

[2] *Ibid.*

[3] *Delhi News,* File 139; September 9, 1857.

[4] *Ibid.*

religion, to go forth and attack the English'[1]. Giving a short report of the action that followed, a British spy said, 'Yesterday the fighting was severe. The Bareilly and Naseerabad Brigades, and in fact all the troops inside the city were engaged. The 61st N.I. and 20th L.N. lost between 30 killed and wounded. Every regiment lost some. The 8th Irregulars dismounted and fought on foot at the Batteries. They too lost 200 killed and wounded. The reports to-day in Durbar stated the entire loss at 500 killed. This number does not include the wounded. The Hindus and Musalmans have interchanged oaths binding themselves not to desert. Nevertheless, 25 sowars made their escape to-day'[2].

The scene which is now unfolding itself before the reader's eyes is the last and longest of the many tragic scenes in the drama of the war in Dehli. It begins with the rain of bullets in the Royal Palace and the streets of the city, the breaching and cracking of its ramparts, the bombardment of its gates, the battering of its bastions, the transformation of its different parts into a vast armed camp packed with sepoys, the ceaseless thundering of guns day and night, the heaping of dead bodies in the streets, the desertions of individual sepoys and groups from the body of the Army, the spread of confusion and consternation in all circles—and closes with the exhaustion of guns in the Fort and the gunpowder in the magazine, the enemies' advance into the city, their capture of the Qudsia Bagh, Kashmiri Gate, Kishanganj, Lahori Gate and finally of the Jamii' Masjid and the Fort. Writing on 9th September a British spy says, 'The guns still maintain a fire from the Cutchery Bastion. Since yesterday all passage by

[1] *Ibid.*

[2] *Delhi News,* File No. 140, September 9, 1857.

the Kashmiri Gate has been closed. The round shot and shell from the British Batteries fall there like rain. Several travellers and some sepoys of the 9th Native Infantry were wounded at Col. Skinner's House. The Bastion at the Kashmiri Gate has been much shaken and the wall of the city is breached in several places. The Shah[1] Bastion between the Mori and Kabul Gates is also much battered and the guns on it are completely silenced[2]. All last night the troops remained under arms at the Kashmiri Gate. They muster very strong from the Kashmiri Gate, Lall Diggi and Darya Ganj to the Delhi Gate. The Chandni Chowk up to the Ajmeri Gate is much less frequented. The rebels for the most part are quartered in the shops and houses along the street leading from the Kashmiri Gate to Dehli Gate. Inside the city there are no preparations for resistance but eight guns were yesterday mounted on the Palace walls by the garrison of Salimgarh. In yesterday's conflict the Neemuch cavalry suffered severely. Muhammad Shafi, second in command of the Bareilly Brigade, was wounded. The casualties amongst the cavalry were considerable[3]. The Kotwal of the City went round at night and ordered the inhabitants of every street to be armed and ready; directly the English made their appearance they were to slay them. The soldiery made the King come out of his privacy and abused him in terms not to be described. The King wept bitterly and exclaimed, 'For God's sake, take my life'[4]. He surrendered all the money and was frantic with grief. All the brigades of the City are standing.

[1] 'Shah' is incorrect. The name of this bastion was *Siah Burj i.e.* Black Bastion. *Vide* Zaheer Dehlawi—D.G., p. 109.

[2], [3] *Delhi News,* File No. 140, September 9, 1857.

[4] *Idem,* File No. 141, September 9 and 10, 1857.

The rebels are constructing an inner battery behind the Shah Bastion and another close to the Budergah[1] Gate and the compound of Baboo's[2] house which will contain two guns. The 9th N. I. went up to the King and declared their unwillingness to fight any more saying, 'Fate has been fulfilled. Now we will issue from the Kashmiri Gate and yield up our lives. Send up such support as you may deem proper. Great consternation prevails: there are no guns left in the Fort. The guns are made to do double duty, sometimes in the Fort and sometimes at the Kashmiri Gate. The barracks are repaired as quickly as possible, and every man who shows his face, whether merchant or shopkeeper, is seized and made to work. . . .[3]

On 10th September the British spy in the city found the guards stronger than usual and every preparation made for resisting an assault. One heavy gun was mounted at each gate. At the Diwan-i Amm there were four guns and six ammunition tumbrels. 'The citadel of Salimpur is well fortified and guns are mounted on all sides. There is a strong muster of troops from the Kashmiri Gate to the Lahori Gate; and in the main streets every house is filled from top to bottom with sepoys. The cavalry are encamped about the Bank[4], the Lall Diggi[5] and flour mills[6]. There is also a large party of them in the Masjid near the Dehli Gate. Others are scattered here and there over the

---

[1] The correct name given by Zaheer Dehlawi (D. G. p. 109) is Badrrau Gate or Badr Gate.

[2] This is the corrupt form of 'Wood house' *i.e. Lakrion ki tal* mentioned by Zaheer Dehlawi (D. G. p. 109).

[3] *Delhi News,* September 9, 1857

[4], [5], [6] For Bank and Lall Diggi see the map facing p. 274. The 'flour mills' were destroyed in the course of the war and cannot be traced.

City. In every gate there is a gun, and inside the Kashmiri Gate there are four guns[1] in position. The *mujahideen* are collected in a body, ready for action'[2]. . . .

On 11th and 12th September the British spy reported saying, 'The Rebels on the whole are pleased with the ardour now displayed and declare that if they fought from the outset with the same spirit the affair should not have been so protracted. All traces of the English would have been swept from the page of history. At night strong guards are posted at the bridge of boats and upon the battlements about the Kashmiri Gate. . . . Between the Kabul and Kashmiri Gates they are constructing a large Battery. More guns have been mounted on the walls and at the city gates. The cavalry shows better heart just now than the Infantry. The sowars of the 9th and 13th Irregulars and the 4th Regiment Cavalry are always forward. They vow their intention of meeting the assault at the gate. The infantry who try to escape are brought back by the sowars. Yesterday Abbas Mirza came in from Lakhnao. He brought some jewels and gold mohurs. The King has established a mint at Katra Mashroo. A new rupee from this mint was brought for inspection to-day. The silver of the King's howdah and sticks of the office and utensils are sent to the mint to be turned into rupees for the use of the Army. A man came to Mirza Mughul and offered for a reward of 9,000 rupees to inveigle the British force into an ambuscade where they might be easily killed.

---

[1] For the guns at the gates of the city see the aforesaid map which has been prepared largely on the basis of the sketch given by Raja Nahr Singh of Ballabgarh. (*Vide* Muir, W.—R.I.D., vol. I, p. 535).

[2] *Delhi News,* September 10, 1857.

Aminu'ddin and Ziyau'ddin, sons of Nawab Ahmad Bakhsh, are prevented by order of the King from leaving Dehli. The city people hear that Musalmans are killed without mercy by the British but Hindus are spared' [1]

Meanwhile the British were making strong and active preparations for the final assault on Dehli. On 6th September they received fresh reinforcements from Mirath; on the 7th came the Jind contingent[2] and good many of the Muzbee[3] Sikhs also joined the British standard. The same day a new battery called Brind's Battery was erected under the command of Kaye and opened such a severe fire on the Mori Gate Bastion that the Bastion was completely demolished. In the afternoon of 8th September the British captured the Ludlow Castle and Qudsia Bagh; and both these places were immediately utilised as sites for the erection of batteries whence firing began and continued day and night. Unable to withstand the British shells, the Badshahi Army brought forward their own guns and enfiladed the British batteries, and they opened fire at the British Camp from the City walls. By the night of 13th September the British made two breaches near the Kashmiri Gate Bastion. 'Before the 14th of September', says Muinu'ddin Hasan, 'the bastions upon which the English concentrated their fire had become dust[4]. In the morning of Monday, 14th September,

[1] *Delhi News*—File 141, September 11 and 12, 1857; Turab Ali, Kalloo and Mohan Harkara, British spies, reporting.

[2] 'His Highness the Raja having made a particular request that they should be employed when the attack on the city took place', says Keith (*Delhi-1857*, p. 265).

[3] 'Muzbee' is derived from the Arabic word *mazhab*. Forrest (H.I.M., vol. I. p. 126) gives it as 'the name of a class of Sikhs originally of low caste'.

[4] Metcalfe—T. N. N., p. 69.

five British columns stormed the city, closing upon it from different directions. The first column commanded by Nicholson marched down the Qudsia Bagh to storm the breach near the Kashmiri Gate Bastion. The second column commanded by Col. Jones proceeded to storm the breach of the Water Bastion. The third column commanded by Col. Campbell assaulted the Kashmiri Gate after blowing it up. The fourth column under Major Reid advanced from Sabzi Mandi towards Kishan Ganj and Paharipur, and made a thrust at the Kabul Gate. The fifth or reserve column under Brigadier Longfield awaited the result of the attacks and bided time to take possession of the posts assigned to it immediately as the other columns entered the city. The Kashmiri Gate was relentlessly blown up with dynamite by Lieutenant Salkeld who was soon crushed to death by the patriots of Dehli. But the Gate lay in ruins, and the storming party of the British Army soldiers burst in. They took possession of the large buildings in the neighbourhood, and then rushed along the rampart to the Mori Gate Bastion and the Kabul Gate in the face of a very obstinate resistance. This was small comfort to the British assailants, for although they had seized a large belt stretching from the Water Bastion to the Kabul Gate including the Church and the College, the Badshahi troops had smashed 4th British column which comprised the Gurkhas and had been striving under Reid's command to enter the city by the Lahori Gate and seize the Kishan Ganj zone. And the Badshahi troops continued to hold possession of the principal parts of the city including the Lahori Gate Bastion and other bastions as well as the Fort.[1] 'The mutineers', says

[1] (i) Charles Ball—H.I.M., I., p. 499.
(ii) Forrest—H.I.M., pp. 131-135.

Muinu'ddin Hasan, 'defended Jami' Masjid and checked the English advance. The English fell back on the Cashmere Gate. A further stand was made by the mutineers at Pulbin Bund[1] and at the Calcutta Gate. The fighting continued for five days through the city[2]. But on Monday, the first day of their assault, the British gained little ground. In the words of Forrest, 'When the day closed only a portion of the walls of Dehli were in our possession. . . . The little ground we had gained had been won at a heavy cost. Eleven hundred and four men and sixty-five officers or about two men in nine were killed or wounded'.[3]

(iii) Rotton—N.S.D., pp. 261-264.
(iv) Sidgwick—I.M., pp. 74-75.
(v) *Illustrated London News*, November 21, 1857, p. 514.

[1] This is a typical example of the corrupted forms of proper names frequently found in Metcalfe's edition of Jiwan Lal's diary. I am of opinion that 'Pulbin Bund' stands for '*Bund* (*Band*) *Gali*' commonly known as 'Gali Sarband' which was a small street near Begam Bagh and Chandni Chowk. (*Vide* Map of the War in Dehli p. 274). The fight that took place in the Begam Bagh and Chandni Chowk area is described by Zaheer Dehlawi (D.G., pp. 109-123); and the traces of the stand made by the inhabitants in the small street near Chandni Chowk that were seen even after the fall of Dehli are noticed by Charles Ball (H.I.M., vol. II., p. 167).

[2] Metcalfe—T. N. N., p. 70.

[3] Forrest—H.I.M., vol. I., pp. 146-147.

On 14th September there was a very stiff hand-to-hand fight in the streets between the British troops and the inhabitants of Dehli. Zaheer Dehlawi (p. 113), the eye-witness says, 'Thousands of people collected, each wielding a stick or broken lathi or sword and with the help of a gun which they had managed to carry from the Lahori Gate to the Kotwali, they made an attack on the British troops and drove them back'. So many were killed that Zaheer Dehlawi saw heaps of dead bodies along the road from the Jami'

Now the British erected their guns and mortars at the places they had gained, and fired ceaselessly at the Palace, the Jami' Masjid and the streets and houses in the city. Early in the morning of 16th September they stormed and captured the Magazine as well as Kishan Ganj. In the course of the next two days (17th and 18th September) they advanced slowly, encountering vehement opposition at every step. On 19th September a party of British troops having rushed from the Kabul Gate attacked the Burn Bastion which fell into their hands the same day. 'In the evening', says Muinu'ddin Hasan, 'General Bakht Khan, collecting a force, went to the King and begged him to fly to Lucknow with him. He also offered to collect the scattered rebel forces outside the city and again fight the English. But the old king refused his help. Bakht Khan then marched for Lakhnao with all the forces he could collect'.[1]

In the morning of Sunday, 20th September, the British took possession of the Lahori Gate and the neighbouring Bastion. Then they captured the Jami' Masjid. 'The Jumma[2] Musjid', says Rotton, 'which resisted an assault on the memorable 14th of September, and from which we had to retire, now fell an easy prey before our victorious arms'.[3] This done, they

---

Masjid to the Kotwali. This is confirmed by Muinu'ddin Hasan who says, 'At the Kotwali a gun had been planted and fired by some sowars and bad characters. This fire fell in the midst of the English advancing column, killing and wounding upwards of fifty of them'. Metcalfe—T. N. N., p. 70.

[1] Metcalfe—T. N. N., p. 70.

[2] Jumma Musjid' also misspelt by Metcalfe (*vide* T. N. N., pp. 23, 98) is incorrect. It should be Jami' Masjid.

[3] Rotton—N.S.D., p. 315.

seized the Fort, blowing up the gate. Col. Jones wrote to General Wilson announcing the capture of the Palace in these words, 'Blown open the gate and got possession of the Palace'.[1] The Fort including the Palace, according to Rotton, 'was well-nigh deserted; few men found within were indiscriminately slain'.[2]

When Bakht Khan left Dehli in the evening of 19th September no trace of the Badshahi Army had remained. All had fled; and Zaheer Dehlawi gives an eye-witness account of the flight of the Purbiyas from the city.[3] The night of 19th September Emperor Bahadur Shah spent practically alone in the Fort. Before daybreak he left and fled to the Dargah of Nizamu'ddin; so did the Princes but they went straight to Humayun's Tomb.[4] At the sacred tomb of Hazrat Nizamu'ddin Auliva Bahadur Shah burst into tears and spoke his mind to Shah Ghulam Hasan, custodian of the Dargah.[5] Then he entrusted to his care the

---

[1] *Idem,* p. 316.

[2] *Ibid.*

[3] Zaheer Dehlawi—D.G., p. 112. Also see Charles Ball who, in the same context says, 'But Pandy don't stand so firmly as people expected'.

[4] This is my conclusion based on a study of all the available evidence. Zaheer Dehlawi appears confounded on this point. At one place (p. 116) while mentioning the Emperor's flight to Humayun's Tomb he gives us to understand that the Princes also went there. Subsequently (p. 124) he says that the Princes were arrested at the Dargah of Nizamu'ddin. But a local enquiry that I recently made shows that while Emperor Bahadur Shah's arrival at the Dargah straight from the Fort is strongly believed and in fact proved (*vide* Photo in the Preface), there is no evidence of the Princes' arrival, or of their arrest, in the precincts of the Dargah. The Princes' flight direct from the Fort to Humayun's Tomb is attested by Muinu'ddin Hasan. (Metcalfe—T. N. N., p. 70).

[5] *Vide* Preface.

Sacred Hairs in a Box[1] which he had carried from the Fort. Afterwards he too proceeded to Humayun's Tomb where he was taken prisoner the same day.' In his diary Keith reports this event saying, 'The King brought in by Hodson. See the old scoundrel'.[3] Writing about the same day, Muir says, 'The King, the Begum Zinat Mahal are close prisoners; and to-day[4] the Princes Mirza Mughul, Abu Bakr and Khair Sultan were brought in by Hodson from Humayun's Tomb, and shot at the Dehli Gate. The bodies are now lying at the Kotwali'.[5] According to Zaheer Dehlawi thirty Princes—sons, sons-in-law and grandsons—of Emperor Bahadur Shah were arrested. Then they were taken outside the Dehli Gate and beheaded; their severed heads were sent to the Emperor.[6]

---

[1] *Vide* Photo in the Preface, p. xv.

[2] 'On 21st September' says Rotton (p. 318) 'Hodson went out accompanied by a native who knew the Royal family and took the person of His Imperial Majesty Shah Bahadur Shah and brought him in, a prisoner to Palace'.

[3] Keith—*Delhi-1857*, p. 301.

[4] *I.e.* 21st September.

[5] Muir, W.—'State Papers', vol. I, p. 369 quoted by Forrest—H. I. M., vol. 1, p. 148.

[6] Zaheer Dehlawi—D. G., p. 315. Also see Appendix H

CHAPTER X

SOURCES

Long is the list of the sources on which this work is based. While all are contemporary, some are published, others unpublished. *First* in the list stands the Royal diwans[1] which have been mentioned above.[2] Hakim Ahsanullah Khan who was in charge of the Royal publications expressed his personal appreciation of these, saying

[3] چه دیوان رهنماے جن و انسان - همه لب لباب نص قران

> What a marvellous Diwan! it is a guide to humanity and genii. The whole is an essence of the Revelations in the Quran.

That is, the poems or ghazals comprising the said diwans inspire the reader with an ardour for morality and spiritualism like the Holy Quran. Composed by Bahadur Shah in the capacity of *Qutb-i Alam*[4], a Sufi saint of high standing verging on 70, his ghazals are absolutely free from erotomania. *Ghazal* means speaking in the language of love but Bahadur Shah spoke, in metaphor, of his devotion to God—a subject on which he is known to have lectured to his disciples[5]—as well as of the anguish of his heart. Thus, what might appear to a superficial reader as erotic poetry

[1] A *diwan* is a collection of poems.

[2] *Vide* p. 44 *supra*.

[3] MS. *Roz-namcha Bahadur Shah,* last page. Naziriya Library, *Dehli*.

[4] Literally 'pole of the universe', *Qutb-i Alam* is a technical term for a higher sufi dignitary. *Cf.* p. 36 *supra*.

[5] *Vide* Photo p. 91 *supra*.

are really Bahadur Shah's verses not only of devotion but also of lamentation, describing his sufferings at the hands of the British.[1]

Secondly the Court Diary[2], which may be seen in the Naziriya Library, *Dehli,* already described.[3] Another but different kind of Court Diary commonly known as *'Diary Bahadur Shah'* is found in the *Khulasa Akhbar* manuscript at the National Archives of India. It speaks magniloquently of the British Government, *e.g.*,

مشہور است کہ نواب گورنر جنرل بہادر بسیار عالی
مراتب و رحیم و کریم و خندہ پیشانی و عرض فریاد
غربا فی شنوند و بداد ہر یکے مسلوک می شوند

(It is widely known that the Nawab Governor-General Bahadur enjoys a very lofty and exalted position with cheery countenance and lucky stars. He is extremely merciful and benign, and gives a careful hearing to the petitions and submissions of every one and administers justice to all.)

This manuscript too has been discussed above.[4]

---

[1] *Vide* Appendix C.

[2] Regarding the Court Diary a question was put to Hakim Ahsanulla Khan at the Military Tribunal: Question: Was a Court Diary of occurrences at the Palace kept by order of the King during the rebellion?

Answer: The Court Diary was kept up as usual according to the custom which had long preceded the outbreak.

(Pr. Tr. B. S., p. 93). Also see Metcalfe (T. N. N., p. 3) who says. '. . . he (Jiwan Lal) procured for me the official Court Diary, kept by the Moulvi or Royal Chaplain of the King's private mosque in the Palace. (Metcalfe--T. N. N., p. 3).

[3] *Vide* p. 95 *supra,* footnote.

[4] *Vide* pp. 95, 96 *supra.*

Another Court Diary is found in the *'Precis of Palace Intelligence'* in English, the manuscript of which, now at the National Archives, runs into 800[1] pages, each page being about 11″ long and 9″ wide with an average number of 30 lines and 250 words. It gives information about the private life of Bahadur Shah and throws light on the social and cultural aspects of the Palace life. A perusal of it will convince the reader that the Royal Palace, then, was not the hotbed of corruption as is commonly believed. The entries are arranged in a chronological order ranging from Monday, 6th January 1851 to Monday, 1st January 1854. Most of these show[2] that Bahadur Shah was a man of regular and active habits. He never missed his daily rides and recreations and was fond of Nature and hunting. One entry of Sunday, 5th December 1857, shows his connection with the Sepoys. It runs as follows: 'Two sepoys of the 50th Regiment were presented to His Majesty by Hameed Khan Jamadar; and offering muzzers and sweetmeats constituted themselves his disciples. His Majesty read them a lecture on the knowledge of God and gave them a rosary and *roomal'*. The same entry also shows his interest in gardening.

Thirdly the records at the National Archives; these are of three kinds—(i) the Mutiny Papers, (ii) Foreign Department Papers and (iii) Spies' Reports.

(i) The Mutiny Papers are those papers which were found by the British soldiers in the different apartments of the Royal Palace after the fall of

[1] MS. Foreign. Miscellaneous (4); N. A.

[2] The entry of Thursday, 18th March, 1852 says, 'His Majesty visited the Qoodsea Bagh by the road through the Salimgarh entrance to the Fort for excercise and returned to the Palace., Friday, 19th March: 'His Majesty visited the Roshan Ara and Sirhindi Gardens by the road through the wicket and returned to the Palace.'

Dehli. Many of these were burnt by them. Those which survived were put into bundles[1] of various sizes; bundles are called 'Boxes' in the Press-List which was later prepared and published.[2] And the papers in all the Boxes amount roughly to 10,000 in number. They deal with different aspects of the civil administration and military affairs during the period of war, and bring into relief the active part played in it by Bahadur Shah. They also serve as a corrective to the spies' reports.[3] Box 49 contains papers giving abstracts of the Parwanas whereby the Emperor and his officers desired different persons in the State to attend to the wants of the mutineers. Box 39 contains some papers which illustrate the personal interest the Emperor took in the maintenance and welfare of his Army and the measures he adopted to establish peace. Box 60 contains a paper which, bearing the seal of Sipah Salar Mirza Mughul, gives the text of a long letter written by the Emperor to the Army Officers reiterating the sacrifices that he had been making for the sake of

---

[1] Nominally grouped in 201 bundles (*Press-List of Mutiny Papers,* 1857, p. i), in fact they are in 199 bundles only; the bundles or Boxes No. 200 and 201 contain pre-Mutiny Papers with very few exceptions.

[2] Calcutta, 1921.

[3] Box 151 contains letters written by Hakim Ahsanullah Khan to Raja (Lala) Devi Prasad asking him to arrange for the supply of provisions for the Badshahi Army proceeding to fight the English. His language bears the stamp of sincerity, and he presses strongly on Raja Devi Prasad the importance of the task. The same Box also contains a letter from Bahadur Shah to Lala Bhola Nath, Diwan of Bharatpur, asking him to bring the State (*Raj*) into line and join the war. On points like these the spies' reports are different; and being mercenary in spirit cannot be relied upon.

the sepoys. Box 65 contains many Papers connected with the *mujahideen* and their petitions to the Sahib Alam Mirza Mughul; Papers No. 5-11 give the enrolment list of several regiments of the *mujahideen*. Box 94 contains a Paper giving the text of a firman enjoining upon the sepoys the duty of maintaining discipline and an *esprit de corps*.

(ii) Foreign Department Papers; these are the records of the Select and Secret Committees of the East India Company's Government which had control over all the military and political affairs. For instance, F. C. No. 113-119 of 27th May 1859 gives the names of the Mughul Princes executed by order of the Dehli Commissioner and of those who died during the trial or after the pronouncement of sentence as well as of those who were banished from India. F. C. No. 68 of 31st December 1858 gives the story of Bahadur Shah's imprisonment and death. Another Foreign Department Paper (Secret No. 102-3 of 29th May, 1857) contains a translated copy of a Proclamation issued from the Iranian Government Press, Teheran. 'It has doubtless been disseminated with a view to exciting a fanatical spirit of opposition to us throughout Persia, Afghanistan and India', says Felix Jones, Political Agent, Persian Field Force, Persian Gulf.

(iii) Spies' reports; these were very small cossid[1] letters written on little scraps of paper con-

[1] 'Cossid' is the corrupt form of the Arabic word *Qasid* meaning 'messenger.' 'The cossid letter' says Keith (*Delhi-1857*, p. 335) 'is written on a paper most wonderfully thin and opaque although very tough, the secret of making which was then hidden in India . . . This paper when rubbed, instead of breaking into holes, assumes a texture resembling chamois leather, and a string only 3 inches wide is found able to support a quarter of a hundredweight without

taining the secret information obtained from and about the Badshahi Army, Palace and the City of Dehli by the Indian spies (*jasus*) employed by the British Intelligence Department. Hodson showed one such letter to Keith saying, '. . . . . . this was brought out in a very ingenuous way: two pieces of cloth being stitched together so as to imitate tape, and then this wrapped up in them, the manufactured tape being used to fasten the buttons of a jacket. These letters . . . are generally put in the hollow of a stick or sewn in the sole of a shoe'[1]. Out of an army of such spies—some of their names being Gauri Shankar, Fath Muhammad, Turab Ali, Kalloo, Mohan,—each spy, firm at his post, obtained hourly news; and writing the same artfully on thin pieces of paper mentioned above, sent these to the British officers like Greathed at Dehli, Barnes at Ambala and to others[2] at other places. These spies also travelled long distances incognito and personally[3] communicated to the British officers the secrets they ferreted out; in this manner they made a living by selling news. And they competed with each other regarding the quality, quantity and price of the news. 'Please reward the bearer of

yielding . . . . In 1841 a small fold of it was presented to Oxford University Press; and upon it 24 copies were printed of the smallest Bible, then in existence . . . Experiments for producing similar paper were undertaken at the Oxford University Press mills at Wolvercote; and in 1875 an edition was published by this Press . . . exactly similar to the 24 copies printed in 1842.'

[1] Keith—*Delhi-1857*, pp. 243-244.

[2] *E.g.* Eden, Neill and Havelock.

[3] Keith—*Delhi-1857*, p. 147.

this letter'[1]; 'I have sent both these harkaras in the hope of getting reward[2]; 'Send money at the hands of the harkara'[3]; 'Who can send you greater and more correct news than myself'[4]; 'I have received six rupees in all by instalments'[5]; 'paid four rupees as house rent[6]; there is a balance of two rupees only[7]; 'one woman will have to be employed as maid servant'[8]—these are some of the phrases used at the end of the spies' reports and need no comment. One of these reports says, 'Mirza Ilahi Bakhsh and Zinat Mahal Begum will even now procure the desired aid from the garrison[9]. Obviously the spies who made these reports were required to approach the persons specially in request; and holding out great temptations they bargained with them. How false and misleading these reports are likely to have been is shown by the typical report of 19th July, 1857 to the effect that 'the inhabitants of Dehli were all with the British'[10]. That the inhabitants were *not* with the British is proved by the demonstrations of the People's War in Dehli which began after the disaster of Najafgarh[11] as well as by the Urdu Press.[12]

---

[1], [2] Mutiny Papers; Box 16, and Box Nos. 18 and 23-24, July 28, 1857.

[2], [4], [5], [6], [7], [8] *Idem*

[9] *I.e.* 'a letter should be written and addressed by the British officers personally to Mirza Ilahi Bakhsh and Zinat Mahal Begum; and the spies were sure that such a letter would bear fruit.' Keith—*Delhi-1857*, p. 335.

[10] *Vide* pp. 258-260, *supra*.

[11] *Idem*, pp. 253-258.

[12] The subject matter of all the Urdu Papers, too much to be quoted here, testifies to the peoples' hatred of the English.

Most of the spies' reports are in Urdu and a few in Persian; fewer still are seen translated into English. But a complete English translation of the reports that were sent from Dehli to Ambala is found in the form of *Typed Scripts Of The Delhi News* at the Records Office of the Panjab Government, Simla.[1]

Fourthly the Persian, Urdu and Hindi newspapers: The most important of these—*Saiyedul Akhbar, Zubdatul Akhbar, Dehli Urdu Akhbar, Sadiqul Akhbar, Sirajul Akhbar, Mazharul Haqq, and Buddhi Prakash*—were published from Dehli and Agra; others were published from Mirath, Banaras, Indore, Lahore and Simla.[2] *The Sirajul Akhbar* named after Emperor Siraju'ddin Bahadur Shah was a Court Gazette or Court Journal[3], which like almost all other papers continued its publication during the period of war (May to September 1857).[4] The general notion that the

---

[1] *Delhi News,* 1857 (May to September) 1857.

[2] *Report of the Press Commission,* Part II. History of Indian Journalism, pp. 48-53.

[3] Chunni Lal, the news-writer for the public, was questioned regarding this paper at the Military Tribunal.

Question: Was a Court Journal kept by order of the Prisoner during the rebellion?

Answer: Yes, one was kept; and it was published at the Royal Lithographic Press in the palace: before the outbreak it contained chiefly items of intelligence connected with the Palace, but other matters too were occasionally admitted to it. It was called *Sirajul Akhbar* or the 'Sun of Intelligence.' (*Pr. Tr. B. S.*—p. 90).

[4] Mutiny Papers, Box No. 1, May 9-15, 1857; *Idem,* May 16-22, 1857; *Idem,* July 18-24, 1857; *Idem,* July 25-31, 1857; *Idem,* August 1-7, 1857; *Idem,* August 8-14, 1857; *Idem,* August 15-21, 1857; *Idem,* August 22-28, 1857; *Idem,* August 29—September 4, 1857.

Sirajul Akhbar was an unimportant paper and that only 34 copies were printed once a week (Sunday)'[1] is not correct. It is evident from the photostats with me[2] that this paper was published daily; and on comparing it with the other papers, particularly *Sadiqul Akhbar* and the *Dehli Urdu Akhbar,* I find that they quoted profusely from the *Sirajul Akhbar*. The following items of news which were published during the War by the *Sirajul Akhbar* were considered so important that they were read out, in English translation, at the Military Tribunal which tried Bahadur Shah[3].

> 11th July 1857.—From the Court Gazette, the *Sirajul Akhbar*. It is ascertained that the King held a Court. The nobles of the realm received admittance in the order of precedence. Particulars of the operations against the accursed hostile force, of the arrangements for carrying on the war, and of the signal valour of the heroes comprising His Majesty's Army were submitted for His Majesty's information. An order was issued to Ghulam Nabi Khan to have the house belonging to the Jhajjar Nawab, situated in the section of the city known as Darya Gaṇj, cleared out for the accommodation of the wounded. Some funds were bestowed on the *Mujahideen* for their expenses.
>
> 12th July 1857.—A petition was received from Saiyed Ali and Baqir Ali, chiefs of Banaras, submitting that they had made a great slaughter of the doomed infidels, and that they now desire to

[1] John Lawrence, quoted in the *Report of Press Commission,* p. 49.

[2] These photostats (*cf.* footnote 3) and a few more I have been able to purchase at the National Archives, *Dehli.*

[3] *Pr. Tr. B. S.,* pp. 115-116.

wait on His Majesty. A favourable answer was written immediately.

13th July 1857.—Information of the capture of Agra through the blessings of God was communicated in a petition from the General Bahadur. His Majesty had a salute of 21 guns fired, and the musicians played upon their English flutes, clarionets and drums, in token of rejoicing on the occasion. Two spies with English letters were apprehended to-day and were sent to Mirza Mughul for investigation in reference to them. A petition was received from the officers of the Jhansi Regiment, reporting the slaughter of the immoral infidels; and an answer was written.

15th July 1857.—A royal missive was received to his address by Bakht Khan, directing him to go out and meet the Jhansi force which was expected to come in next morning, and to have them encamped outside the Ajmeri Gate.

16th July 1857.—The officers of Jhansi attended and presented their swords and pistols in token of their devotion. His Majesty with extreme munificence bestowed 2,000 rupees for their immediate expenses.

17th July 1857.—A report being made that two regiments of infantry had arrived from Ambala, orders were issued that Mirza Mughul was to assign them quarters amongst the regiments which had previously come.

18th July 1857.—Several spies of the English were apprehended at the graveyard, and were brought in as prisoners.

2nd August 1857.—A petition arrived from the Governor-General Bahadur Muhammad Bakht

Khan that the treacherous enemy (English) had been compelled to retreat. An order was passed on it that it should be deposited in the office.

4th August 1857.—General Sidhari Singh of the Neemuch troops and other illustrious officers having paid their respects, submitted their plans for driving the English away from the Ridge; and His Majesty continued conversing with them on the subject.

5th August 1857.—The Emperor issued two orders. the one to the address of Nawab Walidad Khan Bahadur, in answer to his petition, intimating that troops will be sent to him after the capture of the Ridge; and the other to the Raja of Alwar, directing him to send his reply* together with a *peskash*[1].

---

[1] This is my rendering. I do not agree with the translation given in the *Proceedings of the Trial of Bahadur Shah* (p. 115) which runs as follows: 'The king issued two orders . . . . . the other to the Rajah of Alwar, directing him to forward his tribute with a petition'.

It should be recalled that on 12th May, 1857, Bahadur Shah had sent a letter, among others, to the Raja of Alwar soliciting aid in the War against the English. (*Cf.* Metcalfe —T. N. N., p. 85).

Now he wanted to remind him and expected a reply, since replies to his letters from Gwalior, Dholpur and Bharatpur had come. (*Vide,* Keith—*Delhi-1857,* p. 63). Alwar had not replied as yet.

I have compared the original Persian text of the respective issues of the *Sirajul Akhbar* mentioned above (Mutiny Papers, Box 1, vol. 13, Nos. 23, 20, August 1-7, 1857 and No. 23, August 22-23, 1857) with the English tsanslation given in the *Psoceedings of the Trial of Bahadur Shah*. In theses extracts wherever I have substituted my own rendering I have indicated the same spot by means of an asterisk.

6th August 1857.—The Emperor was occupied listening to the account of bravery and valour of the troops, when a trooper arrived and reported that the Valiant Army had crowned the heights of the Ridge. The Emperor immediately gave orders for the despatch of reinforcements and ammunition.

7th August 1857.—It was reported that the Army having gone into the batteries was fighting hard as usual.

25th August 1857.—His Majesty inspected two orders prepared in the Royal secretariat, the one addressed to Bahadur Ali Khan, Hasan Ali Khan, Durga Prasad and Bhup Singh—officers of the troops at Peshawar—directing them to make all haste in coming to the Royal presence and to bring a suitable amount of treasure with them, and the other to the Prince Royal Mirza Muhammad Kochak, ordering him to distribute the pay of the Nasirabad force. After inspection these orders were sealed with the special seal and despatched agreeably to the Royal permission; His Majesty then proceeded to bestow consideration on the following petitions: First—A petition from Tahawwur Ali Khan, son of Muhammad Abdul Ghaffar Khan, resident of Mustafabad otherwise called Rampur, professing fidelity and allegiance, and avowing his intention of coming to the Royal presence. Secondly—A petition from Raja Nahar Singh of Ballabgarh making professions of heartfelt fidelity, allegiance, zeal and goodwill. Thirdly—A petition from Waris Muhammad Khan of Bhopal reporting the saughter of 56 of the accursed English, and enclosing copy of a proclamation issued to the residents of the city and country to engage in like manner in the destruction of the damnable infidels, and moreover soliciting the honour of a royal missive. Fourthly—A petition from Kashi Rao Holkar of Indore, expressive of his devotion and zealous activity in the service of the Emperor, avowing his fixed purpose and determinate resolve to ruin and exterminate the English, clever in all villainy, and forwarding five of the heads of enemies killed. Fifthly—A petition from Muhamad Amir Khan, son of Ghulam Muhammad son of Abdu-s Samad Khan of Dojana.

The officers of the Army submitted that as Muhammad Bakht Khan, Governor-General Bahadur, had gone with His Majesty's victorious troops in the direction of Alipur to fight against the infidel enemy and was now engaged in active operations against them, it was necessary that reinforcements should be sent to his assistance. On this represenation, orders were accordingly issued that a further portion of the troops should be sent in that direction.

The officers of the troops at Teliwara complained that no force was sent to relieve them.

26th August 1857—The Army officers submitted that reinforcements should be sent to the aid of the troops, engaged in fighting the enemy; and orders were issued that the soldiers of all the platoons and cavalry contingents should go out in a body. Then the Emperor inspected the following three orders prepared in the Royal secretariat:

(i) An order to the Army Officers directing that one-half of the forces should proceed to the Najafgarh battery and the other to the Teliwara Battery.

(ii) An order to Mirza Muhammad Zaheeru'ddin Bahadur regarding his investment with power to forgive offences and to consider the whole Army under his orders.

(iii) An order to Thakur Chaman Singh, to bring in more men of his caste.*

A petition having been received from Prince Azim Bahadur posted at Hansi representing his difficulties in consequence of the arrival of the enemies' forces and requesting that reinforcements including artillery might be sent to his assistance, the Emperor gave orders that a special Royal missive in reply should be sent.

27th August 1857.—Baldeo Singh Kundla Kush was honoured with the gift of a pair of shawls as treasurer (*fotadar*) of the Infantry (*platoon jangi*) . . . The Emperor then examined the following six orders which had been prepared in the Royal secretariat, and after inspection permitted their being attested with the special seal and despatched:

(i) An order to Mirza Muhammad Khizr Sultan Bahadur, assuring him that he was invested with full powers in regard to the raising of money and that no representations from any other person in this matter would be heeded.

(ii) An order to Mirza Mughul Bahadur and Mirza Khizr Sultan Bahadur, and the Officers and members of the Court, that is the Body of Advisers (*Ahl-i Shura*) to the effect that money having been twice received from the merchant, Ramji Das Gurwala, he was on no account to be subjected to any further demand.

(iii) An order to Mirza Abul Hasan alias Mirza Abdullah Bahadur in answer to the petition of Amir Khan of Dojana, directing his attendance at the Court.

(iv) An order to Kashi Rao Holkar of Indore directing his attendance at the Royal Court.

(v) An order to Raja Nahar Singh, Chief of Ballabgarh, intimating that a dun horse had been received, and directing him to entertain no fears of being molested by the victorious (Badshahi) Army.

(vi) An order through Fath Ali Khan to Tahawwuar Ali Khan son of Abdullah Khan of Rampur directing his attendance. Some cavalrymen and foot soldiers communicated particulars of the success and valour and enterprise of the troops, particularly of the Nimuch force; they also communicated that the zamindars of the neighbourhood of Najafgarh had rallied (to the Royal standard). But the Emperor felt indisposed and he immediately ordered the Court Physician to be present.

28th August 1857.—Having discharged the usual religious observances, the Emperor permitted the Court Physician to feel his pulse, and then came into the Diwan-i Khass where the nobles and chiefs of the realm paid their respects. Khwaja Ismail Khan of Kalpi came forward and presented the offering (*nazr*) usual on admission to the Royal presence . . . . The following four orders were attested with the special seal, and issued agreeably to His Majesty's commands.

(i) An order to Muhammad Shafi, Brigadier, in

answer to his petition, assuring him that His Majesty was not displeased or angry with him, nor did he entertain any suspicion against the Nimuch troops.

(ii) An order to Mirza Rahat Bakht Bahadur to pay up the rent of the Imambara which goes to meet the expenses of *Nazr Nisar*.

(iii) An order to Ahmad Ali Khan, Chief of Farrukhanagar directing him to send some matchlocks (*bandooq*).

(iv) An order to Bahadur Jang Khan in regard to the theft in his territory of a string of 14 camels.

The above items are also seen in the other Papers. Says Prof. Sajjan Lal, 'They relayed news of the success of the armies . . . . . . broadcast the various proclamations and news of the promised help from Iran, Kabul and Russia . . . . gave people hope and courage and exaggerated the weakness of the enemy'[1]. This was also true of the following news which was 'relayed' and is seen in the *Sadiqul Akhbar,* a powerful organ of public opinion.

6th July 1857.—An order attested with the Royal Seal was issued to the Commander-in-Chief Bahadur, investing him with the management of the daily allowances to the army and placing the direction of all military matters of government in his hands.

7th July 1857—A petition from Raja Gulab Singh, ruler of Kashmir, reporting having established his sway throughout the country appertaining to Lahore and a second from Dost Muhammad

[1] Sajjan Lal—*Dehli Urdu Newspapers and the Freedom Struggle*, p. 38.

Khan, requesting permission to come to the Royal presence, were received under cover of one from the General Bahadur. Orders directing the despatch of missives in answer were issued.

9th July 1857.—A report was made that General Bakht Khan had sent a force fully equipped and appointed to chastise the enemy, and that this force had fought with signal bravery. Couriers continued arriving every moment with reports of the progress of the fight.

Fifthly the lectures and poetry of the revolutionary philosophers and poets and the *Jihad Nama* : The following were the leading revolutionary philosophers and poets—Fazl Haq, Imam Bakhsh Sahbai, Muhammad Baqir, Mirza Rahimu'ddin Haya, Khan Bahadur Khan Masruf, Faiz Ahmad Ruswa and Maulvi Muhammad Zaheer Ali. Fazl Haq who is commonly known as Maulvi Fazl Haq Khairabadi[1] ceaselessly roused by means of his lectures, the sepoys and the people against the British[2] who seized him after the fall of Dehli and exiled him as a life prisoner to the Andaman islands, where he died in 1861/1278: Before his death he wrote in prison with the help of charcoal on small pieces of cloth an Introduction to the Indian Revolution of 1857 (*Muqaddamatu-s Sauratu-l Hindiya*) which he managed to send to India at the hands of a fellow-prisoner, Mufti Inayat Ahmad who was released in 1860. The manuscript of the said *Muqaddama* was handed over by Mufti Inayat Ahmad to Abdul Haq Khairabadi, son of the above-mentioned Fazl Haq. It was published in 1947 at Bijnor.

[1] *I.e.* a resident of Khairabad, Sitapur district.

[2] *Delhi News*, No. 273/3731. File No. 127; August 31, 1857.

A few extracts from this *Muqaddamatu-s Sauratu-l Hindiya* which I have translated into English are given in this book.[1]

Imam Bakhsh Sahbai worked as Professor of Persian at the Dehli College before the outbreak of the Mutiny. He wrote several books, amongst which his *Kulliyat* may still be seen containing his appreciation of Emperor Bahadur Shah. He was a silent and steady worker, but was not outspoken like Fazl Haq. He was suspected of treason by the British and was shot dead after the fall of Dehli.[2]

Maulvi Muhammad Baqir, A Shia Mujtahid of Dehli, who built a mosque called *Khajur Wali Masjid*[3] in the Chhota Bazar of Kashmiri Gate, was a pioneer in the field of free Indian journalism. In his Dehli *Urdu Akhbar*[4], founded in 1836, he used to criticise the British and their administration; and during the war of 1857 in Dehli he left no stone unturned to rouse the people against them. In his paper of 16th August 1857 he announced the printing and publication of the Jihad Pamphlet (*Risala-i jihad*[5]) and urged his readers including the Hindus (*Ahl-i watan*) to buy copies and distribute the same to all. And he appealed to everyone irrespective of religion to join the war which he

---

[1] *Vide,* Appendix H.

[2] Abdul Haq—*Marhoom Dehli College,* p. 149.

[3] This mosque bears an inscription dated 1856/1272.

[4] For the *Dehli Urdu Akbar see Press Commission Report*, vol. II, pp. 40-50 and Sajjan Lal's Paper—I.H.R.C. vol. xix, 1952, pp. 1528-193.

[5] *Vide* (i) *Dehli Urdu Akhbar,* August 16, 1857.
(ii) *Dehli Urdu Akhbar*, dated 3rd January, 1841 and Mutiny Papers, Box 2, May 31, 1857; July 5, 1857; July 19, 1857; August 9, 1857; August 23, 1857.

considered a unique opportunity to expel the English from the country. Maulvi Muhammad Baqir was shot dead by Hodson after the fall of Dehli.

Khan Bahadur Khan Masruf of Rohilkhand inspired a spirit of revolt in the country by means of his poetry, his pen-name being Masruf. He was charged with treason by the British Government, but he escaped to Arabia.[1]

Faiz Ahmad Ruswa[2] also composed some revolutionary verses and is said to have been put to death by the British. A typical verse runs as follows:

بت خانون مین دیا پھرا اذانین -
ناقوس بھی کعبہ مین بجایا
لیکن نہ کسی نے یون بھی پوچھا
بے وقت یہ راگ کس لئے گایا ؟

(I went about giving the call for prayer in the idol houses. I rang the Hindu bell even in the Ka'ba, but no one enquired why I sang this song at an odd hour.)

Maulvi Zahoor Ali was the 'Thanadar' and Rais of Dadri. He was jubilant over the event of 12th May 1857 and immortalised it in verse announcing the new coinage of Emperor Bahadur Shah. The following are some of his typical verses, the first verse being a chronogram:

سکہ زد در جہان بعون الاہ — حامی دین حق بہادر شاہ

Verily Bahadur Shah, defender of Faith, struck coins in the world by the grace of God.

---

[1] *Qamusu-l Mashahir,* II, p. 216.

[2] (i) *Idem,* p. 122.
(ii) Lala Siri Ram—*Khumkhana-i Jawed,* vol. III, p. 408.

بشرق و غرب زده سکه همچو مہر و ماہ -
ابوظفر شہ عالی بہادر شاہ

The Great and exalted Emperor Abu Zafar Bahadur Shah struck coins like the sun and the moon in the east as well as in the west.

بدہر سکہ شاہی زدہ بہادر شاہ -
بحق اشہدان لاالہ الا اللہ

For eternity Bahadur Shah struck the coins of kingship by virtue of the creed—'There is no God but God'.

بدہر سکہ شاہی زدہ بفضل الہ -
ابوظفر شہ گیتی ستان بہادر شاہ

By the grace of God, Emperor Abu Zafar Bahadur Shah, capturer of the world, struck coins of kingship for the world.

Furthermore the ulama came together and joined hands in declaring jihad against the British. And the Jihad was declared in this manner. The revolutionaries approached the ulama with a set of questions and demanded *fatwa*. The ulama held a joint meeting at the Jami' Masjid and decided in favour of jihad. Then a document[1] was prepared in which the

---

[1]*NAQL-I ISTIFTA*

(Copy of a petition for fatwa)

'Question—What do the Ulama of the Faith order in this matter: now the Englishmen are storming Dehli and they are bent on killing the Musalmans and seizing their property. In these circumstances, is Jihad incumbent on the inhabitants of the city or not? Please give the ruling and explain. May God recompense you!

Answer—In the given case as recorded in the question above, Jihad is absolutely incumbent (*Farz-i 'Ain*) on all the

questions were written and the answers too. This document known as *Jihad Nama* was then signed by 30 ulama,[1] one after the other, each attaching also his personal seal to it. Of these thirty which may be seen clearly, two are very prominent, namely Mufti Muhammad Rahman Ali Khan the Siraju-l ulama and Sadru-l Fuqaha, and Muhammad Ali Husain, Qaziu-l Quzat (Chief Justice) who subscribed himself as servant of the Sacred Shari'at (*Khadim-i Shara' Sharif*).

Tracing the genesis of this Rising and the Jihad movement from 1816 onwards, Hunter has proved the existence of a regular Muslim organisation on the Punjab Frontier for passing up men and arms from Bengal to the Badshahi Army. He observes, 'In 1853 several of the native soldiers were convicted of correspondence with the (Muslim) traitors'[2]. Then he

inhabitants who are capable of fighting. In fact the inhabitants of this city now can fight because of the abundance of troops amidst them and because of the weapons of war that they possess in large numbers. In these circumstances there is absolutely no doubt that Jihad in all respects is incumbent on them. On the inhabitants of the suburbs who are distant and far off, Jihad is in the given case optional (*Farz-i Kifaya*). Should the inhabitants of the city of Dehli become indifferent or lax in the matter, then Jihad in that case would become compulsory even on the suburban people; and in this manner and order, Jihad would successively become absolutely compulsory on all the dwellers on the earth from east to west. Should the enemy try to kill and destroy the habitations, Jihad would become compulsory on the dwellers in the said inhabited areas also, subject of course to their ability (power) to fight.

Signatures and Seals [1]'

[Translated by the writer from the *Sadiqul Akhbar*—Mutiny Papers, Box 4-6, July 27, 1857.]

[2] Hunter—*The Indian Musalmans,* pp. 3, 15, 83.

gives names of the Musalman ringleaders, *e.g.* Saied Ahmad of Rai Bareli and Yahya Ali of Patna; at Patna there being a regular propaganda centre where a team of Musalman zealots including Abdul Ghaffar, the bursar of the Propaganda centre, and Muhammad the Meat Supplier to the British forces, worked jointly to crush the British. Hunter also says that the Muslim disaffection and conspiracy had spread from the Punjab to Bengal. 'In Bengal the Muslim terrorists were known as 'Faraizi' (from the Arabic word *fariza* meaning duty), their leader being one Shariatullah who preached at Dacca a holy war against the British in 1828. And before the final outbreak in 1857 there had been at least two risings of the Faraizis against the British—one in 1831 and the other in 1843. On the eve of the outbreak of 1857 the Faraizis of Lower Bengal were amalgamated through the efforts of Yahya Ali with the Wahabis of Northern India; and both fought shoulder to shoulder against the British on the field of battle and later stood the trial jointly as culprits in the British courts of justice'[1].

Sixthly Persian manuscripts:

(i) *Panj Ahang* of Asadullah Ghalib, a courtier of Bahadur Shah. A manuscript of the *Panj Ahang* transcribed in 1867/1284 at Kanpur exists in a private collection[2] of Calcutta. Although printed twice over before the outbreak of the Mutiny, all the copies of the *Panj Ahang* were destroyed in the course of the war of 1857. In 1875/1292 the Nawal Kishore Press brought out a new edition as part of the *Kulliyat-i Nasr-i Ghalib* which I have used. I have also used the above

[1] *Idem.*

[2] Modak Collection, Calcutta.

manuscript and compared it with the printed edition. The most remarkable feature of the book in my opinion is Ghalib's censure of the British Government and his appreciation of Bahadur Shah. Referring to the British Government he says,

بد اوری سرو کارم بجمعے افتاد است -
که برگزیده چرخ اند در ستمگری
چو فتنه جمع قانون عالم آشوبی -
چو غمزه صاحب فرنگ مردم آزاری

(My affairs are in the hands of such notorious people whom Destiny has made the model of tyranny. Like infidelity they are the embodiment of the causes of world disturbances. They squeeze; and while squeezing they look like habitual tormentors of mankind.)

On the contrary Ghalib spoke highly of Bahadur Shah. In fact he adored him and composed an eulogium in his honour which has been incorporated in an earlier chapter.[1]

(ii) *Nusrat Nama-i Government* — a Persian manuscript of Ghulam Husain Khan written in 1858/1274—is mentioned by Khwaja Hasan Nizami who published its Urdu translation in 1930. Ghulam Husain Khan, son of Nawab Faizullah Beg, was a pensioner of the British Government and helped them much during the war of 1857 in Dehli. After the fall of Dehli he wrote this book with the object of announcing the victory of his British masters, as is indicated by its title—*Nusrat Nama-i Government* *i.e.* the book of the Government's Victory. The author

[1] *Vide* p. 49 *supra.*

censures Bahadur Shah for joining hands with the mutineers. And he expresses concern for the safety of the British Government and prays for their complete victory. He stresses the fact that Bahadur Shah charged the Sepoys to expel the adversaries[1] (*mukhalifeen*), and make his own coin current. He gives a short account of the Royal Durbar of 12th May 1857; and while describing the distribution of commands in the new Army, he says that a subordinate command was held by Zinat Mahal Begum.[2] The author also says that Bahadur Shah felt depressed on hearing of the mishap that had befallen this Army in the battle of Badli and broke out saying, *'Bismillah hi ghalat hui, agey khuda khair karc* ('the very beginning is wrong; may God protect in future!').

Barring the information regarding Zinat Mahal Begum's command in the Army, there is nothing new in this manuscript.

(iii) There is also some Persian element in the Newspapers[3] of 1857; and there are over 4.000 Persian manuscript folios[4] of different sizes in the Mutiny Papers at the National Archives. But the Persian element in the Spies' Reports is negligible.

---

[1] *I.e.* the English.

[2] There is nothing strange about this. All accounts agree that Zinat Mahal Begum was a woman of masculine spirit and build; she was also ambitious and had been disappointed by the British. The author tells us that Jawan Bakht, the son of Zinat Mahal Begum and Bahadur Shah, was made wazir. If this is true—and surely it is true for it has been confirmed by other sources too—then Zinat Mahal Begum's acceptance of a command in the new Army at least provisionally was by no means impossible.

[3] All the issues of the *Sirajul Akhbar* are in Persian. *Vide* Mutiny Papers, Box I and 4-6; March 1 to August 29, 1857.

[4] I myself counted these folios in September 1957.

Seventhly; works in Urdu:

(i) *Dastan-i Ghadr* of Zaheeru'ddin Hasan of Dehli commonly known as Zaheer Dehlawi, a youngman of 22 years of age at the time of the outbreak of the Mutiny. He had been connected with the Royal Palace since the age of eight. At the age of thirteen Emperor Bahadur Shah appointed him *Darogha Mahi Maratib*—a special distinction with the fish insignia, then conferred on nobles of high standing—and granted him the title of Raqimu'd-Dawla.[1]

Zaheer Dehlawi was a poet as well as a musician. His gift of poetry won him the appreciation of Ajit Singh, uncle of Maharaja Narendra Singh of Patiala. Ajit Singh who was then living in Dehli awarded Zaheer Dehlawi a gold watch with a gold chain and a robe of gold brocade.[2]

In one of his poems included in the *Dastan-i Ghadr,* Zaheer Dehlawi gives a touching account of the plunder of Dehli at the hands of the Telingas. For this reason he did not like them; and being thoroughly under the influence of the Indian Princes[3] through whose support he was saved from death at the hands of the British, he did not consider the Rising of 1857 a national rebellion.

(ii) *Tarikh-i Uruj-i Ahd-i Saltanat-i Inglishiya* of Zakaullah contains an eye-witness account of Bahadur Shah's reign and of the War of 1857 in Dehli. Zakaullah was a British servant; and true to his salt, he belittles Bahadur Shah and speaks of him disparagingly like the other Indian writers[4] who

---

[1] Zaheer Dehlawi—D. G., pp. 3-6.

[2] *Idem,* pp. 75-76.

[3] *I.e.* rulers of Rampur, Jaipur, and Alwar.

[4] *E.g.* Jiwan Lal and the spies.

were either afraid of incurring British displeasure or expected some recognition at the hands of the British Government. The British Government awarded Zakaullah the title of Shamsu-l Ulama; and perhaps it was due to this honour that C. F. Andrews felt drawn towards him.[1] He claimed him as his personal friend and wrote his biography. Whatever be his other qualifications, Zakaullah was certainly a historian. In his book before us he has not suppressed facts though he could not give up his bias against Bahadur Shah. He says that during the short reign of Bahadur Shah there was no communal strife at all and that he maintained peace. Bahadur Shah had banned cow-slaughter completely. As a result during the four months and four days (12th May to 16th September, 1857), no cow was slaughtered in the city of Dehli, not even on the Bakar-'id day which fell on 2nd August.[2] The cow-butchers were hard hit; they were oppressed and even slaughtered. This caused some reaction; and Muslim zealots, particularly Hakim Ahsanullah Khan resented this.[3] But Bahadur Shah was adamant; and, thanks to the support given by Maulvi Fazl Haq and his own son Mirza Mughul, he carried the day. Zakaullah's book *Tarikh-i Uruj-i Ahd-i Saltanat-i Inglishiya* has become rare. No library in Calcutta, Patna and Dehli could procure me a copy. I found one in Rampur and another with my friend Janab Imdad Sabiri of Dehli.

(iii) *Sarkashi-i Bijnor* of Syed Ahmad Khan which he wrote while he was Sadr Amin of Bijnor during the Mutiny. Testifying to the part that the

---

[1] *Vide*—Andrews, C.F.—*Zakaullah of Delhi,* p. 19.

[2] Zakaullah—T.U.A.S.I., p. 660

[3] Metcalfe—T. N. N., p. 170.

inhabitants of Bijnor, Najibabad, Nagina, Barampur, Dhampur, Chandpur, and Bareilly had played in the War of 1857, Syed Ahmad says that shortly after the announcement of Bahadur Shah's rule, Mahmud Khan of Bijnor—Syed Ahmad calls him *Na* Mahmud Khan—received a Royal firman which is reproduced verbatim in the said book. It is worded in elegant Persian, which hardly anyone other than the Emperor, could command. This firman was taken from Dehli to Bijnor by one Amdu Khan in the company of Lala Mathra Dass, father of Lala Bankey Rai, the royal treasurer. It ran as follows:

> Date 21 July, 21 *Julus*—'Whereas the English have fled away from Bijnor, Mahmud Khan the applicant should look after the Collectorate Treasury; and subsequent to his defraying necessary expenses of the army and Tahsil administration, he should send the balance to the Royal treasury at Dehli under the supervision of the Royal servants, Mathra Dass and two other functionaries, deputed for the purpose'.[1]

Among the reforms that Mahmud Khan made in the administration of Bijnor, the author mentions the restoration of the Royal maund (*mann*) weighing 100 rupees which the British Government had abolished. The *mann* now restored by Mahmud Khan bore the Royal Seal which is reproduced by Syed Ahmad Khan in his book. Another firman of Bahadur Shah similarly worded in elegant Persian was sent on 27th July 1857 to Mir Sadiq Ali and Rustam Ali of Chandpur, vesting them with authority to administer Chandpur and collect the revenue which, after meeting the

[1] Syed Ahmad—*Sarkashi-i Bijnor*, pp. 42-49.

necessary expenses, they were ordered to send to the Royal Treasury at Dehli.[1]

At the end of the book the author makes a personal appeal to the inhabitants of Bijnor in particular and to all the people in general, not to revolt against the British Government which he praises highly.

(iv) *Asbab-i Ghadr* of Syed Ahmad Khan. In the course of this book which was written in 1858 and translated into English in 1873, the author discusses the causes of the rebellion of 1857 and says that the people became disaffected and disloyal to the British Government for various reasons. They had begun to think that 'all the laws were passed with the object of degrading and ruining them and to deprive them of their religion. . . At last there came the time when all men looked upon the British Government as slow poison, a rope of sand, a treacherous flame of fire'. The author is of opinion that the outbreak of 1857 was much more than a Mutiny and that it was not confined to the army alone, but he does not believe that there was 'any national league in India to overthrow the foreign government.'[2]

(v) *Tarikh-i Baghawat-i Hind* of Pandit Kanhiya Lal. Pandit Kanhiya Lal had been a silent witness of the War of 1857 in Dehli which he rightly calls *Mahariba-i Azeem* (great war). *Mahariba-i Azeem*[3] is also a chronogram yielding the year 1273. This book reproduces two documents—Munshi Rajab Ali's letter of 30th July 1857 addressed to Hakim Ahsanullah Khan and the Proclamation commonly attributed to Bahadur Shah.[4]

(vi) *Sarguzasht-i Ghalib* and *Dastambu* of Asadul-

---

[1] *Ibid.*

[2] Syed Ahmad—*Asbab-i Ghadr,* pp. 2-9.

[3], [4] Kanhiya Lal—T. B. *Vide* p. 13 *supra.*

lah Ghalib (1807-1868). In both these books Ghalib has touched on the distress that the War of 1857 had entailed. The *Sarguzasht* also gives a sketch of the author's meeting with Bahadur Shah. In 1856/1272 Ghalib joined as usual the annual gathering of the poets that used to be held in the Fort under the Emperor's chairmanship. The gathering over, he[1] expressed his doubts regarding its continuation in the succeeding years. Obviously he had foreseen the impending war of 1857. He was aware of the intensity of feeling that prevailed in the city against the Firangi. As soon as the war broke out Ghalib went underground and was heard of no more until the fall of Dehli. After the fall of Dehli the British traced him out, arrested him and charged him with treason on the plea that he had been a courtier of Bahadur Shah and had composed legends for his coins, *i.e.*

بزر زد سکہ نصرت طرازی -
سراج الدین بہادر شاہ غازی -

(Siraju'ddin Bahadur Shah Ghazi struck gold coins as a sign of victory

سکہ بہادر شاہ شاہ ہندوستان -
بفضل ایزدی زیور جہاں -

The coins of Bahadur Shah are by the grace of God an ornament to the world)

To save his skin Ghalib disowned authorship and said that the legends in question had been composed by Muhammad Ibrahim Zauq and were published in the *Urdu Akhbar* by his friend Maulana Muhammad Baqir.[2]

---

[1] *I.e.* Ghalib.

[2] Hasan Nizami—*Ghalib ka Roz-namcha*, p. 42.

The *Dastambu*—meaning bouquet—was written in unmixed Persian after the fall of Dehli. It contains some views and observations of the author about the Mutiny. Completely under the influence of the British whom he was now anxious to please, he not only condemned the sepoys as 'brute mutineers' but also expressed an appreciation of the British Government. But he plainly stated *that the common people had joined the war against the British*. He also described the ceremonial submission of the royal house of Lakhnao to Emperor Bahadur Shah saying, 'A ten-year old boy, son of Wajid Ali Shah, was raised to the throne of Lakhnao by Sharfu'd-Dawla who became the wazir. Then Sharfu'd-Dawla sent a very precious *nazr* to Dehli for the Emperor, seeing which Bahadur Shah's hopes revived and he became sanguine about his victory in the war'[1].

(vii) *Lal Qila Ki Aik Jhalak* of Nasir Nazir.

Born a few years after the war of 1857 Nasir Nazir was cradled in its aftermath. Devoted to Bahadur Shah and keenly interested in the welfare of the Royal family, he heard from his childhood upward stories of the 'Ghadr'[2] from those who had seen it through with their own eyes. He collected and compiled those stories in the form of a small book entitled *Lal Qila Ki Aik Jhalak* (A Glance of the Red Fort).

The most important of the authorities of this book is Nannhi Khanam, a daughter-in-law of Ahmadi Khanam, the Lady Superintendent of Bahadur Shah's kitchen. Nannhi Khanam lived all her life in the Fort along with her mother-in-law. Many a time she attended on Bahadur Shah at the dining table. She

---

[1] *Idem*, p. 66.

[2] *I.e.* Mutiny.

was also a close friend of the mother of our author, Nasir Nazir. The book gives some interesting points of information which have been confirmed. A copy of this book is available at the National Library, Calcutta.

Eighthly the contemporary works in English which are shown in the bibliography[1]. Here it is proposed to mention two only, namely the *Proceedings of the Trial of Bahadur Shah* and *Two Native Narratives of the Mutiny in Delhi.*

The *Proceedings of the Trial of Bahadur Shah* printed in 1895 at Calcutta is a book of 177 pages of fairly big size which I used at the National Archives of India. Another copy of the same book entitled *'Trial of the Ex-King of Delhi'* exists at the National Library, Calcutta. The book gives a full account of the trial as well as of the evidence of witnesses and the defence of Bahadur Shah. It proves by documentary evidence that Bahadur Shah was at war with the British. In this connection the numerous letters written to the Emperor by Raja Nahar Singh of Ballabgarh are particularly notable[2]. Further light is thrown by a letter of Jamna Das, a landholder of Mathura who offered to give nearly 2,000 warriors together with ten lakhs of rupees to the Emperor on receiving Royal patronage and ammunition. He also offered his personal services for 'making efficient arrangements so that the Emperor's government may be firmly established'. The Emperor read Jamna Dass's petition[3] very carefully and issued suitable orders directing his sons to deal with the matter. Bahadur Shah's directives to this effect speak volumes for his intelligence and

---

[1] *Vide* p. 435 *infra.*

[2] *Pr. Tr. B. S.* pp. 31-40; No. 58-77.

[3] *Idem.* p. 26; No. 54.

presence of mind in his old age and in the midst of his unearthly and numerous afflictions. Another landholder—Bhatia of Faridabad—similarly offered to send into the Royal treasury Rs. 50,000 from the Tahsil of Palwal; for this purpose he petitioned the Emperor to grant a military escort. The Emperor ordered his son Mirza Mughul to do the needful.[1] Then Mirza Ghulam Husain Risaldar of 18th Regiment came over from Peshawar to join the Emperor's service and submitted a petition saying, 'Hearing of the fame of Your Majesty's auspicious accession I have come from Peshawar after a thousand difficulties and have presented myself at Your Majesty's door[2] . . .' Similarly petitions came from Mohan Pandey Subadar and Ishwari Prasad Pathak Jamadar[3]. Some instances of Bahadur Shah's hostility to the British and the details of his role in the War are also found in the evidence of Hakim Ahsanullah.[4]

Two Native Narratives of the Mutiny in Delhi.—These are two Urdu diaries of Munshi Jiwan Lal and Muinu'ddin Hasan Khan edited and translated into English by C. T. Metcalfe. Jiwan Lal is described by Metcalfe as 'an educated native gentleman, closely associated with the court life of the King of Dehli for many years before the Mutiny, and during the time of the outbreak. His father Girdhari Lal, a lineal descendant of Raja Raghu Nath, Prime Minister of Aurangzeb, had been Munshi or writer, first to Sir David Ochterlony and afterwards to Sir Charles Metcalfe, when Agents to the Governor-General at the court of the Mogul. Later in life, being appointed as

[1] *Pr. Tr. B S.*, p. 13, No. 28, 14th July, 1857.
[2] *Idem,* p. 68, No. 48.
[3] *Ibid,* No. 49.
[4] *Idem,* pp. 161-177.

Accountant of the numerous pensions paid by the British Government to the King's family, he became a kind of go-between, taking confidential messages from the Governor-General's Agents to the Mogul. He for many years lived in daily contact with the King and his family. . . During the actual Mutiny at Dehli and siege of the city, he was resident within the walls. . .' 'After British power was re-established' Metcalfe continues, 'Jiwan Lal was made an honorary Magistrate and Municipal Commissioner, and died. . . regretted by those British officials who had known his worth and goodness. No more trustworthy or loyal native servant has the British Government ever had, and no more trustworthy or reliable source of information could be obtained than the record he has left behind of the summer of 1857. On the occasion of the Imperial Assemblage at Dehli he gave me the original diary he had kept. . .'[1] But it should be noted that immediately after the outbreak of the Mutiny, Jiwan Lal began to act as a British spy. He was arrested under the orders of Mirza Mughul whom he had offended by denouncing the Sepoys as 'mutineers' and 'faithless traitors'[2]. Later he was also charged with failure to pay a fine of Rs. 50,000. Says he, 'Nazir Ali. . . now in charge of a police station came to arrest me with a letter from Mubarak Shah Kotwal accompanied by a hundred soldiers with unsheathed swords. They got into the house by rush as the gate was being opened for the water carriers to bring in water. I was then arrested and placed in a palanquin, and taken under the guard of soldiers with drawn swords to the Kotwali. I found there Mubarak Shah who treated me with respect. He was previously a Customs officer who had now trans-

[1] Metcalfe—T. N. N., pp. 2-3.

[2] *Idem*, p. 179.

ferred his allegiance to the King. He told me that my fears were unfounded, as he too was a servant of the English. He showed me an order issued by order of Mirza Khizr Sultan addressed to him ordering my arrest together with that of Munshi Sultan Singh. . . To deceive us, the order stated that we were required for consultation. I and Munshi Sultan Singh were then taken to Mirza Mughul. On arrival a Subahdar, who was standing, tried to stab me with a dagger, shouting out: 'This is the man who sends news to the English''. I was rescued by the crowd who explained I was summoned to be made to pay money. . . I was then taken upstairs to Mirza Mughul. There I saw a great crowd of people assembled in a strange irregular fashion. On one side sat Mirza Mughul, reclining on pillows. There were present Hamid Ali Khan, Raja Salig Ram, Hakim Abdul Haq and other officials of the King's Court. In front, stretched on a bed, was the notorious Kooray Singh, Brigadier-Major of the rebel Sepoy Army. . . .; about 25 other bankers were sitting there under arrest; I was directed to sit in the row with them. Lala Gham Lal, Lala Nashi Lal, Lala Sant Lal, my friends, came there to get me released. Shortly afterwards Mirza Ahmad Jan went to Mirza Mughul and whispered something in his ear, upon which the latter summoned Sant Lal; and, with a show of condescension and leniency, told him I was to pay 5,000 rupees down at once or I should be imprisoned. The demand for money was made in the same way from the others; and at last we poor writers were threatened, guns being placed on our shoulders and fired. But we made up our minds to die rather than yield to the threats of these rebels. We were kept in suspense as to our fate, while the rebels deliberated from the morning till 4 in the afternoon, when Mirza

Ilahi Bakhsh appeared quite unexpectedly. He induced Mirza Mughul to grant him a private interview; and I believe, used such arguments on our behalf, that we were poor clerks, living on the pay we received; that English rule was not yet abolished. The English might retake the city, and these poor clerks might prove of assistance to him should he then fall into the hands of the English. Mirza Mughul replied that I was sending information to the English, and offering prayers for their success'.[1]

That Mirza Mughul was perfectly right in his estimate of Jiwan Lal's role and character is proved by Jiwan Lal's own words recorded at an earlier stage. Says he, 'Then came a man and reported that the Budmashes were naming me as being the Mir-Munshi to the Agent of the Governor-General, and as one worthy of death, and offering to point out my house . . . Terrified and horror-stricken, I ordered the gates to be locked. The house had been built in the days of the Emperor Firoz Shah, and was of solid stone. and as strong as a fort. The doors and windows were all closed. There were underground apartments into which my family entered, and there remained concealed. I arranged all the servants for watch and ward, both in front and behind, with orders to admit no one . . . I was moved by the thoughts that for many years I had eaten the salt of the English Government and wished it well, and now was an opportunity to do all that was possible with heart and soul for those I had served. So I sent Sakun[2] with instructions to ascertain if I could be of any service to Sir John Metcalfe and my other patrons . . . and to inquire about several Englishmen, in the same office as myself, who lived in the city

[1] Metcalfe—T. N. N., pp. 77, 187-188.

[2] 'Sakun' was the name of a servant.

in Dariya Ganj and about the Kashmiri Gate . . . He was to urge them . . . to come to my house where . . . I would guard them like the apple of my eye, or the soul in my body. I would personally attend to them; Sakun should conduct them through by-lanes to my house . . . With a view to obtaining news of the rebels' doings, I engaged the services of two Brahmins, Giridhari Misser and Heera Singh Misser, and of two Jats who were deputed to bring me information from time to time of all that happened at the city gates and inside the Palace by night as well as by day, in order that I might keep a true and faithful account of all that passed for the information of the high officers[1] of the State'.[2]

It is now clear that Jiwan Lal was not the man who could give correct information about the great events of 1857. He had organised a private Intelligence Agency and collected news about the City, the Royal Army and the Palace and also about the Emperor whom, above all, he wanted to finish to be able to enjoy British favour. Every day he collected news through his spies and hirelings; and after writing the selected items he sent a copy of the same regularly every day to the British Camp. A diary of this kind is surely no better than the Spies' Reports. It is dangerous material because it was skilfully prepared by a man of much greater skill and learning than the spies. A layman cannot discover the poison hidden in it; he cannot grasp Jiwan Lal's artistic way of twisting facts. In the first instance he views the Mutiny from the communal point of view and presents it as a rising of the Musalman fanatics who were out to kill the Hindus

---

[1] *I.e.* British Officers.

[2] Metcalfe—T. N. N, pp. 77-78.

after killing the English. Consequently he gives the day-to-day occurrences a religious colouring; and the news, though arranged datewise, is not only truncated, disconnected and incomplete but interspersed with highly exaggerated—and perhaps even concocted—notices of Hindu-Muslim conflict.[1] In the second instance he depicts Bahadur Shah as insincere to the Sepoys and faithless. Instances can be given *ad nauseam*.[2] But the situation will be perfectly clear to the reader when, on glancing through another narrative in the same book,[3] he will realise that Muin'uddin Hasan's[4] approach to the subject is entirely different

---

[1] Metcalfe—T. N. N., pp. 98 *seq.*, 7, 230.

[2] Only one instance may be given here. In the entry of 2nd June Jiwan Lal says, 'The King sent for Mirza Mughul, Mirza Abu Bakr, and Mirza Abdullah and rebuked them for continuing to work with the Sepoys and sympathise with the sepoys. This piece of news is torn from the Emperor's long letter written to Mirza Mughul (*vide* pp. 209-217 *supra*). Read without reference to the background, the given news would exhibit Bahadur Shah as faithless and insincere to the sepoys. Tearing the idea from the text of said letter, Jiwan Lal clothed it in an absolutely different language and presented it to the reader as a fresh incident, thus making it impossible for the naked eye to see any connection between it and the previous occurrence. (Metcalfe—T. N. N., p. 111).

[3] Metcalfe, T. N. N., pp. 27-74.

[4] Muinu'ddin Hasan had been a Police Inspector in British service before the outbreak of the Mutiny. After the outbreak he gave up British service and came to the Emperor who appointed him Kotwal of Dehli. Later he became a colonel in the Badshahi Army and held charge of a squadron. After the fall of Dehli he fled from India to Arabia; and when he returned after a few years he was tried. But in view of the fact that he had saved the life of Metcalfe and that his real object throughout the period of service under the Emperor of Dehli was to serve the British cause, he was acquitted. Then he was asked by Metcalfe whether he possessed any

from that of Jiwan Lal. While Muin'ddin Hasan gives a brief but connected and complete account of the Mutiny and the War—and he too was loyal to the British and a traitor[1] to the Emperor and the country—he does not view the events from a religious or communal standpoint, nor does he endeavour to humiliate or caricature Bahadur Shah. There is no trace in the whole of his narrative of a Hindu-Muslim conflict.

---

papers connected with the occurrence of 1857. He said that as Police Officer he used to keep a *Roz-namcha* or diary of daily occurrences . . . 'And so through the troublous time' says Muinu'ddin, 'I had kept a record of daily events . . . . My patron comforted me, saying that time had smoothed away many obstacles to writing a true history, and that I need no longer fear personal consequences. Paying my respects I promised to write of every true occurrence of which I had been an eye-witness, and of every fact with which I was acquainted'.

Afterwards Muinu'ddin Hasan handed over his diary to Metcalfe with the request that it should not be published during his lifetime. He died in 1878. Then Metcalfe wrote an introduction; and having edited and translated the two diaries he intended to publish them. But he died leaving the task incomplete in 1892. It was completed by his wife T. J. Metcalfe who published the book in 1898.

[1] He says: 'I felt I had incurred suspicion and that my life and my family were in danger. It was necessary to take some decided measure. In all hours of difficulty and danger, action is better than inaction—a golden rule. It struck me that if I were to maintain my influence and position in the city, I too must become a mutineer, and checkmate the designs of those who would destroy me. When two men are contending, the one who is the less energetic must be worsted. I determined to go at once to the Palace, and offer my services to the King.' (Metcalfe—T. N. N., p. 55).

APPENDIX A

A SCENE FROM THE TRIAL OF BAHADUR SHAH IN THE DEHLI FORT

'A paper marked A is now produced, enclosed in its original envelope on which is the Dehli post-office stamp of 25th March 1857 and another stamp of the Agra post-office of 27th March 1857. The Judge Advocate explains that this important document was found among the papers of the late Mr. Colvin, Lt.-Governor at Agra. The translation is read out as follows:

'Nourisher of the poor! May your prosperity continue! Your Highness!

The arrangements for the despatch of letters from the King of Dehli to the King of Persia through the Pirzada Hasan Askari have been stated in a former petition. . . . I am a mendicant of itinerant habits and have since learned for a certainty that two men with letters from the King of Dehli through the said Hasan Askari proceeded about 3 or 4 months ago towards Constantinople in company with a caravan going to Mecca. Hasan Askari has now assured the King of Dehli that he has certain information that the prince royal of Persia has fully taken possession of and occupied Bushire and that he has entirely expelled the Christians or rather has not left one alive there and has taken many of them prisoners; and that very soon indeed the Persian army will advance by the way of Kandhar and Kabul towards Dehli. He told the king also that His Majesty was altogether too careless about corresponding with the King of Persia. The King then gave Hasan Askari 20 Gold Mohurs and requested him speedily to despatch letters to Persia and directed him to give the gold mohurs to the man who should take the letters for the expenses of his journey. Hasan Askari accordingly took the money and returned to his house, and has prepared four men to carry the letters, making them assume the coloured garments of religious mendicants, and it is reported that they will leave for Persia in a day or two. The petitioner has not been able to ascertain their names. In the Palace, but more specially in the portion of it constituting the personal apartments of the King, the subject of conversation night and day is the early arrival of the Persians. Hasan Askari has, moreover, impressed the King with the belief that he has learned, through a divine revelation, that the dominion of the King of Persia will to a certainty extend to Dehli or rather over the whole of Hindustan and that the splendour of the sovereignty of Dehli will again revive as the sovereign of Persia will bestow the crown on the King. Throughout the Palace but particularly to the King this belief has been the cause of great rejoicing so much so that prayers are offered and vows made while at the same time Hasan Askari has entered upon the daily performance at an hour and a half before sunset of a course of propitiatory ceremonies to expedite the arrival of the Persians and the expulsion of the Christians. It has been arranged that on Thursday several trays of victuals, wheat-meal, oil, money in copper coin and cloth, should be sent by the King in aid of these ceremonies; and they are accordingly brought to Hasan Askari . . . .

'Your petitioner keeps learning these matters from certain of his friends who have admittance to the presence of the King of Dehli and who are moreover in the habit of visiting Hasan Askari also. Actuated by goodwill, I have communicated the above particulars. It rests in the province of the ever-enduring Government to make necessary and effectual arrangements'.

Petition of the well-wisher Muhammad Dervish, dated 24th March, 1857.

Hakim Ahsanullah—recalled and examined by Judge Advocate.

Question—You have heard the petition of Muhammad Dervish read. Do you know anything of the trays of food . . . said to have been sent by the King in aid of the ceremonies performed by Hasan Askari?

Hakim Ahsanullah—Yes, all these things were usually sent . . .

Question—You have mentioned that Jat Mall was one of the court spies. Did the King pay him for the news given?

Answer—He was not a servant of the King; he was a news-writer on the part of the British Government.

Question—How was it then that you came to get secret information from him; and how being known as Government news-writer was it that this man was entrusted with such a secret?

Answer—Jat Mall used to go about the Palace collecting all sorts of news and having heard the matter asked me what I knew of it at which time I was ignorant of the subject, and it was only subsequently that I heard it confirmed.

Jat Mall formerly news-writer to the Lieutenant Governor of Agra is called.

Question—Did you know a man of the name of Hasan Askari here?

Answer—Yes, I did.

Question—Was he frequently in attendance on the Prisoner?

Answer—Yes.

Question—Relate what you know of his transactions with the king.

Answer—He used to come and repeat incantations over the king, and after praying, breathe on him; he used also to profess to be possessed of miraculous gifts from heaven, the gift of prophecy, the power of interpreting dreams. (The Prisoner here voluntarily declares his belief that Hasan Askari did really possess the powers here attributed to him)

Question to Jat Mall—Did you Jat Mall! ever hear any particular dream which this man Hasan Askari interpreted to the king?

Answer—Yes, about the time the Persian forces came to Herat I heard that Hasan Askari communicated one of his own dreams to the king to the effect that he had seen a hurricane approaching from the West which was followed by a great flood of water devastating the country, that it passed over and that he noticed that the king suffered no inconvenience from it but was borne up over the flood seated on a couch. The way in which Hasan Askari interpreted this dream was, that the king of Persia with his army would annihilate the British power in the East, would restore the king to his ancient throne and reinstate him in his kingdom and at the same time the infidels, meaning the British, would be all slaughtered.

Question—Do you know whether through the means of this man Hasan Askari, letters were sent to the king of Persia or communications kept up with him?

Answer—Yes, I do know that letters used to be sent. About a year and half or two years ago, a caravan was going to Mecca. A man of the name of Sidi Qambar who was chief of the Abyssinians in the Palace asked permission to accompany it as a pilgrim. This was granted, and . . . . he was given a year's pay in advance, and . . . . the Prisoner . . . . sent a petition addressed to God to be posted on his account on the walls of the shrine at Mecca. After *some* 8 *or* 9 *days I heard that Sidi Qambar's going to Mecca was only a pretence and that in reality he had started direct for Persia with letters from the king of Dehli to the King of Persia. I heard this from Khwaja Bakhsh, a messenger of the king's, and from one of the Prisoner's armed personal attendants whose name* I do not recollect. I acquainted Capt. Douglas with this matter at the time, who said it was a very serious business and directed me to make every possible inquiry about it *because such correspondence on the part of the king of Dehli was interdicted* . . . . I continued my enquiries and some 20 days afterwards I learned . . . . that *Haidar Husain,* commandant of the Prisoner's artillery, and *Hasan Askari had some letters written; and having them authenticated in some way had them despatched to Persia by Sidi Qambar. . . . .*

Sir Theophilus Metcalfe examined by Judge Advocate:

Question—Some short time before the outbreak in May last was there any paper stuck up on the walls of the Jami' Masjid purporting to be *a proclamation from the King of Persia*?

Answer—Yes, it was a small dirty piece of paper with a naked sword and shield depicted—one on the right and the other on the left of it; and the purport of it was that the king of Persia was about to visit this country and he called upon all the faithful followers of the Prophet Muhammad to join with him in extirpating the English infidels, and offering landed estates and other large rewards to all who would do so; it was further stated that there were 500 men in Dehli at the time of putting up the placard who were devoted to his interest.

Question—Did you ever hear that the subject of the advance of the Persians upon Herat was much discussed among the natives?

Answer—Yes, very much so; and frequently in connection with the idea of Russian aggression upon India. Every native newspaper had at this time its correspondent in Kabul and there was a constant communication kept up with the North, every newspaper having its weekly quota of information from thence.

Hakim Ahsanullah was then questioned regarding

the communication *between Bahadur Shah* and (*Nasiru'ddin Qajar*) *king of Persia*.

Answer— . . . . about two or three years ago I remember reading in Muhammad *Baqir's Gazette that Mirza Najaf, one of the Prisoner's nephews, had gone to the Persian court and had been received by the King of Persia with much courtesy and kindness.*[1]

---

[1] *Vide* (i) *Pr. Tr. B. S.* (2nd, 3rd and 8th February 1858); pp. 72-75 and 84-85

(ii) *Idem,* Supplement to *Pr. Tr. B. S.*, p. 161.

Appendix B

PROCLAMATION OF THE SHAH OF IRAN

The royal proclamation of the Shah of Iran Nasiru'ddin Qajar, a contemporary of Bahadur Shah, was issued and printed towards the close of 1856 and its copies were circulated throughout India[1] and added to the current of agitation. It is held by some historians to have been one of the causes of the Mutiny.[2] 'By means of this,' says Kaye, 'the Persian Government endeavoured to raise manifold excitements in our 'Northern Frontier'[3]. The Shah sent forth to Dehli Iranian emissaries who called upon the Musalmans of all sects to unite against the Firangis[4]. Copies of this Proclamation were posted on the principal walls of Dehli and inside the Jami' Masjid. 'It was bruited abroad also that . . . . Dost Muhammad the Amir was really the friend and vassal of Persia and that the amity he had outwardly evinced towards the English was only a pretext for beguiling them to surrender Peshawar to the Afghans'[5].

The following is the English translation of that Proclamation:

'Whereas the British Government through the power acquired by the conquest of India and the advantages thereby gained has framed its politics and has pursued a course of aggression to the end that all the East be added to its dominion; and for the

---

[1], [2] Metcalfe, C. T. . . . . T. N. N. . . .p. 6.

[3] Kaye . . . . H. I. M. I, p. 353.

[4] *Ibid*

[5] *Op. cit.* p. 354.

purpose of accomplishing this and advancing the performance of it the British Government attempted the conquest of Afghanistan; and although it was overwhelmed by a complete repulse in this attempt, nevertheless it caused great destruction and mischief in the countries of Afghanistan and took possession of Lahore, Peshawar and several other dependencies of that country; and this is the proceeding and politics of this Government to obtain complete dominion in Persia; they try to prohibit the intercourse with the Sirdars of Afghanistan who are our neighbours and co-religionists and have always been our allies; and this is with a view to open to themselves a road to Persian soil so that whenever they wish, they could advance their troops from every side into Afghanistan and all the countries bordering on Persia; and even if they found they possessed the power to reduce the Government of Persia to the state of the Rajas of Hindustan and to destroy the religion of Islam in Persia in like manner as the religion of the Musalmans of India. And in order to carry out this design, the British have commenced invading the kingdom of Persia; they have occupied themselves in deceiving the vulgar, and through deceipt and bad faith, and an improper mode of proceeding, whilst our Government have never resented it, and presuming upon our supposed weakness they have carried their ill practice and bad faith to such an extent that they have tried to seduce persons in the employ of the Persian Government to enter the service of their embassy and also endeavoured to bring Princes and Moonshees of the kingdom under their authority; and they have employed strategems and artifices, so that, by false pretences and improper proceedings, they have tried to bring to pass that which they desire, and by degrees all their machinations have come to light. Unexpectedly they brought troops to the soil of a power of Islam, and having thus gained a footing took possession of one of the forts of Islam which was on the seashore, and was only held by a small number of troops as its fixed garrison and thus no army being present they occupied it; and when they saw that, if they advanced from the seashore they would flounder about like fish on dry land, they have stuck there, for they knew that if they advanced the blows of the sharp sword of the heroes of Islam would not leave breath in the soul of one of them.

'But His Majesty the *Shahinshah* has taken advantage of this breach of faith of the British Government to make manifest his royal will and pleasure; and his orders have gone forth that countless armies are to be assembled on the boundaries of every country; and victorious troops have been directed towards the frontiers to drive out the enemies of the faith. . . . . . .

'But whereas the victorious army of the State have not drawn the sword upon the enemy, we have not permitted the eager multitudes to leave their homes; and in the direction of Fars, we have appointed the Amiru-l Umara Mirza Muhammad Khan *Kashakimi Bashi* and Mir Ali Khan Shujau-l Mulk and several other generals and commanders with 25,000 men; and in the direction of Mohumerah, the Prince Nawab Samsamu'd-Dawla with 20,000 fine troops; and in the direction of Kirman, Jafar Kulah Khan Mir and Ghulam Husain Sipahdar with regiments and cavalry . . . and in the direction of Cutch and Makran towards Sind, and from the direction of Afghanistan the Nawab Ahsanu-s Saltanat with 300,000 men and . . . . . the

Afghan Sardars—*viz*. Sardar Sultan Ahmad Khan, Sardar Shah Doolah Khan, Sardar Sultan Ali Khan and Sardar Muhammad Alam Khan . . . . . . have been ordered towards India; and they are hopeful that, by the blessing of Divine aid, they may be victorious.

'And it is necessary that the Afghan tribes and the inhabitants of that country who are co-religionists of the Persians and who possess the same Quran and Qibla . . . . should also take part in the Jihad . . . . And this should also be made known to all the people of Afghanistan that the Persian Government has no intention of extending its conquests in that direction except to the government of Qandhar which should be given over to Sardar Rahim Dil Khan . . . and the government of Kabul and its dependencies should be vested in its chiefs and they should join in the jihad against the enemies of Islam.

'And we are hopeful that after the publication of this proclamation, Dost Muhammad, amir of Kabul, who always was desirous that the Persian armies should extend their conquests to Afghanistan and who wished to be strengthened by their alliance should also unite with us against this tribe of the wanderers from the path of righteousness and that he should become one of the leaders of the faithful in this jihad and that he should become a *Ghazi* in Hindustan . . . . .

'And this proclamation is published for the information of all true believers; and please God the followers of Islam in Hind and Sind will also unite with us and take vengeance upon that tribe[1] (British).'

---

[1] *Vide* (i) J. Cave-Browne—*The Punjab and Delhi in 1857*. vol. I, pp. 359-360.

(ii) Mutiny Papers, Box 195, Nos. 1, 2, 3, 4, 5, 6, 8, 9, 10, 13-16, March, April, May, July, August and September 1857.

(iii) *Pr. Tr. B. S.* p. 157.

FACSIMILE OF AN EPITOME OF THE ABOVE PROCLAMATION IN ORIGINAL PERSIAN OF NASIRU'DDIN QAJAR, SHAH OF IRAN, FROM THE TEHERAN GAZETTE OF 1856 A.D. (1273 HIJRA, 18 MILADI)

stating that Mirza Aqai Etimadu'd-Dawla Nuri Sadr-i Azam of Iran sent copies of this Proclamation to several prominent men of Hindustan and this encouraged the outbreak of rebellion in India. After the treaty when England complained to the Iranian Government about thus exciting rebellion in India they replied that it was a measure adopted during war time.

facing p. 332

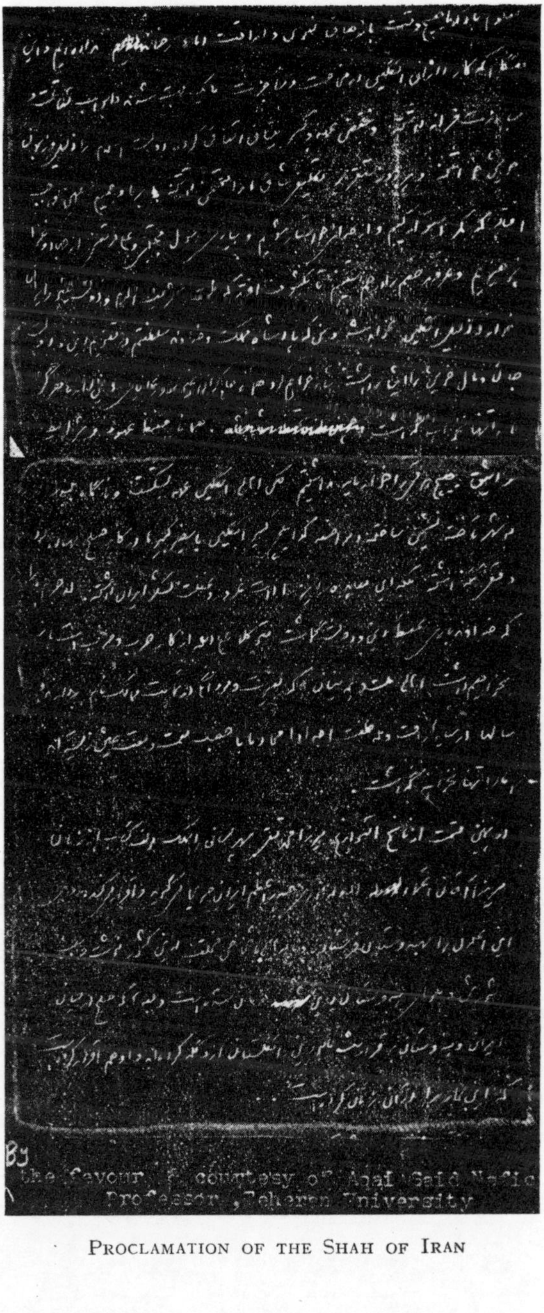

By the favour & courtesy of Aqai Said Nafici
Professor, Teheran University

PROCLAMATION OF THE SHAH OF IRAN

Appendix C

SOME OF THE ANTI-BRITISH VERSES[1] OF BAHADUR SHAH ZAFAR

I Composed before the War of 1857

کہا پوچھتے ہو کج روئ چرخ چنبری
ہے اوس ستم شعار کا شیوہ ستم گری

What! do you enquire about the crooked ways of Fate? It is oppressive in its nature and cruel in its practice.

کرتا ہے خوار تو انہیں جن کو ہے برتری
اوسکے مزاج میں ہے یہ کیا سفلہ پروری

It humiliates particularly those who are more exalted; it is the nature of Fate that it supports and patronises the mean.

کھاے ہے گوشت زاغ - فقط استخواں ہما
کیا منصفی ہے زاغ کہاں اور کہاں ہما

---

[1] It should be noted that Bahadur Shah is speaking in metaphors; but in spite of the metaphors it is easy to understand that through these verses he has asserted his position as the *de jure* sovereign. He is sorry to find that while he is not supported and is in trouble, his enemies whom he compares with thistles and trees of prickly thorns (*nakhl-i mughilan*) are flourishing. He considers himself a prisoner of the British and says, 'Circumstances are so unfavourable that if I decide to take even one step forward I would have to meet with ten obstacles, each preventing me from achieving my object'.

The crow[1] enjoys meat while the phoenix[2] has to live on mere bones. What justice! There is no comparison whatever between the phoenix and the crow.

بالعکس هیں جہاں میں جہاں تک هیں کار و بار
شیوہ کیا ہے الٹا زمانہ نے اختیار

All the affairs of this world are topsy-turvy; the world has adopted perverse ways.

ہے موسم بہار خزاں اور خزاں بہار
آئی نظر عجب روش باغ روز گار

Spring is replaced by autumn and autumn by spring; such strange scenes are staged in the garden of this world

جو نخل پر ثمر هیں اٹھا سکتے سر نہیں
سر کش هیں وہ درخت کہ جن میں ثمر نہیں

Those of the trees which are fruit-bearing cannot raise their heads; the trees which raise their heads are those which bear no fruit.

باد صبا اڑاتی چمن میں ہے سر پہ خاک
ملتے هیں دمبدم کف افسوس برگ تاک

Breeze throws dust on its head in the garden; the vine trees wring their hands in sorrow, every now and then.

---

[1] 'Crow' stands for the Englishmen who were then known as 'men of black heart. *Vide Sadiqul Akhbar,* 2nd July 1857; and *Saptahik Hindustan of New Delhi* dated December 2, 1957, p. 16 for facsimile.

[2] 'Phœnix' is a fabulous bird whose shadow, it is believed, is auspicious and anyone, on being favoured with it, secures the throne. Here 'phoenix' stands for Bahadur Shah

غنچے هیں دل گرفته - گلوں کے جگر هیں چاک
کرتی هیں بلبلیں یهی فریاد درد ناک
شاداب حیف ! خار هوں - گل پائمال هوں
گلشن هوں خار - نخل مغیلاں نهال هوں

The buds are afflicted with sorrow; the hearts of the roses are lacerated and the nightingales are chirping painfully as if telling in sad melancholy tones—'Alas! the thorns flourish while the roses are trampled; the garden is transformed into thorns while the tree of prickly thorns is thriving.

جائیں فلک کے احاط سے هم کہاں
هووے گا سر په چرخ یهی جائینگے هم جهاں

Where can we[1] go out of the vault of the sky? There will be this vault of the sky over our head wherever we go.

جو آگیا هے اس محل تیره رنگ میں
قید حیات سے هے وه قید فرنگ میں

Whoever has come into this weird place is a prisoner of the Firangis as long as he lives.

یه گنبد فلک هے عجب طرح کا قفس
طاقت نهیں هے ناله کی جس میں ایک نفس
جنبش هو ایک پرکی تو پر ٹوٹ جایں دس
ره جاے دل میں دل کی نه کس طرح هوس
کیا طائر اسیر وه پرواز کر سکے
جس میں نه اتنا دم هو که پرواز کر سکے

[1] This is the Royal 'we'. By means of this and the following verse Bahadur Shah expressed the agony of his heart.

This vault of the sky is such a strange cage that one has not the power to raise in it cries even for a moment.

If I move an inch I would suffer breakdown in ten points; the longings of my heart would surely then remain unfulfilled.

How can a caged bird fly? He has no strength to fly.

کیا کیا جہاں میں ہو چکے شاہان ذی کرم
کس کس طرح کا رکھتے تھے ساتھ اپنے وہ حشم
آخر گئے جہاں سے تنہا سوے عدم
دارا کہاں؟ کہاں ہے سکندر؟ کہاں ہے جم
کوي نہ یاں رہا ہے نہ کوی جہاں رہے
کچھ اے ظفر رہے تو نکوی یہاں رہے

Many kings of might and majesty have been in this world.

What powerful armies of different kinds did they possess!

At last they left this world and departed alone.

Where is Darius? Where is Alexander? Where is Jamshed?

O Zafar! barring good deeds which might remain, nothing will survive in this world.[1]

—: o :—

اس ستمگر نے مجھے جرم وفا پہ مارا
کوئی لینے کا نہیں نام وفا میرے بعد

[1] *Diwan-i Awwal,* pp. 382-383. Nawalkishore Press, 5th edition (1918).

This tyrant has killed me on account of my faithfulness, considering it a crime. After me, faithfulness will not be considered worth a mention.[1]

کیا ھم نے ظفر جا کے جب تیرا مذکور
تیری طرف سے اونہیں بدگمان پایا

O Zafar! whenever we remembered thee to them, we found them mistrustful of thee.[2]

تمہاری دوستی میں مرگئے لاکھوں نہ رحم آیا
تم ھی ھو دشمن عالم - بھلا مانو برا مانو

Lakhs of people have perished in their attempt to cultivate friendship with you, but you did not relent. Verily you are an enemy to the whole world; whether you like this epithet (*dushman-i 'alam*) or not.[3]

کیا جو تم نے میرے ساتھہ اپنے دل سے وہ پوچھو
مجھے بس چپ ھی تم رہنے دو کھلواتے زباں کیوں ھو

What you have done to me! This is a story on which you may draw out your own heart. Let me remain silent. Why do you make me speak plainly?[4]

میں خوب جانتا ھوں نا معتبر ھیں بالکل
تم لاکھہ عہد نامے قول و قسم سے لکھو

I know full well that your words are absolutely unreliable. You may write a lakh of pledges under solemn oaths; matters little.[5]

---

[1] *Diwan-i Awwal*, p. 87
[2] *Diwan-i Duwum, p.* 164
[3] *Diwan-i Chaharum*, p. 122
[4] *Idem*, p. 120
[5] *Idem*, p. 114

اب جو لکھتا ہے وہ کاہے کو لکھتا تھا کبھی
دیکھ لو اوس بت بے پیر کا پہلا کاغذ

Whatever he (Governor-General) now writes, he never wrote before; you may look into the previous letters of this accursed fellow.[1]

ملتے ہیں ہم سے پہ دل سے عداوت رکھتے
جانتے ہم تو نہ ایسوں سے محبت رکھتے

They meet us in a friendly manner but cherish enmity at heart. Had we known this before, we would never have made friends with them.[2]

پاسکے رمز و کنایہ کوئی کیا اوسکے ظفر
جس کی ایک بات میں سو طرح کا پہلو نکلے

How can one get at their allusions and references, O Zafar! A single word of theirs is capable of yielding a hundred different meanings.[3]

نہ ہم راہ وفا بھولے نہ تم طرز ستم چوکے
جو اپنی بات تھی اوس سے نہ ہم چوکے نہ تم چوکے

We never lost remembrance of the way of faithfulness, and you did not neglect your special pursuit of tyranny. According to the characteristic habit of each, neither diverted from his path: nor you, nor we.[4]

نہ کر بد عہد یاں پیماں شکن ! انصاف کر دل میں
کئے تھے میرے ساتھ کیا کیا قول و قسم تونے

---

[1] *Diwan-i Chaharum,* p. 44

[2] *Idem,* p. 223

[3] *Diwan-i Suwum,* p. 144

[4] *Idem,* p. 116.

O breaker of pledges! do not be repeatedly untrue to your word. Do justice, looking into your heart; and recall what remarkable assurances you had given me before.[1]

تمہاری بات کا کہا کوی اعتبار کرے
کہ قول دے کے کئی بار تم ظفر سے پھرے

How can Zafar rely on your word for you have turned your back on your word of honour several times[2]?

II Composed after the War of 1857

گئی یک بہ یک جو ھوا پلٹ کہ نہ دل کو میرے قرار ھے
کروں غم ستم کا میں کیا بیاں میرا غم سے سینہ فگار ھے

The wind having suddenly changed what shall I relate regarding my grief and injuries! My heart is wounded with grief.

کیا رعایا ھند تباہ ھوی کہو اُون پہ کیا یہ جفا ھوی
جسے دیکھا حاکم وقت نے کہا یہ تو قابل دار ھے

How cruelly have the Indian subjects been ruined! Is it possible to conceive what oppressions they have endured? Whomsoever the ruler of the day beholds, he sends him to the gallows, saying 'He surely deserves to be hanged'.

یہ ستم کسی نے بھی ھے سنا کہ دی پھانسی لاکھونکو بے گناہ
ولے کلمہ گویوں کی طرف سے ابھی دل پہ اُون کے غبار ھے

Has anyone heard of such oppressions as hanging innocent people by hundreds of thousands?

---

[1] *Diwan-i Awwal,* p. 271

[2] *Diwan-i Duwum,* p. 89

They have yet malice in their hearts against the Musalmans.

نه دبایا زیر چمن اُونهیں - نه دی گور اور کفن اُونهیں
کیا کس نے یارو دفن اُونهیں - بے تهکانه اون کا مزار هے

Those whom they have killed have neither been interred in gardens, nor have they had any grave or winding-sheet. Who could have given them burial? No trace can be discovered of their graves.

یه وبال تن په پڑا نهیں ڈر ذرا جان جانے کا
بچے غم سے - نکلے جو دم خدا! همیں زندگی اپنی پهاڑ هے

I have been so afflicted that I do not fear to die. If I were to die I would be saved from grief. My life, O God! is a heavy burden to me.

شب و روز پهول میں جو تلیں کهوں خار غم سے جب کهلیں
اونهیں طوق قید میں جب ملے گویا بدله گل کے وه هار هے

Those who used to live amid flowers day and night are (clad) in thorns. What shall I say regarding their agonies when their wounds, pressed by the thorns, gape! And the iron collars put round their necks look like a substitute for the garland of flowers.

یه سلوک کرتے تهے اور سے کهوں کیا وه جیسے جور سے
وه هیں تنگ چرخ کے دور سے رها تن په اون کے نه تار هے

Those who used to treat others kindly, conferring gifts, their misfortune now baffles description. They are in great misery under the afflictions of cruel Fate; they have not a thread left on their backs.

نہ تھا شہر دہلی - وہ تھا چمن دلی - سب طرح کا تھا وہاں امن
وہ خطـــاب اسکا تو مٹ گیـا - فقط اب تو اُجڑا دیـــار ہے

Dehli was not a city but a garden of hearty pleasures (*Chaman-i Dili*) with all kinds of security and amenity. That epithet of Dehli is obliterated. Now Dehli is a ruined waste land.

یہاں حال تنگ خوشی کا ہے - وہ کرشمہ قدرت رب کا ہے
یہاں بہار میں تو خزاں ہوئی - وہاں خزاں میں اونکو بہار ہے

Here, now, there is no joy at all: such is the wonderworking of Fate! For us spring has turned into autumn. For them (Englishmen) autumn has become spring.

کھٹکا نہیں ظفر تجھے حشر کا - جو خدا کہے تجھے برملا
تجھے ہے وسیلہ رسول کا - وہ تمہـــارا حامی کار ہے

O Zafar! you should have no fears of standing before the Divine Tribunal and of being called to account openly by God on the Day of Judgment since you can count on the intercession of the Prophet. He is your supporter in any case and saviour.*

---

*Regarding the above verses of Bahadur Shah II the Political Agent of Bhopal says in the course of a letter dated 14th July, 1862 addressed to Major R. I. Meade, A.G.—G. for India:

'. . . . . I have the honour to transmit a copy of some stanzas of the ex-King. This ode, I am told, is sung or recited by the minstrels of India and can be heard in any town of importance throughout the North-West Provinces. From stanzas 3, 8, and 9 I am of opinon that the composition is of more recent date and that it has been attributed to the ex-King by the faction of which he was the head for reasons apparent'.

(N.A., F.D. Pol. A. No. 3/4, August 1862.)

Appendix D

EVIDENCE OF MUKAND LAL, PRIVATE SECRETARY OF BAHADUR SHAH II, AT THE EMPEROR'S TRIAL

'The King of Dehli has for some two years been disaffected against the Government and was disposed not to respect his obligations to the English. The particulars are as follows:

'When Mirza Haider Shikoh and Mirza Murad, sons of Mirza Khan Bakhsh son of Mirza Sulaiman Shikoh, came here from Lakhnao they in concert with Hasan Askari arranged and suggested to the King that he should have a letter prepared and despatched to the King of Persia. This letter they suggested should represent that the English had made the King a prisoner and had put a stop to all those marks of respect to which as king he was entitled and had suspended the appointment of an heir-apparent. It was further represented that his wishes in reference to the appointment of any particular son as heir-apparent were not attended to. Under these circumstances the letter was to request that such an understanding might be established that mutual interchanges of visits and letters might be the result. Sidi Qambar who was one of the King's special armed retainers was presented with 100 rupees through Mahbub Ali Khan for the expenses of his journey and was despatched in the direction of Persia with a letter that had been prepared in the King's private secretariat office. After this, Mirza Haidar and his brother returned to Lakhnao, and having despatched his brother Mirza Najaf, a distant relation of the King with Mirza Bulaki son of Mirza Musharrafu'ddin son of Mirza Agha Jan to Persia reported the same to the King in writing.

'It is now about three years since some infantry soldiers stationed at Dehli became the disciples of the King through Mirza Ali whose duty it was to receive and present all petitions, and also through Hamid Khan Jamadar. And on that occasion the King gave each of them a document containing the names and order of those who had preceded him in the direct line, disciples to each other, himself included, together with a napkin dyed pink as an emblem of his blessing. The agent of the Lieutenant-Governor, hearing of this occurrence inquired regarding it, and for the future prohibited the King's making any more of the men of the army his disciples. *It may be said that from that day a sort of understanding was established between the army and the King.*

'Some 20 days before the commencement of the late rebellion, intelligence was received here that the troops at Mirath were about breaking out in open mutiny, but it had not been heard that they were to come here. When the troops arrived, they first came under the palace windows and told the King that they had come to him after killing all the English at Mirath and that they would slay immediately those that were here, and they further said that they would for the future consider the Prisoner their King . . . . They further said that the whole army would obey the King's orders.

'The King said that if they had a disposition to come they should prepare themselves for all consequences, and if they were so prepared they were at liberty to come and take the management of matters in their hands.

'While this disturbance was going on, these traitors got into the city; the special armed retainers joined them and Kadir Dad Khan, a resident of Kabul, slew the Resident Mr. Fraser while some of the infantry soldiers with others of the King's retainers went to the apartments of the commandant of Palace Guards and slew him there. After that the English were killed all about the city wherever they were met with. The same day proclamation was made by beat of drum throughout the city that God was the ruler of the World and Bahadur Shah was sovereign of the country and had the supreme authority.

'The next day the 12th when the troops from Mirath and those at Dehli had coalesced, the King took his seat on the throne, a salute of guns was fired, and Mahbub Ali Khan the minister, was ordered to give the whole army a feast. Accordingly they were all supplied with confectionary, the native officers receiving in addition a present in money. Formerly a silver throne had been kept in the Diwan-i khass on which the King used to take his seat on state occasions; but since 1842 the presentation of the usual offering by the agent of the Lieutenant-Governor on occasions of interviews and salutes was disallowed. This throne was then removed and placed in a recess in the passage below the King's sitting-room, and since that time was in disuse till the 12th May when it was brought out again, and the King took his seat on it, as on a throne'.[1]

---

[1] (*Pr. Tr. B. S.* pp. 149-159.)

Appendix E

GUARANTEE OF HIS LIFE TO BAHADUR SHAH WAS NOT THE RESULT OF ANY KIND OF INTRIGUES ON HIS PART

This is proved *first* by the following correspondence[1] between C. B. Saunders, offg. Commissioner, Dehli (*Dehlee*) and (a) G. E. Edmonstone, Secretary to the Government of India, (b) Major General Wilson,[2] C. B., and (c) W. M. Stewart, Adjutant-General, Dehli (*Dehlee*); *secondly* by the British account[3] of the 'Grant of pensions to Mirza Ilahi Bakhsh and his family for services rendered during the rebellion'.

(i) In his letter of 31st December 1857 addressed to G. E. Edmonstone, Secretary to the Government of India, Saunders refutes the allegation that 'the life of the King of Dehlee was conditionally spared by Wilson in compliance with his (Saunder's) recommendation'. After discussing the circumstances in which the guarantee of Bahadur Shah's life was accorded under dire necessity, he says, '. . . . As in the above correspondence I have emphatically denied any personal participation in granting the guarantee of

---

[1] N. A., F. C. 1859, No. 1785.

[2] It should be noted that Wilson who was the conqueror of Dehli was invested with authority to pardon mutineers except those who had murdered Europeans (*vide* S. C. No. 7-11, Mutiny Papers). After capturing Dehli (20th September 1857) he directed that 'the King of Dehli be sent to Allahabad, if any British officer has promised to spare his life, otherwise he is to be tried under Act XIV of 1857 and sentence carried out at once'.

(*Vide* Mutiny Papers, S. C. No. 186, 30th October 1857).

the King of Dehlee of his life; it was not without considerable surprise that I read the letter from Major-General Wilson to your address in which he distinctly asserts that it was in compliance with my recommendation that he gave his consent to the measure which had also been previously recommended to him by my predecessor, the late Mr. Greathed . . . . I did not receive until after the Ex-King had been made over a prisoner to me any of the official documents in the possession of Mr. Greathed at the time of his decease, nor had I read the instructions which had from time to time been sent to him and was perfectly ignorant of what the views of the Government of India or of the N. W. Provinces were with reference to the treatment of the Royal Family of Dehlee or other measures of State Policy, and it was not therefore probable that I should have volunteered my opinion on the subject unless I had been called on to give it. I did, however, consider it to be my duty immediately after the fall of Dehlee to urge most strongly upon the General the necessity of organizing a force to pursue the fugitive columns of the Enemy and to secure the destruction if possible of all those who had taken prominent part in the rebellion.

It must be borne in mind that the Infantry and perhaps more specially the artillery of the force had been for nearly three weeks without rest fighting almost without intermission or relief both in the trenches and in the city and were totally unfit for further immediate exertion. I therefore suggested that the cavalry—which, not having undergone the same harassing duties as the other branches of the service and from having remained outside the city had not been subjected to the same demoralizing influence as the rest, were in a position to be more readily made available for the pursuit—should be immediately sent to scour the country to the south of the city. *Had it been found practicable to carry out these views, I am confident that the King's person might have been secured without the offer of any guarantee.*

The General, however, refused—and I have no doubt on military grounds very properly so—to send the cavalry unsupported by Infantry and Artillery in pursuit of the flying Enemy as the nature of the ground from the number of old ruins and walled enclosures which would give shelter and protection to the fugitives rendered it unsafe to employ that arm of the service alone on such duties. He was however equally alive to the necessity of organizing a flying column for the pursuit and gave directions for equipping a force for the purpose which it was not found practicable to despatch for several days and not until too late to be of any use in pursuing the Enemy down the right bank of the Jumna.

It was under these circumstances and these alone, when I found that no force could be at once sent to pursue the Enemy and arrest or destroy the leading members of the rebellion, and not till after the person of the King had been on the strength of the guarantee secured that I can be said as stated by the General to have approved of the measure, for certainly I did consider that it was far preferable to have secured his person whether with or without a guarantee of his life than to allow him as I have before stated to be carried off by the Mutineers to become a rallying point for the disaffected.

From the tenor of the General's letter to myself I cannot but perceive that while admitting his error, he is somewhat impressed with the idea that I am anxious to throw the whole responsibility upon him. Had I been before aware that he had reported to Government that he had consented to the measure upon my recommendation I might perhaps from motives of delicacy have been unwilling to have contradicted the assertion however unfair or unjust I might have deemed it. But the case is now widely different in total ignorance of what the General had written either to Government or to Sir John Lawrence; and in answer to a requisition from the Governor-General in Council founded upon assertions contained in the Public Prints, I submitted a full and correct statement of the circumstances under which the guarantee was accorded. I therein stated mere matters of fact, and in justice to myself I denied any personal participation in the Guarantee . . . . . .

27th December, 1857. Sd. C. B. Saunders,
offg. Commissioner, Dehlee.

My dear General,

I have received the accompanying copy of a letter from Mr. Edmonstone calling upon me to submit such an explanation as I may be prepared to offer with reference to a statement which you appear to have made to Government that the life of the Ex-King of Dehlee had been conditionally spared by you in compliance with my recommendation.

I feel sure that in making the above statement you had no wish whatever to throw the responsibility of the measure off your shoulders on to mine, and that if you had called the circumstances under which the guarantee was accorded to your recollection more carefully you would have written differently on the subject.

You will I think remember on recalling the subject to your recollection that I was not present on the occasion when Captain Hodson applied for and obtained your permission to guarantee the King his life but was at the time absent at Mr. Greathed's funeral. The only other person present besides Captain Hodson and yourself was I believe Captain Stewart, the Asst. Adj. Gen. who has authorized me to state that he heard all that passed on the occasion having taken a part I believe in the conversation.

This occurred on the afternoon of the 20th September, Mr. Greathed having died at midnight on the 19th. The whole of the morning of the 20th you were engaged in giving your instructions for the attack on the Palace which came off in the middle of the day. I had no conversation with you relative to the apprehension of the King and his family, nor did I join you at the Palace that day but proceeded early in the afternoon to cantonments to attend the funeral of my predecessor, Mr. Greathed. I cannot therefore be held responsible for having recommended you to offer the guarantee.

On my return from the funeral I met Captain Hodson outside the city near the Cashmere Gate cantonments. As *he passed me he checked his horse and called out that he was off to make arrangements for securing the King's person through Ilahee Bukhsh as he had received your permission to guarantee the King his life.* This was the first I heard of the probability of the King's person being secured, and I certainly had nothing whatever to do with counselling you to the measure. Whether Mr. Greathed had recommended you to offer the King his life or not I know not, but I think it highly probable that he did so, as he informed me on the day before his death that he had Mr. Colvin's authority to grant him his life.

Under the circumstances I have mentioned I feel sure that you will readily admit that upon a more careful recollection of what took place you were in error in stating that you offered the guarantee of his life to the King upon my recommendation and will moreover allow that it was Captain Hodson and not myself who was the party authorized by you to grant the King his life on condition of his giving himself up unreservedly.

I shall feel highly obliged by your sending me an early reply as I am anxious to submit my Explanation without loss of time and I do not wish to do so without first communicating with you on the subject

I am . . .

Meerut, 28th December, 1857. Sd. C. B. Saunders.

My dear Saunders,

I am quite sure that I gave no orders in any political question without the advice of the Political Agent with the Force. I had Mr. Greathed's recommendation to guarantee the King his life and it struck me when writing to Mr. Edmonstone on the 23rd October last that I had yours also; I may have been mistaken in supposing I had received your recommendation on the 20th September. On such a day of excitement I may very probably have made such a mistake, but I am quite sure that you approved of the measure afterwards and that when the King was brought in I told you that he was your prisoner and that you must do what you considered best for his safe custody.

I only directed that not more than ten attendants should be allowed for him and the Begum.

I considered then the King had been only a tool in the hands of the Mutineers and that it was a wise political measure to secure his person and prevent his being carried off by the Rebels. This was also, I believe, your opinion.

I can assure you that I have no wish whatever to throw responsibility on anyone's shoulders, and as Mr. Greathed is dead and I have no evidence of my conversation with him on this subject and you object to taking any responsibility on your part you are perfectly at liberty to throw the whole on my shoulders. In fact I do not see how anyone else can be called upon; as commanding the Forces the whole power and responsibility rested with me. I could ask advice, but could act upon it or not as I thought right.

Believe me . . . .

To — Sd. A. Wilson.

C. Saunders Esqr.,
offg. Pol. Agent,
Delhee.

Delhee,
29th December, 1857.

My dear Stewart,

I have been called upon by direction of the Governor-General in Council to submit any explanation which I may be prepared to offer with reference to the accompanying copy of a letter from Major General Wilson to the address of the Secretary to the

Government of India dated 23rd October last reporting that *the life of the Ex-King of Dehlee was conditionally spared by him* in compliance with my recommendation.

As I believe you were present when Captain Hodson applied for and obtained permission from General Wilson to guarantee the King's life, I shall feel obliged by your stating for my satisfaction and for the information of Government what took place on that occasion and whether I was present or had anything to do with the offer of the guarantee.

I should also feel obliged by your honouring me whether in the subsequent conversations which I believe you have had with General Wilson and other officers of the Headquarters Staff at Meerut relative to the circumstances under which the guarantee was accorded, you have heard my name mentioned either by the General or others in connection with the above as having recommended the measure.

Yours,——

To Sd. C. B. Saunders.

Capt. W. M. Stewart,
Asst. Adj. Gen.,
Dehlee.

Dehlee,
29th Dec., 1857.

My dear Saunders,

I did not hear all that passed in the Diwan-i Khass between the General and Hodson as I continued writing at my own table for some time after Hodson began talking. Having occasion to speak to the General I went up to him and found him engaged with Hodson upon the guarantee question. *The latter urged him to grant the King's life, and after considerable hesitation the General appeared with reluctance to give his consent.* I did not join in the conversation for obvious reasons.

There was no one with the General during Hodson's interview. In fact, there was no one in the verandah except myself and I was at my own table which was as you may remember at some distance from the General.

I have often heard the General talk of the guarantee matter but I have never heard him place any portion of the responsibility of the measure on you. I am aware however that Mr. Greathed was always prepared to give the guarantee and had communicated his views to the General who finally acted upon them.

Yours,——

To Sd. W. M. Stewart.

C. B. Saunders,

Commissioner. . . .

(ii) GRANT OF PENSION TO MIRZA ILAHI BAKHSH AND HIS FAMILY FOR SERVICES RENDERED DURING THE REBELLION[1]

(a) Letter from R. H. Davies,
Secretary to the Govt., Punjab
and its Dependencies.

[1] Mutiny Papers; F. C. No. 38/43, 26th August 1859.

To

The Secretary of the Government of India,
Foreign Department,
dated Lahore, the 8th August, 1859.

Sir,

. . . . Mirza Ilahi Bukhsh is a member of the Royal Family of Delhie. During the siege of the city in 1857, he is believed to have exerted himself in our favour by his counsel to the leaders of the rebellion; at any rate *he did good service by enabling us to capture the Ex-King after the fall of the city* since it is stated that it was by his persuasions that the Ex-King did not accompany the rebel army in its flight from Delhie. . . . .

Sd. R. H. Davies,
Secretary to Govt. Punjab

(b) Letter from C. B. Saunders,
Commissioner,
dated Delhie, the 13th June 1859.
To R. H. Davies.

Sir,

. . . . Mirza Ilahi Bukhsh is a man of the Royal House of Timur and a descendant of Alamgir II. His daughter was married to Mirza Fakhroo, the eldest son of the Ex-King and heir-apparent to the Crown who died about 9 months before the outbreak.

Mirza Ilahi Bukhsh performed a most undoubted service in detaining the Ex-King and preventing him from taking his departure with the rebel army where his name would have become a rallying point for the disaffected and rebellious throughout the country.

The late Major Hodson entered into correspondence with the Mirza immediately after the assault of Delhie in order to effect the capture of the Ex-King through Maulvi Rajab Ali and Turab Ali; and it is admitted on all sides that Major Hodson's success in effecting the above important object was mainly brought about by the influence of the Mirza who is therefore in my opinion entitled above all members of the Royal House to the favourable consideration of the British Government.

Sd. C. B. Saunders,
Commissioner.

(c) Letter from Dy. Commissioner of Delhie,
To Commissioner of Delhie.

Dated Delhie, the 4th Aug., 1858.

Sir,

. . . . The services which Mirza Ilahi Bukhsh rendered to our cause in preventing the King of Delhie going away with the Rebel Troops are, I believe, admitted on all sides. *The late Captain Hodson himself told me that the Mirza had rendered excellent service. . . . .*

It is at all events certain that he did do his best to detain the King from going with the Rebels and there is every reason to believe that to his exertions is to be attributed the fortunate result of his capture. . . . .

Sd. Philip Egerton,
Dy. Commissioner.

(d) Letter from C. Wood of India Office, London,
To the Governor-General of India.

Dated London, 1st Dec., 1859.

My Lord,

. . . . Mirza Ilahi Bukhsh's claim upon the liberality of the British Government was based upon positive acts of service.

It was mainly through his instrumentality that the Ex-King was dissuaded from flying with the rebel army after the capture of the city by the British troops, a circumstance which is truly said to have contributed to the earlier suppression of the rebellion in that part of the country.[1] . . . .

Sd. C. Wood.

---

[1] Italics is mine.

APPENDIX F

PETITION OF NUR MUHAMMAD KHAN, RISALDAR, 10TH IRREGULAR CAVALRY[1]

Dated 29th August 1857.

To

The King, 'Shelter of the World'. Nourisher of the Poor.

My Corps, the 10th Regiment of Irregular Cavalry, was stationed at Peshawar in the Cantonments of Nowshera. Five of the Officers, Keshri Singh, Qalandar Khan etc. combining with the infidels and practising deceptions on the men, had us called out to a parade, and had our arms, such as carbines, swords etc. taken from us. Cheerfully enduring the greatest hardships and difficulties for two months, we slaves have now come to your Royal presence to defend the faith and to offer up our lives in protecting your Majesty's throne. Moreover, the English having placed their guns in position against us, we abandoned all our property, money and three months' arrears of pay, and having accomplished the journey, have now presented ourselves at your Royal door to sacrifice our lives. Most of the Troopers of the 10th Irregular Cavalry have gone to their homes, but their residence is near. If I am authorised I shall immediately call them in, and set up the Corps at once, when it will remain in attendance and will employ itself night and day, in giving effect to Your Majesty's orders. It will besides join in the attacks against the batteries and the members will willingly sacrifice their lives, if necessary. This alone

[1] *Pr. Tr. B. S.* p. 63, Military Papers, No. 37.

is your slave's ambition also. Let a written order be bestowed that he may at once enrol the Troopers of the 10th Irregular Cavalry.

About 50 of them are now present with your slave. On obtaining Your Majesty's order he will enrol the rest. It was necessary, and I have therefore submitted it. (Prayers for the King's prosperity.) Secondly if Your Majesty's orders are kindly bestowed on your slave and some horses are given to him, he will remain in attendance . . . .

Autograph order by the King in pencil

Be assured that favourable provisions will be made for you.[1]

PETITION OF COLONEL AHMAD KHAN[2], STATIONED AT GHAZIU'DDIN NAGAR. DATED 9TH SEPTEMBER, 1857

To

The King, Nourisher of the Poor!

Respectfully sheweth,—That leaving your imperial presence, your slave came to Ghaziabad, and here learned that yesterday, the 8th of September, some Europeans assisted by the Jats, burned and sacked Pilkhowa and 3 or 4 neighbouring villages. The force engaged in this destruction was comprised of about 30 Europeans, 300 Jats . . . and 4 guns. They are still encamped there, and the farmers of the surrounding country fearing similar devastation, and feeling their helplessness, are paying the revenue. Moreover definite intelligence has been received to-day that near 50

---

[1] *Pr. Tr. B. S.* p. 63, Military Papers, No. 37.

[2] *Idem.* p. 64, Military Papers, No. 38.

Europeans and Jats with 2 or 3 guns have assembled at Begamabad with the intention of destroying the bridge over the Hindan and of desolating Ghaziabad; and have cut off the supplies which used to be taken to Dehli and Pilkhowa etc. It is therefore prayed that, with kind consideration, Your Majesty will send some Royal (*Badshahi*) troops accompanied by guns in this direction for the punishment of the infidels so that full chastisement may be inflicted on them and the collection of the revenue of the State may be commenced. If, however, delay shall occur the bridge over the Hindan will be broken and the enemy will desolate Ghaziabad. Furthermore there is a very strong fortress of masonry at the village of Mukimpur near Pilkhowa in which there are about 50 or 60 maunds of old gunpowder. Should the Europeans get into this fortress, their expulsion afterwards will be very difficult and a second artillery centre (*dam dama*) will come into existence, and I shall then be utterly unable to counteract their operations. If my Regiment of Infantry accompanied by guns could be thrown into the said fortress, by to-morrow the English might be well punished and would certainly be routed with deserved chastisement. But Your Majesty being master, it is your prerogative to decide. Such orders as may be issued will be carried out. (Prayers for the continuance of the King's power.) Petition of the slave, attested with the seal of Ahmad Khan, stationed at Ghaziabad.

Autograph order by the King, in pencil

Mirza Mughul will adopt measures agreeably to this petition.[1]

[1] *Pr. Tr. B. S.* p. 64, Military Papers, No. 38.

Appendix G

'A LYING INVENTION OF THE ENGLISH'

With the above headline Prince Khizr Sultan, son of Emperor Bahadur Shah II, sent the following order to the Bombay army on 11th August 1857:

To

The Officers, Subadars, Chiefs and Others of the Whole Military Force Coming From the Bombay Presidency.

Dated 11th August 1857.

'To the effect, that the statement which some person has made to you, of the defeat of the Royal Troops (*Badshahi Sipah*) at Dehli, is altogether a false and lying fabrication, contrived by the contemptible infidels, namely, the English. The true story is that nearly eighty or ninety thousand organized Military troops are now present here, nearly ten or fifteen thousand Regular and other Cavalry. These troops are constantly engaged, night and day, in attacks upon the infidels and have driven back their batteries from the ridge. In three or four days hence, please God, the whole ridge will be taken when everyone of the base unbelievers will be humbled and ruined, and will be sent to hell. You are therefore directed immediately on seeing this order to use every endeavour speedily to reach the Royal Presence, so that joining the army of the faithful, you may give proofs of your zeal and may establish your claims to renown. Consider this imperative.

Order
from Mirza Khizr Sultan to the Bombay Army
dated 11th August 1857.

giving assurance that the report of the defeat of the Royal Army (*Lashkar-i Badshahi*) is *A Lying Invention of the English* who will themselves be exterminated in three or four days'[1].

Was this a lie invented by political malignity? Or was it a white lie? Or was it a lie of a darker complexion which like a few others of its kind embodied in the following telegram and letter calls for research?

Telegram from M. Tucker, Benares to Lord Canning, Calcutta No. 246 dated 24th June, 1857.

'There was a telegram late last night from Agra saying that the walls of Dehli had been knocked down, that the mutineers were entirely dispirited and that the King of Dehli wished to throw himself on British protection. Major Erskine had written to the Resident at Indore to telegraph to Agra the Governor-General's message to securing the King and his papers, pending his orders'[2].

And the letter dated 4th July 1857 written by General Reed, Commander-in-Chief of the British besieging force at Dehli to Sir John Lawrence, Chief Commissioner of the Panjab, ran as follows:

'One of our Gumashtas who was in Dehli contrived to make his escape yesterday and brought a message from the King that if we would guarantee his life and pension he would open the gates for us; how far this is to be depended upon remains to be proved; but we have been so busy with their attack upon our rear that

[1] *Pr. Tr. B. S.* No. 29, p 60.
[2] Forrest, G. W.—S.L. D. S.P., vol. I p 307.

there has been no time to consider it; he has evidently been made a tool of and it might stop an immense deal of blood granting his pension for the remaining years of his life which cannot be many. The private statement of Futteh Muhammad Gumashta—4th July, 1857, has just been placed in my hands as follows: About a fortnight ago Boolakie Doss, a Buneeah and friend of mine hinted to me that the Hakeem Haissan Oollah Khan wished to come to terms with the British but I did not attend to him as I thought nothing would be done. However he came to me eight days ago, and told me the Hakeem was most anxious to see me. Two days after I went to the palace to wait on the Hakeem who took me into a private apartment at the top of a high building; no one was present but the Hakeem, his mooktear Boolakie Doss and myself. The Hakeem at once asked me if I fully understood what he had desired Boolakie Doss to tell me; I said that I did, but that I would not give him much hope of being able to do anything. Then he said that the King was most desirous of making terms with the British and that if a promise (a formal one) were given him that his pension of 1 lac of rupees a month and his former position should be secured to him he would have the jerdarojah opened for the admission of the British troops. The Jerdarojah is a private entrance into the palace under the Summund Boorj on the riverside. The King also offered to arrange to have any other of the city gates opened at any time the British might wish. A written agreement to assist the British in every way in obtaining possession of the city would be given with the Royal Seal attached. I promised to submit the offer as it was made and make known the answer.

The substance of this will be sent to you by telegraph to-day so that you will probably have replied to it before you receive this. Mr. Greathed has also been requested to make it known to the Lieutenant-Governor, N. W. Provinces. If we enter into terms with the King it will be necessary to obtain a material guarantee that his part of the conduct will be faithfully performed. I doubt his (King's) ability to have one of the city gates opened as they are all in the hands of the insurgents whatever may be his power in the palace'[1].

The above telegram and letter are considered as evidence of a plot on the part of Emperor Bahadur Shah to sabotage his own army. 'The mutineers did not know that the King had opened negotiations with the English as early as June'[2], says a modern historian. And it has been concluded that 'after scarcely a month had elapsed since the Mutiny and less than two weeks after the British forces were encamped on the Ridge before the walls of the city of Delhi . . . . at the very moment when the sepoys were fighting in his name and shedding their blood for defending the city, he (Bahadur Shah) began to intrigue secretly with the British General offering to admit the British troops into the city, secretly through a gate, if they agreed to continue his pension and *status quo*'[3].

But no walls of Dehli were knocked down till the 14th of September, nor was the Royal army entirely dispirited until then, nor did the Emperor throw himself on British protection until the close of the war. As for the plot it should be noted that Bahadur Shah played no part in it. Both the gomashtas received their information directly from Hakim Ahsanullah Khan who had wished to come to terms with the British. That he

[1] Majumdar, R. C.——S.M.R., p. 122.

[2] Sen, S. N.—*Eighteen Fifty-Seven*, p. 95

[3] *Vide* footnote 1 *supra*.

claimed to do so on the part of his Royal master is no evidence of the Emperor's personal initiative in the matter, particularly when read in the light of the radical differences[1] that existed between Hakim Ahsanullah Khan and Bahadur Shah. Furthermore the story of the above plot should be compared with its counterpart in the *Delhi News* which says, 'The news-writer in Delhi suggested to the King to throw open the gates and admit the English force, as by that course though he might lose his life his family which have great claims on the British would be saved. He consented but Hakim Ahsanullah Khan stepped in and did not allow the plan to be executed'[2]. According to the first story, it may be recalled, Hakim Ahsanullah Khan is extremely anxious to see the gumashta and proposes in the name of the King to open the gates for the admission of the British troops; the King is in the background. According to the second story the King is in the foreground while Hakim Ahsanullah Khan is in the background. And immediately as the King agrees to the plan of opening the gates, Hakim Ahsanullah Khan springs from the rear and does not allow the plan to be executed. How amusing!

In fact each story or each part of the two stories neutralizes the other, and both are rejectable. Says Rotton the contemporary British chaplain and observer, 'The closing day of August 1857 was as gloomy as any out of the 31 which constituted that month. Report confidently affirmed that the King was desirous of treating with the English. The terms which he offered were the continuance of his pension and *service for the sepoys*. And if there be the least grounds for believing

---

[1] *Vide*, pp. 52, 53 *supra*.

[2] *Delhi News*——July 28, 1857.

this report, what conscience Shah Bahadur Shah and his supreme council must have had. . . . It was reported that when the King and Council of Delhi received the answer of the British Camp that there could be no treating with the mutineers and rebels and that nothing but unconditional surrender would be listened to, they expressed themselves determined to offer the most vigorous resistance and fight to the very last. I simply give this as the talk of the camp, my means of information on such a subject being necessarily limited. But judging from the acts of the mutineers on the 1st of September, I thought this conclusion on the part of the enemy not only possible but more probable inasmuch as the fire from the hostile batteries directed against our own batteries was certainly nothing lessened but everyone considered it was rather increased'.[1]

Another contemporary evidence which appears in the name of Colvin may also be noted. It runs thus: 'There was a hollow pretence of negotiations entered into by the King of Delhi. It was noticed in the Lieutenant-Governor's letter to the Governor-General of July 30, 1857 in these words, "The overture to which Greathed alludes was one from the old King made no doubt in fraud." Nothing further has been heard of any overtures from the Palace until a letter of the 22nd from Greathed this morning. In it he says, Yesterday an emissary came in from the Chief Lady of the Palace offering her good offices'[2].

In another letter of August 29, 1857 Colvin says, 'Rumours have more than once reached this Government that overtures have been made by the King of Delhi.'[3]

[1] Rotton——N. S. D. pp. 214-215

[2] Muir——R. I. D. vol. I, pp. 78-145

[3] *Idem*

Now the records show that in the given period or from mid-June to 4th July 1857, Emperor Bahadur Shah was as busy as he had been since the outbreak of the Mutiny, establishing peace and discipline in the city and protecting it against the English and attending personally to sundry matters. On or about 18th June—the day he is supposed to have opened negotiations with the English 'to sabotage his own army'—he wrote to his son Mirza Mughul the commander-in-chief, directing him to issue parwanas to the officers of sappers and miners for digging trenches.[1] On 19th June he wrote to the Kotwal directing him to report on the riot committed by the Telingas.[2] On 20th June he directed him to appoint guards to look after the bullock carts carrying saltpetre for gunpowder.[3] On 21st June, he ordered Mirza Mughul to secure tents from the volunteer and other regiments and hand them over to the Mukdoom regiment.[4] On 23rd June he desired the commander-in-chief to see that no one might seize the provisions sent to the trenches.[5] On 26th June he sent instructions to the commander-in-chief to direct the officers of the cavalry to vacate a garden they had been occupying.[6] The same day he also learnt that certain deserters had come from Lakhnao and joined his Army.[7] On 27th June he despatched 20 sepoys and 10 sowars to Badarpur to act as guards and directed the Thanadar there to send them back if and when not required.[8] And the same day he wrote to the

[1] Mutiny Papers, Box 152, No. 8

[2] *Idem*, BoR 63, No. 6.

[3] *Idem*, Box 152, No. 10

[4] *Idem*, No. 11

[5] *Idem*, No. 12

[6] *Idem*, Box 69, No. 29

[7] *Idem*, Box 70, Nos. 135-136

[8] *Idem*, No. 13

commander-in-chief directing him to supply boats to ferry the expected Bareilly troops across the Jumna as the bridge had been damaged by the floods[1]. On 1st July when he heard from Mirza Mughul that the boats were ready for ferrying the Bareilly troops he wrote, directing him to station the troops outside the Ajmeri Gate and at the Turkoman Gate. The Royal autograph to this effect still exists.[2] On 2nd July he directed the Army officers to vacate the shops of one Badru'ddin the seal-engraver; and on the 3rd he attended to a similar affair petitioned by Khwaja Khairiyat Ali, a clerk in the office of General Bakht Khan. On 4th July one Saiyed Muhammad applied to him soliciting protection of his house against the violence of the sepoys, attached to the Jullunder Regiment.[3] Then a complaint was made to him against Prince Mirza Abu Bakr.[4] The Emperor looked into both the matters immediately ordering the commander-in-chief to make inquiries. The same day the sons of Ahmad Singh,[5] Hasan Ali Khan and Hamid Ali Khan who had attended the Royal durbar on the previous day waited on the Emperor in connection with the news announced at the durbar that the troops at Kalpi and Udeypur had mutinied and murdered their English

[1] *Idem*, No. 14.

[2] *Idem*, Box 199, Nos. 16, 105.

[3] Mutiny Papers. Box 199, Nos. 112 and 114.

[4] *Idem*, Nos. 116, 119.

[5] Presumably a Hindu amir who rubbed shoulders with Hasan Ali Khan, chief of Jhajjar and Hamid Ali Khan, a wazir of Bahadur Shah. Ahmad Singh's name reminds the writer of the mixed Hindu-Muslim names like Ram Ghulam, Mata Din, Dilasa Ram in mid-19th century and Malik Kachhan, Malik Chhajju, Kamal Bhatti, Rukn Chand and many others of the 13th and 14th centuries.

officers and were proceeding to Dehli.[1] About the same time a firman having been issued by the Emperor, General Bakht Khan read it out to 20,000 of the inhabitants of Dehli, assembled for the purpose at Chandni Chowk.[2] The Royal army then received fresh reinforcements from Rampur and Nagina and took up their quarters at the Fatehpuri mosque.[3]

These are but a specimen of the numerous activities of the Emperor's according to the records. According to Jiwan Lal reinforcements having come to the Royal Army in the given period from Bhopal and Banaras, the Emperor sent a division of 2 regiments of infantry and 200 cavalry with two guns to engage the troops of the Maharaja of Jind. And when it was reported that the troops who had marched from Dehli to fight the English were returning because of the inclemency of weather he was displeased, and indignantly ordered that the 'troops who had failed to drive away the English should leave the city and go elsewhere'. Then a victory of the Royal arms was announced, the Jind troops being repulsed. It was also announced that the commander-in chief of the English had been killed in a fight near the Kashmiri Gate and that a rift had appeared in the British ranks, the English and the Gurkhas being at loggerheads. Then fresh reinforcements from Gwalior (*Gawaliar*) reached the Royal camp and the Royal Army succeeded in getting the upper hand in a fight at Baghpat. Subsequently it was reported that all the inhabitants of Dehli waited on the Emperor to pay their respects, that the English had failed in their attempt to blow up one of the bastions of the city and that the dues of the Royal Army had been paid from the Royal treasury. And

[1], [2], [3] Metcalfe—T.N.N., pp. 128—138.

when the Army officers complained of the inconvenience they were subjected to in camping during rains outside the city, the Emperor permitted them to reside in the city till the rainy season should pass. This done, badges engraved with the Emperor's name were issued to the Guards of the Thanas in the city. On 29th June, according to the same news-writer, the Royal Durbar was thickly attended by the amirs and military officers, and news was announced of the arrival of fresh reinforcements from Nimuch, Banaras and Kanpur as well as of some treasure from Nimuch. The same day some Bareilly officers presented themselves to the Emperor and reported that their troops would arrive in Dehli in the course of three days. On 30th June a fight took place at Sabzi Mandi with the British troops who were defeated. Then many officers of the Royal Army attended the Royal durbar and 'expressed their loyalty and determination to fight the English to the best of their ability', dwelling at some length on the prowess of the sepoys. About the same time 500 of the *mujahideen* returned triumphantly from the battlefield and presented to the Emperor an elephant which they had seized from the British camp. Then a mine dug by a British spy near the Kashmiri Gate was discovered. The spy digger was caught and hung before the Kotwali on a tree, and a Royal proclamation was read out publicly that all those who were friendly to the English would be treated in the same manner. On 1st July two messengers arrived from Bijah Bai with a *nazr* of one lakh of rupees for the Emperor. They had been also conveying for him a letter and some important papers which were seized by the Gujar plunderers on the way. Then news reached the Palace of the arrival of the Bareilly troops on the banks of the Jumna. The Emperor saw them across the river through a telescope and was impressed by their imposing cavalry and elephantry[1]. Their arrival inspired him with fresh hopes of victory and created an atmosphere which should have militated against the alleged opening of negotiations with the British. A glance at the telegrams which the British officers had been exchanging during the same period in feverish haste will convince the reader that the British were then in the direst straits,[2] and were making frantic efforts[3] to enter the city by acquiring control of any gate or wicket of the Fort; and Sir John Lawrence is reported to have suggested a plan to build or utilise an underground passage

---

[1] Metcalfe—T.N.N. pp. 128—138.

[2], [3] Telegram of 6th June 1857 reports that the British were making frantic efforts for entering the city of Delhi. (*Vide* P-L. p. 65).

Tel. No. 73 of 8th July 1857 communicates the requisition made by Brig. Chamberlain Delhi, for any trustworthy cavalry for Delhi, saying, 'If Gulab Singh's troops are to be trusted they may be sent but they should be sent quickly to Delhi.'

Tel. No. 342 of 8th July 1857 shows that Sir John Lawrence asked for immediate reinforcements for Delhi and wired to the Commissioner of Peshawar to send more Multani and Peshawar cavalry for Delhi. (P-L. p. 147).

Telegram of 9th July 1857 says 'Funds needed for Army before Delhi.'

Tel. (Ser. No. 339) dated 18th July 1857 from Brig. Wilson, commanding Delhi, Field Force to Sir John Lawrence, Chief Commissioner, Punjab:

'Brigadier-General A. Wilson who has succeeded Maj.-Gen. Reed in the command of Delhi reports to the Chief Commissioner the state of affairs at Delhi, represents the necessity for more troops without which no attempt can be made to assault the city of Delhi. Adds that unless speedily reinforced the force under his command will be so rèduced by casualties and sickness that nothing will be left but a retreat to Karnal. The disaster attending such an unfortunate proceeding Gen. Wilson cannot calculate'. (*Vide* P.L. p. 167).

through a house opposite the Church.[1] It follows that the alleged overtures were not made by Bahadur Shah; on the contrary these were the overtures made by the British officers and spies. The spies were compelled by the nature of their trade to tell lies and to colour their statements. Each spy or team of spies was assigned a particular duty ranging from the task of inducing any of the influential members in the Royal Palace to agree to open one of the gates to finishing the Emperor. They acted accordingly. And the British officials fully exploited the situation that resulted or was created for instance by a telegram which announced that great mischief to the British cause was being done by the Indian Press and stressed the need for controlling it[2]. The British officers who found the Indian Press beyond their control took instead to making hostile propaganda against the idol of the Indian Press, namely Bahadur Shah; and the British spies invented the much-needed canard which, on being incorporated in the official letters and telegrams became indistinguishable and has been considered as sound material of history. But in the eyes of Bahadur Shah these lying inventions were like many of his pseudo-friends 'a pitcher of poison with a mouth coated with sweets' (বিষকুম্ভং পয়োমুখং)[3]

[1] P-L. p. 65.

[2] Tel. P-L. o.38. Tel. (Ser. No. 300) of 26th May 1857.

[3] *Cf.* a communication of 21st September 1857 saying, 'The King is in the Jami' Masjid determined to die with his fanatics. Other reports say he is in the Palace which is likeliest . . . . . At Hathras the native report is that before the Palace was evacuated the King poisoned himself . . . . likely enough'. (Muir—R.I.D. Vol. I, pp. 78, 102, 111, 145).

APPENDIX H

MAULVI FAZL HAQ AND THE MUQADDAMATU-S SAURATU-L HINDIYA

At the Raza Library, Rampur I lighted upon an anonymous Arabic manuscript[1] which, on reading the contents, I was able to identify. It was a copy from a manuscript prepared on the basis of an autograph of Maulvi Fazl Haq. As he himself says he wrote it in a state of mental anguish and under tortures of rigorous imprisonment[2] in the Andaman Islands. A little before his death which took place in 1861 he managed to send it to his son Abdul Haq Khairabadi[3] who arranged the scattered pieces of the autograph[4] and produced a fair copy from which several other copies were made by the scribes. One of these went to Rampur, another to Habibganj, another to Aligarh and another to Mecca. But everywhere the contents were kept strictly private until 1947 when Maulvi Abdush Shahid Khan Sherwani of Aligarh published the text of the Aligarh copy together with an Urdu translation; and finding that the author had given no name to it he named it *Baghi Hindustan*[5] (Rebel India) which was improved

---

[1] MS. 129 Raza Library, Rampur. For the colophon see the photo on the adjoining page.

[2] *Vide* pp. 373, 381, 390 *infra*.

[3] *I.e.* a resident of Khairabad in the Sitapur district of Uttar Pradesh.

[4] It is said that Maulvi Fazl Haq wrote it on rags and irregular scraps. *Vide Baghi Hindusthan,* Preface.

[5] Abdush Shahid Khan Sherwani—*Baghi Hindustan.* Madina Press, Bijnor (1947).

upon by Maulana Abul Kalam Azad. He had received the Meccan copy and named it *Sauratu-l Hindiya* (Indian Revolution). Since it does not give the complete story of the Indian Revolution and is but a kind of introduction, a suitable name in my opinion would be *Muqaddamatu-s Sauratu-l Hindiya* (Preamble to the Indian Revolution) for it was intended by the author for the sake of his friends and relations in India who were busy preparing a protest[1] against the unfavourable verdict of the British Court, 'exiling Maulvi Fazl Haq as a life prisoner to the Andaman Islands'[2]. Consequently those of his associations and deeds which were likely to prove him a criminal in the eyes of the British were either suppressed or presented in a lurid light. For example, Bahadur Shah with whom he had previously identified himself[3]—attending his court, presenting

[1] It should be noted that on being sentenced to transportation for life Maulvi Fazl Haq contested the prosecution charges against him. In a memorial written in Urdu, duly sealed and signed by him, and addressed to the Lt.-Governor of North-Western Provinces he denied the Government's charge that he was one of the leaders of the revolt. He submitted that he was Fazl Haq of Khairabad and that the Commission had made a mistake in punishing him in place of the rebel Fazl Haq who was a resident of Shahjahanpur. But the Government could not be convinced of his innocence and his conviction was upheld. He again addressed an appeal on 9th February 1860 to the Secretary of State for India, but this also met the same fate as that of his first endeavour. Then the prominent Muslim citizens of Calcutta made efforts to get his release by submitting a memorial to the Governor-General, but the Government refused to rescind the order. *Vide* For. Pol. Sept. 1860; Sec. Cons. Nos. 556-558.

[2] *Vide* Memorial of Calcutta Muslims to the Governor-General. N. A. For. Pol. Sept. 1860. Cons. Nos. 556-558.

[3] *Vide* (i) Metcalfe—T.N.N. pp. 196, 217, 223, 224.
(ii) *Delhi News*, September 1, 1857.

nazr, giving advice and promoting the war—was now disowned and even disparaged[1]; some misleading information was also given about him.[2]

[1] Fazl Haq's opinion regarding Bahadur Shah's ignorance about the affairs of the world (*vide* p. 384 *infra*) cannot be taken literally. There are many documents in the National Archives which show that Bahadur Shah was alert and well-informed. He was fully conscious of his responsibilities and never shirked his duty and did not fear dangers and opposition that threatened him. As a result he was trusted by all classes of people; even the weakest person in the State looked up to him for the redress of wrongs. Sahu, a gardener, applied to him for the redress of his grievances stating that his brother Mamraj had been killed by the English and prayed for the maintenance of his children (Mutiny Paper, Box No. 259). Again Kidar Nath and Man Singh, grocers of Ghaziabad, applied to him seeking redress against the extortions practised on them by Khwaja Muhammad Ahsan, Governor (*Amil*) of Ghaziabad and Ahmad Khan, *Risaldar* at Ghaziabad. The Emperor immediately redressed the grievance making Khwaja Muhammad Ahsan and Ahmad Khan deposit in the Royal Treasury the sum that they had taken from the complainant and he also demanded an explanation of their conduct. (Mutiny Paper, Box 94, No. 4). See also Box 16, No. 20; Box 33, Nos. 9, 16, 17, 19, 20, 21, 22, 24, 25; Box 43, Nos. 31, 35. 36, 37; Box 57, Nos. 179. 186. 203. 211-212, 352, 426-427, 446. Box 58, No. 76. Box 59, Nos. 215, 318; Box 60, Nos. 8, 9, 566; Box 62, Nos. 137, 144; Box 63, Nos. 42, 57; Box 67, Nos. 3, 21, 91, 140; Box 68, No. 26; Box 69, Nos. 7, 8, 9, 11; Box 71, No. 110; Box 85, No. 2; Box 102, No. 36; Box 103, No. 259; Box 110, Nos. 214, 215, 221, 222, 223, 224, 225, 226, 227, 228, 229, 230, 231, 232, 233, 234-35, 241, 242, 243-45.

[2] According to Maulvi Fazl Haq (Rampur MS. 129, F. 16a, 18a; also see p. 386 *infra*) the Emperor had moved with all his family much before the close of the war to 'a tomb at a distance of 3 miles . . . . Along with him had gone his amirs and camp followers, each with his family and dependents . . . As soon as they had left the city . . . the English and their troops dashed into it'. This has remained unconfirmed. In fact all available evidence is to the contrary. It

It must be remembered that the Arabic manuscript namely the *Muqaddamatu-s Sauratu-l Hindiya* was a continuation of the defence campaign of Maulvi Fazl Haq who had not lost hope of his release and had

---

has been conclusively proved that on or about the 20th of September 1857 Bahadur Shah fled from the Fort to the shrine of Nizamu'ddin Auliya. This is also attested by Sir Richard Temple who saw Bahadur Shah after the fall of Dehli. The italicised part in the following note from his pen will help to clarify the point at issue. 'I visited him' says he 'in his place of confinement . . . . It was a strange sight to see the aged man seated in a darkened chamber of his palace. The finely chiselled features, arched eyebrow, aquiline profile, sickly pallor of the olive complexion, nervous twitching of the face, delicate fingers counting beads, muttering speech, incoherent language, irritable self-consciousness, demeanour indicating febrile excitability—altogether made up a curious picture, upon which no spectator could look unmoved who was acquainted with Asiatic history. Here sat the last of the Great Moguls, the descendant of emperors two centuries ago ruling the second largest population in the world, who had himself . . . been treated with regal honours. He was now to be tried for his life by judges whose forefathers had sued for favour and protection from his imperial ancestors. I looked at the lattice window where at the dawn of that fatal 11th May he stood to hear the vows of allegiance from the mutineer troopers as they stood in the dry fosse below; at the cabinet whence he issued edicts as if the Mogul empire had been restored; at the hall of audience where he reproached his new followers for their rudeness in the imperial presence; at the old tree in the palace precincts where the European prisoners were executed with his sanction; *at the shrine whither he fled for asylum when he found that the British had stormed the city gates*. His own signatures, annotations, and orders after the outbreak showed him to have possessed more capacity than would have been expected from a man who had been immured all his life as a titular king in his ancestral place'. (Temple, Sir Richard—*Men and Events of My Time in India*, pp. 135-136.)

intended thus to obtain it. To understand the said *Muqaddamatu-s Sauratu-l Hindiya* aright it would be necessary now to glance at the following proceedings of the British Court which had convicted Maulvi Fazl Haq.

Maulvi Fazl Haq was charged as follows:

Charge: Rebellion and instigation of murder.

1st Court: In having during the years 1857 and 1858 been a leader in the Rebellion and instigator to revolt and murder at Delhi, in Oude and in other places.

2nd Court: In having at Bondee, during the month of May 1858 taken a prominent part in the councils of the rebel chief, Mammoo Khan.

3rd Count: In having at Bondee, during the month of May 1858 been an instigator to murder in the instance of one Abdool Hakeem, a Government servant.

The Prisoner pleaded not guilty, and the Trial proceeded. The Court found the Prisoner guilty as follows:

1st: Having during the years 1857 and 1858 been an instigator of Rebellion and a propounder of Doctrines, calculated to encourage murder.

2nd: Having at Bondee in year 1858 taken a prominent part in the Councils of the Rebels assembled there and specially of the Rebel Chief Mummoo Khan, and having then propounded doctrines calculated to encourage murders.

And on March 4th 1859 sentenced him to detention as a State Prisoner in transportation beyond seas for the term of his natural life and to confiscation of the whole of his property.

Remarks

This man's case may be considered to have two phases. He was known to be a leading adviser of the rebel Chiefs in Oude in 1858, and after his seizure on account of his former connections in Delhi, reference was made to that place, and from the letter of the Commissioner of Delhi and the depositions forwarded by him, it appears that the prisoner had borne precisely the same character in Delhi in 1857. The case as regards his conduct in Delhi cannot be considered to be completely and regularly proved because the witnesses have not been before the Court, and the prisoner has not had an opportunity of meeting and rebutting their evidence. But if the case in Oude be made good, the evidence taken at Delhi may be accepted as strongly corroborative and confirmatory of the general conduct and character of the prisoner. He was therefore charged

1st: Generally as Instigator throughout the Rebellion

and

2nd: Particularly as an Instigator in Oude in 1858.

There seemed at one time to be very strong evidence to convict him of instigation amounting to direct attempt to murder. But the Court have hesitated to convict him of this crime, because the persons denounced were not actually murdered and it is not certain that the prisoner did not finally acquiesce in sparing them on certain conditions. But nevertheless the Court considers it proved that the Prisoner did on that occasion, very distinctly and officiously propound doctrines which had a direct tendency to encourage murder in many cases. He quoted and perverted texts from the Quran, insisted that the persons who had served the English were apostates and that their death was required by the law; and even went so far as to tell the rebel chief that if he spared them he was himself a criminal in the eye of God. The Court has given the prisoner the benefit of the doubt whether in the particular case these denunciations may not have been in some degree intended to compel, as the alternative of death, the abandonment of the English cause and adhesion to the rebels. But it is sufficiently clear that such doctrines are eminently calculated to lead to such bloody scenes as have characterized this Rebellion and, from the whole of the evidence, the Court consider it quite established that the prisoner was as a counsellor and adviser, an active Instigator of the Rebellion. He bore that character at Delhi, and he had certainly acted up to it in Oude. He at one time attempted to make something of the fact that there were two notable Fazl Haqs among the Oude Rebels, but that is now quite cleared up, since it appears that one was ex-Tahsildar of the Bareilly District and lately a Chuckladar and leader of rebel troops whereas the present prisoner is quite identified as the person who was not a man of the sword but a man of council and was the leading member of a sort of rebel privy council at Bondee. It seems doubtful whether the prisoner held any regular office, whether this Council was really of an Official character, but there seems to be no doubt of the fact, notorious at the time, that a few persons were the habitual advisers of the Begum and the rebel chiefs and were known in the Rebel Camp as the *Arbab-i Shoora* or masters of consultation, and sometimes by the English name of the *Cutchery Parliament* and that in this council the prisoner was prominent.

It also appears from direct evidence that he was high in the confidence of Mummoo Khan the rebel chief and much consulted by him, as on the occasion on which he propounded the murderous doctrines.

The prisoner is evidently a very clever man, but either from an unscrupulous ambition or extreme bigotry has assumed the place in the rebel councils above described. He is a most dangerous character—one who may at any time do infinite harm and one whose removal from the country, justice and security demand.

He is a resident of Oude but comes of a family which owed everything to the British service, and himself at one time occupied a good position in that service. He has, however, for many years past, abandoned the British service and served in honourable capacities several native States—Oude, Rampur and Alwar. He has always been a notable well-known man. Most of the witnesses who had not before seen him have all their lives frequently heard of Maulvi Fazl Haq. At the time of the outbreak, he was serving in Alwar. He subsequently voluntarily came into Delhi and thence forward continued to follow the fortunes of the Rebellion. He is a man who must be most severely punished and carefully excluded from India. But considering his advanced age, his position in life and his character as an Oude subject and for very many years past a servant of Native States, not of the British Government, we have thought it proper that he should be treated as a state Prisoner, not as an ordinary convict.

Sd. G. Campbell, Jud. Commr. of Oude.
Major Barron,
Offg. Commr. of the
Khairabad Div.

True Copy[1]
March 4, 1859.

The above proceedings should be read together with the petition of Maulvi Fazl Haq addressed to Lord Canning, a few extracts from which are given below:

(i) The humble petition of Maulvi Fazl Haq sentenced by the Special Commissioners of Lucknow to transportation for life and confiscation of property.

'That your petitioner having in violation of the terms of the Royal Proclamation of amnesty been condemned to suffer transportation for life and confiscation of property and having in vain appealed successively to all the authorities in India for justice, or at least on consideration of his advanced age for clemency, now throws himself at your feet for redress.

'Your petitioner refrains from submitting any other papers for perusal than a copy of the Judgment of the Special Commissioners of the last petition presented by him to the Government of India in which it is established by reference to the very terms of the Judgment that he has been tried, convicted and sentenced contrary to the intent of Her Majesty's amnesty and of an intercessary address presented by the principal

[1] For. Pol. Cons. 3rd June 1859. Nos. 387-89; pp. 43-47.

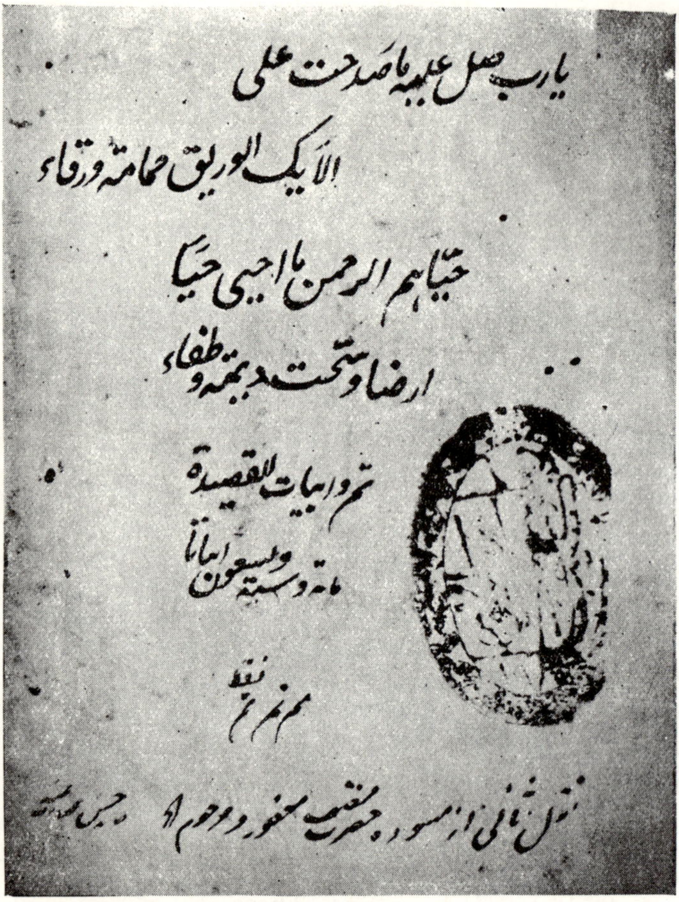

يارب صل عليه ما صدحت على

الأيك الوريق حمامة ورقاء

حياهم الرحمن ما احيى حيا

ارضا وسحت ديمة وطفاء

تم وابيات القصيدة

مائة وتسعون ابياتا

تم تم تم فقط

نقل ثاني از مسوده حضرت مصنف مغفور و مرحوم ... حميد حسن عفى عنه

THE *ecriture* ON THE LAST PAGE OF THE RAMPUR *MS.* OF THE *Muqaddamatu-s Sauratu-l Hindiya*

O God! pour blessings on him (Prophet) as long as the ring-dove sings at the tall tree covered with green leaves. May the Merciful God greet them (the Prophet and his Decendants) as long as there remains a single living creature on earth and as long as there is abundant rainfall to water the earth fully,

Finished; and the verses of this *qasida* are 190.

The end.

This is the second copy from the draft of the late revered Author

[Hamid Hasan (copyist) may Allah forgive him!]

Mahomedans of Calcutta to the Government of India for his liberation. He will merely for the better understanding of the facts of the case recapitulate his movements, the proceedings of the local officer and Government regarding him and the endeavours he made to obtain a removal of the sentence passed on him. . . . . .

'It is evident that your petitioner is not punished for crime but is to be removed from the country to prevent his doing harm at any time, though what harm a man of his advanced age can do is difficult to imagine. . . . . .

'Having thus proved the trial, conviction and sentence to be altogether illegal because in violation of Her Majesty's proclamation as well as contrary to evidence and the rules of law as is manifest from the terms of the Judgment itself, your petitioner submits whether your Lordship will lend the sanction of your honoured name to so flagrant a breach of faith, law, justice—and all for what? to crush an old man by sending him to die away from his family and deprive them of the trifling property. . . . .'

Now a few extracts from the *Muqaddamatu-s Sauratu-l Hindiya* as translated by the writer from the original Arabic may be read. These are given below together with the Arabic text as found in the Rampur manuscript which I have also compared with the Aligarh copy.

'I hereby write this while I am a prisoner, broken, debarred and wistful. I am suffering from all kinds of unbearable hardships and am looking forward even for a momentary relief which is easy for my Creator to award. I am in chains and have been made crazy, fallen as I am into the trap of troubles in spite of the fact that I had been brought up in ease and had been enjoying prosperity from the beginning. I am expecting release from my torture under God's mercy through earnest prayers. I am a prisoner in terrible fright and distress in the hands of a frowning tyrant who has stripped me of all that I had of comeliness, style and garments and has inflicted on me all kinds of atrocities and untold miseries which are like thick layers of mischief. I have been a prisoner in a desperate condition, have lost all hope of release and am terrorised by a jailer who is rude and stone-hearted. But I have not given up hopes of divine mercy. Gentle, simple and afflicted as I am—a victim of oppression—I have fallen in the clutches of a fierce, accursed Satan-like wicked man; I am in despair, utter want and misery on account of the tyranny of a cruel and brutal oppressor and torturer. I am hopelessly depressed and involved in unparalleled hardships which are beyond human imagination. And I have been treacherously thrown into the most rigorous imprisonment and bloody tortures. I am in the prison of a white-skinned man of black heart, blue eyes, stern looks, brown hair and an unprincipled and crafty mind. He has stripped me of garments and put on me roughest clothing of canvas. I am utterly dismayed and have been imploring God since I have been banished through rigorous and tight imprisonment from my country and people whom I am pining to see. I have been sentenced summarily without a defence and without any consideration. I am very sad and sorrowful since I have been deprived of all associates and of the benefit even of a single servant. My limbs are broken under the worst kind of rack. I am like a lonely exhausted lion, melancholy, gloomy and . . . .

. . . . He (jailer) has imprisoned me, treated me with cruelty and inflicted on me all sorts of tortures in order to break my morale on account of my adherence to and firmness in, faith and religion and because of my reputation as one of the notable ulama. All this the English did with the object of destroying the system of learning and burying the banner of knowledge and effacing it even from paper and books. That Revolution ruined homes and made the country and its inhabitants a target of bolts from the clouds of sorrows. . . . . .

. . . . The English of Great Britain filled their hearts with malice which they cherished secretly after they had established their rule over India. . . . They surrounded it from all sides and humiliated its eminent nobles extremely, leaving not a single man capable of presenting an opposition. They broke their pledges most treacherously and enforced their usual coercion and fraud. . . . . .

. . . . Verily the differences of religion and communities are like virulent diseases which mortify the body of kingdoms and bring about changes in the State, provinces and governments. Hence they tried their utmost and strained every nerve to remove these differences by means of their tricks and contrivances. . . . .

. . . . They appointed certain priests and clergymen to give wrong education and mislead and misguide the people. They even sent to every village and town a group of these ecclesiastics to create doubts by means of fabricated lies in the minds of the inhabitants regarding their own religion. . . . .

. . . Matters came to such a pitch that many of the rebel troops took refuge in the capital of Dehli which was a famous city thickly populated and the home of many Timurides. There they installed a man who had previously been their head and had a staff and a wazir. But he was an extremely old man who was in reality ruled by his wife and the wazir who was truly dominant, was an ally of the English and was deeply attached to them, viewing all others than the English and particularly their enemies with strong hatred. The same was true of his household and of a group of his close relations and kinsmen who did whatever they wanted while professing submission to him. He was a ruler who knew nothing and who did nothing but the undesirable. Neither he ordered anything by his own decision, nor did he order anything publicly or in private, nor was he capable of doing good or harm. He appointed some of his own sons and grandsons to command the troops although they were cowardly foolish and unfaithful and shunned the society of men of wisdom and probity. . . .

In these circumstances rose for action—for waging a holy war and fighting a bitter fight and to attain martyrdom—a body of brave Musalmans from some villages and towns on the strength of a *fatwa* and explicit orders issued by the pious and notable ulama and well-known jurists who proclaimed that jihad was incumbent. . . . .

Since there were in Dehli many of my relations and family members and inasmuch as I had been called there in the hope of bettering the situation—whatever Destiny had decreed being as yet a sealed book—I started in the direction of Dehli which had been my headquarters. There I put up and met my people. To the people in general I gave the best advice I could think of; but they did not accept my advice and did not act accordingly. When the English captured the city and neither the (Royal) army nor the inhabitants remained in it and when the edibles in it became scarce and we could not get water even—the enemies having controlled all supplies—I stayed there five days and nights. Then I came out together with my family and children leaving behind my books, my equipments as well as my property for want of conveyance. I pursued a road in expectation of safety relying on God, God alone being the saviour.

After capturing the city and its environments with the help of the white majority the English became anxious to seize the Emperor and his sons and grandsons who had continued residing in the place where Destiny had planted them, cherishing false hopes held out to them. In that tomb the Emperor was complacent and contented and had a following. There he was made a prisoner and put in chains together with his sons and grandsons and taken in this condition to the city. On the way one of the chieftains bulleted them. Their bodies were flung over there and their severed heads put in a tray were presented to the Emperor. Later even those heads were smashed and thrown away.........'

فان كتابى هذا كتاب اسير كسير خسير علے ما فات عنه
حسير مبتلے بكل عسير لايطاق ولو فى آن يسير منتظر
لفرج علے ربه يسير و مكبول مخبول واقع فى احبول علے
الدعة والسعة فى بدء فطرته مجبول - يرجو النفس من
كربة من نفس ربه بدعاء مقبول - و محبوس فى باس بيس
و بوس وكل إلى ظلوم عبوس - عراه عما كان له من رى
و زى و ملبوس و ابتلاه بشجون مشجون فى مضايق

شجون - هى مجامع فتن جون - منحيس منبس من الخلاص متائس نظرا الى تحكم منحيس منبس فظ غليظ القلب لاكنه من رحمة ربه ليس بيؤس و غرير سلس ضرير .... و جابر جائر بائر تعس من ظلم جابر جائر شكس شرس و بائس ائس منى لشدائد لاينتهى اليها قياس فائس و مغتر معتر فتن باشد احتباس و احمر باس فى اسر ابيض اسود الكبد ازرق عباس اصهب الشعر متلون. لباس - جرده عما كان له من لباس وكساه اخشن كساء و كرباس .... و عاجز جازع فازع الى ربه فازع نزيع من اسرته بالاسر بالاسر نازع اليهم نا زع قضى عليه بلا مدع و منازع و سادم نادم عادم لكل منادم و خادم فت فى اعضاده باشد مصادم و نجيد فريد طريد عنى فجلى من ارضه، و بلده و كئيب غريب كريب عنى فانى عن اهله و ولده -

ضامه ظلوم و جاره وانى ء عنه اهله و جاره وخلى عنه و عنهم و جاره فما رثى له احد ولا اجاره - اسره فقسره و كسره بكل ضرب من الايلام لتصلبه و بغضه فى الايمان والاسلام واشتهاره انه من العلام الاعلام و وما لدرس رسم الدرس و طمس علم العام حتى من قرطاس والطرس ذالك لواقعة فازعة تركت الديار بلاقع و جعلتها لصوائب المصائب مواقع امطرت على اهلها من غموم الغموم صواعق و صواقع.......من قصتها ان النصارى البراطنة الاولى شحنوا صدورهم بالشحناء الباطنة بعدما تسلطوا على ممالك الهند و اقطارها و قراها و امصارها واستولوا على حدودها و ثغورها واحاطوا باعجازها

و صدورها و ذللوا اعزة رؤسائها بالاستقصاء و لم يذروافيها من يبدی لهم قرنه بالكيد والزور - وانقضوا ماكان لهم من الايد والزور .... ان اختلاف - الثلل فی الاديان والملل من اقوی العلل فی بقاء التسلط وحدوث الحول فی الولايات والدول فجدوا كل جد ...... لرفع هذا الاختلاف بابتداع الحيل ...... و دنوها للتعليم والتلقين والتضاليل والتفتين انفارا من الرهبانين والقسيسين بل ارسلوا فی كل قرية و بلد طايفة منهم ليلقوا الناس بفرية فی ريب و مرية ..... فاوی من الجيوش المنحرفة الی دارالملك دهلی التی هی مصر مشهور وبلد معمور ومثوی لجمع كثير من ال تيمور فامروا بها من كان من قبل بينهم رئيساً له عملة و تامور وهو غمر قد رد الی ارذل العمر وهو فی الحقيقة لزوجته و تاموره مامور وكان عامله الذی كان فی المعنی عالياً للنصاری موالياً فی حبهم غاليا ولمن عداهم لاسيما لعداهم مبغضاً قاليا وكذا امر عشيرته و شرذمة من عشيرته الاقربين من سريرة و سريرته يفعلون مايشاؤن و يعملون بآرائهم و فی طاعته يراؤن وهو امر لايعلم امرا ولا يعمل الا امرا ولايامر برأيه امرا ولا يفقه خيرا ولا شرا ولايحكم بشی جهرا ولا سرا ولايملك نفعاً ولاضرا وقد امر ذالك الامر علی الجيوش بعض من له من الاحفاد والابناء وكانواهم من السفهاء الخوان الجبناء المتنفرين من العقلاء الاعداء -

و قد انتهض من بعض القری والبلاد جمع من المسلمين الجلاد للجدال و الجلاد والغزو و الجهاد طمعاً فی نيل الثواب والاستشهاد بعدالاستفتآ والاستشهاد من العلماء

الزهاد و افتائهم بوجوب الجهاد وبفتاوى ايمة الاجتهاد
...........واذكان فى دهلى كثيرمن عيالى و اهلى ومع
ذلك كنت مدعوا وكان الافلاح والافراج مرجوا والفرج
والفرح مظنوناً وما قدر فى الغيب مكتوباً مكنوناً توجهت
تلقاء دهلى مما كان محلى فالقيت بها رحلى ولاقيت
بها اهلى واشرت الى الناس بما اقتضى رأيى وقضى به
عقلى - فلم ياتمروا بما اشرت ولم ياتمروا بما امرت فلما
استولى النصارى على البلد ولم يبق فيه من الجيوش
ومن سكانه احد وعازت فيه الاقوات ولم يتيسرلنا الماء الفرات
اذ قد استبد به العداة مكثت فيه خمسة ايام وليال ثم
خرجت مع اهلى وعيالى بعد ترك مالى من كتبى
ونشبى ومالى لعوز مايكفى لنقل احمالى و اخذت للنجاء
سبيلا متوكلا على الله وكفى بالله وكيلا -

والنصارى بعد استيلائهم على البلد وسواده بسواد
بيضانهم عمدوا الى اخذ الملك و اولاده و احفاده و هم لم
يبرحوا مستقرهم والقضاء مكنهم فى ذلك المكان واقرهم
وهم مستوثقون بمن غرهم باكاذيبه وسرهم و كان فى
تلك المقبرة مغروراً مسرورا محشوراً محفورا فاضحى
ماسورا محسودا مكمودا مصفودا و اخذوا من معه من
الابناء والاحفاد مقترنين فى الاصفاد و ذهبوا به الى البلد
مع من معه من الاهل والولد فاغتال احد من عظمائهم
هو طرخان او بطريق ابنائه واحفاده بالبندق فى اثناء الطريق
واهدوا رؤسهم مقطوعة الى رئيسهم فى خوان موضوعة
و تركوا جثثهم منبوذة ثم نبذوا تلك الرؤس مجذوذة -

From a glance at the above sources of information the reader may now pass to a perusal of the following conclusions reached by the writer.

Maulvi Fazl Haq (1797/1212-1861/1278) son of Maulana Fazl Imam Khairabadi, chief judge (*Sadru-s Sudur*) of Akbar Shah's time, was really a gifted *allama* and doctor of law and literature; he was also a thinker and a philosopher who believed strongly in the need for a firm Hindu-Muslim alliance in order to drive away the English from India. At the age of 28 (1825/1241) he was appointed Cutchery Chief (*Sarrishtadar*) at the Dehli Residency which post, however, he resigned after a few years for he did not like British service. Then with a view to rouse the princes and people of India against British rule he took to travelling and visited Jhajjar, Sharanpur, Tonk, Rampur and Oudh. In 1848 he accepted service at Lakhnao and held the office of *Sadru-s Sudur* until 1856 when on seeing the tragic scenes which had followed the British annexation of Oudh he resumed his journeys, doing the necessary propaganda work to uproot the British Government. In this connection he also came to Alwar where he stopped until the outbreak of May 1857. Then he came back to Dehli[1] and did his utmost to

[1] The date of Maulvi Fazl Haq's arrival in Dehli cannot be fixed with certainty for the Maulvi Sahib himself had shrouded it in mystery. He pleaded alibi and said that throughout the 4-month-long war he had remained at Alwar. The British spies would have us believe that he had arrived in Dehli on 16th August 1857 and continued attending the Royal durbars till 7th September and that he was also a member of the Administrative Court (*vide* Metcalfe—T.N.N., pp. 196-224 and the *Delhi News*, September 1, 1857). But from the trend of language used by Zakaullah (p. 687) as well as by the Judge (For. Pol, June 3, 1859; pp. 43-47), it would appear that Maulvi Fazl Haq had arrived in Dehli shortly after the outbreak of the Mutiny.

promote the war. He also drew up the constitution (*Dastur-ul amal-i Saltanat*) for the government of Dehli —a fact mentioned vaguely by Zakaullah as if the said constitution was never completed and did not see the light of day. But its first item, namely the 'ban on cow-slaughter' was certainly carried out. According to the spies' reports Maulvi Fazl Haq worked ceaselessly to rouse the sepoys and Mughul princes to fight the English and turn them out of the country. After the fall of Dehli he fled to Khairabad whence he was brought as a culprit under a warrant of arrest to Lakhnao. There he was tried. And the judge referred to him 'as a learned man exercising great influence over the masses and highly placed in life'; he also charged him with having instigated the Rebellion and to have kept it alive. Then he was sentenced to transportation for life and banished to the Andaman Islands. Through a fellow-prisoner Mufti Inayat Ahmad by name who was released in 1860, he managed to send his manuscript to India, and the same was published in the year of India's partition with a foreword from the pen of Muhiu'ddin Ahmad surnamed Maulana Abul Kalam Azad who observed, 'The late Abdul Haq Khairabadi copied this treatise personally and sent the copy thus made to my father at Mecca; that manuscript is still preserved in my library'[1].

Like the defence of Bahadur Shah already

[1] It was in response to my request for this manuscript and the like that the Director of Archives sent me on 21st March 1958 two enlargements relating to the erection of a mausoleum at the tomb site of Bahadur Shah at Rangoon. I take it that the aforesaid manuscript from the personal Library of the Maulana has not reached the Archives. I take this opportunity to thank the Director for the said enlargements.

noticed,[1] the defence of Maulvi Fazl Haq was also intended to defeat the prosecution. He pleaded alibi, asserting that throughout the period of war (May to September 1857) he had stayed at Alwar and that he did not come to Dehli until the close of the war. But the judges were not convinced and persisted in having the sentence passed on him executed. In fact the line of defence adopted by the Maulvi Sahib was intended to whitewash his conduct in the eyes of the British,[2]

[1] *Vide* p. 156 *supra*.

[2] Writing in Urdu under the heading of 'Maulvi Fazl Haq and the *Fatwa-i jihad* of 1857' (*vide Tahreek* of *Dehli* August 1957, pp. 10-15) Maulana Arshi of Rampur says that Maulvi Fazl Haq had nothing to do with the *Fatwa-i Jihad* published in the *Sadiqul Akhbar* of 27th July 1857 (Mutiny Papers, Box 4-6; vol 4, July 27, 1857). It is true that the said *Fatwa* does not bear Maulvi Fazl Haq's signature, but it is not true that 'he had not been the leader of the Rebellion'. In fact he was a leading philosopher of the Indian Revolution of 1857; and through his philosophy he gave the movement life and strength. He also prepared the way for the outbreak of the Revolution by resigning British service in good time and travelling to different places, presumably with the object of rousing the people and princes against British rule. (*Vide* For. Pol. Cons May 13, 1859, 306-308; For. Pol. Cons. May 13, 1859. 659-660; For. Pol. Cons. June 3, 1859, 387-394; For. Pol Jan 13, 1860, No. 4; Pol. Procdgs. Sept. 1860, 556-558. Part A; Home Judicial, Cons. June 10, 1859 No. 1). If Jiwan Lal be credited Maulvi Fazl Haq also held command of troops in the Royal Army and was desired once in the course of war to use them in order to collect revenue (Metcalfe——T.N.N., 198).

Fazl Haq appears as Fazlul Haq in the *Trial of Ex-King* of *Delhi* (p. 182) and similarly also in a Persian letter of his (Mutiny Papers, Box 100, No. 96 of July 26) addressed to Mirza Mughul, the Commander-in-Chief, asking the latter to communicate to him (Fazlul Haq) all that passed between him and General Bakht Khan during their interview. Maulvi Fazlul Haq also directed the Royal Secretariat to write letters to (i) Hasan Bakhsh Uzbegi—an officer whose duty it was to

and the same was true of his remarks about Bahadur Shah.

---

realize the revenue of the Aligarh district, (ii) Faiz Ahmad who was appointed to realize the revenue of Bulandshahr district and (iii) Walidad Khan who was charged to aid the above two men in realizing the revenue. (*Vide Tr. of the ex-King of Delhi,* p. 183). In a word Maulvi Fazl Haq is identical with Fazl Haq who is subsequently mentioned as having directed the Royal Secretariat to write a letter to his own son Abdul Haq charging him to make arrangements for realizing the revenue of Gurgaon district. And it must also be noted that Maulvi Fazl Haq (Fazlul Haq) is mentioned uniformly as a 'rebel'. (*Idem,* pp. 183, 184).

Appendix I

SOME UTTERANCES OF EMPEROR[1] BAHADUR SHAH II DURING THE WAR OF 1857 IN DEHLI

Viewed in the light of the Arabic saying الفضل ماشهدت به الا عدا[2] the following utterances of Bahadur Shah II throw considerable light on his character and his role in the war. They also tend to unmask the myth behind the disparaging words used for him by Maulvi Fazl Haq, and reproduced in the preceding appendix[3].

May 20, 1857. *'The Holy War (jihad) is against the English. I have forbidden it against the Hindus'. (Bahadur Shah)*

Explanation: One Maulvi Muhammad Saiyeed reported to the Emperor that 'the standard of holy war had been erected for the purpose of inflaming the minds of the Musalmans against the Hindus. The Emperor answered that such a jihad was quite impossible and such an idea an act of extreme folly for the majority of the Purbiya soldiers were Hindus. Moreover such an act would create internecine war, and as a result would be deplorable. It was fitting that sympathy should exist among all classes. It was

---

[1] Culled from Jiwan Lal's collection of the spies' reports (Metcalfe——T.N.N. pp. 98-219) the Royal utterances are reproduced here verbatim with this much of difference that the term 'king' has been replaced by the usual title 'Emperor'.

[2] *I.e.* Excellence is that which is attested by the enemies.

[3] *Vide* p. 384 *supra*

pointed out that the Hindus were leaning towards an alliance with the English and had no sympathy with the Muslims and were already holding themselves apart. A deputation of Hindu officers arrived to complain of the war against the Hindus being preached. The Emperor replied saying:

THE HOLY WAR IS AGAINST THE ENGLISH; I HAVE FORBIDDEN IT AGAINST THE HINDUS[1]

July 2, 1857. *'It is no use my giving orders as they are never obeyed and I have no one to enforce them but my decree is that the English should be caused not to exist'.* (*Bahadur Shah*)

Explanation: Nawab Ahmad Quli Khan went out to receive the Bareilly force. Hakim Ahsanullah Khan, General Samad Khan, Ibrahim Ali Khan, Ghulam Ali Khan and others were present. Muhammad Quli Khan with Muhammad Bakht Khan, commander of the Bareilly force, solicited orders for the employment of the same. The Emperor's orders were that the inhabitants of the city must not be plundered. Then he said, 'It is no use my giving orders as they are never obeyed and I have no one to enforce them but my decree is that the ENGLISH BE CAUSED NOT TO EXIST.[2]

July 19, 1857. *'If I be altogether victorious . . . I shall visit the tomb of Salim Chishti'.* (*Bahadur Shah*)

Explanation: General Muhammad Bakht Khan reported to the Emperor that the English sergeant and

[1] Metcalfe——T.N.N. p. 98.

[2] Metcalfe——T.N.N. pp. 133-134.

two English soldiers who had been brought to Dehli had been executed on the river-bed of the Jumna. The Emperor as if under divine inspiration suddenly said, 'If I be altogether victorious . . . I shall go to Agra and make a pilgrimage to Ajmer and visit the tomb of Salim Chishti if the Most High be willing and will fulfil all my desires'.[1]

July 21, 1857. *'I have no money to give you'. (Bahadur Shah)*

Explanation: Six hundred jihadis (*mujahideen*) from Tonk arrived and reported that two thousand more men were on their way to join the Royal camp. The Emperor replied, 'I have no money to give you'.[2]

July 30, 1857. *'I ask you for money as a loan; I do not want to take it as a tax'.* (*Bahadur Shah*)

Explanation: At four o'clock in the afternoon Ranji Mal and Puttia Mal merchants waited on the Emperor at the durbar; and after making their obeisance Ranji Mal placed his turban at the Emperor's feet and pleaded that he had not a penny in the world left. His banking firm was at Lakhnao and his house had been plundered; he had nothing to give the Emperor. His Majesty replied, 'I ask you for money as a loan: I do not want to take it as a tax. See, my friend Jyoti Prasad has advanced 30,000 rupees to the English; on what grounds do you demur to lend me money?'[3]

---

[1] Metcalfe——T.N.N. p. 155.

[2] *Idem*, p. 160.

[3] *Idem*, p. 174.

July 31, 1857. *'Bravo! well done!'* (*Bahadur Shah*)

Explanation: A number of the officers of the Nimuch force appeared at the durbar and reported that they had marched to Alipur at two o'clock in the night and reached Bisari Bridge about eleven o'clock (in the day) where they came under artillery fire. They quickly destroyed the entrenchment thrown up by the English; they then mended the bridge, and returned and had an engagement with the plunderers (English) in which about two hundred men on both sides had fallen. The Emperor cried, 'BRAVO! WELL DONE!' and gave the officers great praise'.[1]

August 3, 1857. *'The Royal treasury is empty'.* (*Bahadur Shah*)

Explanation: A petition was received from the troops at Gwalior to the effect that 2,000 men were ready to march to Dehli if the Emperor would give the order. The Emperor said in reply, 'The Royal Treasury is empty'.[2]

August 2, 1857. *'You will never capture the Ridge'.* (*Bahadur Shah*)

Explanation: General Bakht Khan attended (the durbar) and reported that in consequence of the heavy rains the troops that had gone in the direction of Basi had found the whole country flooded and had returned. The Emperor, on hearing this, became very angry and said, 'You will never capture the Ridge'.[3]

---

[1] Metcalfe——p. 175.

[2] *Idem,* pp. 178-179.

[3] *Idem,* p. 177.

August 2, 1857. *'My desire is that you all leave the city and go to some other central point'.* (*Bahadur Shah*).

Explanation: The same day the Emperor summoned his officers to the Diwan-i Amm in the evening and addressed them saying, 'All the treasure that you brought me you have expended; the Royal treasury is empty and without a pice. I hear that day by day the soldiers are leaving for their homes. My desire is that you all leave the city and go to some other central point. If you do not, I'll take such steps as seem to me most advisable'.

In answer to this address, the officers tried to cheer His Majesty and exclaimed, 'By the help of God we will take the Ridge yet'.[1]

August 2, 1857. *'May all the enemies of the Faith be killed to-day! May the Firangis be destroyed root and branch!'* (*Bahadur Shah*)

Explanation: The Diwan-i Amm was filled this day with the brightness of the Emperor's presence. Mirza Aminu'ddin Saadat Ali Khan Vakil, Fazl Hasan Khan and Maulvi Sadru'ddin Khan . . . . were present. The value of the *nazrs* presented to-day was 126 rupees and 9 gold mohurs. The conversation turned for a long time on fighting. Then the Emperor recited some verses—Celebrate the festival of the 'Id-i Qurban by great slaughter. Put our enemies to the edge of the sword—spare not'.[2]

August 4, 1857. *'We have here 60,000 men in the city but they have not been able to win a clod of dirt from the English'.* (*Bahadur Shah*)

[1] Metcalfe——T.N.N., p. 178.

[2] *Idem*, p. 177.

Explanation: The Emperor ordered pay to be distributed to the soldiers. He further requested that every officer of any position in the Army should be summoned to appear before him. General Bakht Khan in accordance with this command came to the durbar and explained that the officers had gone out with an escort of 400 cavalry and the local zamindars to make themselves acquainted with the various positions they were to occupy and he added, 'Now I shall be victorious; if God wills. I shall prosper. My plan is to attack the English at Alipur'.

A message came to the Emperor from Gwalior that the whole army was willing to place itself under his command. 'Reply,' said the Emperor impatiently, 'as I said before; there is no money for their support. We have here 60,000 men in the city but they have not been able to win a clod of dirt from the English'.[1]

August 4, 1857. *'Go with haste and be victorious on the Ridge'.* (*Bahadur Shah*)[2]

Explanation: Whilst the Emperor was in the private apartments a deputation of officers came with the complaint that Hakim Ahsanullah Khan was in communication with the English and that it was he who had caused the proclamation to be made that 1,400 jihadis from Swat had reached the halting place and would arrive in the city that day. The officers stated that from inquiries they had ascertained that the men were Pathans enlisted by the English who, to make themselves masters of the city, were coming to fight the Purbias and kill them. The Emperor replied to the officers saying, 'I have no information of any such

[1] *Idem,* p. 181.

[2] *Ibid.*

proclamation and am certain that Hakim Ahsanullah is not concerned in any such treachery. On the contrary I know that the Akhund of Swat had deputed a trustworthy agent to act as his deputy and had placed his own sword in his hands with an order to destroy the English in the name of God and the Prophet'. . . . . . The Emperor sent for the officers and Mirza Mughul; and after flattering the former said, 'I am satisfied that the man who made the proclamation was an agent of the English . . . . ; it is intolerable that the inhabitants of the city should be harassed and threatened by the soldiers who came to the city with the avowed object of destroying the English and not their own countrymen. These soldiers are always boasting that they are going out of the safety afforded by the fortifications to destroy the English and yet are always returning to the city. It is quite clear to me that the English will ultimately recapture the city and will kill me.' The officers seemed impressed with the Emperor's words; they besought him to be brave of heart and invited him to put his hand on their heads, for without doubt they would be victorious. There were about 150 officers present, and as they passed before him he placed his hand on the head of each man. Then His Majesty uttered a prayer and said, 'GO WITH HASTE AND BE VICTORIOUS ON THE RIDGE'.

August 8, 1857. *'Every princely house has its vicissitudes and my turn is now coming'.*

(*Bahadur Shah*)

Explanation: The Emperor said this 'impressed by the fact that he had been treated with disrespect by the sepoys the preceding day'.

---

[1] Metcalfe——T.N.N. p. 190.

August 14, 1857. *'Unless the English are driven from the Ridge you will never be victorious'.*[1]

(*Bahadur Shah*)

Explanation: The Emperor entered the Diwan-i Amm. Hakim Ahsanullah and others attended. General Muhammad Ghaus made a private report to His Majesty who replied, 'Unless the English are driven from the Ridge, you will never be victorious'.

August 18, 1857. *'Look to your troops; go out yourselves to fight and lead them against the English'.*[1]

(*Bahadur Shah*)

Explanation: This was the Emperor's retort to Maulvi Fazl Haq who had advised him to leave the city and go away to save himself and his family from general massacre at the hands of the English.

The Emperor's words, if reported correctly, would show that Maulvi Fazl Haq also held command of some troops.

August 18, 1857. *'Do not demand money except from the soldiers in the city.'*[2]

(*Bahadur Shah*)

Explanation: 'Mirza Aminu'ddin Khan and others on whom a requisition for money had been made waited on Mirza Mughul, and represented to him that they had not got the money to pay up. They repeated their inability to pay, on which Mirza Mughul said to his Silver Stick[3] in waiting 'Arrest that man', pointing to

[1] *Idem,* p. 198.

[2] Metcalfe——T.N.N. p. 199.

[3] Metcalfe has not given the Persian term for "Silver Stick".

Aminu'ddin Khan, 'and put him under guard till he pays the money,' Aminu'ddin, roused by this impertinence, drew his sword, and challenged anyone to touch him. . . . Leaving Mirza Mughul's house, he went to the Palace, and told the King what had happened, and that he would be killed rather than have money extorted from him. The Emperor asked him to be seated, and told him he would be protected from these demands in future which pacified him. General Bakht Khan was present at the interview, and said the demand was unjust, for the pay of the Army should be demanded from the Army. The Emperor said to the General, 'Do not demand money except from the soldiers in the city'. Orders were sent to Mirza Khizr Sultan not to concern himself with money matters.

August 22, 1857. *'It is much to be regretted that in place of your silencing the English fire, I see their batteries getting nearer every day'.* [1]

(*Bahadur Shah*)

Explanation: After the morning durbar the Emperor visited the Fort of Salimgarh and ordered the battery to fire a few rounds. Then he said to the artillerymen what has been reported above. The gunners answered, 'No fear, Your Majesty! we are getting the better of them'.

August 22, 1857. *'If the sepoys would only leave the city and employ themselves in collecting the revenue, I should be in a position to pay them and to protect the lives and property of the citizens'.* [2]

(*Bahadur Shah*)

[1] Metcalfe—T.N.N., p. 203.

[2] *Ibid.*

Explanation: The son of Nawab Muhammad Mir Khan represented to the Emperor on the part of several bankers that twice had the sepoys extorted money from them and again were now demanding money from them. The Emperor replied as above.

August 24, 1857. *'Go, may God protect you! Show your loyalty by attacking the English; destroy them and return victorious'.*[1] (*Bahadur Shah*)

Explanation: The Emperor said this to General Bakht Khan when the latter announced that he was going to attack the English and came to take leave of His Majesty.

August 25, 1857. *'Take this and forget your hunger'.*[2] (*Bahadur Shah*)

Explanation: His Majesty went on the river in a boat manned by some men of the Sapper Regiment and watched the artillery fire directed on the English from the Fort. . . . . . . More demands were made for pay by a deputation of officers. The Emperor went into his private apartments and brought out jewellery and gave them to the officers, saying, 'Take this and forget your hunger'. But the officers refused, saying: 'We cannot accept of your Crown jewels but we are satisfied that you are willing to give your life and property to sustain us'.

August 29, 1857. *'No one has censured your conduct and I am quite satisfied to leave the chief command in your hands.*[3] (*Bahadur Shah*)

Explanation: 'A letter came from General Bakht

[1] *Idem,* p. 206.

[2] *Idem,* p. 205.

[3] *Idem,* p. 212.

Khan stating that many persons were giving the Emperor about the war advice which was of no value, yet His Majesty was displeased with his generalship. He proposed in future to concern himself only with the command of the Bareilly column.' The Emperor replied, 'No one has censured your conduct and I am quite satisfied to leave the chief command in your hands'.

August 31, 1857. *'No, refer this matter to the Military Court; they are responsible'.*[1] (*Bahadur Shah*)

Explanation: A spy reported that the English were preparing more batteries on the Ridge and would destroy the whole city and the troops encamped outside the city walls. The Emperor, on hearing this, ordered the Military Court to sit and consult what should be done. More complaints came (?) from the sepoys that they were starving as the shopkeepers had refused all supplies for want of payment. Mulahi Lal Mutasaddi[2] reported that no more sulphur could be purchased. He suggested that urgent letters should be sent to the Nawabs of Farrukhabad, Jhajjar and Bhoali to supply this; but His Majesty said, 'No, refer this matter to the Military Court; they are responsible'.

September 1, 1857. *'There is no necessity to plunder. I will sell my horses, elephants, silver and gold ornaments of state, and pay the Army. If you intend to plunder the city, kill me first. Afterwards you can do as you please'.*[3] (*Bahadur Shah*)

[1] Metcalfe——T.N.N. p. 214.

[2] The text (p. 214) has 'Muthridi' which appears to be a corrupt form of 'Mutasaddi', a Persian term for a government functionary, a clerk or an accountant.

[3] Metcalfe——T.N.N. p. 216.

Explanation: The officers again and again urged upon His Majesty to make some arrangements about the pay, threatening to plunder the city. The Emperor replied, 'There is no necessity to plunder. I'll sell my horses, elephants, silver and gold ornaments of state and pay the Army. If I do not do so, you can all leave and abandon the city, the more so, as I never summoned you. . . . . Kill me first . . . .

September 3, 1857. *'Again I write to you to send the money without delay, also a contingent of 500 foot-soldiers with two field-guns and five maunds of opium; otherwise I'll impose a fine on you of one lakh of rupees'.*[1] (*Bahadur Shah*)

Explanation: A petition came from the Raja of Bullubgarh, complaining that 'Hakim Abdul Khan is demanding five lakhs from me for the expenses of the war'. The Emperor replied as above. It should be noted that opium was needed for the use of the sepoys; many of them were addicted to it.

September 4, 1857. *'Sell them, and divide the proceeds among yourselves for pay'.*[2]

(*Bahadur Shah*)

Explanation: Certain officers of the Nasirabad camp had given His Majesty a great deal of annoyance the preceding night regarding their pay. The Emperor ordered all the silver goods to be made over to them, uttering the words already reported.

[1] Metcalfe—T.N.N. p. 218.

[2] *Idem* p. 219.

Appendix J

LIST OF THE MUGHUL PRINCES (*SALATEEN*) WHO WERE EXECUTED BY ORDER OF THE DEHLI SPECIAL COMMISSIONER FOR REBELLION[1]

1. Mirza Nadir Bakht son of Mirza Iqtidar Bakht
2. Mirza Moula Bakhsh son of Mirza Rahim Bakhsh
3. Mirza Kurreem Bakhsh son of Muhhoo Mirza
4. Mirza Abu Abbas Mirza son of Mirza Muzaffar
5. Mahmood Shikoh son of Mirza Abbas Shikoh
6. Mirza Husain Bakhsh son of Mirza Qadar Bakhsh
7. Mirza Ahmad Bakhsh son of Mirza Qadar Bakhsh
8. Mirza Abidoodin Abbas (Mirza Manjhley) son of Mirza Zahooru'ddin
9. Mirza Musheeru'ddin son of Mirza Qadar Bakhsh
10. Mirza Moinu'ddin son of Mirza Ala Bakhsh
11. Mirza Qadar Bakhsh son of Mirza Makhoo
12. Mirza Qutbu'ddin son of Mirza Qadar Bakhsh
13. Mirza Nooru'ddin son of Mirza Abboo
14. Mu'izzu'ddin son of Mirza Medhu
15. Mirza Inayat Husain son of Mirza Iqtidar Bakht
16. Mirza Muhammad Bakhsh son of Mirza Ezad Bakhsh
17. Ghulam Muhammadi son of Mirza Karim Bakhsh
18. Mirza Ghulam Bakhru'd din son of Mirza Agha Jan
19. Mirza Ghulam Abbas son of Mirza Agha Jan
20. Mirza Kabiru'd din son of Mirza Qutbu'ddin
21. Mirza Bahadur son of Mirza Baland
22. Mirza Wala Shikoh son of Mirza Balandey
23. Mirza Nannhey son of Mirza Karimu'ddin

[1] Pol. Cons., Nos. 113-119, 27th May, 1859.

24. Mirza Mubarak son of Mirza Munjhley
25. Mirza Bullenday son of Mirza Mukarram
26. Mirza Kaley son of Mirza Agha Jan

Sd. M. A. Davies,
Secretary to Govt. Punjab

Sd. C. B. Saunders,
Commissioner.

21 April 1859

Appendix K

LIST OF THE MUGHUL PRINCES WHO DIED SHORTLY AFTER THEIR ARREST OR SUBSEQUENTLY TO THE PRONOUNCEMENT OF SENTENCE OF IMPRISONMENT FOR LIFE.[1]

1. Mirza Kamran son of Mirza Babur
2. Mirza Babur Shikoh son of Mirza Husain Bakhsh
3. Mirza Ilahi Bakhsh son of Mirza Shuja'uddin
4. Mirza Bahadur son of Mirza Mamman
5. Mirza Husain Bakhsh son of Mirza Sungee
6. Mirza Karim Bakhsh son of Mirza Sungee
7. Mirza Ghulam Imamu'ddin son of Mirza Ali Bakhsh
8. Mirza Muhammad Usman son of Mirza Ghulam Fakhru'ddin
9. Mirza Husain Bakhsh son of Mirza Ali Bakhsh
10. Allah Bakhsh son of Mirza Khuda Bakhsh
11. Mirza Kadir Bakhsh son of Mirza Jan
12. Mirza Ghulam Na'eemu'ddin son of Mirza Nadir Bakht
13. Mirza Ahmad Jan son of Mirza Khurram Bakht
14. Mirza Inhan Sultan son of Mirza Mu'izzu'ddin
15. Miirza Riyazu'ddin (father's name unknown); he died during trial

[1] F.C. Nos. 113-119, 27th May, 1859.

Appendix L

LIST OF THE 13 MUGHUL PRINCES WHO WERE THROWN INTO RIGOROUS IMPRISONMENT AT AGRA IN SEPTEMBER 1857 BUT WERE SUBSEQUENTLY RELEASED AND DIRECTED TO BE KEPT UNDER SURVEILLANCE AT RANGOON ON A MONTHLY SUBSISTENCE ALLOWANCE OF RS. 10 PER HEAD.[1]

1. Mirza Khuda Bakhsh son of Mirza Hyder Shikoh.

   The prisoner was apprehended by Major Burn. There is no record of the circumstances under which the arrest was made, nor is there anything to show that he was implicated in the rebellion. He is a descendant of the house of Timur but in what degree he stands related to the ex-king is not ascertainable. That he was not nearly related is apparent from his not having any allowance assigned to him from the income of the ex-king in which all his near relatives participated. Elahi Bakhsh and Ahsanullah Khan have deposed before me that Mirza Khuda Bakhsh took no part in the rebellion.

2. Mirza Babur son of Mirza Mahrookh.

   The above remarks apply to this prisoner with this difference that in addition to Mirza Elahi Bakhsh and Hakim Ahsanullah Khan, Misser Mukand Lal has also deposed to his being unconnected with the rebellion.

[1] Pol. Cons. Nos. 113-119 of 27th May, 1859.

3. Mirza Nizamu'ddin son of Mirza Babur.
4. Mirza Farrukh Shah son of Mirza Kausar.

The prisoners are nephews to the ex-king but in other respects the above remarks are applicable to their cases; also that the latter was apprehended by the Thanadar of Paharganj.

5. Mirza Muslehu'ddin son of Husain Bakhsh.

The same as No. 4 of this statement but only very distantly related to the ex-king.

6. Mirza Imam Bakhsh son of Mirza Ali Bakhsh.

As No. 5 states that he was in receipt of an allowance of Rs. 10 a month from the income of the ex-king.

7. Mirza Khuda Bakhsh son of Mirza Bugboo.

As No. 6 received Rs. 7 a month.

8. Mirza Nizam Shah son of Muhammad Mubarak Shah.

Own brother to the ex-king; no evidence in the proceedings of the Commission against the Prisoner. The above witnesses exonerate him from any participation in the rebellion.

9. Mirza Chhotey son of Mirza Bakhtawar Bakht.

As No. 7 received Rs. 6 a month; only Mirza Ilahi Bakhsh deposes in his favour. The other two witnesses deny all knowledge of the Prisoner.

10. Mirza Turan Shah son of Mirza Raushanu'ddin.
11. Ahmad Shah son of Mirza Mahmud Shah.
12. Mirza Fakhru'ddin son of Mirza Shakuru'ddin.

These three prisoners were arrested with others in company with Nadir Shah, one of the prisoners who took an active part in the rebellion.

There is no evidence incriminating them. They are not near relatives of the ex-king, nor is it known what allowance they enjoyed. Elahi Bakhsh, Ahsanullah Khan, Misser Mukand Lal and Bakht Ali have all deposed before me that the prisoners were not implicated in the rebellion.

He was arrested on 30th July at the village of Loni by the Tahsildar of Delhee. He is a grandson of the ex-king. This case was appealed to the late Chief Commissioner who on receiving the proceedings recorded his opinion that there was no evidence criminating the Prisoner.

13. Mirza Asghar son of Mirza Shahrookh.

From further enquiries since made nothing has been elicited tending to implicate him in the rebellion. The evidence recorded by me is forwarded in a separate file.

Commissioner's Office, Sd. C. B. Saunders,
Delhi, Commissioner.
The 21st April, 1859.

Appendix M

THE FOLLOWING 13 MUGHUL PRINCES (*SALATEEN*) WERE DIRECTED TO BE SENT TO MOULMEIN AND KARACHI IN ACCORDANCE WITH THE SECRETARY'S LETTER, NO. 490 DATED 18TH JUNE 1859. THEY WERE SENTENCED TO IMPRISONMENT FOR LIFE AND WERE FIRST CONFINED IN AGRA JAIL WHENCE THEY WERE SENT TO KANPUR JAIL AND THENCE TO CALCUTTA AND CONFINED IN ALIPUR JAIL.

They were sent to Calcutta by mistake and the Superintendent of the Alipur Jail was requested under the circumstances to send those who were destined for Karachi to Akyab.

The policy under which their distribution in different jails took place is explained in the following letter from Secretary to Government, Punjab, of 26th August 1859; No. 324.

'I do not however think it expedient that all the connections of the ex-king should be congregated together even though it be at Rangoon. It will be better to divide these men between Moulmein and Karachi, ... Among those to be sent to Moulmein I should specially mention Mirza Nazim Shah, the brother of the ex-king. I would not allow him to go to Karachi.'

No. 39. Memo of the distribution of the 13 Princes (*salateen*) directed to be sent to Moulmein and Karachi in accordance with the Secretary's letter No. 490, dated 18th June 1859.

Names (forwarded to Moulmein)

1. Nazim Shah, son of Muhammad Akbar Shah.
2. Mirza Khuda Bakhsh, son of Hyder Shikoh.
3. Mirza Farrukh Shah, son of Mirza Kausar.
4. Mirza Imam Bakhsh, son of Ali Bakhsh.
5. Turab Shah, son of Mirza Raushanu'ddin.
6. Zahiru'ddin, son of Shakuru'ddin
7. Muslehu'ddin, son of Husain Bakhsh.

Directed to be sent to Karachi

8. Mirza Babur, son of Mirza Mahrookh.
9. Mirza Nizamu'ddin, son of Mirza Babur.
10. Mirza Khuda Bakhsh, son of Mirza Babur.
11. Mirza Chhotey, son of Mirza Bakhtawar Bakhsh.
12. Mirza Ahmad Shikoh, son of Mirza Muhammad Shikoh.
13. Mirza Asghar, son of Mirza Shahrookh.

Commissioner's Office, Delhi Division, 20th June 1859.

Sd. E. L. Brandreth, Commissioner & Superintendent, Delhi Division.

Appendix N

SEVERE IMPRISONMENT

Once Col. Hogge took Jawan Bakht, a youth of 17, for airing against the Prison Rules. He was called to account. A letter from Saunders to Edmonstone, Secretary to the Government of India, dated 20th January 1858, explains the circumstances in which he allowed Hogge to do so.

Extracts from the said letter

Says Saunders, 'I remembered that the Sikh chieftains, Chutter Singh and Sher Singh . . . . . the leaders in the last Sikh campaign who were sent down in strict confinement as State Prisoners to Calcutta were allowed by . . . . . the Governor-General to go out daily for an airing in carriage attended by a European, and I was of opinion that a similar practice in the present instance would not have been forbidden. . . .

'The chief and in fact the only reason why Jawan Bakht was allowed to go out for an airing upon the elephant was to elicit information from him regarding the war. In a demi-official letter which I received from Sir John Lawrence, dated the 24th September 1857, four days after the surrender of the king occurred the following passage, 'Try and get out of the king now that he is alarmed all that you can. Tell him that much will depend upon his making a clean breast'. In compliance with these instructions I endeavoured to elicit from the king and his more loquacious consort Begum Zinat Mahal the information I could obtain from them, but I found it very difficult to gather anything of any value from their conversation, their chief object evidently being to avoid incriminating themselves and at the same time to endeavour as little as possible to inculpate others. With Jawan Bakht the case was different. In the presence of his parents he was perfectly taciturn on all subjects on which we desired to obtain information. He, however, gave us to understand that if he were allowed to go out for an airing he could tell us anything we wished to know. He kept his word and a great deal of useful and important information[1] was elicited from him on subjects bearing upon he Mutiny, the conduct of the War and the complicity of the native chiefs in the Rebellion.

No honours were shown to him or to any other member of his family. It certainly never occurred to me when Col. Hogge obtained my permission to take Jawan Bakht out for an airing that any distinction was likely to be conferred upon him thereby in the eyes of the natives while perambulating the desolate streets of Delhi deserted by almost every living being except a few stray cats in a state of starvation, the dead bodies of our enemies and here and there a guard of our victorious troops'.[2]

Commissioner's Office, Delhi. Sd. C. B. Saunders,
The 26th January 1858. Offg. Commissioner.

[1] No trace of this information could be had even after a careful study that I made of the whole file.

[2] Secret Cons. No. 68 of 31st December, 1858.

APPENDIX O

SYNOPSIS OF THE RELEVANT DOCUMENTS[1] GIVING THE STORY OF BAHADUR SHAH II'S AND HIS DEPENDANTS' JOURNEY AS STATE PRISONERS FROM DEHLI TO RANGOON; THEIR LIFE IN RANGOON PRISON AND THE DEATH AND BURIAL OF BAHADUR SHAH II.

Nominal roll of the state prisoners proceeding to Calcutta.

1. Abu Zafar Bahadur Shah, Shah Ghazee, ex-king of Dehli.
2. Mirza Jawan Bakht, son of the above by ex-queen Zinat Mahal.
3. Mirza Shah Abbas, son of the above by Harem woman.
4. Zinat Mahal, ex-queen of Dehli.
5. Nawab Shah Zamani Begum, wife of Mirza Jawan Bakht.
6. Ruqaiya Sultan Begum, sister of Nawab Shah. Zamani Begum has one female baby.
7. Mumtaz Dulhan Begum, mother of Shah Zamani Begum and Ruqaiya Sultan Begum.
8. Nawab Taj Mahal Begum, a wife of ex-king of Dehli.
9. Sultani
10. Raheema
11. Ishrat
12. Taharat

} Harem of the ex-king.

[1] National Archives, F.C. No. 547, 10th December, 1859; Foreign Dept. Consultation, Nos. 71-73; 10th December, 1858; F. C. No. 66, 10th December, 1858.

13. Mubarakunnisa, mother of Mirza Shah Abbas, Harem of ex-king.

Male attendants

14. Mirza Keisur[1]
15. Abdur Ruhiman[2]
16. Ahmad Beg
17. Inzzur
18. Khwaja Bakhsh, eunuch

Female attendants

19. Sandal
20. Niazoo, foster-nurse of Nawab Shah Zamani Begum.
21. Husaini
22. Kimeean[3]
23. Wafldar[4]
24. Rahat
25. Jumayat
26. Mubarak
27. Sakina Khanam
28. Hurmat Bhai[5]
29. Lutfan

N.B. one or two of the servants have two or three little children;

Left Dehli in the morning of 7th October 1858 *en route* for Allahabad under escort of the 9th Lancers or Troops of European Horse Artillery Police Battalion by land route. The women or female attendants were conveyed in five tilted carts and the ex-king with seven

[1] The correct spelling is Qaisar.

[2] *I.e.* Rahman.

[3] *I.e.* Kariman.

[4] *I.e.* Wafadar.

[5] *I.e.* Bai.

other members of his family were taken in three palanquin carriages pulled by four horses.

They reached Allahabad on 13th November 1858 where 14 members of the above party expressed a desire to go back to Dehli and were detained in the Allahabad Fort. The names of these fourteen are given below;

1. Mirza Keisar } male attendants
2. Jaffar } male attendants
3. Khwaja Bakhsh, eunuch
4. Taj Mahal, wife of Bahadur Shah
5. Sakina Khanum
6. Mumtaz Dulhan, mother-in-law of Jawan Bakht
7. Ruqaiya Sultan Begum, sister-in-law of Jawan Bakht
8. Raheema
9. Taharat
10. Kimeean
11. Wafedar[1]
12. Rahat
13. Jumayat
14. Mubarak

At Allahabad Bahadur Shah's health was examined by a committee of doctors and their finding was this: '......Allowing for the natural functional decay attending his advanced age... his general physical condition is good ......; he is hale and vigorous for his age and free from organic disease. '

At Allahabad the carriages and horses which had conveyed the royal prisoners were disposed of and the proceeds remitted to the Commissioner of Dehli.

From Allahabad the Prisoners were taken to Mirzapur where they embarked on board the *Soorma*

[1] See p. 416 *supra,* footnote 4.

Flat in tow of the Thames Steamer and were accompanied by eleven followers who having received the option determined to go with the Prisoners to their destination.

Edmondstone, Secretary to Government of India, intimates C. Beadon, Offg. Secretary to Government of India that the ex-king of Dehli, his wife and two sons, with 11 followers are on their way down from Allahabad in charge of Lt. Ommaney and requests that the requisite measure may be taken for giving effect to the Governor-General's wishes as to having the State Prisoners conveyed to Rangoon without touching at Calcutta.[1]

Starting from Allahabad on 16th November the State Prisoners reached Mirzapur in the morning of 19th November; and departed on the Govt. steamer 'Thames' on the downward voyage at 2 P.M. the same day. The Steamer was scheduled to reach Mud or Diamond Harbour in about 20 days.

From Mirzapur the Steamer Thames came to Buxar in the morning of 22nd November 1858. It arrived with the State Prisoners at Dinapur in the evening of 23rd November and proceeded again the following day in the morning, touched Monghyr in the morning of 25th November and proceeded downward the same day at noon. Then it touched Rajmahal in the morning of 27th and proceeded downward the same day. It touched Rampur Balliah in the morning of 28th and proceeded downward the same day; touched Womurkolly on 29th and proceeded. Then it touched Khoolnah at 8 A.M. on 1st December 1858 and proceeded shortly after. On Saturday 4th December 1858 it arrived at Diamond Harbour at 9.5 A.M.

---

[1] Foreign Dept., Political, No. 77, 10th December, 1858.

Here at Diamond Harbour the Prisoners were transported quickly from the Steamer Thames and the *Flat Soorma* on board H.M.'s Ship *Megara* (*Magoera*) which started immediately after receiving them at 11.30 A.M. The Megara touched Kedgeree at 2.45 P.M. the same day and left for Rangoon the following day at 6.30 A.M. It arrived at Sandheads at 12 noon of 5th December and reached Rangoon on 9th December 1858.

THE PRISON[1]

Letter

From Major A. P. Phayle, Commissioner of Pegu,
To the Secretary to the Govt. of India.
Foreign Department.

Fort William,
dated Rangoon, 16th April 1859.

Sir,

In acknowledging the receipt of Mr. Under Secretary Simon's letter No. 1220 of 23rd March last, I have the honour to state that owing to the exigency of the moment the ex-king of Dehli and other State Prisoners were located partly in tents and partly in a portion of the main guard which was partitioned off. As there was no convenient residence available for them and in anticipation of their being detained here some time, estimates were prepared and building commenced upon as soon as circumstances would admit; it is now all but completed and in a few days the State Prisoners

[1] Foreign Department, Pol. Cons, No. 547, 13th May, 1859.

will be removed from their present quarters. Their new residence is built of teak and will be raised off the ground with a substantial palisade round. . . . . .

Sd. Commissioner of Pegu.

Then Captain H. N. Davies in the charge of the State Prisoners in Rangoon says in a despatch[1] of 3rd August 1859:

' . . . . The house is situated within a few yards of the Main Guard and like wooden houses of the country is considerably raised off the ground. It is in an enclosure 100 ft. square and is surrounded by palisading 10 ft. high. The accommodation consists of 4 rooms, each 16 ft. square, one of which is allotted for the use of the ex-king, another is occupied by Jawan Bakht and his young Begum, a third is appropriated by Zinat Mahal Begum; to each of these rooms a bathing is attached, Shah Abbas and his mother occupying the remaining rooms. . . . There are two bath rooms . . . . also a place to cook in.

The cost of dieting the prisoners—16 in number—is about 11 rupees a day and an extra rupee is allowed every Sunday and Rs. 2 per head on the 1st of each month to meet their toilette necessities; but pen, ink and paper are strictly prohibited. The public are not allowed to hold intercourse with the prisoners and the servants gain admission under a pass.

The health of the ex-king has improved. . . . His memory is still good when time is allowed him to fix his ideas but his articulation is indistinct consequent upon the loss of the teeth. He certainly does not give

[1] F. C. No. 125, 11th November, 1859.

the impression of being capable of an extended mental energy of capacity, but on the whole he appears to bear his weight of years remarkably well; he passes his days in listless apathy manifesting considerable indifference to all external affairs. This apparently has been his normal state for a long time past and may continue so for some time to come until all of a sudden his career may come to a close.

The ex-king's wife Zinat Mahal is a middle-aged woman. She enjoys very good health; I have had several conversations with her from behind the screen. She frequently enlarges on the step she took at the time of the outbreak at Dehli in writing to the late Mr. Colvin, the Lieutenant-Governor of the N.W. Provinces, begging of him to come to her assistance implying thereby that at that time they were thus helpless even to protect the unfortunate European girl who sought her protection. She also frequently alluded to the loss of her private treasure and jewels and states that Major Hodson pledged his word and gave her a written document as security for the safety of her personal property. . . . She states that her property was not disturbed till after Major Hodson's death when she was required to give up the document he had given her as a protection; she was then dispossessed by Mr. Saunders, the Commissioner at Dehli, of all her valuables to the extent of twenty lacs rupees in value and he refused to return the document.

I have explained to her that on her husband being convicted of rebellion all the property of the family became escheated to the Government and that her establishment being distinct from the King's and her residing in a separate mahal has nothing to do with it.

She seems however to think that the sequestration of her private property is somewhat contrary to custom. . . . She appears to be a woman of masculine turn of mind judging from her conversation and deportment; and of the two most probably she had more to say to the intrigues of the Rebels than her imbecile husband. . . .

In connection with the loss of her treasure a certain Ahsanullah Khan appears to have had a hand; all the prisoners are very bitter against him and assert that this individual who was the king's Hakeem and adviser was the principal person through whose insidious counsel the destruction of the European prisoners was brought about. This is I believe contrary to fact; but it is not improbable that this man may have given some information regarding the secret treasure and thus incurred the enmity of the queen's party. This Hakeem from the account given appears to have gained the confidence of the British authorities at Dehli no doubt with good and sufficient reason, and the spleen displayed by the Begum and her associates only adds to confirm this opinion.

The younger Begum—Zamani—the wife of Jawan Bakht is described as a young and pretty woman probably not more than 15 years old although she has already been the mother of two children. She feels the restraint of prison life more than the others, due to delicate state of her health consequent upon her accouchement which took place shortly after her arrival here. The child was a male one and was still-born. Both the old king and his daughter-in-law are particularly fond of soliciting the services of the Doctor upon every trifling occasion and the young lady is very solicitous of being allowed to go out for an airing occasionally.

The two sons are both healthy and rather promising youths. Both are extremely ignorant, the attainments of the elder (Jawan Bakht) embracing merely a slight knowledge of reading and writing in Persian character and when interrogated on the most ordinary topics their want of knowledge is very apparent; even the boundaries of their native country are wholly unknown to them.

I felt it my duty to record the very laudable desire both these lads exhibit to learn; they have frequently expressed a very earnest wish to acquire a knowledge of the English language in particular and they seem to be fully aware that by so doing they will have adopted the very last course for removing the misfortune if not disgrace attendant on their present state of ignorance and they state they expressed a wish to the Commissioner of Dehli to be sent to England in preference to any other place. Both the parents of the lads have talked to me on the subject and appear anxious that a commencement should be made. The lads are possessed of sufficient intelligence to warrant a hope of speedy progress and have promised me earnestly to apply themselves if Government permits the scheme to be undertaken.

Rangoon, Sd. H. Nelson Davies.
3rd Aug. 1859.

Half-yearly report of the officer-in-charge of State Prisoners, Rangoon, dated 1st July 1861.

'I have the honour to state that the State Prisoners under my charge have enjoyed good health during the past six months. Abu Zafar is generally getting weaker; the Civil Surgeon is of opinion that his tenure of life is very uncertain. Zinat Mahal, the wife of Abu Zafar, has all along enjoyed excellent health. Zamani, the wife of Jawan Bakht, has occasionally complained of slight attacks of fever. She is now well as is also her little girl and there is a prospect of an addition to her family. Jawan Bakht and Shah Abbas, the two sons of Abu Zafar, are in good health; they both attend at my house pretty regularly and study a little English with Mr. Finncane who was formerly Brigadier Sergeant Major here; they are making remarkable progress and may require a superior teacher hereafter. Of all the attendants Ishrat suffered for a long time from painful abscess in her left breast and Ahmad Beg has recently had an attack of fever. Mrs. Davies has occasionally taken Zamani out for a drive and both she and Zinat Mahal have been over to spend an hour or so at our house occasionally. . . .

The prisoners find their quarters rather confined. There is a difficulty in making any alteration in the house.

Nawab Begum, mother of Zamani, Jawan Bakht's wife, has occasionally expressed a wish to visit Rangoon; inquiry has been made whether she really intends visiting her daughter.

Sd./- H. Davies,
in Charge of State Prisoners.

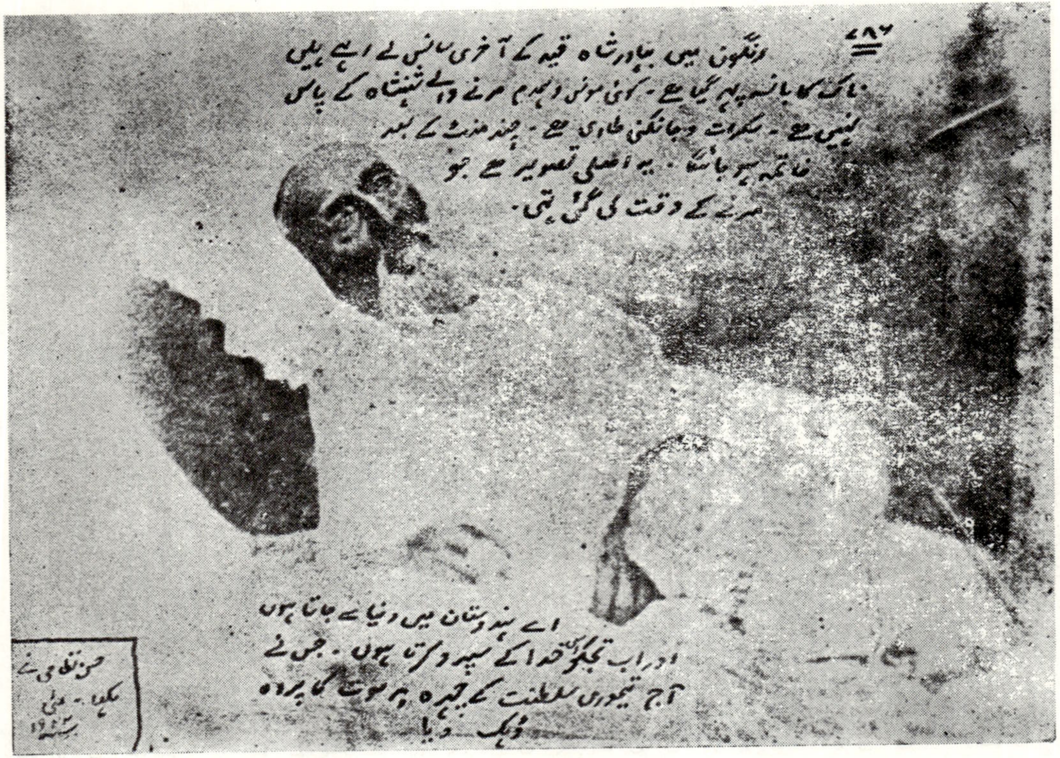

BAHADUR SHAH II IN DEATH AGONY
(From Hasan Mizami Collection)

Death and Burial of Bahadur Shah II[1]

Reports that Abu Zafar Muhammad Bahadur Shah, a State Prisoner, died on 7th November 1862 and was buried the same day.

The Civil Surgeon of Rangaan certified that the ex-King of Dehli was seized with a third paralytic attack on 6th November and died at 5 A.M. on 7th November 1862.

Since Sunday 26th October 1862 according to the statement made by Ahmad Beg his attendant Bahadur Shah felt sneaks (*sic*) and could swallow his food with difficulty. His condition grew worse every day and his condition was reported on Sunday, 2nd November. On Monday 3rd November 1862 the doctor reported that Abu Zafar's throat had become affected; it is very difficult to get broth down even in small quantities. On Thursday, 6th November, the doctor reported, Abu Zafar is evidently sinking from sure decrepitude and apparently paralysis in the region of his throat'.

H. Davies, the officer in charge of the State Prisoners, then ordered bricks and lime to be collected near the spot appointed for his last resting place and made other necessary arrangements.

He expired at 5 o'clock on Friday; all things being in readiness he was buried at 4 P.M. on the same day in the rear of the Main Guard in a brick grave covered over with turf level with the ground; a bamboo fence surrounds the grave for some considerable distance and by the time the fence is worn out the grass will have again covered the spot and no vestige will remain to distinguish where the last of the Great Mughuls rests.

[1] Foreign Department, Political; Nos. 165/164, November

A Mulla assisted at the funeral and the body of the deceased was placed in a teak wood coffin covered with red cotton velvet. A crowd of Mahomedans from the bazaar had assembled near the enclosure; but beyond a general rush to touch the coffin on its being brought out from the palisade round the Prisoners' quarters, no inconvenience was experienced. They were all kept outside the enclosure which had been erected by a few policemen on duty at the entrance. A few bystanders were admitted inside the enclosure in order that the internment might be sufficiently public.

The two sons of the deceased Jawan Bakht and Shah Abbas and male attendant Ahmad Beg accompanied the coffin; no females were allowed to be present, nor were any titles allowed to be rehearsed.

Monday, 10th November 1862.

Sd./- H. Davies, in Charge of State Prisoners.

The death of the ex-king may be said to have had no effect on the Mahomedan part of the population of Rangoon.'

Sd./- H. Davies.

The above reports were but formal and intended to meet a certain political end. They cannot be taken as symbolic of a rapprochement between the aggrieved Emperor or his party and the British. The impossibility of a rapprochement is adumbrated from the outset by Bahadur Shah's verses[1] composed before the Rising of 1857 as well as by his prognostications[2] made during the War and the elegies[3] cited after the fall of Dehli. Hodson—who had shot two of his sons and a grandson, piercing each of them with three bullets and then cutting off their heads which were presented along with the severed heads of 29 other scions of the Royal house dripping in blood to the afflicted Emperor, now a prisoner[4]—had no pity for him. He longed to take his life but regretted that policy forbade him to do so. Wilson, commander-in-chief of the British forces in Dehli, had laid down that policy. He had advised Hodson to make Bahadur Shah prisoner and bring him alive in view of the fact that he was still the cynosure of all the sepoys, Indian princes, chiefs and zamindars and that he was the hero of the long-drawn-out drama of the Mutiny. Like Hodson, Lawrence too thirsted for the blood of Bahadur Shah. As soon as he heard of Bahadur Shah's survival he burst out in anger saying, 'It is a great pity that the old rascal was not shot directly as he was seen. I would not have taken him prisoner'.

Afterwards Bahadur Shah was escorted by the foot and horse-guards to the Fort where he was greeted with jeers and ceaseless shower of abuses from the

---

[1] Appendix C.

[2] *Vide* p. 237 *supra*.

[3] *Vide* pp. 339-341 *supra*.

[4] Appendix H, p. 372.

English military massed therein. Some of them who wanted to see him dead had drawn on the Lahore gate of the Fort a picture which showed him dying on the gallows. He was then made to stand in the midst of his blood-thirsty enemies, one of whom gnashing his teeth stepped forward and struck him on the thigh a blow. Seeing this an Abyssinian slave of the helpless Emperor rushed at the assailant, and gripping him fast threw him on the ground. That faithful slave was immediately set upon and killed by other English soldiers.

Then the stage was set for the trial of this extraordinary prisoner. He was tried before a Military Commission in the Diwan-i Khass where he himself used formerly to hold durbars in full royal glory. Four charges were framed against him. The *first* accused him of encouraging, aiding and abetting the sipahis in the crimes of the Mutiny and rebellion against the State; the *second* of encouraging, siding and abetting his own sons and other inhabitants of Dehli and the north-west provinces of India to rebel and wage war against the State; the *third* of having proclaimed himself reigning king and sovereign of India and of assembling forces at Dehli and of encouraging others to wage war with the British Government; the *fourth* of having on the 16th May felonously caused the death of 49 people of European descent and of having subsequently abetted others in murdering European officials and other English subjects. During the 42-day-long trial the aged, afflicted prisoner went through all the heart-rending tribulations in the course of which he even fainted. In the end he was declared a traitor—guilty of all the four charges. He was supposed to have forfeited his crown and was punished with exile and life imprisonment. He was taken under heavy guards to Rangoon and thrown into a prison where no one was allowed to see him, not even a *hakeem* whom the Royal prisoner needed badly.

After his death the British troops trampled upon his grave while mounting guard over it until it was completely effaced; thus was fulfilled Bahadur Shah's prediction:

پس مرگ قبر پہ اے ظفر کوئی فاتحہ بھی کہاں پڑھے
وہ جو ٹوٹی قبر کا تھا نشاں اوسے ٹھوکروں سے اڑا دیا

(After the death of Zafar! where can one recite the *Fatiha*? For even the sign of a broken grave that had remained is obliterated through tramping and treading heavily up and down.)

As a result the grave of Bahadur Shah became indistinct and remained unknown for many years. When in 1903 some of his Indian devotees arrived in Rangoon with the object of invoking blessings on his soul and performing *Fatihakhwani*[1] at his grave, they could not find it. After making some efforts and through local guidance they tentatively fixed upon a space under a withered lotus tree as the site of the much sought-for grave. There the *Fatihakhwani* was performed, and subsequently attempts were made to raise a magnificient mausoleum there. To this effect an entreating appeal was made to the Indians and Burmese in general and a plan was drawn up of the proposed mausoleum. A printed copy of this appeal as well as of the projected mausoleum has been recently received at the National Archives of India as part of the Maulana Abul Kalam Azad collection. The translation of the said appeal made by the writer from the original Urdu text is given below:

---

[1] Commemoration Service.

An entreating appeal

An entreaty for the construction of the mausoleum of His Majesty Abu Zafar Siraju'ddin Bahadur Shah Zafar; the mercy of Allah on him!

The Mughul Empire: In India the sun of the Mughul Empire shone for 330 years. At last in 1858 a dark cloud sprang from the west (Europe); and drowning that sun spread over the whole of India.

Imprisonment of Zafar Shah: Bahadur Shah, the awakener of the memories of the zenith of the Mughul Empire, was brought in a deplorable condition to Rangoon and imprisoned there. Such was the result of the Revolution which transformed him completely. Describing his own condition he said

نہ رہا وہ رنگ نہ بو رہی نہ گلوں کی خوبی و خو رہی
جو خزاں کے ہاتھوں تباہ ہے وہ یادگار بہار ہوں
یہی حال گلشن دہر ہے کبھی مہر ہے کبھی قہر ہے
جو کبھی چمن تھا وہ پھول ہوں جو کبھی سمن تھا وہ خار ہوں

Neither has remained that colour, nor that odour; nor have the flowers their former elegance and beauty, I am the memento of that spring which has been ruined at the hands of autumn. Such are the ways of Fate; sometimes it is kind and sometimes indignant. I am the flower of the once-flourishing garden, now reduced to a thorn.

Death: Having suffered from the pangs of sorrow and grief, thus unmasking the faithlessness and crooked ways of this world the Emperor breathed his last in 1862.

facing p. 430

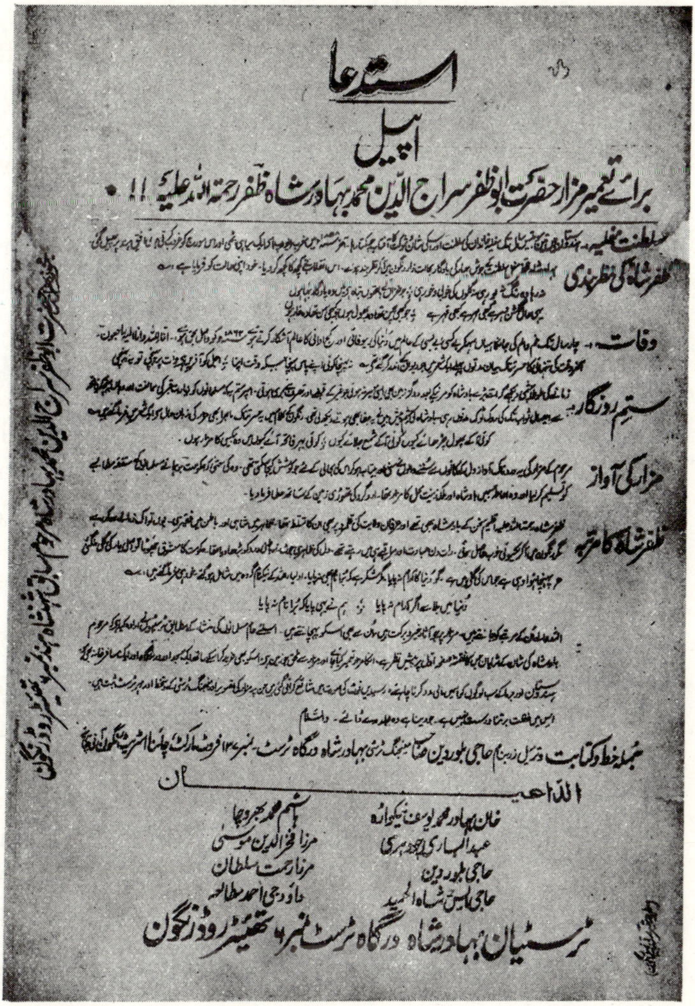

استدعا

اپیل

برائے تعمیر مزار حضرت ابوظفر سراج الدین محمد بہادر شاہ ظفر رحمۃ اللہ علیہ !!

الداعیان

ٹرسٹیان بہادر شاہ درگاہ ٹرسٹ نمبر۶ تھئیٹر روڈ رنگون

An Entreating Appeal

'To God we belong, and to Him is our return'
(Holy Quran, Sura II, verse 156).

Many years before his death, the Emperor had depicted the tragic scene of his death in a verse which forms part of his *diwan* and runs as follows:

نہ پہنچا کوئی اپنے پاس پہنچا جبکہ وقت اپنا

اجل کو آفریں ہے وقت پر پہنچی تو یہ پہنچی

As the hour of death drew nigh, nobody came to us. Hurrah for Death! it was Death alone who arrived in time.

Tyranny of the Times: Look at the mischievous ungratefulness of the Times! After his death such a great Emperor could not obtain even a 2-yard-long piece of land, free from foreign occupation and control. Furthermore the Musalmans were prohibited for many years from visiting his grave and there even prevented from invoking blessings on his soul by reciting the Fatiha. . . . Visualising this tyranny in a forecast of his the Emperor had composed in Rangoon the following among many other verses:

کوئی آ کے پھول چڑھائے کیوں؟ کوئی آ کے شمع جلائے کیوں؟

کوئی بہر فاتحہ آئے کیوں؟ میں وہ بیکسی کا مزار ہوں

Why should anyone come to my grave with an offering of flowers? Why should anyone visit my grave to recite Fatiha? Such an embodiment of misery I shall become, on dying!

Voice from the grave: A voice proceeded from the grave of the afflicted Emperor and was heard by those who were capable of hearing it.

They were seized by agony and became restless; and left no stone unturned in their endeavour for the maintenance of that grave. As a result even the then Burmese Government were moved and accepted the prayer made jointly by the Musalmans to that effect. They gave away for that purpose the plot containing the graves of the Emperor and Queen Zinat Mahal together with the surrounding piece of land.

Real Worth of Zafar Shah: Zafar Shah—may God have mercy on him!—was a king of the domain of literature and at the same time a ruler of the dominions of spiritualism. Outwardly he was a king, inwardly he was a fakir. In this way he passed his life until his arrival in Rangoon when he gave himself to the pursuit of a single purpose. All the hours—day and night—he spent in prayer and meditation. To all appearances his broken heart had heightened the torment of his soul. When the beloved sweetheart of kingship was torn from his embrace, he drew to his bosom the Supreme Divinity, thus rising to the eminence of a real saint, as the saying goes: The real saint is he who lives in God'.

ع - پہنچا ہوا وہی ہے جو اوسکی گلی میں ہے

Although Zafar Shah enjoyed no worldly comforts yet, thank God! he was given no bad name. He joined the reputed galaxy of the Saints of Allah; and foreseeing this much he himself had said:

دنیا میں بلا سے اگر آرام نہ پایا

ہم نے یہی پایا کہ برا نام نہ پایا

facing p. 433.

PROPOSED MAUSOLEUM OF BAHADUR SHAH II, EMPEROR OF INDIA
Theatre Road, Rangoon

'It does not matter if we enjoyed no comforts in this world. We have at least earned this distinction that we have been given no bad name'.

Spiritual men know the real worth of Bahadur Shah. They recognize him also through the signs of Divine grace and favour that are witnessed at his tomb In view of all this and in full accord with the longing of the Muslims, the trustees of his Dargah have resolved that a mausoleum—a fitting memorial to his high position—be raised on the grave of the deceased Emperor. The plan of that mausoleum may be seen on page one[1]. It is also proposed that the land adjoining the said mausoleum be purchased and utilised for building thereupon a mosque and a public resting place. All the people of India and Burma should join hands in financing the proposed construction. Receipt books have been printed bearing a picture of the desired mausoleum along with the signature and seal of the managing trustee.

This matter must not be taken lightly. Whatever you want to give, please give at once.

All correspondence and remittance of money should be addressed to Haji Billouru'ddin Sahib, Managing Trustee, Bahadur Shah Dargah Trust, 178, Fruit Market China Street, Rangoon.

APPEALERS

Khan Bahadur Muhammad Nekwara, Abdul Bari Chowdhuri, Haji Billouru'ddin, Haji S. Shah al-Hamid, Hashim Muhammad Bharocha, Mirza Fakhru'ddin

[1] *I.e.* facing page 433 of this book.

Musa, Mirza Rahmat Sultan, Daudji Ahmad Matali'—Trustees of the Bahadur Shah Dargah, Trust No. 6, Theatre Road, Rangoon.

But the British Government disapproved of the idea of the proposed mausoleum[1], and it was dropped *sine die*. At last Bahadur Shah's blood which according to popular belief surges after a *qarn*,[2] cried; and the cry was heard. In 1934 his tomb was built on a humble and moderate scale, as if by miracle, in its present form and goes under the name of *Dargah Bahadur Shah*.

[1] See Photo of the proposed Mausoleum facing page. 433. *Of Rangoon Daily*, Bahadur Shah Number 1957.

[2] *I.e.* a period of 30 years.

Select Bibliography

Anderson—*Tarikh-i Bahadur Shahi* (translated). Calcutta, 1860

Andrews, C. F.—*Zakaullah of Delhi* (1929)

Atkinson—*Prints of War in India*, 1857-58

Bahadur Shah—*Diwan-i Sani;* Royal Press, Dehli, 13th (His Majesty, the Shadow of God; the Caliph of God; Lord of the World, Abu Zafar Bahadur Shah Ghazi Badshah; may Allah perpetuate his empire and rule!) year of the glorious reign, 1266 Hijra (1850 A.D.)

Bahadur Shah—*Kulliyat-i Zafar; Nawal Kishore Press* (1887)

Bahadur Shah—*Khiyaban-i Tasawwuf, Dehli* (1259/1843)

Charles Ball—*History of the Indian Mutiny*, Vols. I-II (London 1858-59)

Dutta, K. K.—*Biography of Kunwar Singh and Amar Singh* (1957)

Edward Thompson—*The Other Side of the Medal* (London 1925)

Fonveille—*Des Sentiments de Justice et d'Humanite de l'Angleterre dans la Question Indienne* (1857)

Forrest, G. W.—*A History of the Indian Mutiny*, Vols. I-II (1903)

Forrest, G. W.—*Selections from Letters, Despatches and other State Papers preserved in the Military Department of the Government of India*, (1857-1858), Calcutta, 1912

Frasoo—*Zafaru-z Zafar or Fath Numa-i Angrezi*

Graham, G. P. I.—*The Life and Work of Syed Ahmad Khan* (1909)

Greathed, H. H.—*Letters written during the Siege of Delhi* (1858))

Hindu, A—*The Mutinies and the People* (1859)

Holmes, T. R. E.—*A History of the Indian Mutiny* (1898)

Holloway, J.—*Essays on the Indian Mutiny* (1864)

Kaye, J. W.—*A History of the Sepoy War in India* 1857-1858, Vols. I-III

Kaye and Malleson—*History of the Indian Mutiny of* 1857-58, Vols. I-VI (1898)

Leasor, James—*The Red Fort* (London, 1856)

List of Documents for 1857, National Archives of India

Majumdar, J. K.—*Raja Ram Mohan Roy and the last Moghuls* (1939)

Mangin, C. T.—*La Revolte au Bengale en 1857 et 1858*

Martin, Ch.—*La Puissance Militaire des Anglais dans l'Inde et l'Insurrection des Cipayes* (1859)

Metcalfe, C. T.—*Two Narratives of the Mutiny in Delhi* (1898)

Press-List of the Mutiny Papers, 1857, (1921)

Press-List of the Mutiny Papers of 1857-1858 in the Punjab Secretariat; (1925)

(A collection of all the telegrams referring to the actual course of the Mutiny from May 1857 to April 1859)

Rotton, J. E. W.—*The Chaplain's Narrative of the Siege of Delhi* (1858)

Russell, W. H.—My Diary in India (1860)

Showers, C. L.—*A Missing Chapter of the Indian Mutiny* (1888)

Sidgwick, F. R.—*The Indian Mutiny of 1857*

Spear, P.—*Twilight of the Mughuls* (1951)

Syed Ahmad (Sir)—*Tazkira-i Ahl-i Dehli* (1955)

Trial of Ex-King of Delhi—For Rebellion against the British Government and murder of Europeans during 1857. Calcutta, 1868

Young Keith—*Delhi-1857*, London, 1902

Zaheer Dehlawi—*Dastan-i Ghadr*, Lahore

SELECT NAMES OF PERSONS

A

B

C

D

E

F

G

H

I

J

K

L

M

N

O

P

Q

R

S

T

NAMES OF PLACES AND TITLES OF BOOKS

A

B

C

D

E

F

G

H

I

J

K

L

M

N

O

P

Q

R

S

T

V